PSYCHOLOGICAL FOUNDATIONS OF MUSICAL BEHAVIOR

PSYCHOLOGICAL FOUNDATIONS OF MUSICAL BEHAVIOR
Third Edition

By

RUDOLF E. RADOCY

*Professor of Music Education
and Music Therapy
The University of Kansas
Lawrence, Kansas*

and

J. DAVID BOYLE

*Professor of Music Education
and Music Therapy
The University of Miami
Coral Gables, Florida*

CHARLES C THOMAS • PUBLISHER, LTD.
Springfield • Illinois • U.S.A.

Published and Distributed Throughout the World by

CHARLES C THOMAS • PUBLISHER, LTD.
2600 South First Street
Springfield, Illinois 62794-9265

© *1997 by* CHARLES C THOMAS • PUBLISHER, LTD.
ISBN 0-398-06720-1 (cloth)
ISBN 0-398-06721-X (paper)

Library of Congress Catalog Card Number: 96-31867

First Edition, 1979
Second Edition, 1988
Third Edition, 1997

With THOMAS BOOKS *careful attention is given to all details of manufacturing and design. It is the Publisher's desire to present books that are satisfactory as to their physical qualities and artistic possibilities and appropriate for their particular use.* THOMAS BOOKS *will be true to those laws of quality that assure a good name and good will.*

Printed in the United States of America
SC-R-3

Library of Congress Cataloging-in-Publication Data

Radocy, Rudolf E.
    Psychological foundations of musical behavior / by Rudolf E.
Radocy and J. David Boyle. — 3rd ed.
        p.   cm.
    Includes bibliographical references and index.
    ISBN 0-398-06720-1 (cloth). — ISBN 0-398-06721-X (paper)
    1. Music—Psychology.   I. Boyle, J. David.   II. Title.
ML3830.R15   1996
781'.11—dc20
                                                            96-31867
                                                            CIP
                                                            MN

PREFACE TO THE THIRD EDITION

Since publication of the second edition in 1988, knowledge relevant to musical behavior's psychological foundations has increased dramatically. Important research and writing have come from recognized music psychologists as well as from individuals with primary interests in other disciplines, including psychology, sociology, philosophy, music theory, and music education. The authors believe that cross-disciplinary contributions are important because these researchers and writers bring varying perspectives to the study of musical behavior.

The openness and objectivity of individuals who study musical behavior and evaluate research and writing from varying perspectives nurtures true cross-disciplinary exchange, thereby facilitating improved knowledge of the pertinent variables. Such knowledge is important in and of itself, but its greater value comes when musicians, psychologists, and teachers apply it to enhance the development of children's and older students' musical abilities, sensitivities, and enjoyment. The ultimate application of whatever knowledge is gained from the discipline generally called "psychology of music" should be to enrich people's lives individually and collectively through musical experience.

The authors have resisted the temptation to change this edition's title to include "psychology of music." The reason is that the book's focus remains on *people* and the factors that influence their interactions with music and musical phenomena. With increased understanding of people's interactions with music in diverse cultures, investigators are increasingly aware that people, individually and collectively, probably have more influence on human interaction with music than the music per se.

Of course, the authors do not suggest that knowledge of musical structure is *un*important for understanding people's interactions with music. Indeed, a certain understanding of musical structure is essential for studying human musical responses. That people respond differently to different musics and structural attributes of music is well documented. Composers, performers, and users of music long have understood that even subtle changes in music's structural attributes may evoke quite different responses in listeners. A premise of this book is that a reader's lifetime of experience with music in any society or culture, and particularly experience with music of Western cultures and a basic understanding of Western musical structure, will provide sufficient knowledge for the purposes of understanding this book.

Much recent research and writing has focused on understanding music cognition. A particular focus of research in music cognition has been on pattern recognition, both melodic and rhythmic, with special emphasis on identifying the cognitive processes underlying perception. Music increasingly is recognized as a unique type of intelligence, and much research related to music perception and cognitive processing is designed to increase understanding of musical development as an intellectual endeavor. The authors agree that musical intelligence is a requisite of musical behavior and that an understanding of the perceptual, cognitive, and other psychological processes which underlie musical intelligence is basic to understanding musical behavior. An intent of this third edition is to emphasize the importance of this perspective.

As we have noted previously, however, the psychological foundations of musical behavior encompass much more than perceptual and cognitive processing. Investigators conduct research relevant to understanding musical behavior under a variety of rubrics, and much of their work does not focus on cognitive processing. Systematic musicology (i.e., the study of various systems that function in music) has much to offer students of musical behavior. Its subfields of psychoacoustics, psychomusicology, and sociomusicology examine musical behavior from particular perspectives. Psychological aesthetics, focusing on variables underlying the affective or feeling response to music, has much to offer, and philosophical aesthetics provides invaluable insights into musical meaning and response. Much music education research provides data relevant to understanding musical behavior, particularly musical development and learning. Educators increasingly are concerned with understanding the interactions between learning through enculturation processes and learning through formal instruction. With increased sophistication of physiological recording equipment and new developments in techniques for examining neurological and other physiological reactions to music, there is renewed interest in physiological research as an avenue for understanding musical behavior and integrating music into therapy and healing.

While music has been an integral part of society throughout history, recent developments related to music as a sociocultural phenomenon suggest that music's availability, nature, and usage in its social and cultural contexts strongly influence the musical behavior of both an individual and a society. Certainly, music's virtually worldwide ubiquitousness via various electronic media, both alone and accompanying film or video, either as background music or as music intended for conscious listening, has had a major influence on the enculturation process related to music, musical behavior, and the influence of music on many nonmusical behaviors.

The authors recognize that the factors influencing musical behavior are highly complex, and that research from many disciplines may contribute to understanding musical behavior. The various areas of research, however, are not discrete; students must consider results and conclusions from different areas and approaches to research on musical behavior in relation to those from other areas and approaches. Further, disciplines not concerned directly with musical behavior, but which seek to develop understanding of general cognition and behavior, offer many insights into musical behavior. In short, individuals seeking to understand musical behavior must draw from many disciplines. A premise of this book is that such eclecticism greatly will enhance one's understanding of musical behavior.

Constraints of time, space, and resources necessarily limited this revision's scope and breadth. Consequently, the authors have exercised their professional judgments, based on teaching courses and conducting research and other scholarly inquiry, regarding content. Naturally, some arbitrary decisions were necessary, and the book reflects the authors' scholarly biases. As with previous editions, time and changing emphases in the field will make some material obsolete or seem trivial. Given their chosen content, however, the authors have tried to make this book comprehensive, comprehensible, and contemporary. Traditional areas of study continue to be represented, but the authors have attempted to incorporate recent research and contemporary psychological perspectives while not losing sight of the book's primary concern: to facilitate the reader's understanding of variables underlying musical behavior.

ACKNOWLEDGMENTS

M any individuals contribute to the successful completion of a text through their suggestions for content, criticism, encouragement, and toleration for delayed completion of other tasks. The authors are indebted to their professional colleagues, particularly Dr. George Duerksen, Director of the Music Education and Music Therapy Division of The University of Kansas, and Dr. William Hipp, Dean of the School of Music at The University of Miami, for their encouragement and support from the authors' respective universities. The authors appreciate the many instructors who have selected the first or second editions of *Psychological Foundations of Musical Behavior,* in English or in Japanese, and provided valuable feedback for preparation of the third edition. Many students, especially students in the authors' classes at The University of Kansas, The Pennsylvania State University, and The University of Miami, have identified strengths and weaknesses for the authors to address. Administrative and technical support from Ms. Lois Elmer was essential in maintaining the writing process. Finally, the authors are grateful to their loving wives Dr. Wanda Lathom-Radocy and Dr. Arlene Boyle, for their loving support and encouragement.

R.E.R.
J.D.B.

CONTENTS

PSYCHOLOGICAL FOUNDATIONS
OF MUSICAL BEHAVIOR

CHAPTER ONE

INTRODUCTION

Purpose

This book provides the reader with a comprehensive overview of human musical behavior, viewed from a psychological perspective. Music has been a component of human culture since before recorded history. Organizing sound for functional and aesthetic purposes provides many fascinating, although occasionally unanswerable, questions. Description, prediction, and explanation of musical composition, performance, and listening behavior are continuous challenges. This book focuses questions and general interests in such description, prediction, and explanation for the benefit of psychologists, musicians, educators, and anyone else with a serious interest in music.

Understanding human musical behavior is useful for the performing musician, whether in the studio, on stage, in the classroom, or in a commercial setting. Why do people prefer certain sounds over others? How relevant is precise pitch discrimination? What psychoacoustical processes underlie musical perception? What cognitive processes operate to make a stream of sonic events music? Are some individuals naturally "musical"? Why is a deviation from stereotyped performance practice a "stroke of creative genius" when done by a well-known conductor but "failure to understand the style" when done by an amateur? Can business employ music in successful marketing strategies? Does the master performer differ in some way from the struggling student, or is it just a matter of more practice? Knowledge of human musical behavior in diverse manifestations and situations is essential for addressing these and other numerous questions.

Contemporary musicians and educators, struggling to balance conflicting philosophies and societal demands, may find utility in developing understanding and familiarity with human musical behavior. Does music really motivate and/or sedate students? What physiological changes may occur while listening to music? Why are children more receptive to "different" music in the primary grades than in later years? How related is musical ability to intellectual or manual abilities? Again, although this book does not promise definitive answers, the information provided may focus relevant inquiry.

Scope

Music psychology's traditional domains include psychoacoustics, measurement and prediction of musical ability, functional music, cultural organization of musical patterns, music learning, and the affective response to music. Since about the mid to late 1970s, music cognition has been a dominant domain. The chapter organization recognizes the traditional domains as well as the importance of the more contemporary emphasis on cognition, especially regarding psychoacoustics, musical preference, learning, and the psychological foundations of rhythm, melody, and harmony. The chapter on music as a phenomenon of people, society, and culture reflects contemporary interest in music's various roles as a catalyst for social behavior and its diverse sociocultural functions. Music psychology traditionally has given less attention to performance and creative activity than to listening and associated behaviors; in contrast to earlier editions, the authors have added a chapter to address these areas of increasing interest.

Musical behavior is one aspect of human behavior. Consequently, it must be subject to whatever genetic and environmental factors influence all human behavior. Throughout, the book expresses a concern for what people *do* with musical stimuli, in natural as well as laboratory settings.

Behavior, as used herein, means the activities of living dynamic human beings. Such activity is directly observable and is of interest either in itself or as external evidence of some internal state. *Cognition,* the internal processes of memory and "thinking," may be behavior in a covert sense, but the only way to study covert behavior with relative objectivity is to study its overt manifestations. *Perception* is a process of sensing the environment; it obviously is essential for behavior. Perception may be studied only through evidence of its results. Musical behavior includes performance, listening, and creative activity involved in composition and improvisation. The study of musical behavior thus necessarily includes related cognitive and perceptual processes. That which people *do* with music is musical *behavior.* So, too, is that which music *does* to people.

As Gaston (1968, p. 7) indicates, musical behavior is studied through psychology, anthropology, and sociology. This book primarily reflects a psychological approach, as psychology is the study of human behavior. Nevertheless, the authors have not hesitated to look beyond the general body of psychological literature. Sociology, anthropology, philosophy, music history, acoustics, and business are germane areas from which the authors have drawn material.

Preview

As with the two prior editions, in planning this book the authors considered the dynamic (in the sense of moving and everchanging) aspects of music performance and listening as well as important influences of prior experiences on present behaviors. No human musical activity results solely from willful interaction with music. Cultural influences, learning, and biological constraints are as crucial as motivation, reward, and any "inherent" properties of the musical stimulus. Gaston's (1957, p. 25) statement, made almost two score years ago, remains significant:

> To each musical experience is brought the sum of an individual's attitudes, beliefs, prejudices, conditionings in terms of time and place in which he lived. To each response, also, he brings his own physiological needs, unique neurological and endocrinological systems with their distinctive attributes. He brings, in all of this, his total entity as a unique individual.[1]

Chapter Two examines diverse views of why people have music and considers music's functions for individuals, its social values, and its importance as a cultural phenomenon. While the focus is on Western music, certain ethnological research suggests that commonalities of musical function exist across different cultures.

Much of the world's music exists primarily to further some nonmusical purpose, such as selling something, sedating or stimulating people, enhancing a story told through film or television, or facilitating and enriching ceremonies and rituals. Chapter Three considers such "functional music." It also provides a basic discussion of music as a therapeutic tool.

Music would not exist if people were unable to perceive and process certain psychoacoustical phenomena, such as pitch, loudness, and timbre. Accordingly, Chapter Four discusses basic descriptions and relationships involving psychoacoustical phenomena and gives considerable attention to perception, judgment, and measurement, as well as physical and psychophysical events.

Music is a time-based art form; some organization of the durations of

---

[1]This is a direct quote of material written at a time when generic use of masculine terms in reference to unspecified individuals or humanity in its entirety was customary. The present authors have made every effort in their original writing to avoid exclusive reference to one gender when they are discussing unspecified individuals or humanity in general.

sounds and silences necessarily is present in all music. Chapter Five discusses rhythmic behaviors and what is involved in producing and responding to rhythms. The authors believe that rhythmic response is learned; no person "has rhythm" on an absolute inherent basis.

Definitions and opinions regarding melody and harmony differ; whether those properties exist in all music is debatable. Nevertheless, they are vital considerations of much Western music, and musicians and nonmusicians use the terms freely. Research in cognitive psychology suggests that the mental organization of music depends, in part, on structural aspects involving melody and harmony. Chapter Six considers horizontal and vertical pitch organization, tonality, scales, and value judgments, as well as related pedagogical issues.

Chapter Seven examines basic aspects of musical performance, improvisation, and composition. It considers characteristics of the expert performer, performance anxiety, creative and recreative aspects of making new music, and related philosophical and pedagogical issues.

Chapter Eight is concerned with the "chills up the spine" effect and other indications of an affective response to music. Physiological changes may occur in experiencing music, but what is their nature? What is the influence of training? What makes "beautiful" music "beautiful"? The chapter discusses several approaches to studying the affective response to music, with particular emphasis on developments in psychological aesthetics.

Musical preference is the subject of Chapter Nine. It examines existing preferences and tastes and discusses musical and social variables of which musical preference is a function.

Chapter Ten represents a major change from prior editions. The chapter closely relates the development and prediction of musical ability, music learning as a form of human learning, and musical abnormalities. Music as a form of intelligence, diverse approaches to assessing musical ability, and a developmental sequence receive attention. On the basis of what research and theory say regarding human musical learning and development, the authors offer some practical suggestions for music education.

Chapter Eleven speculates regarding future research directions. It primarily warns against overzealous interpretations of limited research.

All chapters reflect the authors' bias that music is a human phenomenon. Individuals bring their prior experiences to the performance and listening situations, where such experiences interact with all the dynamic aspects of human intercourse. Much remains to be learned regarding musical behavior. Its complexities at times may overwhelm the student, teacher, and researcher, but seemingly far-fetched and distantly related ideas may begin to appear with surprising frequency. In the last analysis, musical behavior is but one dimension of human behavior, albeit a very important one for many people—it is no more, and no less. As Gaston (1968, p. 21) said, "Music is not mystical nor supernatural—it is only mysterious."

References

Gaston, E. T. (1957). Factors contributing to responses in music. In E. T. Gaston (Ed.), *Music therapy 1957* (pp. 23–30). Lawrence, KS: Allen Press.

Gaston, E. T. (1968). Man and music. In E. T. Gaston (Ed.), *Music in therapy* (pp. 7–29). New York: Macmillan.

CHAPTER TWO

MUSIC, A PHENOMENON OF PEOPLE, SOCIETY, AND CULTURE

People have examined music from many perspectives, including historical, psychological, philosophical, sociological, and cultural anthropological, as well as the more specialized domains of ethnomusicology, sociomusicology, and sociology of music.[1] There appears to be consensus that society and culture have much influence on the musical behaviors of individuals within given societal and cultural groups and subgroups.

Nettl (1956, p. 6) notes that music is present in all cultures, at diverse levels of civilization. Merriam (1964, p. 218) states that

> the importance of music, as judged by the sheer ubiquity of its presence, is enormous and when it is considered that music is used both as a summatory mark of many activities and as an integral part of many others which could not be properly executed, or executed at all, without music, its importance is substantially magnified. There is probably no other human cultural activity which is so all-pervasive and which reaches into, shapes and often controls so much of human behavior.

The preceding statement, while made by a person concerned with the study of music outside Western traditions, accurately reflects music's place in contemporary society. The ever-presence of music, whether in the concert hall, supermarket, home, church, school, commercial media, or elsewhere, provides evidence that the statement is equally as true for "sophisticated" as for "primitive" societies.

For the most part, musical behavior is interhuman, interpersonal, or social (Mueller, 1963). According to Dasilva, Blasi, and Dees (1984, pp. 3–5), music may be social in several senses: (a) Performing, creating, hearing, and interpreting music involves the use of shared social constructs— grammars and symbols, (b) music involves composers, interpreters, and listeners, and (c) music is communal in nature; i.e., it

---

[1]Sociology of music focuses primarily on any aspect of musicmaking that influences or is influenced by society (Lundquist, 1982, p. 107). Sociomusicology's interests and concerns are ultimately *musical.* Sociology of music, however, "is not about music but society" (Dasilva, Blasi, & Dees, 1984, p. 1). Nevertheless, each field of study offers insights into the effects of society on musical behavior.

8

takes place in "communities," limited circles in which particular interpersonal and intergroup relationships exist. Dasilva et al. argue that musical behavior, or "conduct" as they prefer, can not be understood without examination of the social processes involved. Sloboda (1985, p. 240) also maintains that social influences are essential to any full explanation of human conduct.

Why Music?

Because people create music, they presumably create it for some purpose, i.e., music serves some function within the society in which it is created. Perhaps more accurately, the musical *experience* rather than the music *per se* is functional. As Portnoy (1963, p. 113) suggests, music's value lies not in the musical structure but in the effect it has on people. Thus, from this perspective, music that is of no use to people or has no effect on people might be considered valueless.

The authors base the present discussion on the recognition that music is created by and for people. For Gaston (1968, p. 15), "Music is the essence of humanness," not only because people create it, but because they create their relationships to it. Gaston maintains that the human brain, which distinguishes people from other animals by making possible speech and abstract thinking, also enables "significant nonverbal communication in the form of music." Sloboda (1985, p. 268) and Dowling and Harwood (1986, pp. 236–237) also recognize that biological development has been essential to music becoming such a vital part of society and culture. As Roederer (1995, p. 12) notes, artistic creativity and appreciation are unique to human beings.

Most readers probably agree that musical behavior is unique to people, but there may be less consensus regarding *why* music exists. While most philosophical inquiry regarding the question examines music as an art form with aesthetic value, anthropologists and ethnomusicologists suggest that music exists because of its enculturational functions (Johnson, 1985, p. 54; Nettl, 1985, p. 69). Music also is recognized as serving additional functions.

Several writers (e.g., Adorno, 1976; Dowling & Harwood, 1986; Gaston, 1968; Kaplan, 1990; Merriam, 1964; Nettl, 1956; Sloboda, 1985) have presented views regarding music's functions, and this section reviews those functions from three perspectives: (a) cultural anthropological (Merriam, 1964), (b) sociological (Kaplan, 1990), and (c) psychological (Gaston, 1968). As will be evident, the functions identified within each perspective and across the three perspectives are neither discrete nor exhaustive.

Merriam's Functions of Music

For Merriam, *functions* denotes the reasons, particularly the broader purposes, for engaging in musical activity. Although he recognizes that there are differences in the ways or situations in which people *use* music in nonliterate and literate societies, he maintains that music essentially serves the same functions regardless of the society, culture, or its level of sophistication. These functions include (a) emotional expression, (b) aesthetic enjoyment, (c) entertainment, (d) communication, (e) symbolic representation, (f) physical response, (g) enforcing conformity to social norms, (h) validation of social institutions and religious rituals, (i) contributions to the continuity and stability of culture, and (j) contributions to the integration of society.

Music as *emotional expression* provides a vehicle for expression of ideas and emotions which might not be revealed in ordinary discourse. It can convey either individual or group emotions. The social protest songs of the 1960s allowed young people a socially tolerable outlet for expressing anti-Vietnam war sentiments. Songs have been a part of many other movements in which people sought to express social and political displeasure, e.g., the American civil rights movement, the political upheaval in South Africa, and the Beijing demonstrations for democracy. On a more personal level, young people often express feelings of love through song. Music also is used to express grief, joy, reverie, fright, and virtually any conceivable emotional feeling.

Music as *aesthetic enjoyment,* which is examined more fully in Chapter Eight, essentially involves the contemplation of music in terms of its beauty, meaning, and/or power to evoke a feelingful experience. The exact nature of music's function as aesthetic enjoyment has been a matter of philosophical consideration throughout the history of Western civilization. No doubt people will continue to debate the "real" meaning of the aesthetic function, but an aesthetic experience essentially involves seriously contemplating and responding feelingfully to some object or event in terms of its beauty, meaning, and/or power to evoke a feelingful experience. Whether the feelingfulness of the aesthetic experience results from the organization of the sounds themselves, the sounds' "expressive qualities," something external that the sounds might symbolize, or even from the listener's previous associations with the music also will be subject to continual debate. Regardless of the exact nature of and bases for the aesthetic function, making music and responding to its beauty, meaning, or power appear important to most people.

Music functions as *entertainment* in virtually all societies. Distinguishing between the entertainment function and the aesthetic enjoyment function, Mussulman (1974, p. 140) suggests that entertainment "engages the attention agreeably" and "amuses or diverts" while art is concerned with aesthetic principles. Whether a given musical experience may both entertain and give rise to aesthetic experience has been questioned, but the function served may vary for individual listeners. At least for the last half of the twentieth century, "popular" music, in the broadest sense of the term, apparently is intended to serve an entertainment function, while art music is intended to serve an aesthetic function, although the authors recognize that popular music may give rise to aesthetic contemplation and experience and that much art music is entertaining. Certainly, music to entertain is a major industry in itself, and when commercial values (e.g., planned obsolescence so that new music and recordings may be sold) begin to override artistic values, one may question such music's potential to serve the aesthetic function. However, one can not deny that highly commercialized undertakings such as Andrew Lloyd Webber's musicals *Jesus Christ Superstar, Evita, Cats,* and *The Phantom of the Opera* resulted in aesthetic experiences for millions of people. Or were these people just being entertained?

Merriam suggests that music's function as *communication* is perhaps the least understood of his ten major functions. Merriam is adamant that music is *not* a "universal language;" rather, he contends, music is shaped in terms of the culture of which it is a part. Even within a culture, that which music communicates usually is imprecise. Its communicative meaning particularly depends on the extent to which individuals within the culture have shared experiences regarding the musical idioms and what they convey. Even then, it is unlikely that individuals with shared experiences will derive the same meaning from a given musical experience. As suggested previously, any mood or emotion conveyed by music also depends on a variety of factors external to the music itself. A listener's personality and other attributes that contribute to his or her uniqueness as an individual, the mood he or she holds just prior to the musical experience, any word meanings conveyed by the music (if any exist), and the listener's attitudes toward music in general and the particular music heard all affect any mood or emotion resulting from the musical experience.

In virtually every culture, music may function as a *symbolic representation* of other things, ideas, and behaviors. In serving this function, whatever music symbolizes or represents must be of a nonmusical nature. These things, ideas, and behaviors may include cultural values, other group or individual values, abstract ideals, or occasions which hold particular affective meaning. A national anthem may symbolize a nation's values and traditions. Protest songs often symbolize social or political movements, and school songs and theme songs of other organizations have symbolic value for members of those organizations. Theme songs for individual performers, for radio and television shows, and even for products promoted in advertising jingles also have a certain symbolic value, although it is doubtful that the symbolic representation in these instances reflects the profundity of cultural symbolism that Merriam suggests.

Music gives rise to *physical response,* and every society uses music to accompany dance and other rhythmic activities. Music elicits, excites, and channels crowd behavior, although the type and extent of the behavior also is shaped culturally. Chailley (1964, p. 62) suggests that an important part of religious ritual in primitive societies was to draw the worshiper "out of himself, to excite him and . . . to put him in a state of ecstasy." Chailley also argues that religious ritual that uses music solely for creating tranquility and contemplative meditation is against human nature. Perhaps the music of contemporary Christian rock and gospel groups, which by its very nature tends to elicit more physical response than traditional church music, is capitalizing on this basic movement function of music.

According to Merriam, *enforcing conformity to social norms* is one of music's major functions, particularly in primitive cultures. Merriam notes that the songs of social control play an important part in many cultures by providing either direct warnings to erring members of the society or by indirectly indicating what is considered proper behavior. Protest songs often point out the improprieties of society as well as the proprieties. Many songs for young children, including both traditional folk songs and certain songs specifically devised for preschool and early elementary children, serve to reinforce the values and ideals that parents, schools, and society wish to instill in young children.

Closely related to the preceding function is the use of music to *validate social institutions and religious rituals.* Songs which emphasize the proper and improper in society and songs which tell people what to do and how to do it serve this function. Songs of fraternal organizations, church youth groups, and many other organizations that wish to establish and preserve their traditions and ideals also serve this function.

Perhaps all of the foregoing functions are related to Merriam's ninth musical function, the *contribution to the continuity and stability of culture.* As Merriam (1964, p. 225) states,

> If music allows emotional expression, gives aesthetic pleasure, entertains, communicates, elicits physical response, enforces conformity to social norms, and validates social institutions and religious rituals, it is clear that it contrib-

utes to the continuity and stability of culture. . . . Music is in a sense a summatory activity for the expression of values, a means whereby the heart of the psychology of a culture is exposed without many of the protective mechanisms which surround other cultural activities.

He goes on to suggest that music's very existence provides a normal and solid activity which assures members of the society that their world is continuing in the right direction. Music continues to serve this function today: Since the 1950s, American adolescent subculture has had various forms of music with which to identify, music that teenagers feel is "their" music. Folk songs from the "old country" may provide immigrants and their descendants with a cultural link to the past. In addition to their religious and entertainment functions, traditional Christmas and Hannukah songs provide a certain stability across generations.

Perhaps music's most important function from Merriam's perspective is its *contribution to the integration of society.* If nothing else, music draws people together: It invites, encourages, and in some instances almost requires individuals to participate in group activity. People who might otherwise never interact will work together in making music. Farrell's (1972) study of the meaning of the choral experience for adult amateur singers and Hylton's (1980) study of high school choral groups both revealed that social interaction was a highly meaningful aspect of the choral experience. Mills's (1988) study of the meaning of the high school band experience yielded similar results. In short, musicmaking brings people from differing sociocultural, religious, occupational, and musical backgrounds together for a common musical and social experience.

In summary, Merriam's ten musical functions reflect an anthropological perspective and suggest that since its beginnings, music has helped and served people by (a) integrating individuals into society, (b) teaching the society's institutions and rituals, and (c) generally contributing to cultural stability and continuity. While the nature and forms of music vary from culture to culture, and the directness with which various cultures have *used* their music functionally also varies, Merriam's functions continue to have merit in contemporary cultures.

Kaplan's Social Functions of the Arts

Kaplan is both a sociologist and a musician, and while he intends his social functions of the arts to reflect all of the arts, they seem particularly descriptive of music's functions. Kaplan's (1990, pp. 28–38) functions include art [read *music*] as (a) a form of knowledge, (b) collective possession, (c) personal experience, (d) therapy, (e) moral and symbolic force, (f) incidental commodity, (g) symbolic indicator of change, and (h) a link between the past, present, and scenarios of the future.

Art as *a form of knowledge* is an aesthetic knowledge based on the "essence of originality in putting together things, objects, ideals, sounds, forms, and space and time relationships in ways that have not been done before, but on the principle of beauty" (p. 20). Such knowledge also involves subjectivity, the essence of which is undefinable. This subjectivity, Kaplan maintains, gives art its strength and reason for being.

The arts may be the *collective possession* of a state, church, fraternal organization, political group, or other social group and may be useful in some ritual or to commemorate some special events. When arts are used in this way, they serve both to "identify the persons who watch or listen with the intended group interests and values" (p. 30) and to fulfill some particular social, political, or propaganda end.

The arts as *personal experience* may provide a means by which an individual can remove himself or herself from a group, thereby weakening personal reliance upon the group (p. 30). Music and arts from other eras even allow a certain escape from the present and an opportunity to experience the past. Kaplan maintains that art as personal experience also may provide the "opportunity for relaxation, memory, fragmentary or sustained enjoyment, contemplation, or any other subjective mood or need" (p. 31).

The arts, and particularly music, as *therapy* have evolved over the past half century into respectable professions. Kaplan notes that in the very process of singing or playing an instrument, "something happens." That which happens is often difficult to explain, but Kaplan suggests that a handicapped individual's mere participation in a group musicmaking experience involves a type of communication, something which often is not possible for such individuals through normal verbal discourse. Kaplan suggests that in a period of growing anxieties in society, the medical profession may show an increasing interest in such symbolic communication as the arts offer.

The arts value as *moral and symbolic forces* may articulate concepts that are "external to the arts but important to society: God, freedom, love, bravery, youth, joy, or sadness" (p. 32). Kaplan notes that the arts may teach "proper responses or attitudes towards values and institutions of the society" (p. 32) and acknowledges that the arts as symbolic and moral forces can not be distinguished clearly from *collective possession,* citing particularly music's long history as a tool of propaganda. However, he goes on to note a more general sense in which art is a symbolic force in all societies: as *play.* He maintains that it is more than a figure of speech when we say we "play" music or are "playing" an instrument, and suggests that participation in music and the other arts "transcends the immediate needs of life and imparts meaning to the action" (p. 33).

As a sociologist, Kaplan is interested particularly in the arts as *incidental commodity*. He notes applications of the arts in radio and television for which profit is a primary motive. He views musicians and other artists who work in these media simply as employees engaged for a specific task. Kaplan's comprehensive model for the arts in society sees the roles of creators and distributors of art as intertwined and involved directly with the arts as a commodity. While this particularly is the case for music in the various popular and entertainment idioms, it also is evident for some art music. In short, music is both a process and product through which many individuals in today's society are able to realize commercial gain.

Kaplan also views the arts as *indicators and forerunners of social change* and notes that this function "is so obvious that it risks being ignored" (p. 34). Music both shapes and is shaped by society, and students of music history are cognizant of music as a reflection of the life and social conditions of the various historical eras. Contemporary youth music provides a notable example of a group's social values being both reflected in and promulgated by the group's music.

Perhaps the most important function of the arts for Kaplan is their role as a *link between the past, present, and scenarios of the future*. Contrasting the creativity of artists with the creative efforts of scientists, Kaplan notes that artists produce works that might be tested or evaluated subjectively rather than empirically by their colleagues and the public. He suggests, however, that it is the "subjective nature of the arts, and its accumulative nature as a part of every culture, that gives it the unique stability to which the scientist may turn for his own sense of stability in his objective, experimental world" (p. 37). He maintains that great works of art such as Beethoven's *Ninth Symphony* will continue to be heard by future generations, thus serving as a link from the past, through the present, and into the future. Such an important function, Kaplan argues, makes music "a basic form of knowledge and a major cultural value" (p. 37).

Gaston's Fundamental Considerations of People in Relation to Music

Gaston's (1968) "fundamental considerations" focus more on music's functions for the individual than for culture or society. The eight considerations include (a) the need for aesthetic expression and experience, (b) the influence of the cultural matrix on the mode of expression, (c) the integral relationship between music and religion, (d) music as communication, (e) music as structured reality, (f) music's relationship to the tender emotions, (g) music as a source of gratification, and (h) music's potency in a group.

Gaston views the *need for aesthetic expression and experience* as essential to the development of humanness and considers sensitivity to beauty and the making of beauty to be one of humankind's most distinguishing characteristics. Gaston goes so far as to suggest that individuals who are insensitive to beauty—whether in music or some other medium—are not achieving their full potential as human beings and may even be handicapped.

While not a function per se, the view that the *cultural matrix in which an individual lives determines the mode of expression* is fundamental to Gaston's functions of music. While music serves similar functions in nearly all cultures, *individuals* usually respond only to functional music of their own culture, i.e., they learn the music of their own culture and generally react to it in terms of the way their particular society reacts to it.

The *integral relationship of music and religion* is evident in virtually every culture. Gaston believes the primary reason for this is that religious services and music performances have some common purposes, the greatest of which is their valence for drawing and bonding individuals into a group. Music and religion go together to defend against fear and loneliness. Music also seems to be particularly appropriate for invoking the supernatural, a concern of many religious rites.

For Gaston, the importance of *music as communication* is in its value as nonverbal communication, which provides music its potency and value. Gaston maintains that people would not need music if they could communicate verbally that which is easily communicated musically. Even the best verbal descriptions of feelings elicited by music fail to communicate the feelings adequately. Perhaps it is because music's meaning is wordless that philosophical explanations of music's meanings are inadequate.

That *music is structured reality* should be evident to any student of music theory. The fact that music is a time-based auditory phenomenon does not make it any less sensorily tangible than objects which people touch, see, taste, or smell. Gaston maintains that music therefore is a particularly valuable therapeutic medium through which individuals who have withdrawn from society may reestablish contact with a structured reality.

Gaston's contention that music *is derived from the tender emotions* is reflected clearly in most popular music, as well as in most religious music, folk songs, art songs, and patriotic music. Most such music reflects a concern for other individuals, and the predominant theme is love in one of its various manifestations—love of one another, love of country, love of God, etc. Such music also may provide an individual with a feeling of belonging, thus providing a sense of closeness to others and the alleviation of loneliness.

> In our culture, as well as in others, *music is nearly always an expression of good will, a reaching out to others,* and is so interpreted. Music, then, is a powerful expression of the interdependence of mankind, and from the lullaby to the funeral dirge, an expression of the tender emotions. (Gaston, 1968, p. 25).

The recognition of music *as a source of gratification* is particularly apparent in children and adolescents, although adults certainly may attain a sense of gratification from musical experience. Gratification is a by-product of achievement per se rather than competition, and music provides opportunities for achievement in noncompetitive situations. The self-esteem which results from musical accomplishment contributes greatly to an individual's state of well-being.

That *the potency of music is greatest in the group* should be self-evident. Music is a social phenomenon which invites and encourages participation. Music provides group activities which bring together individuals who otherwise might not come in contact with one another. Group musical experience provides people with opportunities to interact in intimate yet ordered and socially desirable ways.

While Merriam, Kaplan, and Gaston view the functions of music from different perspectives, many commonalities exist among the functions they describe. Also, the various functions are not discrete; given musical experiences may serve different functions for different individuals and even more than one function for a given individual. The important point is that musical experiences serve a variety of functions for most people in virtually every culture and society. While some cultures, particularly Western ones, may place greater emphasis on an aesthetic function, all functions contribute to music's importance in society.

Another Perspective

While the functions of music noted by Merriam, Kaplan, and Gaston offer plausible reasons for music being such an important aspect of virtually all cultures and societies, some recently proposed views on music's functions in society and culture suggest that biological development (Sloboda, 1985, pp. 260–268) and music's *biological adaptive value* (Dowling & Harwood, 1986, pp. 236–237) were instrumental in making music so valuable for the human species.

In raising the question "Does man *need* music?" Sloboda (p. 266) notes that individuals can go without music for very long periods without showing any noticeable ill effects. He suggests that perhaps *cultures* rather than individuals need music and that the "need" might be more direct in nonliterate cultures than in today's complex contemporary societies.

> Primitive cultures have few artifacts, and the organization of the society must be expressed to a greater extent through transient actions and the way people interact with each other. Music, perhaps, provides a unique framework with which humans can express, by the temporal organization of sound and gesture, the structure of their knowledge and social relations. Songs and rhythmically organized poems and sayings form the major repository of human knowledge in non-literate cultures. (Sloboda, 1985, p. 267)

Sloboda goes on to speculate that human mental processes, which he views as a product of evolution, have led to a natural propensity to behave in adaptive ways, including a propensity to use language and music. He maintains that evolution supplied a *motivation* for music, making it "natural" and enjoyable for people to indulge in it.

Advocating a similar position, Dowling and Harwood (1986, pp. 236–237) suggest that we should consider evolution in terms of the *gene pool of groups* rather than in terms of *individual adaptations.* They agree that music is valuable to human groups and note that as humans evolved over hundreds of thousands of years in small groups, singing and playing music served as a "cohesion-facilitating group activity—an expression of social solidarity" (p. 236). They recognize music as a powerful symbol of cultural identity, especially since musical style tends, like language, to reflect a highly stable set of culturally transmitted shared behaviors. They maintain that music's *biological adaptive value* is reflected in its value to human societies. Furthermore, they maintain that even with changes in social structures and other developments that have come with industrialized societies, including some division of labor between "musicians" and "consumers," music's sociocultural values and the underlying distribution of musical abilities are essentially the same as in more primitive societies.

The answer to the question "Why music?" continues to be in terms of the many important functions which music serves in society and culture. Perhaps understanding the role of biological evolution in the development of human adaptive behaviors provides at least a partial answer as to "how" music became so important to human society and culture.

What Makes Some Sounds Music?

Studies of the development of musical behavior suggest that differential responses to musical sounds and other sounds become evident during infancy (Dowling, 1984; Fridman, 1973; Michel, 1973; Moog, 1976).

Virtually every child and adult "knows" what music is—at least the music of his or her surrounding culture. An enculturation process assures that early in life children develop a concept of music, albeit vague, ill-defined, and largely nonverbalized. That individuals' concepts reflect cultural bias is readily apparent, although the authors believe that most individuals will recognize another culture's music as music, even though it may sound "strange."

Whatever the culture, music involves an organization of sounds and silences. That organization encompasses various pitches, loudness levels, and timbres, all of which occur within a rhythmic framework. Music is a time-based art form; the pace at which a listener hears a sequence of sounds and silences is determined by the organization across time. While a person may elect how much time to spend on viewing a work of visual art, and may read an excerpt of literature at varying rates, subject to limits of comprehension and maintaining a narrative flow, the person listening to music must accept the durational sequences embodied in the performance.

Many combinations and varieties of sounds are possible in music: When one considers the range of perceptually just noticeable differences in pitch, loudness, and timbre, the possibilities are virtually infinite.

Of course, all sounds are temporal, and all sounds have a certain loudness level and sound quality or timbre. One can argue that all sounds, even obvious noises, have a certain pitch level, even though the pitch may be rather indefinite and continually changing. Despite the definition of music as organized sound and silence, one may hear discernible organization in sounds generally considered nonmusical, e.g., speech, certain machinery sounds, and many natural sounds, especially if they have a repetitive quality. Some contemporary music—*musique concrete*—incorporates sounds of nature and other environmental sounds into a recognized musical style.

So why are some sounds more likely to be organized into and heard as music more than others? Psychologists, theorists, philosophers, and musicologists have considered that question and offered various answers, ranging from physical explanations in terms of the harmonic structure of musical sounds to psychological characteristics. Others (Beament, 1977; Gaston, 1968) even suggest that the basic differences in what people will recognize as music ultimately are a function of physiology or biology.

Blacking (1973, p. 10) argues that music could not exist if people had not developed a capacity for structural listening, i.e., the ability to perceive *sonic order*. He goes on to argue that understanding music involves both sound (the object) and person (the subject); for Blacking, the key to understanding music is in subject-object relationships, the activating principle of organization (p. 26).

No one answer to the "what makes some sounds music" question will be acceptable to everyone, but obviously some sounds must be easier to organize into music than other sounds. One basic difference between most natural sounds and most sounds deliberately created for music is that natural sounds are "constantly changing from instant to instant in the frequencies present and in the amplitudes of the frequencies" (Beament, 1977, p. 7). Beament notes that music primarily involves sounds with sustained constant frequencies (heard as fixed pitches) without which melodic and harmonic music could not occur. He maintains that fixed pitches "are virtually an *artefact* [sic] *of man.*"

Using fixed pitches in music is virtually universal, and psychophysiological explanations of music processing support the need for such use. Roederer (1995, p. 179) maintains that fixed pitches are essential for perceiving music. A tone must last a minimum amount of time in order for the brain to process it as a tone. Sounds of continually changing frequencies do not allow sufficient processing time. In everyday terms, it is easier to identify pitches of sounds which have a certain minimal duration than sounds of pitches that pass by quickly.

Roederer suggests that recurring patterns of a relatively small number of fixed pitches organized into scales have come to be used for music within given cultures because

> it is easier for the brain to process, identify, and store in its memory a melody that is made up of a time sequence of discrete pitch values that bear a certain relationship to each other ... rather than a pitch-time pattern that sweeps continuously up and down over all possible frequencies. (p. 179)

While the use of fixed pitches appears to be an attribute of sound that most music employs, one should note that the range of sounds used in music has other attributes for which "reasons for being" are inadequate. For example, Sloboda (1985, pp. 253–259) recognizes other musical universals. He notes that virtually all music occurs with respect to fixed *reference* pitches, such as a drone or tonal center. He also notes that the octave is a "privileged" interval, frequently used in nearly all music, and that scales in virtually all cultures do not divide into equal sized intervals. A fourth universal involves the use of pulse or meter to provide *time reference* points. Sloboda argues that both pitch and time reference points are essential for people to coordinate their behaviors in such a way as to make music a structured social phenomenon.

Consensus regarding answers to "Why music?" or "Why is this music while that is not?" may never be attained. It appears, however, that any answer must encompass more than the objective ordering of sounds. The answers also must recognize that music is a human construct, with certain psychophysical, perceptual, cognitive, and behavioral potentials for interacting with sound constructs. Finally, the answers must recognize that musical sounds vary from culture to culture, yet serve many similar functions within all cultures.

The eventual answer to "What makes some sounds music?" must be in terms of the *function* of sounds within a given cultural context. Musical sounds are (a) created or combined by a human being, (b) recognized as music by some group of people, and (c) serve some function which music has come to serve for humanity. Ultimately, musical sounds are those sounds that people are willing to accept as such.

Origins of Music

Obviously, the study of music's origin is fraught with many difficulties, not the least of which is music's temporal nature, which allows anthropologists and archaeologists few artifacts for determining the nature of early people's musics and still fewer clues to music's origins. Such a void has given rise to myth, legend, speculation, conjecture, and theory. People have handed down myths and legends through many cultures, perhaps from prehistoric times, but certainly from the cultures of antiquity and many primitive cultures that anthropologists and musicologists have studied.

In the nineteenth and early twentieth centuries, scholars demonstrated a renewed interest in searching for music's origin. Revesz (1954, p. 218) suggests that perhaps Darwin's (1874) theory of evolution stimulated the renewal. Although many have questioned the sophistication and accuracy of the nineteenth and early twentieth century scholars' speculations regarding music's origin (e.g., Blacking, 1973; Chailley, 1964; Nadel, 1930; Nettl, 1956; Revesz, 1954; Wallaschek, 1893/1970), these speculative theories still hold a certain fascination and even plausibility for many.

Chailley (1964, pp. 1–11) and Wallaschek (1893/1970, pp. 259–262) summarized some of the myths and legends, most of which suggest that some supernatural being gave music to people. One Hindu myth holds that Brahma, the supreme spirit of the universe in Hindu theology, invented music as the goddess of speech, Saraswati. A Chinese legend dating back to the third century B.C. says that the Chinese musical scale came from six tones sung by a magical bird, called Fung-Hoang. Durant (1963, p. 723), however, offers a different, non-avian account of the origin of Chinese music; he ascribes music's origin to the legendary emperor,

Fu Hsi. Japanese tradition holds that music came from the gods themselves, perhaps devised to lure the sun goddess from a cave into which she had retreated.

The Sumerians had the goddess Nina as the patroness of music, while the Assyrians called their goddess of love, Ishtar, "the harmonious and sweet-toned flute" (Chailley, p. 6). Greek mythology recognized several gods and goddesses associated with music: a goddess or Muse of song; Athena, creator of the flute; the god Pan, who created the pipes of reeds; and Hermes, who created the shepherd pipe for himself and the lyre for Apollo, the god of music (Portnoy, 1963, p. 241). Perhaps the most far reaching Greek myth about music was that of the "harmony of the spheres," which originated with the Pythagoreans and subsequently became the basis of Plato's philosophy of music.[2]

The Hebrews were among the few people of antiquity who considered music's origin to be historical rather than supernatural. The Bible credits music's invention to Jubal, a seventh generation descendant of Cain, the elder son of Adam and Eve. "He was the father of all such as handle the harp and organ" (Genesis 4:21).

Many speculative theories of music's origin are rooted in music's potential for facilitating communication, at least in a broad sense of the term. Several of the communication-related theories postulate a close relationship between the development of language and music. Other theories, which will be discussed prior to the communication theories, include the *mating call* or *Darwinian theory*, a *theory of imitation*, a *theory of rhythm*, and a *worksong theory*.

The mating call theory holds that music's origin is rooted in human sexual instincts and that the earliest form of music was a form or extension of a mating call (Darwin, 1874, p. 652). Although highly criticized by many (Nettl, 1956, pp. 134–135; Revesz, 1954, pp. 224–227; Sloboda, 1985, pp. 265–266), proponents of the theory cite the mating calls of some animals and songs of birds that serve a sexual function—sounds or songs used in seeking a mate. Critics of the theory, however, note that (a) birds "sing" outside of mating season, (b) there is an absence of music-like mating calls among apes, and (c) if the theory were true, music of today's primitive cultures should be preponderantly love songs related to seeking a mate.

The theory that music originated from human attempts to imitate bird songs predates the mating call theory. Support for this theory generally

---

[2]Essentially, harmony of the spheres refers to characteristic music of heavenly bodies, a part of the divinely ordained "celestial" music, with which people might interact through mathematics. For further information regarding this view, see Walker (1990).

is based on the tendency of some birds' songs to use fixed pitches and some recurring intervals. Revesz, however, notes that no primitive cultures have songs which imitate bird calls; further, he asserts that the utterances of birds are merely reactions to biological states. Instinct dominates bird songs and animal sounds, whereas music created by people reflects purposeful and conceptual behavior.

The theory of rhythm stresses the close relationship between dance and song (Revesz, p. 227). Proponents of this theory cite the importance of rhythm to both music and dance. However, no one has demonstrated that music evolved from sounds used to accompany dance, and, indeed, dance, as organized movement, does not require music any more than music, as organized sound and silence, requires dance. Sachs (1943, p. 21) argues that *"music began with singing"* and observes that many primitive people do not have musical instruments to accompany their dance.

Attributed to Karl Buecher, the work song theory suggests that early people's need to coordinate work efforts provided the impetus for music. Buecher's theory apparently was based on his study of Western folk songs, which revealed a number of work songs. Nettl (1956, p. 134), criticizing the theory, notes that most primitive cultures do not have work songs, and even when they do work in groups, rhythmic efficiency is not evident.

Variously called the *speech theory* (Wallaschek), the *theory of expression* (Revesz), and the *theory of impassioned speech* (Nettl), a theory of expressive or emotional speech suggests that as a person becomes more emotional in his or her speech, the speech patterns take on more the characteristics of music—those of fixed intervals, their transposability to various pitch levels, and their use of rhythmically articulated tone combinations (Revesz, p. 219). Critics of the theory argue that speech sounds manifesting emotion have little in common with music or song; neither do these sounds serve any musical function. Also, speech may be highly expressive of emotion yet fail to reflect the essential characteristics of music.

The *theory of melodic speech* holds that music evolved from the accentuation and intonation of human speech. Essentially, this theory suggests that recitative-like speech preceded and eventually evolved into music. Another version of this theory is that tonal modulation in speech eventually became song. Sachs (1961, pp. 34–36), highly critical of this supposition, notes that in many languages, past and present, sounds "are not only long and short or stressed or accented, but also, in a musical sense, ascending, level, descending, or medium, high, or low" (p. 35). He notes that tonal differences are essential in understanding Chinese or Siamese;

changing pitch levels of otherwise similar words may change the meaning entirely.

Revesz is a proponent of the view that music originated from early humans' need to communicate more effectively over long distances. His theory, labelled the *calling signal theory*, suggests that shouts or calls of individuals trying to communicate over long distances take on musical characteristics, particularly fixed pitches and varying loudness levels. Nettl disregards this theory because his study of primitive cultures found no use of fixed pitches in calling signals.

Nadel (1930, pp. 538–542) theorizes that people devised music in an effort to communicate with the supernatural. Throughout history, people have integrated music, ritual, and religion and absorbed them into the mythology of many cultures, thereby giving this theory a certain credence. Ostensibly, a function of much religious music is communication with the spirits, a god, or supreme being. Nettl, however, argues that this theory is unprovable and supported only by circumstantial evidence.

Nettl offers a theory suggesting that early communication in primitive cultures was neither music nor speech. Such communication, he contends, possessed three elements common to both music and speech: pitch, stress, and duration. In his view, neither fixed pitches nor definite vowels and consonants existed; rather, the sounds were grunts, cries, and wails that sounded like neither speech nor music. Nettl conjectures that through a long, gradual stage of cultural differentiation and specialization, language acquired the characteristics of vowels and consonants while music acquired the characteristics of fixed pitches. This process of differentiation involved three stages: (a) undifferentiated communication, (b) differentiation between music and language, and, eventually, (c) differentiation among various styles of music.[3]

Despite the richness and variety of speculative theories about music's origin, contemporary scholars generally are skeptical of them, particularly when they consider music's temporal nature and the lack of artifacts or documentation to corroborate the theories.

As an alternative to the early speculative theories, later writers have offered more recent socio-biologically based views of music's origin. Blacking (1973) argues persuasively that "we shall learn more about music and human musicality if we look for rules of musical behavior which are biologically, as well as culturally, conditioned and species-specific" (p. 100). Gaston (1968, pp. 7–17) and Sloboda (1985, pp. 241–268)

---

[3]Infants' early pre-speech sounds, a combination of babbles, wails, and other sounds, some of which are tonal, may be a microcosmic reenactment of the long term evolutionary process that Nettl's theory suggests. Young children eventually differentiate between language and music.

concur. Such a view suggests a certain evolutionary basis for music's origin, but in a much different sense than the mating call notion.

Gaston argues that the beginnings of human culture go hand in hand with human biological development and stresses that biological and cultural evolutions were part of the same process. He notes that with the development of the brain's cortex, primitive people could suppress rage and hostility, a prerequisite for the development of society. Cortical development freed the primitive female from blind instinctive behavior that would cause her to accept just any male at each period of estrus. The cortical became dominant over the endocrine factor.

These two aspects of biological development, suppression of rage and selective mating, fostered the beginnings of family with its resulting division of labor, modified aggressive behavior between male and female, and increased communication. "All this leads to a uniqueness in humans, among all animals, of the mother-child relationship, without which there would be no culture as we know it" (Gaston, p. 11). Human infants' almost total dependence on their mothers for a long period of time required mothers to devote much time to child care, while the fathers in these primitive hunter-gatherer societies provided food and protection.

Gaston speculates that as the primitive mother sought to soothe her child and express feelings for it, her soothing efforts assumed the rhythmic character of lullabies. Such lullabies may have been one of the earliest forms of music.

Whether or not one accepts Gaston's speculation regarding music's origin as an outgrowth of the mother-child relationship in the earliest families, it is evident that music did become an important part of early human culture. The views of Sloboda (1985, pp. 265–268) and Dowling and Harwood (1986, pp. 235–238), discussed in a previous section of this chapter, support the view that music's origins are rooted in the development of primitive society.

Music in Society and Culture

Whatever music's origin, music is human behavior that occurs within a cultural context. Through an enculturation process, each social order develops its institutions and artifacts for perpetuation of itself, and music's existence is one of the few things common to all cultures (Nettl, 1975, p. 71). In much of European and American society, there is a curious paradox: Music is readily available, yet that very availability may make many people take music for granted. Music is a type of commodity, to be used at the pleasure of the consumer. Perhaps this results from a dichotomization of society into a relatively small group of music makers and a relatively large group of music listeners, many of whom listen passively rather than actively. Despite music's importance to people, many people may not readily recognize its importance.

Previously, this chapter noted that music serves some common functions in most societies even though musical styles and forms vary from culture to culture. Through its functionality to society, music is an integral cultural component, serving as both a cohesive and perpetuating force. On the other hand, music also reflects cultural values and temperaments. Weber's (1958, p. xxvi) analysis of music's rational and social foundations even suggests that the difference between Western music and that of other (particularly Eastern) cultures is rooted in Western people's temperament and their drives to rationalize and understand environmental phenomena. Nettl (1975, p. 93) agrees that a society's character and quality of life greatly influence its music, but he notes that other factors, e.g., technological level, types of raw materials available for instrument construction, amount of contact with other cultures, and attitudes toward cultural change or continuity, also influence the development of a culture's music.

Recognition of cross-cultural "universals" (Dowling & Harwood, 1986, pp. 238–239) does not negate the fact that sociocultural content influences musical behavior. While music obviously has some similarities and serves similar functions in different cultures, individual musical behaviors vary greatly from culture to culture. Just why such variation exists is difficult to explain; Sloboda (1985, pp. 244–248) makes a strong case for the use of notation as an explanatory variable, especially regarding differences between oral and literate cultures. In an oral culture, learning is bound inextricably to fundamental human interactions; individuals gain knowledge through custom and ritual. In literate societies, knowledge is not limited to memories of oral discourse and direct experience; symbol systems, such as notation, allow storage of knowledge. That storage allows recreation of prior knowledge with the aid of the symbols, but it also puts a certain psychological distance between an individual and the accumulated knowledge of the culture that created the symbol system. Furthermore, individuals may be selective regarding aspects of knowledge and more objective in examining that knowledge than individuals operating in an oral culture tradition, where learning and knowledge are more of an integral part of one's self.

Sloboda discusses how differences between directly recalled and symbolized knowledge might affect musical traditions and behaviors in the two types of cultures. In oral cultures, music, like verbal knowledge, is subject to mutation over time: Relatively exact knowledge of particular pieces of music that might be gained through repeated examination of scores and listening to recordings (a way of preserving sound, considered an extension of notation) is virtually impossible. Sloboda suggests several implications of oral/literate differences for musical behavior: (a) memory processing strategies and structures of individuals in the two cultures will differ, (b) the "architectural" complexity of an oral culture's music necessarily will be limited, (c) the nature of a literate culture's musical *content* may be examined separately from musical *context,* and (d) notation leads to *selecting* some aspects of sounds for preservation and discarding others.

Culture clearly affects musical behavior. Conversely, music may influence the culture. Lomax (1968, p. 133) summarized music's cultural role by suggesting that music is a human vehicle for expressing what is most basic in intersocial relationships. Lomax's examination of music in different cultural settings revealed that a culture's favorite music "reflects and reinforces the kinds of behavior essential to its main subsistence efforts and to its central and controlling institution" (p. 133).

Research and writings conducted over several decades (Bindas, 1992; Blacking, 1973; Frith, 1988; Hamm, Nettl, & Byrnside, 1975; Kaplan, 1990; Lomax, 1968; Merriam, 1964; Nettl, 1956; 1975) continually support the hypothesis that music is an integral part of culture. Two once "classic" psychology of music texts (Farnsworth, 1969; Lundin, 1967) adopted the view that music is a cultural and social phenomenon.

The emergence of music sociology, psychomusicology, ethnomusicology, and anthropology of music as discrete fields of study further attests to musical behavior as an integral component of human society and culture. Students of musical behavior, therefore, must be cognizant of the context in which such behavior occurs.

Summary

1. Music is present in all cultures.
2. Music is unique to human beings.
3. Merriam's ten functions include (a) emotional expression, (b) aesthetic enjoyment, (c) entertainment, (d) communication, (e) symbolic representation, (f) physical response, (g) enforcing conformity to social norms, (h) validation of social institutions and religious rituals, (i) contributions to the continuity and stability of culture, and (j) contributions to the integration of society.
4. Kaplan's functions include art [read *music*] as (a) a form of knowledge, (b) collective possession, (c) personal experience, (d) therapy, (e) moral and symbolic force, (f) incidental commodity, (g) symbolic

indicator of change, and (h) link among the past, present, and scenarios of the future.

5. Gaston's eight considerations include (a) the need for aesthetic expression and experience, (b) the influence of the cultural matrix on the mode of expression, (c) the integral relationship between music and religion, (d) music as communication, (e) music as structured reality, (f) music's relationship to the tender emotions, (g) music as a source of gratification, and (h) the potency of music in a group.

6. There is increasing recognition that music's importance in society and culture depends in part on human biological evolution that made possible adaptive behaviors such as language and music.

7. Music of all cultures involves the organization of sounds with varying pitches, loudness levels, and timbral qualities within a rhythmic framework.

8. Fixed pitches are an attribute of music.

9. Sounds are music when they are created or combined by a human being, recognized as music by some group of people, and serve some function for people.

10. Most myths and legends regarding music's origin suggest that some supernatural being gave music to people.

11. Some theories regarding music's origin include the (a) Darwinian theory, (b) theory of rhythm, (c) work song theory, (d) theory of imitation, (e) theory of expression, (f) theory of melodic speech, (g) communication theory, and (h) Nettl's theory of an undifferentiated method of primitive communication.

12. More recent views include (a) Gaston's view that music developed with the beginning of family and (b) the view that music served a need for primitive societies by providing a framework for communicating the structure of social relations.

13. Whether an oral or a literate culture, a culture's characteristics affect the culture's music.

14. Music reflects a culture's values, attitudes, and temperament.

References

Adorno, T. W. (1976). *Introduction to the sociology of music* (E. B. Ashton, Trans.). New York: Seabury Press.

Beament, J. (1977). The biology of music. *Psychology of Music, 5* (1), 3–18.

Bindas, K. J. (Ed.) (1992). *America's musical pulse.* Westport, CT: Greenwood Press.

Blacking, J. (1973). *How musical is man?* Seattle: University of Washington Press.

Chailley, J. (1964). *40,000 years of music?* (R. Myers, Trans.). New York: Farrar, Straus & Giroux.

Darwin, C. (1874). *The descent of man* (rev. ed.). Chicago: Rand McNally & Co.

Dasilva, F., Blasi, A., & Dees, D. (1984). *The sociology of music.* Notre Dame, IN: University of Notre Dame Press.

Dowling, W. J. (1984). Development of musical schemata in children's spontaneous singing. In W. R. Crozier & A. J. Chapman (Eds.), *Cognitive processes in the perception of art* (pp. 145–163). Amsterdam: North-Holland.

Dowling, W. J., & Harwood, D. L. (1986). *Music cognition.* Orlando, FL: Academic Press.

Durant, W. (1963). *Our Oriental heritage* (Vol. 1, *The story of civilization.* New York: Simon and Schuster.

Farnsworth, P. R. (1969). *The social psychology of music* (2nd ed.). Ames: Iowa State University Press.

Farrell, P. (1972). *The meaning of the recreation experience in music as it is defined by urban adults who determined typal singer profiles through Q-technique.* Unpublished doctoral dissertation, The Pennsylvania State University.

Fridman, R. (1973). The first cry of the newborn: Basis for the child's future musical development. *Journal of Research in Music Education, 21,* 264–269.

Frith, S. (Ed.) (1988). *Facing the music.* New York: Pantheon Books.

Gaston, E. T. (1968). Man and music. In E. T. Gaston (Ed.), *Music in therapy* (pp. 7–29). New York: Macmillan.

Genesis 4:21

Hamm, C., Nettl, B., & Byrnside, R. (Eds.) (1975). *Contemporary music and music cultures.* Englewood Cliffs, NJ: Prentice-Hall.

Hylton, J. B. (1980). *The meaning of the high school choral experience and its relationship to selected variables.* Unpublished doctoral dissertation, The Pennsylvania State University.

Johnson, G. T. (1985). Learning from music. In *Becoming human through music* (pp. 53–68). Reston, VA: Music Educators National Conference.

Kaplan, M. (1990). *The arts: A social perspective.* Rutherford, NJ: Fairleigh Dickinson University Press.

Lomax, A. et al. (1968). *Folk song style and culture.* Washington, DC: American association for the Advancement of Science.

Lundin, R. W. (1967). *An objective psychology of music* (2nd ed.). New York: Ronald Press.

Lundquist, B. L. (1982). Sociology: A status report. *College Music Symposium, 22* (1), 104–111.

Merriam, A. P. (1964). *The anthropology of music.* (n. p.) Northwestern University Press.

Michel, P. (1973). Optimal development of musical abilities in the first years of life. *Psychology of Music, 1* (2), 14–20.

Mills, D. L. (1988). *The meaning of the high school band experience and its relationship to band activities.* Unpublished doctoral dissertation, University of Miami.

Moog, H. (1976). The development of musical experience in children of preschool age. *Psychology of Music, 4* (2), 38–45.

Mueller, J. H. (1963). A sociological approach to musical behavior. *Ethnomusicology, 7,* (3), 216–220.

Mussulman, J. A. (1974). *The uses of music.* Englewood Cliffs, NJ: Prentice-Hall.

Nadel, S. (1930). The origins of music. *Musical Quarterly, 16,* 531–546.

Nettl, B. (1956). *Music in primitive cultures.* Cambridge, MA: Harvard University Press.

Nettl, B. (1975). Music in primitive cultures: Iran, a recently developed nation. In C. Hamm, B. Nettl, & R. Byrnside (Eds.), *Contemporary music and music cultures* (pp. 71–100). Englewood Cliffs, NJ: Prentice-Hall.

Portnoy, J. (1963). *Music in the life of man.* New York: Holt, Rinehart and Winston.

Revesz, G. (1954). *Introduction to the psychology of music* (G. I. C. deCourcy, Trans.). Norman, OK: University of Oklahoma Press.

Roederer, J. G. (1995). *The physics and psychophysics of music: An introduction* (3rd ed.). New York: Springer-Verlag.

Sachs, C. (1943). *The rise of music in the ancient world, east and west.* New York: W. W. Norton.

Sachs, C. (1961). *The wellsprings of music* (J. Kunst, ed.). The Hague: Martinus Nijhoff.

Sloboda, J. A. (1985). *The musical mind: The cognitive psychology of music.* Oxford: Clarendon Press.

Walker, R. (1990). *Musical beliefs: Psychoacoustic, mythical, and educational perspectives.* New York: Teachers College Press.

Wallaschek, R. (1970). *Primitive music.* New York: Da Capo Press (Original work published 1893).

Weber, M. (1958). *The rational and social foundations of music* (D. Martindale, J. Riedel, & G. Neuwirth (trans. & eds.). (n. p.) Southern Illinois University Press.

CHAPTER THREE

FUNCTIONAL APPLICATIONS OF MUSIC
IN CONTEMPORARY LIFE

As noted in Chapter Two, music has served and still serves many basic functions in society. It is an important human behavior that is an integral part of all cultures. Besides aesthetic and expressive functions, music serves many nonmusical functions.

> Indeed most music is performed for the express purpose of achieving aims wherein the aesthetic is not the primary goal. The *functional music* is far older and more abundant than music played or composed for aesthetic purposes. All primitive music is functional music...[and] even today a majority of the reasons given for school music ascribe to its functional goals. (Gaston, 1951/52, p. 60)

While music's general functions were discussed in Chapter Two, the present chapter examines some specific *uses* of music in contemporary life.

Some of the uses discussed are traditional; i.e., they are similar to the uses of music throughout much of the history of Western civilization: in religious rites and ceremonies, to promote social conformity and interaction, to accompany dance, and generally to contribute toward the continuity and stability of a culture. Other uses are directed more specifically toward particular industrial, commercial, therapeutic, and educational ends.

People long have recognized that different types of music serve different purposes and that many factors serve to influence each person's musical behavior. Nevertheless, the purpose of much functional music is to stimulate or suppress activity. Prior to examining music's uses, therefore, the authors briefly discuss some of music's structural characteristics that enable it to stimulate or suppress. The reader should recognize that an individual's previous experiences with particular musical structures will influence his or her responses to those structural characteristics. Within a given cultural context, people learn to react in certain ways to certain types of music. While the exact nature of the interaction between learning and the structural characteristics is not clear, observations of reactions to the two basic types of music suggest that differential response patterns are real, regardless of the degree of influence coming from learning or from the structural characteristics themselves.

Stimulative and Sedative Music

All music exists on a continuum between highly stimulating, invigorating music and soothing, sedating music (Gaston, 1968b, p. 18). McMullen's (1982) theoretical model of the dimensions underlying music meaning suggest that *energy* and *structure* in music are experienced as forms of *activation* or *arousal.* Music therapists and others using music to influence behavior essentially are concerned with arousing or suppressing activity, and the type of music selected for influencing the desired behaviors generally reflects different structural characteristics, particularly with respect to energy.

Stimulative Music

Music that stimulates or arouses listeners has a strong energizing component. "For most people it is rhythm that provides the energy of music, be it great or small" (Gaston, 1968b, p. 17). Lundin (1967, p. 172) and Farnsworth (1969, p. 83) both suggest that tempo, an important attribute of rhythm, is of primary importance in influencing mood response to music.

Rhythm characterized by detached, percussive sounds tends to stimulate muscular activity. March and dance music usually have definitive and repetitive rhythms that appear to stimulate physical movement. The more percussive, staccato, and accented the music, the greater the apparent physical response to it. Whenever the underlying beat is clearly defined, even a casual listener is likely to respond with some overt physical response.

While rhythm, and particularly tempo, appears to be the dominant energizing factor, dynamic level also may serve as a stimulator. Louder music generally stimulates greater response than softer music. Other musical attributes, such as pitch level, melody, harmony, texture, and timbre, also may help energize music, but the extent to which these variables contribute toward music's driving, energizing force is less clearly understood than for rhythm and dynamics.

Sedative Music

Music which soothes, calms, or tranquilizes behavior appears to rely on nonpercussive and legato sounds. Its melodic passages are usually sustained and legato, and generally have minimal rhythmic activity. The most important rhythmic attribute of sedative music is the underlying beat, which is usually monotonously regular but subdued. Lullabies are a prime example of functional sedative music. They are comprised of sustained legato melodies, with a quiet but steady underlying beat. Lullabies also are usually quite soft, much slower than stimulative music, and quite limited in frequency range.

Differential Response to Stimulative and Sedative Music

Apparently, individuals concerned with using music for functional purposes long have recognized the differential response to the two types of music, but they have not gone to great lengths to corroborate the effects through research.[1] Certainly music used by the military throughout history to incite troops into battle reflects the characteristics of stimulative music, as does music of today's school pep bands and marching bands. On the other hand, melodies used to soothe infants reflect characteristics of sedative music. March music reflects different characteristics than romantic music. Responses to adjective checklists, taken as indicators of mood or character response to music, reveal quite different lists of adjectives for stimulative and sedative music. Applause at concerts generally is much greater for stimulative music than for sedative music.

The bulk of the limited research particularly focused on comparisons of responses to the two types of music was conducted in the 1940s and 1950s at The University of Kansas by some of Gaston's students. His (1951/1952; 1968b, pp. 18–19) reviews of this research revealed that nearly all studies found significant differences in response to stimulative and sedative music. Judges readily classified drawings and paintings by both children and adults according to which type of music the artists heard while creating. Studies of postural response to the two types of music revealed that subjects sat more erect when listening to stimulative music than when listening to sedative music. Clinical observation of sedative music's effects on patients in a hospital ward revealed an "observable sedative effect for the ward as a whole."

Hodges's (1980) review of music's effects on physiological response generally revealed differential response for stimulative and sedative music, although inconsistencies existed among the results of the various studies. With respect to heart rate and pulse rate, (a) some studies resulted in increased rates for stimulative music but decreased rates for sedative music, (b) some resulted in increased rates for any music, whether stimulative or sedative, (c) some yielded rate changes that were unpre-

---

[1]An exception to this might be some of the research conducted by consultants for the Muzak™ Corporation. This research is discussed later in the chapter.

dictable, and (d) some yielded no change in heart rate or pulse rate for any music.

Boyle's (1982) study of 145 university students' verbal descriptions of excerpts of stimulative and sedative music provided additional evidence of differential response to the two types. Subjects were asked to respond to each of six excerpts, three stimulative and three sedative, on a five-point continuum between each of the following pairs of bipolar adjectives: happy/sad, restless/calm, joyous/gloomy, whimsical/serious, vigorous/quiet, majestic/soothing, playful/dignified, and exhilarated/dreamy. (Each adjective pair appears in opposite clusters of the Hevner Adjective Circle, which is discussed in Chapter Eight.) The mean difference in ratings for the two types of music for each pair of adjectives was highly significant ($p < .001$). Such data

> lend support to the theory that affective response to music is related to the activation and energizing characteristics of the musical stimulus. Mood response, which seems to reflect a "disposition to action," apparently is intertwined somehow with response to stimulative and sedative music. Music therapists and Muzak-like corporations undoubtedly will continue to exploit these activation characteristics of music to influence human behavior. (Boyle, 1982, p. 115)

Despite inconsistent results from physiological research, strong evidence from varied sources apparently supports the contention that people respond differently to stimulative and sedative music. Examples of music throughout history, in everyday life today, and in a limited number and variety of research studies reveal differential response to stimulative and sedative music. A discussion of various applications of this knowledge and the subtlety with which it is applied for particular uses comprises the balance of this chapter. Some of these applications capitalize on music's ability to stimulate, while others capitalize on its ability to soothe. These applications are discussed as they pertain to music in ceremonies; "background" music; commercial, industrial, and therapeutic uses of music; music to facilitate nonmusical learning; and music as a reward for behavior change.

Music in Ceremonies

Ceremonial music reflects one of music's earliest functional uses, a use that has continued throughout history and remains an important part of most ceremonies today. Apparently music is viewed as an integral part of ceremony and does much to enhance the formality of such occasions. Virtually all types of ceremony incorporate music in one way or another, be they religious, military, state, athletic, or commercial.

Mussulman (1974, p. 129) notes that music has functioned more consistently and more positively in religious ritual than in any other area of life in Western civilization, even to the extent that religious music now comprises one of the longest and richest traditions of Western music. Music's specific function in religious ceremony tends to vary with its place in the ceremony, as evidenced within Christianity by the principal sections of the highly formalized mass of the Roman Catholic Church. Anglican and Lutheran services also have music as an integral part of their formal services.

Christian churches of a more evangelical tradition, such as the Methodist, Baptist, and Presbyterian denominations, also include music as part of the services, but they appear to place less emphasis on observance of corporate sacraments than do the Roman Catholic, Anglican, and Lutheran services; instead, they appear to involve the congregation much more directly. Hymn singing, an important part of most of these services, is a direct way to draw the congregation into the service.

Music in religious services appears to serve several functions. At times it serves as a signal to stimulate the congregation to respond in a certain way; at other times quiet organ interludes are used to help establish a mood of reverence or tranquility. Congregational singing serves to draw people together, while choir anthems appear to lead the worshipers to reflect on the religion's beliefs and values and its implications for them as individuals. Special music accompanies special religious ceremonies. Certainly weddings, funerals, and special religious holidays are made more meaningful by music designed to enhance the occasions' significance. Some of these uses of music in religious ceremony, however, are more "persuasive" than "ceremonial," attesting further to music's importance in religion.

Perris's (1985, pp. 123–155) examination of music in major world religions focuses particularly on music's persuasive function:

> Music in all worship is expected to heighten the desired emotional effect in the listener, to emphasize the ritual text, especially certain significant words, and to focus the worshipper's [sic] attention on the rite. But the danger of so sensuous a phenomenon as music is that it may be more seductive than the rite itself, and that the musicians may evoke more interest than the priests. If the music in the worship service is "entertaining," is the religious ambience destroyed? How can the worshipper's [sic] attention be shielded from wandering? (Perris, 1985, p. 124)

Perris's juxtaposition of concepts from four major world religions—Judaism, Christianity, Islam, and Hinduism—revealed that, even though some obvious differences exist in how the four religions use music, six underlying factors emerge for consideration when using music in religious service: (a) the words must be comprehensible to the congregation; (b) traditional melody and performance practice should be observed; (c) the musical instruments used must be morally and socially acceptable; (d) music must be used for proper purposes and at proper places in the worship ceremony; (e) music in a worship ceremony should not be misused, i.e., detract from the purpose of the ceremony; and (f) composers' artistic goals should not override theological concerns. Perris notes that this final consideration is a particular concern of Western religious music.

While music in religious ceremony may serve more than "ceremonial" functions per se, these other functions do not negate its importance in heightening the meaning and impact of the ceremony, and music most likely will continue to serve a major role in religious ceremonies throughout the world. Perhaps composers' artistic concerns, which may undermine music's persuasive value, ultimately may enhance its ceremonial value.

Music also has been a traditional part of military and state ceremonies, where, as in religious ceremonies, it has served varied functions. Perhaps military music's traditional function has been to inspire and heighten interest in the military cause and to stimulate troops to battle. That music for the military traditionally has been band music characterized by percussion and fanfare is more than coincidental. Such music appears to have a highly stimulative effect. Even today, most nations' military and state ceremonies include music of the military band rather than string instruments.

Music in military and state ceremony not only is used as a signal to draw attention to a particular part of the ceremony, such as playing "Hail to the Chief" to signal the arrival of the President of the United States, but it also is used to create a feeling of patriotism and to commemorate particular important occasions. Music serves to heighten the occasion's immediate importance as well as to contribute toward its memorableness.

Many occasions other than religious and military also include ceremonial music. Major sporting events are a prime example. The opening and closing of the Olympic Games always involve special music, and the medal ceremonies include playing the national anthems of the gold medal recipients' countries. Major high school, college, and professional sports events open with ceremonial music, and music of marching and pep bands, while not always ceremonial music per se, serves an important function for sporting events.

Nearly any queen (or king) crowning ceremony, whether a high school homecoming event or a Miss World beauty pageant, incorporates music. Folk festivals, while perhaps not ceremony in the ritualistic sense, usually rely on music as an integrative force as well as for heightening the memorableness of the occasion.

From this cursory review, it is apparent that music is an important part of most ceremonies. While research has not examined ceremonial music's effects from a "scientific" perspective, the fact that music has been and continues to be a part of most ceremonies attests to its functional value.

Commercial Music

"Commercial" uses of music refer to using music in some way to make money from music directly or to enhance business through the use of music. The next few sections examine background music, music as a means for advertising, music as entertainment, and music for narration, especially as a way of enhancing a story told in another medium.

Background Music

Music has been a "background" for various activities for centuries. The development of electronic recording and reproduction systems enabled background music to become extremely prevalent in society, whether as a part of a planned audio environment or as the result of happenstance.

The term often connotes some type of "mood music," "easy listening," or "beautiful music," although almost any type of music may serve as a background for something else. Mussulman (1974, p. 93) notes that background music is "intended to be heard but not actively or purposely listened to." Strictly speaking, music which captures a person's attention is failing to function as truly "background" music. Models and theories incorporating deliberate attention as essential to an aesthetic experience with music or to determining musical preference (see Chapters Eight and Nine) theoretically can not apply to background music.

The term "new age" occasionally is applied to some background music. Usually, new age music is instrumental, often featuring solo piano or guitar, quasi-chamber ensembles, synthesizers, or a mix of electronic and acoustic instruments. Describing the style, Pareles (1987, p. 3C) indicates that "almost invariably the tempos are slow, the harmonies simple, the timbres rich, and the recording quality full-bodied and noiseless" and explains that the growing interest in it may be because "it eliminates the most complex, time-consuming, mentally draining part of the musical experience: paying attention." Time may resolve the question of whether new age music is really a style or an alternative label for background music; certainly, it lends itself well to background functions.

Another generic label for background music is "Muzak™." While the Muzak Corporation is indeed the best known major provider of background music in the workplace, the Minnesota Mining and Manufacturing Company and Audio Environment Incorporated also provide significant services; other regional and local vendors exist. Yet, the Muzak label often is attached to any form of relatively unobtrusive music, just as a facial tissue often is called a "Kleenex™," regardless of its actual manufacturer.

Muzak's development. The history of the Muzak Corporation and its social functions is important to the present discussion, and the authors have relied heavily on Husch's (1984) landmark historical study. Major General George Squier, an officer in the U.S. Army Signal Corps during World War I, developed an idea for "wired" radio, a system in which radio signals would travel over electric power lines rather than through electromagnetic disturbances in the atmosphere and beyond ("wireless" radio). General Squier acquired a patent, which he sold in 1922 to The North American Company, a holding company that had created the General Electric Corporation and once financed the American entrepreneur and inventor, Thomas Edison. Shortly after, North American acquired Associated Music Publishers, Inc. as a source of a large music library, which the company could record and distribute over its background music subsidiary. The future Muzak thus was not a "garage business": It was a corporate enterprise from the beginning.

Initially called Wired Radio, Inc., the background music service was reorganized as The Muzak Corporation in 1934. The first transmissions were to homes in Cleveland, Ohio's Lakewood section, but Muzak soon began to concentrate on a type of "functional" music, sent over telephone lines to hotels and restaurants. A partnership purchased Muzak in 1938; by 1941, one of the partners, William Benton, became the sole proprietor. A vice president of The University of Chicago with a background in advertising, Benton had a significant influence on the development of Muzak into its modern form.

The Second World War saw continued growth in Muzak as its recording studios provided materials for the American armed forces and the defense industry. Important to Muzak's future, the war also saw a growing belief that providing background music for workers in offices and industry was beneficial to morale and boosted production. Much in-house literature that purported to document such benefits accrued.

By 1948, a characteristic format of 15-minute segments was in place.

Unlike other providers of background music, Muzak uses the concept of *stimulus progression* extensively. Over a 15-minute period, successive short musical excerpts increase in a *stimulus value,* which is based on the excerpt's tempo, accent patterns, instrumentation, and texture. The degree of progression varies; the corporation purportedly can match stimulus progression curves with worker fatigue curves: During the times of likely worker fatigue, such as the middle of a shift, the musical stimulation is high; during times of likely low fatigue, as at the beginning or near the end of a shift, the stimulation is relatively low. The 15-minute musical segments alternate with periods of silence.

Muzak passed through several owners and adopted ever more sophisticated programming. It made increasing use of industrial psychologists and medical professionals as consultants. Today, Muzak is available through the company's recorded tapes, as well as, to some extent, by direct satellite broadcast. While background music tailored to specific work situations remains the corporation's core business, Muzak also provides a type of "foreground" music, deliberately programmed to capture the attention of potential customers (Hunter, 1983).

Music in the workplace. In examining Muzak's operations, Husch concludes that five generalizations, based on early research, generally provide a rationale: (a) Music generally is a successful way to combat boredom, (b) music in the workplace will increase productivity, (c) music will help improve employees' morale, (d) popular rhythmic music likely will be more effective than other types of music, and (e) proper scheduling is important for maximizing music's effectiveness.

Using music in the workplace to raise morale, coordinate efforts, or stimulate the workers has a long history. During past years, diverse laborers, such as field hands, railroad track layers, sailors, and others, sang and chanted. The possibility exists for work songs wherever people work in groups and can hear each other; as Chapter Two notes, work songs are one hypothesized source (albeit an unlikely one) of music's origins. Yet, Muzak is a very different phenomenon, as Husch carefully describes.

A major difference between Muzak and earlier use of work songs is that the workers do not create Muzak while they work. The music is imposed through Muzak, usually as a result of a management decision. Rhythms and words do not arise from the particular task at hand, as they generally did in the earlier examples of work songs. Muzak's rhythms and implied words (Muzak usually has no audible words) have no necessary connection with the work at hand; workers' job-related physical actions are not a consideration in the music selection process.

Muzak thus has become another standard of operation in the manufacturing or service concern, similar to operations involved in word processing, accounting, or cleaning. It does not address any set of specific procedures or working conditions, and it is unrelated to any particular job site. Muzak has a regularity and predictability along with its mood variations. Rather than a focus on the immediate task, Muzak may encourage fantasy and reminiscence; many of the absent lyrics from Muzak song segments address love and friendliness. Husch goes as far as to suggest that Muzak is a form of auditory social control, which results in a control of symbolic action through alteration of time and space without human interaction. While Muzak is created separately from the people who must work in its presence, it affects an individual's state of mind as he or she works.

Whether Muzak or another source provides the background music, and whether it truly is a form of social control or merely a pleasant diversion, a logical question arises: Does it work? Muzak certainly has its success stories regarding increased product and enhancement of the workplace. According to Kerr (1945), several World War II era studies indicate that music tended to increase the amount of produced material meeting quality control standards. Music especially seemed to enhance productivity in highly repetitive work. A 1974 in-house Muzak brochure, with no author of record, claimed increased productivity and improved employee attitude in companies manufacturing electrical appliances and watches, an electrical utility, and a medical claims processing office. Wokoun (1979) found that Muzak apparently reduced fatigue among automobile workers, particularly during the afternoon.

Music may not always be the important variable in studies which purportedly show effects of background music in work settings. Many variables influence production and morale, both of which need clear indication of how they will be recognized in particular experimental settings ("operational" definitions). In relatively short-term studies, the Hawthorne effect, where increased personal attention results in a positive change in attitude or production, may be a factor. The type of work is a consideration: Music may distract people engaged in relatively intellectual and non-repetitive work. Realistically, all workers may not welcome background music, especially if other people select the music and determine the conditions under which it is heard.

Background music usually is conceived as a group experience, but modern personal headsets enable individual workers to select their own programming from available broadcasts. While some supervisors may object to the "Walkman™ in the workplace"[2] phenomenon because it may remove people from the work environment excessively or interfere with necessary on-the-job communication, many workers engaging in repetitive tasks enjoy them (Powell, 1994).

Will background music enhance productivity, improve morale, and generally make a workplace more pleasant? The answer is a "definite maybe." No one reliably can guarantee that all workers will profit from background music, but unless the music is distracting or annoying, it is not harmful, and if people think that it is beneficial for them, it probably is.

Music in the marketplace. While the workplace is one major setting for background music, it also appears extensively in the *marketplace*. Its purpose essentially is to enhance customers' experiences so that they will spend more money. In a restaurant, the music is intended to promote a pleasant dining atmosphere for the patrons. In a store, background music presumably makes shopping a more enjoyable experience. In a television commercial, music presumably makes the advertised product or service more desirable. In all cases, the business's customers rather than its employees are the "audience" for background music.

Appropriate music may encourage people to spend more time (and money) in a particular store or restaurant. The music might add to a favorable ambience, people might like the particular music, the music might mask objectionable background sounds, or it might signal some favorable judgment to the customers. Experience suggests that stimulative music might elicit a faster pace and thereby move people through a store more rapidly or encourage them to eat faster. Conversely, sedative music might slow the pace through a store and encourage more browsing through the merchandise, and it might encourage diners to linger longer over food and drinks. Providers of background music would have to ensure that customers did not receive the music negatively.

To test the different effects of stimulative, sedative, and no music on shoppers' pace, sales, and customer reactions in a supermarket, Milliman (1982) alternated slow background music (MM $\leq$ 72, mean tempo = 60), fast background music (MM $\geq$ 94, mean tempo = 108), and no background music over a nine-week period. Results indicated that slow music indeed slowed the shoppers' pace: Respective mean observed times for passage between two points for slow, no, and fast music were 127.53, 119.86, and 108.93 seconds; the slow and fast times differed

---

[2]"Walkman" actually is a model of personal radios and/or stereos, contained in headphones, manufactured by the Sony™ Corporation, but just as "Muzak" often is used generically to refer to any background music, "Walkman" often refers to any personal headset.

significantly. Gross sales were highest under slow music conditions and at their lowest under fast music conditions; the difference in sales under conditions of the two tempo extremes was statistically significant. Interviews revealed no significant differences among shoppers regarding awareness of the music conditions, regardless of the actual background music or lack thereof.

In a similar study, Milliman (1986) alternated slow and fast instrumental background music in an "up-scale" restaurant for eight successive weekends. On four weekends, Friday nights featured slow background music and the following Saturday nights featured fast background music. The alternate weekends reversed the music; i.e., Fridays featured fast background music. Results showed that customers spent significantly more time in the restaurant and spent significantly more on alcoholic beverages during slow music nights. The restaurant's gross receipts were significantly higher on slow music nights. Service time and the number of customers losing patience and leaving before they could be seated did not differ significantly between the two music conditions. The amount of food purchased did not differ significantly; apparently the restaurant's greater income on slow music nights was due to people lingering longer over more drinks.[3]

In addition to regulating customers' paces and thereby enhancing the likelihood that they might spend more, music may enhance the marketplace by building a more positive attitude toward cooperative aspects of mutual selling and buying. Music therapists recognize that "pleasant" music may make an environment more attractive and clientele more receptive toward therapeutic uses of music and other therapies. Similarly, music may give people a more positive attitude toward cooperating with others. Fried and Berkowitz (1979) divided eighty university students (forty men, forty women) into four groups. Three groups listened to music for approximately seven minutes; the remaining group "sat still" and heard no music. One listening group heard stimulative music, "One O'clock Jump." Another listened to sedative music (which Fried and Berkowitz labelled as "soothing" music), two of Mendelssohn's "Songs Without Words." Coltrane's "Meditations" was played for the remaining group as "aversive" music. At the conclusion of their group's respective activities, subjects were asked to volunteer to help with another alleged

---

[3]Milliman's restaurant study was concerned with tempo, a very basic musical variable, and the music was *background* music. Restaurants must use care that the style of music complements rather than clashes with the restaurant's ambience. Loud rock music might be inappropriate in a restaurant attempting to present a sophisticated "up-scale" image. Sedative background music might be inappropriate in a Mexican, Italian, Greek or other restaurant with an ethnic theme, where diners expect a broader cultural experience as well as a culinary experience.

experiment as a measure of helpfulness. The sedative and stimulative music created positive moods; the aversive music tended to arouse negative feelings. Subjects who previously heard sedative music were the most "helpful," with significantly greater helpfulness than the aversive music or no music subjects.

In a frequently cited (and often criticized) experimental study, Gorn (1982) paired otherwise similar beige and blue pens with liked music (from the then popular musical comedy *Grease*) and disliked music (Indian classical music). Beyond the .001 level of statistical significance, subjects tended to prefer the pen, regardless of its color, that was paired with the preferred music. In a second experiment, under a condition where subjects knew in advance that they would eventually receive their choice of pens, subjects saw the beige pen while they listened to liked music and saw the blue pen while they heard alleged product information (e.g., the blue pen would not smudge). This time, a majority (71%) preferred the blue pen; product information apparently overrode the favorable music association. However, in a similar experiment where other subjects did not know in advance that they would be asked to select a pen, a majority (63%) selected the *beige* pen. Gorn's study thus suggests that information has less impact in nondecision-making situations; perhaps music which can induce pleasant feelings or emotions is useful in "reaching" uninvolved potential customers. Although Gorn's pen research has attracted considerable attention, Kellaris and Cox (1989) were unable to replicate the results and suggest that limited exposure to music is unlikely to influence product choice.

There seems to be little question that music indeed may place potential customers or clients in a more positive mood, which in turn may make them more likely to purchase particular products or services. The general tendencies of slower music to make people linger longer and preferred music to encourage a more favorable response could be predicted from research in musical affect, musical preference, and music therapy. Of course, the operative verb is *may* — not *will*. A customer with a limited specific purpose in shopping and clear expectations regarding a desired product or service probably is less likely to be influenced by music or any other background condition, as compared with aspects such as quality of product or service, cost, and convenience. Furthermore, a shopping situation is highly complex, and many variables are involved.

Music in Advertising

· Whether the potential consumer elects to enter a place where he or she may spend some money or is at home or somewhere else other than a store or service establishment, advertisers want to persuade that consumer to seek what they have to offer. In radio or television advertising, where the commercials may be quite incidental to the entertainment or information that the listener or viewer seeks, the use of music to attract and hold attention and induce a positive mood toward an advertised product or service is well-established. Indeed, music for radio and television commercial advertising has become a business in itself, even to the point where composers specialize in writing such music. Writing *jingles,* the music for broadcast commercials, has become "a billion-dollar-a-year industry that's growing all the time" (Shea, 1988, p. 49).

Commercials usually last between 15 and 20 seconds. Radio commercials may include both verbal and musical sounds; television commercials may add visual-verbal effects. In either case, the intent is to persuade the audience that the advertised product or service has value and to help them remember it. Commercials usually are brief interruptions within some continuing program;[4] this may help attract attention (toddlers playing in a room with an operating television set often will interrupt their play in response to the change signalled by the onset of a commercial), or it may simply provide the audience with an opportunity to leave the room, read the newspaper, or otherwise ignore the broadcast.

Music may affect a person's mood, which is a relatively temporary state or frame of mind that individuals can recognize in themselves and describe verbally (Eagle, 1971, p. 19). Individuals may be in a happy, sad, depressed, pensive, optimistic, or pessimistic mood, or in other moods. Presumably, a person in an appropriate mood state, whether due to music or to something else, may be more receptive toward a commercial and what it advertises than a person in an inappropriate mood state, whatever those states may be. The association of happiness with a product or service, such as a detergent, shampoo, or lawn maintenance service, that is intended to make life easier or more pleasurable certainly might increase interest in that product or service. A pensive or reflective mood might be especially desirable in a potential customer for life insurance or new tires. Gardner (1985) notes that mood states generally bias evaluation judgments in directions which logically relate to the mood. Favorable service encounters, as in a pleasant trip to a barber shop or beauty salon, may be recalled later in terms of some overall positive impression rather than in details of what was done to the hair. Interactions with a sales staff and the resulting mood may influence the customer's evaluation of his or her purchase, and the program's content may influence persons watching a television program.

Music may be a form of nonverbal communication, which clearly is

---

[4]Of course, programs ("infomercials") exist that are simply one long commercial.

important in advertising, regardless of an advertisement's verbal content. Stewart and Hecker (1988) include as nonverbal aspects the way something is said, facial expression, body movements and spacing, gesture, eye movements, touch, pictures, and symbolic artifacts (e.g., a judge's gavel in a commercial for legal services). The relative importance as compared with verbal information will vary, and context is especially important for understanding meaning of nonverbal information. Stewart and Hecker exemplify context by describing a woman slowly opening her lips to an approaching man. After a brief sensuous buildup, the "enticement" is revealed as not part of a sexy novel but as part of a commercial for a dental practice.

The importance of nonverbal information is supported further by Holbrook and Batra (1987), who identified six descriptive factors from adult women's judgments of 72 television commercials: emotional, threatening, mundane, sexy, cerebral, and personal relevance. They also identified pleasure, arousal, and domination as three dimensions of emotional response to commercials.

Alpert and Alpert (1989) describe the television audience as likely to contain viewers who are far more involved in the programs than in the commercials. As such, they are "potentially uninvolved, nondecision making consumers rather than cognitively active problem solvers" (p. 487). Advertisers may hope to link favorable associations to the advertised products and services via emotionally arousing presentations of music, colors, lighting, or other nonverbal aspects. They may hope that music will influence viewers' moods favorably and thereby lead not only to increased attention to commercials but also to a favorable evaluation of what is being advertised.

The viewer's mood may be influenced far more by program content than by nonverbal or verbal commercial content. A certain "folk wisdom" regarding television advertising is that advertisers should avoid sponsoring overly depressing programs because the sadness will impact negatively on the advertised products. Mathur and Chattopadhyay (1991) studied effects of embedding advertising within programs previously judged through viewer ratings to be sad (a film based on the Nuremberg war crimes trials that followed World War II) and happy (a Walt Disney "classic" film). Commercials were for McDonalds™ food products and for life insurance from Mutual of New York (MONY™). The viewers who saw the happy Disney program seemed to process the advertising more thoroughly than the viewers who saw the sad Nuremberg program. The "happy" viewers showed greater recall.

In a previous study of happy vs. sad programs interacting with emotional vs. informational commercials for catsup, wine, coffee, and breakfast drink, Goldberg and Gorn (1987) found that happy programs elicited a happier mood in viewers. They also elicited greater perceived commercial effectiveness than sad programs, a more positive cognitive response, and better recall. The program-commercial interaction was such that the program effect was greater for those viewing emotional commercials, all of which contained music, than for those viewing the informational commercials. In general, emotional versions of commercials tended to outperform informational commercials regarding felt mood, perceived commercial effectiveness, and intention to purchase. Informational commercials elicited greater recall, but, of course, there was more to recall than in the emotional versions.

Whether or not music indeed does what it should do in arousing favorable associations or building positive moods in the context of a commercial that exists within a program is not easy to evaluate. Judgment of an advertisement's efficacy on viewers' abilities to recall presented information is too limited without giving attention to the nonverbal aspects, including music, which allegedly are building a positive feeling (Haley, Richardson, & Baldwin, 1984). There are numerous investigations of music's effects.

Wintle's (1978/1979) study of the dimensions underlying response to television commercials supports the contention that music does make a difference in a commercial. In a series of three studies in which college students were asked to respond to commercials with and without music, three factors emerged: activity, pleasantness, and potency. In the third study, which paired commercials respectively with a supporting music excerpt, results showed that supporting background music "routinely intensified the dimension positively characterized by a commercial" (Wintle, 1978/1979, 5115-A).

Conceivably, music's effects in advertising may result from classical conditioning, where something linked to a favorable response from a prior association (e.g., "Nice music"—"I like it") becomes a signal for a similar response (e.g., "the advertised product—"Nice music"—"I like it").[5] Gorn's (1982) pen study, discussed above, presumably exploited the idea of generalizing a favorable response to music to a particular product, i.e., the blue or the beige pen.

While educational television programs are not strictly commercials, successful programs must hold the attention of the intended audience, often children, just as a successful commercial must attract and hold

---

[5]Classical or Pavlovian conditioning is described in Chapter Ten. Conditioning occurs in many aspects of human behavior. In the advertising context, the advertised product presumably becomes a signal for a previously conditioned stimulus of favorable music, which in turn elicits some positive response.

attention. Music may attract attention, but it also may be distracting. Wakshlag, Reitz, and Zillman (1982) conducted two experiments regarding music's effects on 50 first and second graders watching educational television. In one experiment, the children watched, singly, 10-minute presentations on mathematics, use of the dictionary, earth/sun relationships, and gravity. The earth/sun film had background music; the gravity film did not. The mathematics and dictionary films, which represented the experimental variable of content, were shown in fast background music (MM = 100–170), slow background music (MM = 36–60), and no background music conditions. No adult was present in the viewing room; channel selection monitoring equipment recorded what each child watched. For both content areas, fast music resulted in significantly more viewing time than slow or no music; there were no effects for part of the program, gender, or grade.

In the second Wakshlag et al. experiment, children watched, in pairs, a program on a Lapland shepherd and a program on submarines; the investigators observed them via a hidden camera. Again, there were no significant gender or grade differences, and this time there were no differences regarding the music condition. However, there was a significant interaction with program time segment. The children's attention declined across the 7-minute programs, and the decline was greatest for fast music. No music showed less decline, and slow music showed little decline; slow music apparently was more effective in maintaining attention. A measure of what the children learned showed that learning was lower in the music conditions, and lowest for fast music. Background music did not influence the children's overall evaluation of the films. The investigators suggest that background music perhaps should be intermittent rather than continuous, as it was in their experiments.

Macklin (1988) considered whether music would distract children or attract their attention and result in a more positive attitude. In one experiment, preschool children viewed mock cereal commercials in one of three conditions: no music, accompaniment by words and music of a professionally-composed jingle, and accompaniment by the jingle's instrumental music minus the words as a background. While lacking statistical significance, results showed that children who experienced instrumental music had more positive attitudes toward the commercial and the alleged brand of cereal. In a second experiment, pre-school children had toys available and were organized into groups of three to view a Tom and Jerry cartoon containing embedded commercials. (Such a situation is more realistic; many American children "watch" cartoons with the television set functioning as an accompaniment to other play and give only occasional attention to the program.) There were no significant differences, except that the children exhibited increased visual attention in the no music condition. While Macklin does not mention it, the increased attention may be an artifact of a sudden change in "background" stimulus; Tom and Jerry cartoons, as many others, include almost continual music throughout.

The time and type of music may influence its popularity with particular audiences; these have implications for the selection of music for commercials. Research in music therapy (Gibbons, 1977) showed that elderly people tend to prefer music which was popular in their youth, and Holbrook and Schindler (1989) found that preferences for popular music are a function of when the music was popular in relation to the listener's lifetime, with the greatest peak of popularity for songs popular around the listener's age of 24. They suggest that social relationships and development of sensitivity may be responsible, and that the age-related phenomenon may exist for other areas.

Rock music of previous decades increasingly is incorporated into commercials to provide an aura of familiarity and identity for the audience and potential customers in their 30s and 40s. Presumably, listeners would identify with the song and then with the advertised product. Shea (1988, p. 49) noted an increase in the market share of Ford Motor Company's Lincoln-Mercury division allegedly due to music and the similar use of rock music commercials by the rival General Motors Corporation (p. 57).

Sullivan (1990) embedded advertisements for a chicken sandwich at a fast-food restaurant and a new entree at a sea-food restaurant within programs consisting of adult contemporary (AC) and easy listening music.[6] (There was no disk jockey talk—just commercials and music.) Listeners of a variety of ages heard the tapes. The AC listeners consistently showed more recall of advertising claims, a better attitude toward the commercials, and a stronger intent to try the food than did the easy listening audience. Sullivan predicted this on the basis of the AC music format being more "involving."

Stout and Leckenby (1988) had 1498 people, 90 percent of whom were female, respond to 50 commercials. The commercials represented nine product categories: flavored coffee, instant coffee, soft drinks, candy,

---

[6]AC radio generally features relatively unabrasive "soft" styles of rock music, with disk jockey presentations that are oriented toward adults, primarily in the 25- to 54-year-old age range. Variation exists; AC stations may stress older songs, "full-service" radio, "romantic" songs, or alternative forms of popular unabrasive music. Easy listening implies less or even no rock, with an emphasis on instrumental music, nostalgia, and targeting to audiences of age 45 or older. Radio format labels may be confusing and inconsistent; Barnes (1988) provides a classification that is useful and comprehensive, albeit subject to evolutionary change.

pudding, muffins, beauty aids, laundry detergent, and a fast-food restaurant. There were 11 different brands, with 2 to 11 commercials per brand. Forty commercials included music. The respondents answered open-ended questions and responded to 52 evaluative statements. Of the 52 statement variables, only five showed any significant differences: Respondents were more positive regarding feeling as if they learned something, feeling not "talked down to," feeling untired of the commercial, and not feeling as if they heard the same thing repetitiously for the commercials with *no* music. BUT they said that they were more likely to *buy* products that had been presented *with* music. There were no significant differences in brand recall. The commercials with music in a major or mixed mode generally were evaluated more favorably than music in a minor mode. Commercials featuring music at faster tempi generally were preferred to those featuring slower tempi.

Alpert and Alpert (1990) considered particular musical characteristics as they investigated music's effects on mood and intention to purchase. On the basis of prior ratings, the investigators selected three friendship greeting cards—a happy, a sad, and a neutral card. Using the stereotypical major-happy/minor-sad dichotomy, the investigators contrasted the major and minor preludes from Book I of J. S. Bach's *Well-Tempered Clavier.* Subjects other than the experimental subjects rated the preludes for familiarity and preferences, and the investigators selected "Prelude III in C# Major" and "Prelude XXII in Bb Minor" as two relatively obscure but strongly preferred contrasting pieces. Forty-eight marketing students, organized into three listening groups, saw brightness-controlled slides of the three card types, with the music condition—happy, sad, or no music—varying systematically. While viewing and listening, the students drew a continuous line across columns characterized by a five-point Likert scale (the investigators call this technique the "mood monitor") to show changes in their moods across time. They also described each card with 10 semantic differential scales, including a "happy-sad" scale to assess perceived mood and a "would buy it-would not buy it" scale to assess purchase intention. A multiple analysis of variance showed no effects due to subject grouping, but there were significant effects on perceived mood due to card and music. In order of perceived happiness, with the happiest combination first, the card-music combinations were (1) happy music/happy card, (2) no music/happy card, (3) happy music/neutral card, (4) happy music/sad card, (5) sad music/happy card, (6) sad music/neutral card, (7) no music/neutral card, (8) no music/sad card, and (9) sad music/sad card. Further analysis showed that when the music condition was controlled statistically, the cards differed significantly, but when the cards were controlled, the music did not differ significantly.

When purchase intention was the dependent variable of interest, the card-music combinations in order of most to least likely to purchase were (1) sad music/neutral card, (2) sad music/happy card, (3) no music/happy card, (4) sad music/sad card, (5) no music/sad card, (6) happy music/happy card, (7 and 8, a tie) no music/neutral card, happy music/neutral card, and (9) happy music/sad card. Sad music was more effective regarding purchase intent, perhaps because of the reasons why the subjects might purchase a card. Obviously, variation in musical structure is important in determining effects; the investigators caution that generalizing from a laboratory-based study such as theirs to a "real" business situation is difficult.

Logically, one should ascertain that the type of music fits with the commercial's overall theme. Garfield (1988) discussed the necessity for unity between image and sound and the importance of not overusing music.

A further complication in fitting music with advertising relates to the viewer's inherent interest in and value for what is advertised. Petty, Cacioppo, and Schumann (1983) noted that the way a potential consumer processes information from an advertisement may vary: If there is high consumer involvement, as there might be in the purchase of an expensive item, "central processing" is involved; with low cognitive involvement, as is likely in determining which soft drink to purchase, "peripheral processing" with less concern for any particular issue and less motivation for a decision is involved.[7] Golden and Johnson (1983) also address cognitive involvement when they distinguish between "thinking" commercials, which make relatively objective appeals to a presumably rational individual, and "feeling" commercials, which appeal more to emotions, perhaps through drama or music. Park and Young (1986) found more effects of cognitive development than of background music in a study where groups of adult women watched shampoo commercials that differed in presence or absence of music, with different sets of instructions designed to arouse different degrees of involvement with shampoo and beautiful hair.

The use of music to enhance advertising probably will be subject to continuing research, as will most applications of functional music. Whether the music attracts attention, reinforces a message, induces a mood, or

---

[7]"Central" and "peripheral" processing in this context refer to the intensity of cognitive involvement. This differs from the use of the terms in the psychoacoustic sense, discussed in Chapter Four, where a "central" process occurs primarily in the neural pathway or brain while a "peripheral" neural process occurs primarily in the sense organ.

simply entertains, the possibilities for music making a product or service more appealing arise from music's deep involvement in human culture.

Music as Entertainment

To "entertain" is to amuse or divert. Many forms of entertainment exist, and the popular music industry, often called the "music business" or even "show biz," is one major form. Music's greatest commercial success may be as a means of entertainment; American popular music has spread over most of the world.

While persons working in popular music may be considered "artists," many appear to develop their art for commercial rather than artistic means. A musical style and image must "sell"; this takes priority over artistic values.[8] As Mussulman (1974, pp. 141–142) notes, artists and composers of popular music are engaged in a commercial enterprise, resulting in music that can survive *intensive* exposure for a relatively short time period, while art music ("classical" music) requires and survives *extensive* exposure. The use of marketing skills, image, and packaging is essential for popular musical success—musical talent is not enough, and, as Frith (1988) describes, in some models of musical success, the actual performance is only one part of a larger enterprise.

The history and function of the contemporary music business is a fascinating potpourri of music, recording technology, multimedia presentations, marketing, copyright law, and educated guesses regarding what will be popular when. A detailed discussion is beyond the scope of this text; the reader is referred to the illuminating descriptive works of Baskerville (1995), Brabec and Brabec (1994), Denisoff (1986), and Fink (1989), as well as Shemel and Krasilovsky's (1990) encyclopedic examination of the music business.

Music for Enhancing Narration

Mussulman (1974, p. 103) argues that one of music's most important uses in Western culture is to enhance the emotional qualities, words, actions, or images in film and television dramas. One might insist that this use of music is more "artistic" than commercial, but the production of television and film music clearly has become a huge commercial enterprise. Composing, performing, and scoring such music is a multimillion dollar business.

---

[8]Of course, many performers would deny this. Performers may need to tailor their performances to a public taste in order to win an audience; once they have some stature, they may be more free to experiment with their own musical beliefs and preferences. Ironically, if a performer becomes *too* popular, he or she may be accused by other performers or cult-like listeners of "selling out."

Music is an organized sequence of sounds and silences. Any music event is sequential, just as is a linguistic event or a movement. A narrative is a representation, a sequence of events, a story. Since music is organized into sequential events across time, music may "tell" about events—i.e., narrate—in a designated order. A "narrator" such as a film or television producer may adjust music to flow along with the sequential order of events that comprises the story. Music thus may narrate in and of itself, as in program music, and it may enhance the narration told by another medium.

Narration through music is possible in part because music is able to function as language, albeit a language less specific than any verbal language. Portnoy (1963, pp. 99–100) suggests that music is a language that can express different ideas simultaneously. Farnsworth (1969, pp. 94–95) believes that music is a language in the sense that it has a grammar and syntax that musicians use to communicate, but he feels that music does not convey detailed messages. Brown (1981) indicates that language, unlike music, is not specific to one sense modality. He finds more similarity between music and sign language than between music and spoken language, because signs represent or suggest their meanings while words usually are connected with meanings more arbitrarily. Furthermore, signs can not exist without some configuration, location, orientation, and movement, just as tone can not exist without some pitch, loudness, timbre, and duration. As the authors discuss in later chapters, cognitive psychologists and music theorists try to show an organizational similarity between music and language due to the existence of an underlying "deep" structure.

Narration through music also is facilitated by cultural stereotypes that attach particular meanings to musical effects, which are perpetuated through use. Such stereotyped expectancies do not require formal musical training for development and may be the essence of music as narrative.

Tonal elements (pitch, loudness, timbre) lend themselves to stereotypical narrative portrayals. For example, certain narrative symbolizations of representations may be appropriate for a certain pitch range, in accordance with experience and tradition. Depiction of the pixie-ish character Till Eulenspiegel in Richard Strauss's tone poem *Till Eulenspiegels lustige Streiche* uses a high pitch level. Sounds suggesting some ponderous giant or impending doom will be low; sounds suggesting something spritely or delicate will be high. Changes in loudness easily suggest something approaching or leaving. A particular timbre or tone color may signify a particular character or set a particular mood: Bassoon tone signifies the broomstick in Dukas's *Sorcerer's Apprentice;* in Prokofiev's *Peter and the Wolf,* the clarinet represents the cat. Low frequency timbres, such as those of the bass clarinet, may suggest a certain sense of mystery and foreboding; electronic sounds may suggest "eerie" effects. Stereotypes arise from perceived or imagined characteristics of that which is portrayed in relation to sonic qualities—one hardly would depict birds in flight with a tuba or a lion stalking its prey with a flute.

Sequential musical aspects (melody, harmony, rhythm, and form) affect music's character and have considerable roles in musical narration. A familiar melody may arouse particular memories and anticipations, as exemplified by the use of nationalistic music, such as "La Marseillaise" accompanying ending scenes and a dramatic confrontation in the classic American film *Casablanca.* Themes (incomplete melodies) may accompany particular characters, as exemplified by Wagner's use of the *leitmotif* in his operas and the use of themes to accompany characters in television situation comedies. A melody's mode may be important; the somewhat hackneyed stereotype of major = happy and minor = sad is one of the most heavily used stereotypes.[9] Ascending and descending melodic lines have obvious narrative utility.

Harmonic intricacy may suggest complexity or simplicity. Consonant harmonies may suggest rest or resolution of conflict, while dissonant harmonies may suggest activity, restlessness, or chaos. A polyphonic texture, which involves two relatively independent melodic lines, may suggest a continuing discourse or conflict.

Rhythm, which must exist in all music, is an obvious narrative tool. Tempo is a critical variable; it is the main distinction between stimulative and sedative music, which respectively may portray stimulative fast-paced activities and slow relaxing activities. Strong accents, especially when they occur at normally unaccented places as in syncopation, can create tension and excitement. Repetitive rhythms can build in psychological intensity. An incessant rhythm combined with a continuous increase in loudness, as in Ravel's *Bolero,* can produce particularly strong feelings of drive, determination, or inevitability.

All music has form, although the form may not be obvious. Unity and variety are the bases for form; repetition of earlier musical material may suggest a sense of completion. In narration, form's role probably differs between narration through music as the principal medium, where longer forms are required, and narration through another medium enhanced by music, where shorter segments are needed. Curiously, Portnoy (1963, p. 130) indicates that novelists may use musical forms to enhance their

---

[9]Other musical characteristics, especially tempo, may override modality. A fast minor work may be "happier" than a slow major work.

work and cites Huxley (1928, pp. 293–294) as an example of complicating plots in analogy with the many voices of a fugue.

One may question whether anything of a narrative nature is inherent in music, especially when there are no understandable words. Do the sounds automatically suggest certain sequences of events, or is learning involved? The authors believe that stereotypes and listeners' basic agreements regarding what they are hearing are from learned associations. Music to depict a large animal? Low pitched sounds. Music to depict a battle? Rapid tempi, full orchestration with rapidly changing higher pitched sounds and rhythmic lower sounds. Certain common utilities of experience and ideas exist regarding objects or events; within a particular culture, these translate into acceptable and appropriate music. Except as a joke, no one indoctrinated into the cultures portrayed by most American films and television would claim that a fast, loud, atonal electronic composition depicts a flower garden on a balmy spring day. A musical narrative in which someone triumphs over adversity can not avoid loud sounds. The melody and harmony appropriate for a love scene probably would not suggest unseen but sensed extraterrestrial beings. A trio of flutes hardly can signal a shark approaching a lifeboat from below. Basically, the reason that music may narrate, by itself or in the context of another narrative medium, is that people can associate acoustical events with real or imagined events in other sensory modes.

Television and films are theaters of illusion. Viewers are not actually in the loving couple's living room, on board the ship on the raging sea, on the plains as the sun sets, or in the police car as it chases the criminals. They are watching and listening to a two-dimensional representation,[10] often in a rather confined area. The media intend to stimulate the viewer to perceive or imagine a sense of reality, often with the aid of music. Mussulman (1974, pp. 103–106) summarizes music's uses in these theaters of illusion as (a) filling silence, (b) imitating or suggesting natural phenomena, (c) masking unwanted sounds, and (d) encouraging empathy for the figures on the screen. In describing one use of music to build suspense by arousing the imagination, Mussulman (1974, p. 106) reflects:

> We are looking over the shoulder of a cowboy who is scanning the distant horizon. Suddenly a lone horseman appears there, silhouetted against the rising moon. Is he friend or foe? The cowboy cannot tell us for sure, but a sudden loud (*sforzando*) dissonance warns us that danger is imminent.

Music unquestionably is a vital part of the film and television industries.

---

[10]Of course, "3D" movies, which exploit stereo-optical effects to give an impression of depth, have been available since the 1950s, and the new "virtual reality" technology seems to place the observer in the action. Even with the impression of depth, the narrator still relies on illusion.

Film music and the film itself may have a symbiotic marketing relationship. Haack (1980) described an emerging promotional alliance in which the film and recording industries work together to popularize a film and its soundtrack. Repetitive musical material in a film provides ample opportunity for implanting music in tonal memory, and on-the-air performance of a film score provides commercial messages for the film. And all because of our learned associations.

Therapeutic Uses of Music

Although healing, soothing, and persuasive effects of music have been espoused throughout the history of Western civilization, only within the past few decades has music come to be systematically used toward therapeutic ends. Michel (1985, p. 5) notes that it has come into widespread use in the United States only since about 1946. The National Association for Music Therapy (NAMT) was founded in 1950.[11] The development of music therapy as a profession has been coordinated and promoted primarily through the NAMT, although another organization, the American Association for Music Therapy (AAMT) exists in the United States, and emerging organizations exist in other countries. Accreditation as a Registered Music Therapist (RMT) or a Certified Music Therapist (CMT) is awarded respectively through the NAMT or the AAMT. To become Board Certified, the RMT or CMT then must pass a national certification examination.[12] The designation RMT or CMT has been "adopted by many levels of government and by private employers as the standard for employment of music therapists" (Michel, p. 11).[13]

The founding principles which underlie therapeutic uses of music, as stated by Gaston (1968a, p. v), were that music in therapy should facilitate

1. The establishment or reestablishment of interpersonal relationships,

2. The bringing about of self-esteem through self-actualization,

3. The utilization of the unique potential of rhythm to energize and bring order.

While these principles remain valid, the potential of music therapy in contemporary society has broadened considerably in scope. Music therapists today are professionally trained individuals who use music as a

---

[11]For a review of music therapy organizations in other countries see D.E. Michel's *Music Therapy, An Introduction Including Music in Special Education* (2nd Ed.). Springfield, IL: Charles C Thomas, 1985, pp. 103–110.

[12]The national certification examination was first administered in November 1985 by the administratively independent Certification Board for Music Therapists.

[13]As of this writing, negotiations are underway between NAMT and AAMT regarding a merger of the two organizations. Some other designation may replace the familiar RMT or CMT.

medium to help influence desirable changes in their patients. Michel (p. 11) notes that today's therapist is no longer restricted to working with patients with specific behavioral, emotional, physical, or mental disorders; rather, today's therapist is viewed as a generalist with special *musical* tools that may be adapted to meet the professionally assessed needs of various patients. Michel notes two particular aspects of the therapist's musical tools: (a) the basic power of the musical stimulus to arouse or soothe activity and (b) music's traditional functional values as a socializing agent and as a symbol or vehicle for expressing patriotism, religion, or fraternity.

The uses of music in hospitals and outpatient treatment settings include a variety of specializations for patients with particular needs. As an activity therapy, music therapy requires the patient to be engaged actively in "doing" music through singing, listening, discussing, creating, playing instruments, or moving. The music therapist usually is a member of a professional team, often headed by a psychiatrist or clinical director, which outlines the particular patient's therapeutic program. The team may select music therapy as the particular activity or as one of several activities for facilitating behavioral changes. A particular value of activity therapy is that it requires an interpersonal relationship between the therapist and the patient, as well as relationships within the group.

The specific music activities for individual patients are determined by the music therapist, who considers many factors, including the recommendations of the therapeutic team, the patient's disabilities and behavioral disorders, the objectives for the therapy, and the patient's musical background and interests. While the therapist may establish musical goals, these are secondary to the behavioral and social goals established by the therapeutic team. The music therapist must select music activities that capitalize on music's stimulative and socializing strengths to actively involve the patient while at the same time subtly working toward effecting the desired behavioral changes.

Unkefer (1990) developed a taxonomy of programs and techniques in music therapy for use when working with people with mental disorders. The taxonomy classifies music therapy activities and interventions into six major categories: (a) music performing, (b) music psychotherapy, (c) music and movement, (d) music combined with other expressive arts, (e) recreational music, and (f) music and relaxation.

Music performing activities may focus on either product or process and may involve either group or individual interventions. Group activities emphasize group cooperation and responsibility, social interaction, and mastery of musical material. Techniques with individuals may focus on improving a client's musical skills (product) or fostering a client's self-expression and ability to interact musically and socially with the therapist or others in the group (process).

Unkefer's second category, music psychotherapy, includes supportive, interactive, and catalytic therapy processes for groups and/or individuals. Supportive music therapy activities foster verbal interaction, social participation, and the practice of healthy behavior patterns. Interactive activities seek to help clients become aware of conscious conflicts and unhealthy defense mechanisms and to gain insight into behavior patterns. Catalytic activities seek to create an awareness of subconscious conflicts and encourage change by reliving and resolving deep conflicts and fears.

In Unkefer's third category, therapy using music and movement may help clients become aware of their body mechanics, increase social interaction, allow expression of feelings and emotions, and increase exercise. In category four, music therapy activities which combine music with other expressive arts such as drawing, drama, sculpting, or writing prose and poetry offer individuals increased opportunities for expression of feelings and emotions. Recreational music therapy activities, category five, focus on cooperative group participation, success-oriented musical experiences, and the development of leisure time musical skills.

Unkefer's sixth category, activities using music to foster relaxation, recognizes four techniques: (a) music used in conjunction with progressive muscle relaxation training; (b) music for surface relaxation and temporary respite from anxiety/stress conditions; (c) music imagery to explore and foster increased self-awareness, which may lead to psychological and physical relaxation; and (d) music as a positive perceptual focus and diversion from anxieties, fear, tension, and unpleasant thoughts.

Documenting music therapy's effects via carefully controlled research is understandably difficult. The clinical approach necessary in music therapy activities lends itself more to case study research than experimental research. Further, since music therapy often is used in conjunction with other therapies and medications, it is difficult to attribute any effects solely to the music; also, the individual therapist's personality is an important variable.

A review of the research literature on particular applications of music in therapy is far beyond the scope of the present discussion, but Standley's (1986) meta-analysis of empirical studies using music in actual medical/dental treatments warrants discussion. She identified 81 studies for possible inclusion in the meta-analysis, but only 30 were included. The others had (a) failed to report empirical data; (b) used simulated diagnosis, treatment, or pain stimuli; (c) used auditory stimuli other than music; or (d) reported results in formats not amenable to replicated data analysis. Using the statistic *Estimated Effect Size* (ES), which represents the proportion of a standard deviation that quantifies the experimental effects of the two conditions, i.e., the difference in the means of the groups receiving musical treatment and the groups not receiving musical treatment, Standley's data revealed that for 54 of 55 variables analyzed, "music conditions enhanced medical objectives whether measured by physiological (ES = .97), psychological/self-report (ES = .85), or behavioral observation (ES = 1.10)"[14] (Standley, p. 79).

From the comprehensive data contained in the 30 studies included in her meta-analysis, Standley (pp. 81–97) identified seven types of music therapy applications and techniques for use in medical settings. Following is a list of the techniques and the function the music is intended to serve for each technique. Readers interested in the therapeutic objectives, populations for whom the techniques are intended, and the procedures involved in application of the techniques should consult Standley's article, a major contribution to the field.

1. *Technique:* Music Listening and Anesthesia, Analgesia, and/or Suggestion

Music Function: To serve as an audioanalgesic, anxiolytic, or sedative.

2. *Technique:* Music Listening/Participation and Exercise

Music Function: To serve as a focus of attention and/or to structure exercise (tempo, repetition, duration, force, or fluidity).

3. *Technique:* Music Listening/Participation and Counseling

Music Function: To initiate and enhance therapist/patient/family relationship.

4. *Technique:* Music Listening/Participation and Developmental or Educational Objectives

Music Function: To reinforce or structure learning.

5. *Technique:* Music Listening and Stimulation

Music Function: To stimulate auditorily and increase awareness of other forms of stimuli.

6. *Technique:* Music and Biofeedback

Music Function: To serve as reinforcer or structure for physiological responses.

7. *Techniques:* Music and Group Activities

Music Function: To structure pleasurable and positive personal interactions.

While music therapy is a relatively new application of music in functional ways, it appears to have a stronger research base than other functional applications of music. Standley and Prickett's (1994) compila-

---

[14]An ES of 1.00 indicates that the experimental group (music condition) scored one standard deviation better than the control group (nonmusic condition). The number of variables analyzed was greater than 30 because some studies included more than one dependent variable.

tion of key articles appearing over a thirty-year period in the *Journal of Music Therapy* offers a comprehensive description of much of that base. Health professionals recognize its value as an activity therapy, and research, training, and other standards for the profession are high, thus strengthening the profession's position within the medical and paramedical community. In conclusion, there is little doubt that the ideals and principles under which music is used in therapy make music therapy one of the most, if not *the* most, valuable functional applications of music.

Music to Facilitate Nonmusical Learning

Many claims are made regarding music's effects on nonmusical learning. Students of all ages often claim that they study more effectively while listening to music. When faced with program cutbacks in schools, many American music educators seek new ways to justify music's position in the curriculum by suggesting that music facilitates learning in other curricular areas. An area for which perhaps the most claims have been made is in teaching language arts, and advocacy articles espousing the benefits of music for learning language abound (e.g., Wolverton, 1991; Snyder, 1994).

A solid research base for these claims is lacking. While some isolated studies yield "significant differences" in favor of approaches using music, there are many more that yield "no significant differences." Whether these differences are real or are due to the approach or design of the experiments has been a concern of some comprehensive reviews of the literature, and this discussion relies heavily on those reviews, particularly that of Wolff (1978). Other reviews include those by Hanshumaker (1980; 1986); his reviews included studies regarding the effects of other arts besides music, and his generalizations therefore must be considered with this in mind.

Music has been used in a number of different ways in attempts to facilitate nonmusical learning. One method, discussed in the concluding section of this chapter, is to use music or musical activities as a reward for having accomplished a given task. This method is a part of a behavioral approach advocated by Clifford K. Madsen and many of his former students. Much of their research is reported by Madsen, Greer, and Madsen (1975) and Madsen and Prickett (1987). While much of the research they report uses behavioral techniques to facilitate musical learning, much uses music as a reinforcer for nonmusical behavioral change.

Of the other approaches involving music to facilitate nonmusical learning, perhaps the most basic is that of examining the effects of musical experience and learning on achievement in other subject areas. Wolff labels this approach as *general learning transfer* in which "the study of music serves as a mental discipline which expedites the learning of other subjects" (Wolff, 1978, p. 3). She also notes that the notion of training faculties of the mind had already been discredited by the time of Thorndike. Other studies have investigated *specific learning* on certain tasks common to music and other subjects. An example of such a study is that of Madsen, Madsen, and Michel (1975) in which tonal cues were used to facilitate verbal auditory discrimination.

Another approach using music to facilitate nonmusical learning is through the use of background music. While few specific claims are made regarding the effects of this type of music on academic achievement, there appears to be enough interest on "how environment can affect the learning process" (Muzak, brochure, no date). Interestingly, a recent study of background music's effects on university students' reading comprehension revealed no statistically significant effects (Kelly, 1993).

Two other recent studies, however, suggest that music can be effective in facilitating academic achievement. Battle and Ramsey (1990) found that presentation of social studies facts to inner-city, sixth grade students via a rhythmic song (rap) is more effective than a traditional presentation of social studies facts. Tanner (1991) observed that an approach to reading that incorporated ITA (Initial Teaching Alphabet) techniques in both reading and music instruction helped second-, third-, and fourth-grade students improve their skills in letter-word identification, passage comprehension, and word attack.

Taking a different approach to the problem, Manthei and Smith (1993) sought to assess via regression analysis the effects of music participation on high school students' mathematical achievement. Studying data from a sample of 1,192 drawn from the pool of 12,000 students participating in the 1980 High School and Beyond survey, the researchers report no statistically significant direct effect of music participation on mathematical achievement; however, based on an analysis of the number of music participants who also were participants in mathematics courses, they did observe an *indirect* positive effect of music participation on mathematical achievement (p. 81).

The literature regarding music's effects on nonmusical learning is diverse, and no attempt is made to review it here. However, readers are encouraged to examine Wolff's excellent review and status report on the topic. She also reviews studies that examine the effects of music experience on self-concept, personality factors, and certain physical activities.

Hanshumaker's 1980 review examines studies related to language development and reading readiness, reading and mathematics, learning behavior and attitude, creativity, socialization, and intellectual development and achievement. His 1986 review essentially is an update of the 1980 review. Generally, Hanshumaker concludes that music has positive effects on language development, reading readiness, and student verbalization. He also notes that daily music instruction has a significant, positive effect on math scores and that creativity and perceptual motor skills are positively affected. A conservative but particularly important conclusion for music educators is that "school time spent on music and other arts activities has no negative effect on academic achievement" (Hanshumaker, 1986, p. 11).

Overall, Wolff is more cautious in her conclusions, although she agrees that there may be measurable effects of music education on the development of cognitive skills and understanding. She acknowledges that most of the research she reviewed reported positive results, but she maintains that the conclusions drawn generally remain unconvincing, primarily due to "obvious inadequacies in the experimental designs and also to the incomplete and equivocal descriptions of the experiments themselves" (p. 21). She concludes her review with the statement that "definitive evidence of the nonmusical outcomes of music education is yet to be provided" (p. 21). The authors concur.

Music as a Reward

As noted in the above discussion, research in which music is used as a reward for behavior change or accomplishment of a given nonmusical task is limited. Vance Cotter (1973) was a pioneer researcher in this area, but as noted above, Clifford Madsen and his students (and former students) have provided the bulk of the research.

The research in this area generally reflects a behavioral approach that views learning as a change in behavior which must be observable. Most of the research reflects careful control and isolation of variables.

Cotter (1973) studied the effects of contingent and noncontingent music on the performance of manual tasks in a simulated workshop situation by 16 moderately retarded adolescent females. Subjects in the noncontingent group, i.e., the one receiving music regardless of their work performance, did not achieve a higher mean work rate, while subjects in the contingent group, for whom receiving music depended on work rate, did increase their mean work rate.

Greer, Randall, and Timberlake (1975) compared the contingency effects of music listening, pennies, and no reward on improvement in vocal pitch accuracy and attendance. No significant differences were observed among the groups' vocal gain scores, although significant differences were found between the nonreinforcement group and the groups receiving music or pennies for attendance. No significant difference was found between the groups receiving music and pennies.

Madsen and Forsythe (1975) examined the contingency effects of individual music listening (via headphones), group music listening, mathematics games, and no reward on sixth graders' mathematical achievement. Results revealed statistically significant differences in favor of the two groups receiving music. A subsequent study, in which the contingency for first graders' math achievement was viewing televised music lessons, also revealed greater achievement for the group viewing the music lessons than for a control group receiving no reward (Madsen, Dorow, Moore, & Womble, 1976).

Madsen and Geringer's (1976) study of the effects of choices of reinforcement indicated that televised music lessons were just as effective as free playing in increasing children's academic skills. Madsen's (1981) later study comparing the effects of televised music lessons and the receipt of books as reinforcement alternatives for achievement in math also revealed that both reinforcers were effective in promoting increased performance in mathematics. Results indicated that the televised music lessons had the added advantage of facilitating achievement in music.

The selected studies cited here all suggest that music can function as a reward for achievement for nonmusical tasks. The extent to which these results can be generalized and applied to other learning situations is subject to conjecture. Madsen and Forsythe (1975, p. 31) acknowledge that studies of this type have several problems, including "Hawthorne" and "halo" effects as well as all of the effects presumed to be operating in school settings.[15] The studies do, however, indicate that music as a reward is equally effective with other contrived classroom contingencies and perhaps has the additional effect of facilitating learning in music.

Summary

This chapter's major points are:
1. Music that stimulates or arouses listeners has a strong energizing component.

---

[15]The "Hawthorne" effect refers to an increase in performance derived apparently because a group perceives itself as receiving special treatment; the "halo" effect refers to a bias in evaluations arising from an evaluator's tendency to allow some general impression he/she has of the person being rated to influence ratings of specific traits.

2. For most people, music's primary energizing component is rhythm, particularly its attribute of tempo.

3. Nonpercussive and legato sounds characterize music that soothes, calms, or tranquilizes behavior.

4. Reviews of the limited amount of research on the effects of stimulative and sedative music reveal differential responses to the two types of music.

5. Music has been a part of ceremonies, particularly religious and military, throughout history.

6. "Commercial" music involves using music in some way to make money directly from music or to enhance business through the use of music.

7. Background music is used informally by individuals as well as for groups of people in public places.

8. The Muzak Corporation has been the most successful proponent and producer of background music.

9. Muzak's "stimulus progression" concept involves 15-minute segments of specially recorded instrumental music, with increasing stimulus values from one composition to another as a result of changes in tempo, rhythm classification, instrumental grouping, and the number of instruments used.

10. Commercial uses of music include background music in the workplace, in the marketplace, in advertising, and as entertainment.

11. Music in industry has been studied primarily in terms of its effects on employee productivity and morale.

12. Whether music attracts attention, reinforces a message, induces a mood, or simply entertains, the possibilities for music making a product or service more appealing arise from music's deep involvement in human culture.

13. Music may serve as narration because people have learned to associate acoustical events with real or imagined events in other sensory modes.

14. Fundamental principles of music therapy are that therapeutic experience should (a) enhance the establishment or reestablishment of interpersonal relationships between a patient and others and (b) help foster the patient's self-esteem.

15. Two basic tools of music therapists are music's (a) power to stimulate or soothe activity and (b) values as a socializing agent and as a symbol or vehicle for expressing patriotism, religion, and fraternity.

16. Unkefer's taxonomy of music therapy programs and techniques for working with people with mental disorders falls into six major categories: (a) music performing, (b) music psychotherapy, (c) music

and movement, (d) music combined with other expressive arts, (e) recreational music, and (f) music and relaxation.

17. Standley's seven music therapy functions include using music to (a) serve as an audioanalgesic, anxiolytic, or sedative; (b) serve as a focus of attention and/or to structure exercise; (c) initiate and enhance therapist/patient/family relationships; (d) reinforce or structure learning; (e) stimulate auditorily and increase awareness of other forms of stimuli; (f) serve as reinforcer or structure for physiological responses; and (g) structure pleasurable and positive personal interactions.

18. Some research continually examines music's effects on nonmusical learning, but results are inconclusive.

19. Music can serve as a reward for completion of nonmusical tasks.

References

Alpert, J. I., & Alpert, M. I. (1989). Background music as an influence in consumer mood and advertising responses. In T. K. Scrull (Ed.), *Advances in consumer research* (vol. 16) (pp. 485–491). Provo, UT: Association for Consumer Research.

Alpert, J. I., & Alpert, M. I. (1990). Music influences on mood and purchase intention. *Psychology & Marketing, 7,* 109–133.

Barnes, K. Top 40 radio: A fragment of the imagination. In S. Frith (Ed.), *Facing the music* (pp. 8–50). New York: Pantheon Books.

Baskerville, D. (1995). *Music business handbook & career guide* (6th ed.). Thousand Oaks, CA: Sage Publications.

Battle, J.B., & Ramsey, D.S. (1990). Music as an aid in learning conceptual facts in the social studies lesson. *Southeastern Journal of Music Education, 2,* 221–237.

Boyle, J.D. (1982). College students' verbal descriptions of stimulative and sedative music. In P.E. Sink (Ed.), *Proceedings of the Research Symposium on the Psychology and Acoustics of Music 1982* (pp. 105–117). Lawrence: The University of Kansas.

Brabec, J., & Brabec, T. (1994). *Music, money, and success.* New York: Schirmer Books.

Brown, R. (1981). Music and language. In R. G. Taylor (Ed.), *Documentary report of the Ann Arbor symposium* (pp. 233–265). Reston, VA: Music Educators National Conference.

Cotter, V.W. (1973). Effects of music on mentally retarded girls' performance of manual tasks. *Council for Research in Music Education, 27,* 42–43.

Denisoff, R. S. (1986). *Tarnished gold.* New Brunswick, NJ: Transaction Books.

Eagle, C. T., Jr. (1971). Effects of existing mood and order of presentation of vocal and instrumental music on rated mood responses to that music. Unpublished doctoral dissertation, The University of Kansas.

Farnsworth, P. R. (1969). *The social psychology of music* (2nd ed.). Ames: Iowa State University Press.

Fink, M. (1989). *Inside the music business.* New York: Schirmer Books.

Fried, R., & Berkowitz, L. (1979). Music hath charms . . . and can influence helpfulness. *Journal of Applied Social Science, 9,* 199–208.

Frith, S. (1988). Video pop: Picking up the pieces. In S. Frith (Ed.), *Facing the music* (pp. 88–130). New York: Pantheon Books.

Gardner, M. P. (1985). Mood states and consumer behavior: A critical review. *Journal of Consumer Research, 12,* 281–300.

Garfield, B. (1988). Too much ad music leaves little room for hitting the right note. *Advertising Age, 59*(1), 46.

Gaston, E.T. (1951/1952). The influence of music on behavior. *University of Kansas Bulletin of Education, 6,* 60–63.

Gaston, E.T. (1968a). Foreword. In E.T. Gaston (Ed.), *Music in therapy* (pp. v–vii). New York: Macmillan.

Gaston, E.T. (1968b). Man and music. In E. T. Gaston (Ed.), *Music in therapy* (pp. 7–21). New York: Macmillan.

Gibbons, A. C. (1977). Popular music preferences of elderly persons. *Journal of Music Therapy, 14,* 180–189.

Goldberg, M. E., & Gorn, G. J. (1987). Happy and sad tv programs: How they effect reactions to commercials. *Journal of Consumer Research, 14,* 387–403.

Golden, L. L., & Johnson, K. A. (1983). The impact of sensory preference and thinking versus feeling appeals on advertising effectiveness. In R. Bagozzi & A. Tybout (Eds.), *Advances in consumer research* (vol. 10) (pp. 203–208). Ann Arbor, MI: Association for Consumer Research.

Gorn, G. J. (1982). The effects of music in advertising on choice behavior: A classical conditioning approach. *Journal of Marketing, 46*(1), 94–101.

Greer, R.D., Randall, R., & Timberlake, C. (1975). The discriminate use of music listening as a contingency for improvement in vocal pitch accuracy and attending behavior. In C.K. Madsen, R.D. Greer, & C.H. Madsen, Jr. (Eds.), *Research in music behavior* (pp. 79–88). New York: Teachers College Press, Columbia University.

Haack, P. A. (1980). The behavior of music listeners. In D. A. Hodges (Ed), *Handbook of music psychology* (pp. 141–182). Lawrence, KS: National Association for Music Therapy.

Haley, R. I., Richardson, J., & Baldwin, B. M. (1984). The effects of nonverbal communications in television advertising. *Journal of Advertising Research, 24*(4), 11–18.

Hanshumaker, J. (1980). The effects of arts education on intellectual and social development: A review of selected research. *Council for Research in Music Education, 61,* 10–28.

Hanshumaker, J. (1986). The effects of music and other arts instruction on reading and math achievement and on general school performance. *UPDATE, The Applications of Research in Music Education, 4* (2), 10–11.

Hodges, D.A. (1980). Physiological responses to music. In D.A. Hodges (Ed.), *Handbook of music psychology* (pp. 392–400). Lawrence, KS: National Association for Music Therapy.

Holbrook, M. B., & Batra, R. (1987). Assessing the role of emotions as mediators of consumer responses to advertising. *Journal of Consumer Research, 14,* 404–420.

Holbrook, M. B., & Schindler, R. M. (1989). Some exploratory findings on the development of musical tastes. *Journal of Consumer Research, 16,* 119–124.

Hunter, B. (1983). It's Muzak through your ears. *American Way, 16*(11), 148–157.

Husch, J. A. (1984). Music of the workplace: A study of Muzak culture. Unpublished doctoral dissertation, The University of Massachusetts.

Huxley, A. (1928). *Point counter point.* New York: Harper & Row.

Kellaris, J. J., & Cox, A. D. (1989). The effects of background music in advertising: A reassessment. *Journal of Consumer Research, 16,* 113–118.

Kelly, S.N. (1993). A comparison of the effects of background music on the reading comprehension of university undergraduate music majors and nonmusic majors. *Southeastern Journal of Music Education, 5,* 86–97.

Kerr, W. A. (1945). *Experiments on the effects of music on factory production.* Stanford, CA: Stanford University Press.

Lundin, R.W. (1967). *An objective psychology of music* (2nd ed.). New York: Ronald Press.

Macklin, M. C. (1988). The relationship between music in advertising and children's responses: An experimental investigation. In S. Hecker & D. W. Stewart (Eds.), *Nonverbal communication in advertising* (pp. 225–243). Lexington, MA: Lexington Books.

Madsen, C.K. (1981). Music lessons and books as reinforcement alternatives for an academic task. *Journal of Research in Music Education, 29,* 103–110.

Madsen, C.K., Dorow, L.G., Moore, R.S., & Womble, J.U. (1967). Effect of music via television as reinforcement for correct mathematics. *Journal of Research in Music Education, 24,* 51–59.

Madsen, C.K., & Forsythe, J.L. (1975). The effect of contingent listening on increases in mathematical responses. In C.K. Madsen, R.D. Greer, & C.H. Madsen, Jr. (Eds.), *Research in music behavior* (pp. 25–31). New York: Teachers College Press, Columbia University.

Madsen, C.K., & Geringer, J.M. (1976). Choice of televised music lessons versus free play in relationship to academic improvement. *Journal of Music Therapy, 13* (4), 154–162.

Madsen, C. K., Greer, R. D., & Madsen, C. H., Jr. (Eds.) (1975). *Research in music behavior.* New York: Teachers College Press, Columbia University.

Madsen, C.K., Madsen, C.H., Jr., & Michel, D.E. (1975). The use of music stimuli in teaching language discrimination. In C.K. Madsen, R.D. Greer, & C.H. Madsen, Jr. (Eds.), *Research in music behavior.* New York: Teachers College Press, Columbia University.

Madsen, C.K., & Prickett, C.A. (Eds.). (1987). *Applications of research in music education.* Tuscaloosa: The University of Alabama Press.

Manthei, M., & Smith, T.M. (1993). The effects of instrumental music participation on mathematical achievement. *Southeastern Journal of Music Education, 5,* 77–85.

Mathur, M., & Chattopadhyay, A. (1991). The impact of moods generated by television programs on responses to advertising. *Psychology & Marketing, 8,* 59–77.

McMullen, P.T. (1982). Connotative responses to musical stimuli: A theoretical explanation. *Council for Research in Music Education, 71,* 45–57.

Michel, D.E. (1985). *Music therapy: An introduction including music in special education* (2nd ed.). Springfield: Charles C Thomas.

Milliman, R. E. (1982). Using background music to affect the behavior of supermarket shoppers. *Journal of Marketing, 46* (3), 86–91.

Milliman, R. E. (1986). The influence of background music on the behavior of restaurant patrons. *Journal of Consumer Research, 13,* 286–289.

Mussulman, J. A. (1974). *The uses of music: An introduction to music in contemporary American life.* Englewood Cliffs, NJ: Prentice-Hall.

Muzak Corporation. (n.d.). How environment can effect the learning process. In brochure, *Muzak and schools.* New York: Muzak Corporation.

Pareles, J. (1987, December 3). Consumers are legitimizing new-age music in a big way. *The Miami News,* p. 3C.

Park, C. W., & Young, S. M. (1986). Consumer response to television commercials: The impact of involvement and background music on brand attitude formation. *Journal of Marketing Research, 18,* 11–24.

Perris, A. (1985). *Music as propaganda: Art to persuade, art to control.* Westport, CT: Greenwood Press.

Petty, R. E., Cacioppo, J. T., & Schumann, D. (1983). Central and peripheral routes to advertising effectiveness: The moderating role of involvement. *Journal of Consumer Research, 10,* 135–146.

Portnoy, J. (1963). *Music in the life of man.* New York: Holt, Rinehart, and Winston.

Powell, C. (1994, July 11). When workers wear Walkmans on the job. *The Wall Street Journal,* pp. B1–B2.

Shea, G. (1988, January). Rock'n'roll is here to sell. *Continental,* pp. 42–43, 49–50, 52, 57.

Shemel, S., & Krasilovsky, M. W. (1990). *This business of music* (6th ed.). New York: Billboard Books.

Snyder, S. (1994). Language, movement, and music—process connections. *General Music Today, 7* (3), 4–9.

Standley, J.M. (1986). Music research in medical/dental treatment: Meta-analysis and clinical applications. *Journal of Music Therapy, 23,* 56–122.

Standley, J. M., & Prickett, C. A. (Eds.). (1994). *Research in music therapy: A tradition of excellence.* Silver Spring, MD: National Association for Music Therapy.

Statistical overview—Update '86. New York: Recording Industry of America.

Stewart, D. W., & Hecker, S. (1988). The future of research on nonverbal communication in advertising. In S. Hecker & D. W. Stewart (Eds.) *Nonverbal communication in advertising* (pp. 256–264). Lexington, MA: D. C. Heath.

Stout, P. A., & Leckenby, J. D. (1988). Let the music play: Music as a nonverbal element of television commercials. In S. Hecker & D. W. Stewart (Eds.), *Nonverbal communication in advertising* (pp. 207–223). Lexington, MA: D. C. Heath.

Sullivan, G. L. (1990). Music format effects in radio advertising. *Psychology & Marketing, 7,* 97–108.

Tanner, D.R. (1991). Initial teaching alphabet, language experience and music. *Southeastern Journal of Music Education, 3,* 1–10.

Unkefer, R. (Ed.) (1990). *Music therapy in the treatment of adults with mental disorders.* New York: Schirmer Books.

Wakshlag, J. J., Reitz, R. J., & Zillman, D. (1982). Selective exposure to and acquisition of information from educational television programs as a function of appeal and tempo of background music. *Journal of Educational Psychology, 74,* 666–677.

Wintle, R. R. (1978/1979). Emotional impact of music on television commercials (Doctoral dissertation, University of Nebraska, 1978). *Dissertation Abstracts International, 39,* 5115A. (University Microfilms No. 790153)

Wokoun, W. (1979). A study of fatigue in industry. New York: Muzak Corporation.

Wolff, K. (1978). The nonmusical outcomes of music education: A review of the literature. *Council for Research in Music Education, 55,* 1–27.

Wolverton, V.D. (1991). Facilitating language acquisition through music. *UPDATE: Applications of Research in Music Education, 9* (2), 24–30.

CHAPTER FOUR

PSYCHOACOUSTICAL FOUNDATIONS

Psychoacoustics is a branch of psychophysics, the study of sensory responses to physical stimuli. To study auditory sensations is to study psychoacoustics. Questions regarding comparative pitches and loudnesses, assigning pitch and timbre sensations to tonal clusters, and, indeed, perceptions of all tonal properties essentially are psychoacoustical questions. Without psychoacoustical phenomena that translate physical disturbances into conscious sensations, music (as we presently know it) could not exist. While "real" music certainly is more than a sequence of individual sensations, and music psychology currently has greater interest in "holistic" processes of music cognition (e.g., melodic recognition, sensitivity to musical forms, rhythmic organization) and generally considers study of isolated tones as excessively atomistic, the authors believe that detailed study of individual tonal perceptions and associated processes remains valuable for understanding musical behavior.

After presenting brief overviews of the production and transmission of musical sounds (which readers familiar with elementary acoustics may want to omit), this chapter addresses the reception of musical sounds and psychoacoustical phenomena organized around the basic psychological tonal properties of pitch, loudness, and timbre. Later chapters will address the organization and cognitive processing of more global musical properties.

Production of Musical Sounds

Vibration—something moving back and forth—is basic to any musical sound. If the vibration is within a certain range of rates and is generally periodic, i.e., vibrates with a relatively regularly recurring motion, people are likely to perceive the vibration as a *tone*, i.e., a sound which is of sufficient regularity and length so that they can hear it with a definite pitch. Irregular vibrations, heard as noise,[1] also are incorporated into

---

[1]"Noise" may be considered as sound which has no definite pitch, or simply as unwanted sound. In music, cymbal crashes and snare drum rolls exemplify "wanted" musical sounds which are "noise" by the pitch criterion.

music. Sources of musical sounds include vibrating strings, air columns, metal plates, metal bars, membranes, and electrical circuits.

Consider a vibrating pendulum, one of the simplest illustrations of vibration and related properties. The pendulum, once displaced and thereby set into motion, will swing back and forth. Although the distance it swings will decrease gradually, the pendulum will swing long enough for an observer to note that it regularly returns to the point at which it began to swing. Every so often, with regularity, it completes a *cycle*. A cycle is the complete journey of a vibrating object from an original point through both extremes of displacement and back to the original point. The time required for the cycle's completion is the *period*. The number of cycles completed in a given amount of time is the *frequency*. The distance between the pendulum's original location and its point of maximal displacement is the displacement *amplitude*. One readily can observe and describe a cycle, period, frequency, and amplitude in relation to a vibrating pendulum.

Although a person can not see (except with measuring instruments such as an oscilloscope or stroboscopic lighting) the individual cycles, vibrating objects producing musical sounds also vibrate in cycles, and with certain periods, frequencies, and amplitudes. Musical sounds, tones as well as noises, generally are a complex of individual vibrations; they contain numerous frequencies. Musical sounds can be analyzed into their component frequencies, but a listener usually hears a tone as having one distinct frequency.

All vibrations are not perceivable as sound, of course. A minimum amount of power (intensity) is necessary, and human ears normally respond to an approximate frequency range of 20 to 18,000 cycles per second (called Hertz, abbreviated Hz, in honor of Heinrich Hertz (1857–1894), who conducted early research with electromagnetism). Individuals vary in their frequency sensitivity, particularly regarding the upper limit. Sounds considerably lower than 20 Hz may be heard under artificial conditions.

The production of musical sounds, then, requires that something be set into vibration. If it vibrates with acceptable frequency and intensity, and those vibrations somehow can be transmitted to a listener, music is possible.

Transmission of Musical Sounds

Transmission, as used here, refers to the *propagation* or spread of a disturbance through the air from a sound source to a listener. We are not considering electrical or electronic transmission or sound's travel through media other than air.

Consider a row of upright dominoes. If they are spaced at a critical distance from each other, a person can produce an amusing ripple effect by pushing the first domino into its neighbor. This is somewhat analogous to what happens when a disturbance spreads through the air from a sounding musical instrument or voice to a listener. The vibrating body disturbs air particles around it. Those particles bump other particles, which in turn bump others. Unlike the dominoes, each particle can move back and forth as long as the disturbance's source continues to vibrate. However, just as the first domino does not travel to the end of the row, no one air particle travels from the musical source to the listener. The *disturbance* travels.

A disturbance spreading through the air is a *longitudinal* disturbance, i.e., the overall disturbance travels in the same direction as the slight movements (displacements) of each particle. (In *transverse* disturbances, the overall disturbance travels in a direction perpendicular to the slight movement of each particle.) A travelling disturbance or a chain of travelling disturbances often is called a wave. A sound wave is a series of disturbances travelling through a medium.[2]

Waves may travel directly from a sound source to a listener. They may encounter a surface which represents a sudden change in properties of the medium; then, the wave *reflects,* although some of its energy is absorbed by the reflecting surface. Reflection represents a sudden change in the direction of wave travel; a gradual change in direction results from *refraction,* a progressive "bending" of the wave resulting from a gradual change in medium properties, such as temperature or density. People may sense sounds from sources not directly aligned with their ears or obscured from view because of *diffraction,* a wave's ability to "go around corners" or pass through a small opening.

A travelling wave in air comprises changing locations of air particles as they undergo bumping and the resulting displacements. Accompanying the continual changes in particle location are changes in air pressure. When particles are compressed more closely together than they are in an undisturbed state, the pressure increases. When particles are spread further apart (rarefacted) than they are in an undisturbed state, the pressure decreases. This means that a periodic pressure fluctuation occurs at any point in a travelling wave in air. Such periodic pressure fluctuations,

---

[2]Unlike light waves, radio waves, and other electromagnetic disturbances, sound waves require an intervening physical substance in order to travel from one place to another. Light can travel through a vacuum; sound can not.

minute though they are, are the form in which Beethoven symphonies, Handel oratorios, rock tunes, and thirdgrade recorder ensemble sounds reach our ears.

Reception of Musical Sounds

From Air to Inner Ear

The periodic pressure fluctuations accompany the travelling wave as it enters the ear. The obvious external or cosmetic portion of the ear is the *pinna;* the "hole in the head" is the entrance to the *auditory canal* or *meatus.* The travelling wave passes through the auditory canal and encounters the *eardrum* or *tympanic membrane,* which separates the outer and middle ear. Resonance, particularly in the approximate frequency range of 20007000 Hz, may increase the sound pressure that the wave exerts as it travels through the auditory canal (Pickles, 1982, pp. 12–13).

The eardrum responds to the pressure fluctuations by moving in and out, something like a drumhead. (Incredibly tiny amounts of pressure change are sufficient to move the eardrum.) Eardrum motion is more efficient when the air pressure is equal on both sides of the eardrum, and the air supplied through the *Eustachian tube,* connected to the back of the throat, assists in the equalization. Three tiny middle ear bones or *ossicles* (hammer, anvil, and stirrup, or malleus, incus, and stapes) connect the eardrum to another membrane, the *oval window,* which separates the middle and inner ear. The *acoustic reflex,* resulting from the contraction of two muscles (tensor tympani and stapedius) connected to the ossicles, may increase the bones' stiffness and thereby help protect the inner ear from damage due to strong sounds.

The oval window's motions create wavelike movements in fluid contained in the snail-shell-shaped inner ear or *cochlea.* The *basilar membrane,* which is one part of the *cochlear duct,* an appendage connected to the cochlear wall near the oval window, detects the fluid movements and in turn moves up and down in a manner which depends on the movements' frequencies. Higher frequencies elicit maximal membrane movement closer to the oval window end or base; lower frequencies elicit maximal movement closer to the "far" end or apex of the basilar membrane. Combinations of frequencies, such as most musical tones, excite the membrane at several locations. Where, when, and how much the basilar membrane is excited provides basic information for perception and organization of the psychological sensations basic to music.

From the time the original vibrating body disturbs the surrounding medium until the resulting disturbance reaches the basilar membrane, the form of energy expended is mechanical. It is a matter of movement. Lying alongside the basilar membrane are *hair cells (audiocilia)*, collectively known as the *organ of Corti*, which sense the membrane's movements and function as *transducers*. A transducer is a device which converts one form of energy to another (microphones and loudspeakers are common examples); the hair cells convert mechanical to electrochemical energy and start auditory signals on their way to the brain.

From Inner Ear to Brain

The basilar membrane's characteristic vibration innervates (excites) the hair cells, particularly as the membrane moves toward the center of the cochlear duct. Estimates vary regarding the exact number of hair cells, but 30,000 probably is a good approximation. According to Moore (1989, p. 26), there are about 25,000 *outer* hair cells, each containing about 140 hairs and arranged in three rows, and about 3500 *inner* hair cells, each containing about 40 hairs. (Outer and inner refer to location in relation to the outside of the cochlea.) The outer cells are more sensitive and respond at lower sound levels than the inner cells. The hair cells differ functionally, as evidenced by the guinea pig's inner cells producing a cochlear microphonic (an electrical discharge obtained by inserting an electrode into the cochlea) proportional to the *velocity* of basilar membrane movement while outer cells produce a cochlear microphonic proportional to the amount of basilar membrane *displacement* (Dallos et al., 1972).

Even a single-tone stimulus activates a large portion of the cochlear neural fibres; two tones which differ very slightly activate respective areas along the basilar membrane that overlap considerably. The boundaries between activated and unactivated areas apparently help signal the stimulus frequency(ies). Intensity apparently is signalled in terms of the number of activated fibres and the frequency of neural discharge (Whitfield, 1967). The basic information regarding frequency, intensity, and waveform properties is passed to and through the neural pathways to the auditory cortex, in rough accordance with the schematic diagram in Figure 4-1 (Whitfield; Roederer, 1995). Although the auditory cortex is the "ultimate destination," neural processing occurs prior to the cortex; some perception necessary for basic musical decision making is completed at subcortical levels. Research with cats and monkeys suggests that neurons in the auditory pathway respond preferentially to various stimulus aspects, such as frequency, duration, and rapid transient properties such as those which characterize beginnings of tones; so, although details are sketchy, a subcortical mechanism for clarifying and enhancing tonal features apparently exists (Moore, 1989, pp. 30–41).

Most hair cells innervate the fibres of the auditory nerve and send signals along the *afferent* neural pathway to the brain. According to Zwicker and Fastl (1990, p. 24), and Wallin (1991, p. 155) more than 90 percent of the afferent fibres make contact with inner hair cells. There also is a "descending" or an *efferent* neural pathway through which the brain can modify the excitability of the hair cells, especially the inner cells (Davis, 1962; Pickles, 1982, pp. 31–32).[3] The afferent pathway includes the spiral ganglion, the dorsal and ventral cochlear nucleus complex, the superior-olivary complex, the nuclei of the inferior colliculus and lateral lemniscus, the medial geniculate body, and the auditory cortex. The efferent pathway includes higher descending neurons and the olivo-cochlear bundle (Gacek, 1972). While the neuroanatomy may be obscure, the afferent pathway is important musically, because that is how information travels to the place where it is organized into music. The efferent pathway is important because, despite its relatively low information handling capacity, it provides a pathway for the brain to "alert" the cochlea for particular sounds.

The purpose of the above abbreviated description of a sound's travel, as a pressure fluctuation and as an electrochemical discharge, from a source to a listener's brain is to help the reader appreciate some of the structures involved. Readers interested in more detail should consult Stevens and Warshofsky (1965) for a highly readable and profusely illustrated description; more technical and physiologically-oriented descriptions are available in standard hearing texts, such as Whitfield, Moore, and Pickles.

Hearing, of course, is more than the operation of the structures and even the neural processes. As Espinoza-Varas and Watson (1989, p. 68) note, "hearing" in the sense of extracting sensory information and making sense of it is an active brain function, which depends on skill, experience, learning, and memory.

Pitch Phenomena

Pitch pervades most music. Unfortunately, the term may be ill-defined and confused with other phenomena. Usually, pitch refers to a tone's apparent location on a high-low continuum. Placement on that abstract continuum in relation to other pitches is learned. In the usual sense,

---

[3]Zwicker and Fastl (1990, p. 24) indicate that efferent neural fibres strongly innervate the outer cells. Later (p. 30), they discuss interaction between the two types of hair cells, so the strong influence on the inner cells may be indirect.

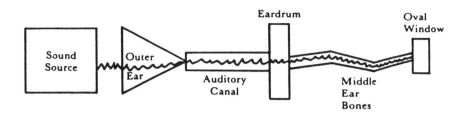

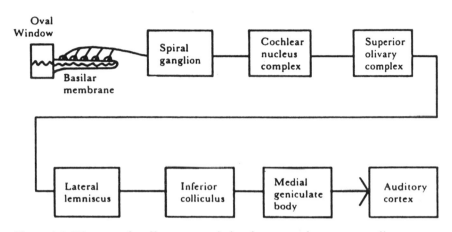

Figure 4-1. Diagram of auditory transmission from sound source to auditory cortex.

pitch is a *metathetic* (place) variable, rather than a *prothetic* (magnitude or strength) variable (Stevens, 1975).

Pitch has other aspects than apparent location. One prothetic aspect is *definity,* the ease with which a pitch may be matched. A flute usually has a far more obvious and definite pitch than a bass drum, for example. Rakowski (1979) calls this definity property pitch strength and suggests measuring it by the variability of subjects' attempts at matching pitches in question to standards. Another pitch aspect, albeit one that is largely meaningless in the context of an isolated tone, is *intimacy, circularity,* or *similarity.* When individual pitches occur in a sequential tonal context, as in a melody or theme, the similarity of any two pitches varies in accordance with tonality (Krumhansl, 1979). Under unusual laboratory conditions involving very specially arranged combinations of frequencies and amplitudes within synthesized complex tones, the height aspect can be suppressed completely in favor of the circularity aspect. A succession of such tones seems to continually ascend or descend, rather like an endless circular staircase (Shepard, 1964; 1982).

The following discussion of pitch phenomena is organized around clarification of its relationship to frequency, various kinds of pitch processing, phenomena resulting from pitch combinations, absolute pitch, and attempts to measure pitch.

Frequency-Pitch Relationship

Frequency, the vibration rate, usually expressed as cycles per second or Hertz, is a physical property of tones; it would exist independently of any human observer. Pitch, a sensation, is a psychological property that requires a human observer. The two properties are not identical, and their relationship is not perfect.

In general, people may experience a pitch sensation from any sufficiently periodic vibration in the range of approximately 20 to 18,000 Hz. The upper limit fluctuates widely with individuals; under special conditions the lower limit may be exceeded: Whittle, Collins, and Robinson (1972) successfully presented highly intense frequencies as low as 3.15 Hz to subjects seated in a cabinet in such a manner that their entire bodies were immersed in uniform sound pressure.

Pitch varies largely as a function of frequency variation, but each minute frequency change does not necessarily elicit a pitch change. Classical psychophysics developed a concept of the *just noticeable difference* (jnd) or *difference limen,* an amount by which a stimulus must change in the appropriate physical property in order for an observer to detect a difference in sensation a certain criterion percentage of the time. The jnd for frequency discrimination (and hence detection of discrete pitches) varies greatly with methodology as well as with people (Woodworth & Schlosberg, 1965); the jnd's size varies with the stimulus frequencies such that it is smaller (in terms of Hz) for lower frequencies (Moore, 1974; Nordmark, 1968). Despite its fluctuation, the jnd usually lies well within the limits necessary for functional musical discrimination. Its exact size is rarely of any musical importance.

Pitch may vary without any change in frequency. Although the effect is rather idiosyncratic and more likely to occur with tones of just one frequency than with typical musical tones, a tone which increases in intensity may be heard as rising or falling in pitch while also becoming louder (Stevens, 1935; Terhardt, 1974b). In *binaural diplacusis,* one tone is heard with a different frequency in each ear. Difficult to research because of its transient nature, the relation of binaural diplacusis to music processing is usually not critical (Sherbon, 1975), although in some clinical instances it may play a role in music perception.

Pitch Processing of Single Pure Tones

A "pure" tone, also called a sine tone or a sinusoidal tone, contains exactly one frequency. Except for some of the sounds produced by electronic means, there are no pure tones in music, although certain flute and organ tones come close to being pure, and a good tuning fork settles into a sinusoidal tone after the initial "clang" dissipates. Most musical tones are complex; even though they usually are heard as having one pitch, they contain a mixture of frequencies. Nevertheless, knowledge of pure tone processing is useful because all complex tones may be analyzed into pure tone components, and investigators have learned much about the auditory system with the aid of pure tones.

Pure tones, limited to one frequency, actually are less clear in pitch than complex tones. For a given duration of sound, a high frequency tone can be determined with greater accuracy than a low one. A certain minimal amount of time is necessary for pitch perception of a given frequency; the greater the frequency, the shorter that time period may be (Kock, 1935).

The place of greatest stimulation along the basilar membrane basically is responsible for pure tone pitch perception. Research (Roederer, 1995; Stevens, Davis, & Lurie, 1935; von Bekesy, 1960; Zwicker, Flottorp, & Stevens, 1957) indicates that stimulations must differ by a certain amount in order for an observer to detect that two separate tones are clearly different or that a continuously sounding tone varying in frequency has changed enough for an observer to detect a pitch change. That amount is known as the *critical band width* (cbw); it is not a precise unchanging value but varies with frequency, intensity, duration, and rate of change.

Pitch Processing of Combined Pure Tones

Tones which contain only one frequency when they leave their respective sound sources may combine in the air and reach the ear in the form of a tonal superposition; a sound wave is shaped by the interaction or interference of each component wave. Any sound wave, in the sense of a pattern of displacements, is determined at any given time by each component's frequency and intensity. When there is only one component, as in a pure tone, the wave is simply dependent on that tone's frequency and intensity. A combination of pure tones creates a superposed waveform, which depends not only on frequency and intensity but also on relative phase.

Phase is the portion of a vibration cycle that is complete at a particular time. Just as the moon may appear as new, a quarter crescent, half, full, or elsewhere at predictable times, a vibrating particle may be at its original position or displaced by varying amounts in either direction. Two vibration cycles of identical frequency may or may not be in phase: Each may be starting its individual cycle at the identical time, in which case they are at zero phase or "in phase" relative to each other. One may be a constant phase behind the other; e.g., one vibration cycle may be at its point of maximal displacement while the other is at the original position of rest. In this case, they are "out of phase." Relative phase influences the superposed waveform. A combined waveform may have less amplitude than either component waveform because of the destructive interference that results from the individual components, in effect, working against each other. Of course, the combined waveform will be stronger than either component when the components are in phase and constructive interference results.

A combination of pure tones will stimulate the basilar membrane strongly at more than one location. If the frequency difference (Δf) between the tones is sufficiently large, the combination is clearly heard as two separate simultaneous tones. If Δf is insufficient, i.e., the cbw is not reached, a sensation of roughness, beating, or, if Δf = 0, unison will result. In terms of frequency separation, Δf may vary from approximately 25 to 2000 Hz, although different studies inevitably give different results (Moore, 1989; Plomp, 1976). One estimate of the actual linear distance along the basilar membrane associated with Δf is 1.2 mm (Roederer, 1995, p. 36).

Thus, frequency discrimination of two simultaneously sounding pure tones also is primarily dependent on the location of basilar membrane stimulation. The jnd for frequency discrimination of two simultaneous tones is considerably larger than the jnd for detecting changes in a single pure tone of varying frequency (Roederer, 1995). However, musicians rarely deal with pure tones.

Pitch Processing of Complex Tones

A complex tone contains more than one frequency. It differs from a combination of pure tones in that the waveform from *one* sound source is complex. A bowed violin string, a plucked guitar string, a blown trumpet, and a human voice all output a complex waveform which is a mixture of individual frequency components, all of which arise from the source's complex vibration pattern and interact to determine the complex waveform.

The complex tone's individual frequency components include a *fundamental* frequency (generally the lowest frequency) and higher frequencies, which may be in a harmonic or inharmonic relationship. In a harmonic relationship, all higher frequency components are in an integral multiple relationship with the fundamental; i.e., nondecimal whole numbers multiplied by the fundamental frequency will give the frequencies of the higher components or *harmonics*. In an inharmonic relationship, the higher components are related in a nonintegral multiple manner. Musical complex tones show varying *degrees of harmonicity*.[4] The more nearly harmonic the relationship, the more obvious may be the pitch sensation, although the ear really is quite robust in detecting a definite pitch sensation despite a certain degree of inharmonicity.

The relative strengths of the particular frequency components vary. Diagrams of complex tones' tonal *spectra*, obtained with the aid of spectrum analyzers or other analytic equipment, show, within limits, the particular component frequencies and their intensity levels. Curiously, the fundamental frequency is not always the strongest (most intense) component, despite the fact that the pitch associated with the complex tone almost always is the pitch elicited by the fundamental.

A complex mixture of frequencies may stimulate the basilar membrane at eight or more locations; such stimulations often exceed the critical band width. Yet a complex tone is heard with one distinct pitch. Why? The basilar membrane serves as an analyzer and information passer for complex tones—the pitch assignment primarily occurs higher in the auditory pathway.

Pitch perception of complex tones is based on the auditory system's ability to use information regarding the pattern of stimulation—placewise, timewise, or both. The sounds to which people are able to assign a definite pitch sensation are periodic, or nearly so: The wave patterns are regularly recurring.[5] The simplest kind of wave (a sine wave) arises from a pure tone; one is diagrammed in Figure 4-2. (Wave diagrams such as this, similar to oscilloscope traces, should be conceived as particular displacement patterns frozen in time.) A complex wave appears in Fig-

---

[4]Unfortunately, partial, harmonic, and overtone occasionally are used interchangeably. A *partial* is any component of a complex tone, regardless of any mathematical relationship or lack thereof. A *harmonic* is any frequency (not necessarily a component of a particular tone) in an integral multiple relationship with the fundamental. (The fundamental itself is the first harmonic; $f \times 1 = f$.) An *overtone* is any harmonic *other than* the fundamental which is in a particular complex tone. Any component of a complex tone is a partial; it may or may not be a harmonic. Any integral multiple of the fundamental is a harmonic; it may or may not be a partial or an overtone (Backus, 1977).

[5]The technical and more restrictive definition of a periodic vibration is that all the frequency components are related harmonically.

ure 4-3. In each case, there is a recurring pattern. Sooner or later, the waveform will repeat itself; it has *periodicity*.[6] The particular structure of the recurring pattern and the rate at which it repeats are extremely important musically.

Figure 4-2. Displacement pattern arising from a pure tone.

Figure 4-3. Displacement pattern arising from a complex tone.

From basilar membrane activity, the auditory system gleans *place* information (where and to what degree the particular stimulations occur) and *temporal* information (the rate at which the stimulations recur). Place information is available over the entire auditory range. Temporal information is available only to about 5000 Hz and would seem to be especially important for musical pitch because musical pitch generally is lost for pure tones beyond 5000 Hz: Sequences of really high tones are difficult to organize as melody (Moore, 1989, p. 191).

A complex tone's usually obvious pitch sensation (some people can hear out individual components) is known as low pitch, periodicity pitch, virtual pitch, residual pitch, and subjective pitch. *Low pitch* probably is the term which is most free of semantic difficulties arising from particular theories or other phenomena. Low pitch perception is not understood thoroughly; two broad classes of models are the *pattern recognition* and *temporal* models.

In pattern recognition models, low pitch is derived from neural signals which correspond to the primary basilar membrane stimulations. Resolution of the separate components of the tonal *spectrum* (the combination of particular frequencies and their relative strengths) is crucial. Pattern recognition models can not account for low pitch detection in

---

[6]Unless the wave is truly periodic, i.e., contains only harmonic components, the pattern will never repeat exactly, but if the amount of inharmonicity is not too large, the repetition is sufficiently periodic for the auditory system.

situations where harmonic relationships are especially complex and frequency components are too high to be resolved (Moore, 1989, pp. 168–171).

In temporal models, low pitch is elicited by the time interval between recurring aspects of the overall pattern, such as the time between waveform peaks. Through a neural process called *fundamental tracking*, a wave's repetition frequency can yield the overall low or periodicity pitch sensation. (For example, a complex tone with components of 50, 100, 150, 200, and 250 Hz will make a wave with an overall repetition frequency of 50 Hz, as will a complex tone with components of 450, 500, and 550 Hz. In each case, the fundamental tracking mechanism yields the pitch sensation corresponding to 50 Hz.)

Temporal models can not account for situations where tonal components do not interact in either ear. Such noninteraction is illustrated by the Houtsma and Goldstein (1972) study where, using earphones, the investigators presented randomly chosen paired upper harmonics, without the fundamental, monotonically (both harmonics to one ear) and dichotically (one harmonic to each ear) to three experienced musicians. The musicians could recognize melodies formed by the "missing" fundamentals in both conditions, even though the harmonics could not combine in either ear in the dichotic condition. Fundamental tracking is a *central* (in the neural network) rather than a *peripheral* (in the cochlea) process.

Moore (1989, pp. 183–187) offers a five stage comprehensive model of complex tone pitch detection which the authors believe is the most comprehensive and logical explanation of the phenomenon. The model incorporates aspects of both pattern recognition and temporal models.

The first stage is analogous to a series of overlapping filters which pass through and/or modify certain aspects of stimulus information. Filters responding to low frequency components resolve individual components and output simple waveforms. Filters responding to high frequency components output complex waveforms, which are based on the interaction of several components and have repetition rates corresponding to the complex stimulating waveform.

The second stage involves transduction (energy conversion). Neurons fire in accordance with basilar membrane motions to represent the temporal structure of the waveform. Particular neurons are "driven" by the waveform's frequency components that are near the neurons' "characteristic frequencies" or frequencies at which the neurons are most likely to fire.

Moore's third stage analyzes the times between firings of each neuron. The fourth stage then compares all those times and searches for common time intervals.

In the final stage, a decision stage selects one time interval. The perceived pitch of the complex tone then is the pitch elicited by the reciprocal of the selected time interval. (Frequency, the number of vibration cycles in a designated time, and period, the time required for one complete vibration cycle, are related as reciprocals; e.g., a frequency of 100 Hz and a period of 1/100 sec are reciprocals of each other.)

Moore's model predicts that lower frequency components would dominate the pitch assignment process: Information for the lower components is less ambiguous than for the higher components since the lower components are more likely to have distinct individual waveforms, in accordance with the first stage. Research (Plomp, 1967b; Ritsma, 1970), however, suggests a *spectral dominance,* in which the components mainly determining the complex tone's pitch vary with the fundamental frequency. In general, the lower the fundamental, the higher the component numbers of important components. The degree of any component's dominance may vary as a function of the component's strength in relation to neighboring components (Moore, Glasberg, & Peters, 1985).

The details of complex tone pitch perception are intricate and under continual investigation. While further details may await discovery, the process is basic to music perception and quite robust. Even tones with significant amounts of inharmonicity and tones with relatively few frequency components may still elicit a clear sensation of one pitch—low pitch. Tonal music would not exist as we know it without the neural processes involved; we would be limited to pure tones or to continual harmony.

Combination Tones

A complex tone's pitch is a single pitch sensation for one tone, from one sound source. The *combination tone* is a third or "extra" tone sensation arising in the presence of two *different* frequencies, sounded together. Combination tones may be experienced from a well-tuned violin double stop, a simultaneous (harmonic) interval on an organ, or two sopranos singing a well-tuned interval. In addition to the two deliberately produced primary frequencies, an observer hears the "extra" sensation. Usually, combination tones with frequencies equivalent to the difference between the two primary tones ($f_2 - f_1$, "difference" tones) are the easiest to hear. Higher-order combination tones such as $2f_1 - f_2$ and $3f_1 - 2f_2$ also may be audible. Theoretically, many other combinations resulting from multiples of the lower tone (f_1) and the upper tone (f_2) are possible.

A true combination tone is not present in the external sound stimulus, although it is perceived as if it were present (Rasch & Plomp, 1982). A combination tone differs from the very strong "extra" sound which one may obtain by feeding two outputs from a synthesizer, electronic organ, or two oscillators into one speaker. In those cases, the "extra" frequency (which often is equivalent in Hz to a difference tone) is an electronic artifact resulting from heterodyning, in which two signals mix and fluctuate in amplitude (Strange, 1972, p. 10). The distortion product produced by heterodyning is physically present in the external sound stimulus.

A true combination tone results from nonlinear cochlear distortion, i.e., a tendency of the basilar membrane to move more than can be accounted for by the auditory stimulus. The primary tones must be at a sufficient intensity level (Plomp, 1965), and audibility of combination tones will vary greatly with people and particular frequency combinations (Plomp, 1976). Research with guinea pigs and monkeys clearly shows that the type of distortion necessary to produce combination tones by in effect causing extra hair cell stimulation at different places is possible (Dallos & Sweetman, 1969; Rhode & Robles, 1974). Rasch and Plomp (1982) refer to cochlear distortion as "nonlinear transmission."

Goldstein (1970) demonstrated that a "cancellation tone" of identical frequency, adjusted for amplitude and relative phase, could cancel a combination tone. This phenomenon is a type of destructive interference; it is similar in principle to some modern noise quelling devices, in which a person wears a headset that outputs signals in opposite phase with frequencies in designated ranges. (Of course, the undesirable noises are environmental sounds, not combination tones.)

Combination tones can interact with physically present parts of the sound stimulus to increase tonal complexity; they can alter the way a tonal stimulus is heard. As such, they may have some musical utility.

Intervals

An interval is a simultaneous or successive sounding of two tones. Musicians often call a simultaneous interval harmonic and a successive interval melodic. Psychology of music has been concerned with apparent consonance, pitch, and interval size.

Consonance-dissonance. Historically, varying uses of the terms as well as different views of what determines an interval's classification have confused the study of consonance and dissonance. Peterson and Smith (1930) asked subjects to evaluate mistuned intervals and report "unnatural" ones, thereby equating certain tunings with consonance. Bugg (1933) reported that subjects were confused when asked to classify intervals on the basis of fusion, smoothness, blending, and purity (all of which have nonauditory connotations) as if they were synonymous. He felt that consonance is not necessarily a pleasantness-unpleasantness dimension; affective reactions to intervals somehow needed to be removed from actual consonance judgments. Four decades later, Terhardt (1974a) divorced *psychoacoustic* consonance (the absence of "roughness") from musical interval sensations: Psychoacoustic consonance is a matter of frequency distance, whereas musical intervals are ratio phenomena. Difficulties with consonance theories and judgments are related to psychologists' and musicians' inabilities to agree regarding a definition.

Musicians generally regard *musical* consonance as a relatively restful and passive auditory sensation, while dissonance is a relatively agitated and active state. Seconds, the augmented fourth, and sevenths currently are considered dissonant in an abstract sense; unisons, thirds, fourths, fifths, and octaves are considered consonant.[7] Such judgments can change with time and context, and Lundin (1947) proposed what remains as the most espoused explanation of musical consonance: It is a matter of cultural conditioning. Prior physical theories, resorting to numerical relationships, beats, fusion, and genetics, all are lacking because of incorrect interpretations of physiology or failure to consider mistuned consonances.

Musicians may merely use consonance and dissonance as additional labels; e.g., "It's a major sixth, so it's consonant;" "It's a minor second, so it's dissonant." Psychoacoustical researchers may prefer nonmusicians as subjects in studies of consonance because of musicians' labelling tendencies. Van de Geer, Levelt, and Plomp (1962) found that nonmusicians evaluated (rather than named) intervals on dimensions of consonancedissonance, euphonious-diseuphonious, and beautiful-ugly. Plomp and Levelt (1965) used nonmusical subjects in producing evidence that consonance-dissonance may be a matter of how partials from the tones comprising a simultaneous interval align along the basilar membrane: Basilar membrane stimulations that are identical *or* are separated by a critical band width promote consonance; nonidentical stimulations *within* a critical band width promote dissonance. In a classic study of *categorical perception,* the phenomenon where differing stimulus objects are categorized identically as long as they remain within certain bounds, Siegel and Siegel (1977) found musicians tending to categorize intervals very accurately but to make few distinctions in interval size within interval categories: Although 77 percent of the intervals were out-of-tune, the six musicians judged only 37 percent as such.

Perhaps the concept of consonance or dissonance should be reevaluated to reflect musical context. Bharucha (1984) suggests that the establishment of a tonal context at the beginning of a musical work generates

---

[7]Centuries ago, thirds and sixths were considered dissonant. Even today, some people refer to those intervals as "imperfect" consonances; the other consonant intervals are "perfect" consonances.

expectancies regarding stable and unstable tones in a melodic context. Unstable tones tend to resolve or be assimilated into stable tones or anchors; consonance or dissonance then may have meaning in accordance with melodic structure. This may be far more salient than labelling or evaluating isolated intervals.

Apparent pitch. An interval comprises two tones. Normally, each tone retains an individual pitch identity within the simultaneous interval. Yet, there may be a certain amount of tonal *fusion,* which for some suggests an intervalic pitch.

Farnsworth (1938; 1969) investigated Stumpf's principle, which said that the lower tone dominates the pitch of any simultaneous interval. Contrarily, Farnsworth found that the upper tone dominates, except for musically untrained individuals and some basses. Since harmony, an extension of intervals, is not a unitary pitch sensation, the whole concept of a single pitch for an interval seems amorphous, although there may be some value in studying dominance of one part of a harmonic section over another.

One mystery in psychology of music is why two simultaneously sounding sources, like two violin strings, usually produce what people hear as an interval, but a single sound source, such as a complex tone or even a noise that is more complicated acoustically than the interval, is heard as one sound. The answer may lie in the brain's ability to use various cues related to localization and transient waveform characteristics (Roederer, 1995, pp. 5862). Deutsch (1982, p. 108) notes that von Helmholtz, a pioneering psychoacoustician, suggested in 1885 that a complex tone sounds as one tone because all of the components start and stop together.

Apparent size. Musical intervals usually are specified by their upper tones' scale degrees (third, fourth, sixth, etc.) in relation to their lower tones, subject to modification by accidentals (minor, major, augmented, etc.). Another way is to specify the interval ratio; each interval in its simplest (just) form has a characteristic frequency relationship between the upper tone and the lower tone. A perfect octave's upper frequency is related to its lower frequency as 2 is to 1. A perfect fifth's upper frequency is in a 3:2 ratio with its lower frequency. Other characteristic ratios are 16:15 for a minor second, 9:8 for a major second, 6:5 for a minor third, 5:4 for a major third, 4:3 for a perfect fourth, 7:5 for an augmented fourth, 5:3 for a minor sixth, 8:5 for a major sixth, 9:5 for a minor seventh, and 15:8 for a major seventh. In performance practice, of course, there is considerable deviation from the simple ratios. In the equally tempered scale, derived by dividing the octave into equally sized semitones (half steps), no interval except the octave has the characteristic ratio. The most exact way to indicate physical interval size is in cents (one cent = 1/1200 of an octave). The number of cents in an interval may be computed via the formula

$$n = 3986.31[\log(f_2/f_1)],$$

where n is the number of cents of the particular interval, f_2 is the frequency of the upper tone, and f_1 is the frequency of the lower tone (Backus, 1977).

All identically named intervals share a perceptual similarity, regardless of their particular frequency components, which aids in identification and musical utility. But if an interval, especially a successive interval, is evaluated rather than simply categorized, its apparent size may vary with frequency range. Evidence is conflicting: Some research (Stevens, 1975; Stevens, Volkmann, & Newman, 1937) suggests that physically identical intervals increase in apparent size with increasing frequency range; Winckel (1967) says that intervals in lower frequency ranges have greater "melodic distance," which implies that they apparently decrease in apparent size with increasing frequency range. Radocy (1978) found that perceived interval size is a highly idiosyncratic function of interaction among the particular interval, interval direction, subjects' musical experience, and frequency range.

Beating

First order beating, a perceptible rise and fall in loudness, is experienced with the simultaneous sounding of two slightly different frequencies. It results from the periodic changes in the superposed waveform. The beat frequency for a mistuned unison is equivalent to the difference between the two frequencies; the greater the frequency separation, the faster the beating. With sufficient frequency separation, the beating becomes roughness. Once the frequency separation is great enough that the difference between the basilar membrane stimulations equals the critical band width, the listener experiences a clear sensation of two simultaneous tones. Beating provides a very obvious clue that two instruments or voices are "out of tune" with each other. However, tuning by eliminating the beats between a reference tone and a tone to be tuned may be ambiguous (to the tuner) because of uncertainties regarding the direction of deviation. After investigation, Corso (1954) long ago suggested that unison tuning may depend more on pitch matching than on beat elimination.

Beating of a mistuned interval other than a mistuned unison, particularly an octave, fourth, or fifth, is *second order beating* (Roederer, 1995, pp. 40–43), which may result from the peripheral interference of combination tones or, especially at lower frequencies, from central neural processing (Plomp, 1976). Also known (unfortunately) as the beating of mistuned consonances, second order beating is more ambiguous than first order beating. Just what fluctuates or "beats" is not obvious. Second order beats are strong when the beating interval is below 500 Hz. The beats become progressively weaker above 1000 Hz. When audible, the beats do not disappear when noise is introduced to cover (mask) possible peripheral effects such as combination tones; evidence strongly suggests central processing of second order beats (Plomp, 1967a).

If a different sound is presented to each ear in such a manner that the sounds can not possibly mix until they reach the neural pathways, *binaural beating* may occur. Perrott and Nelson (1969) found that likelihood of such beat detection varied with frequency, with detection most likely around 500 Hz. The beats may appear as a rapid flutter, or, especially at small frequency differences, a fused sensation may appear to travel around inside the person's head. While binaural beats may appear to have relatively little musical significance, the ever increasing use of headset listening and expanding technology may enable composers and arrangers to exploit binaural presentation and the resulting phenomena.

First and second order beating are musically significant. Piano tuners may count beats to obtain the tempered tuning of designated intervals. Instrumentalists may be confident that they are in tune once first order beats disappear. One reason that one French horn amplified to ten times its output does not sound like ten horns is that the complex beating among the ten horns' outputs adds a "richness" to which listeners have become accustomed. (This is the "chorus effect" (Backus, 1977).)

Absolute Pitch

Absolute pitch, the ability to name a tone without reference to any external standard, may astound people who do not possess it. People with absolute pitch may view their "gift" as quite ordinary and an occasional nuisance. Relative pitch, the ability to name a tone in relation to a known external standard, is quite common among musicians; to label a C as "C" because it sounds a perfect fourth lower than a known F only requires knowing intervalic relationships. Naming the C when only C is heard with no reference is qualitatively different and much less common.

Investigators have suggested that absolute pitch results from sensitivity to tonal chroma[8] (Bachem, 1954), that it results from deliberate

---

[8]Tonal chroma are cyclical characteristics that are consistent across octaves. All tones with a given letter name share a chroma; i.e., all A's have a certain "A-ishness," all B's have a certain "B-ishness," etc.

learning (Corso, 1957; Meyer, 1956), and that it could result from learning and internalizing a reference tone (Cuddy, 1968). Cuddy noted that judgments of piano tones were related specifically to piano experience. Internalizing a particular reference would enable one to display absolute pitch, but differing degrees of accuracy with different performance media suggest that one may learn a "pseudoabsolute" pitch by using auditory cues other than frequency, e.g., timbre characteristics.

A somewhat more contemporary view of absolute pitch development relates learning tonal identification to a critical age period, roughly four to seven years, when pitch has a greater salience, in both speech and music, than it does in later life. Jeffress (1962) noted that some supposedly tone-deaf individuals were from India and spoke a language in which pitch is insignificant. Sergeant (1969) showed that a majority of surveyed adults possessing absolute pitch experienced critical training during the critical period.[9] De Gainza (1970) indicated that isolated sounds attracted her small children, but as they matured form, structure, and tonal relations became more salient than individual pitches. The auditory system can perceive details, but it also can perceive structure, which, in music, becomes more important than the details that foster absolute pitch development. Pitch relationships usually are more important than the actual pitches themselves. The critical period involves an *imprinting* theory, in analogy with the maternal connection a hatched duckling makes with the first moving object it encounters (usually mama duck). During the critical period, a label is highly associable with a tonal sensation, and the correct label-sensation associations, if formed, become absolute pitch.

Investigation of absolute pitch requires using varied stimuli and avoiding relative pitch cues. It is not enough to "come within a second" or label correctly only tones produced by an instrument with which the person is familiar. Many people probably can learn to identify certain tones some of the time, but to then insist that they can identify any tone all of the time is inaccurate. In their detailed discussion of absolute pitch, Ward and Burns (1982) recognize that frequency-pitch relations are acquired early in life and that, despite many attempts, only one person has been able to develop absolute pitch as an adult.[10] If absolute pitch is desirable, more consideration of the means whereby the *labels*

---

[9]Although he has heard tales of individuals not acquiring absolute pitch until adulthood, each person that one of the authors (RER) has met in 23 years of university teaching who has absolute pitch had begun piano study no later than age seven.

[10]Courses of study purporting to be able to teach absolute pitch to anyone are available, but the authors believe that the research base for them and their use to date is insufficient to justify discussion here.

are attached to the pitch sensations, particularly in early childhood, is necessary.

Pitch Measurement

Pitch may be measured in various ways, but any technique must use a human observer (or an apparatus built to simulate one). The stroboscope and digital frequency counter measure frequency, not pitch. Since pitch is defined as a human sensation, it must be measured through human sensation.

Qualitative judgments in the form of pitch matching, as illustrated by intonation judgments and tuning instruments, are one type of pitch measure. Quantitative judgments are illustrated by the mel scale, where 1000 mels equals the pitch sensation of 1000 Hz (Stevens, Volkmann, & Newman, 1937). A table equating frequency in Hz to pitch in mels appears in Stevens (1975). The pitch sensation "twice as high" as 1000 mels (2000 mels) requires a frequency of 3120 Hz, not 2000 Hz. The mel scale generally predicts psychological interval sizes that are larger than physical sizes and larger than the judgments of many listeners, musicians and nonmusicians (Radocy, 1977). The psychological octave often is larger than the physical octave, but the mel scale does not seem to be the answer. The search for a quantitative pitch measure continues.

Loudness Phenomena

Loudness is an obvious but complex property of all sound — if it is audible, it must have loudness. Listeners, even very unsophisticated ones, readily may evaluate musical performances as "too loud" or "too soft." Music educators direct considerable pedagogical effort toward improving student's sensitivity or musicality by urging them to use more effective dynamic contrasts in performance.

Curiously, although human ears are sensitive to about a trillionfold range of sound intensity and to only about a thousandfold range of frequency, minute loudness distinctions have not attained the importance of minute pitch distinctions, at least in Western music. Loudness notation is limited to symbols for dynamic levels and words indicating a gradual change, whereas pitch notation has specific locations on a musical staff. Furthermore, although six basic dynamic levels —*pp, p, mp, mf, f,* and *ff* —have been used for approximately 200 years, few instrumentalists have a dynamic range capable of attaining those six discrete levels. This generally is not due to limitations of performance media. Restricted musical dynamic ranges and solo passages equal in loudness to full orchestral passages, characteristic of films and television, may be partly responsible, but the general artistic demand for a wide range and variation seems restricted (Patterson, 1974). Some modern popular music with its restriction to sounds of a high intensity level minimizes dynamic range as a musical variant.

Our loudness discussion is organized around distinguishing loudness from other properties, measurement of loudness and systematic relations therefrom, masking, loudness summation, and dangers to hearing.

Intensity-Loudness Relationship

Intensity and loudness are not interchangeable terms. *Intensity* is an objectively measured physical property, an amount of power. It often is expressed in power units per unit area, as in watts per square meter (w/m^2). *Loudness* is a subjective sensation of a sound's magnitude or strength. Its perception requires an animate perceiver (or a machine built to simulate one). Devices such as sound level meters do not measure loudness.

The amount of sound intensity is the major determinant of loudness, but the intensity-loudness relationship is not on a simple one-to-one basis. A minimal perception time, varying from 10 to 500 msec and beyond, is necessary for a sound to build to its maximal perceived loudness (Scharf, 1978, pp. 205–206), and loudness may vary further with the time it takes for a sound to reach its maximum intensity (Gjaevenes & Rimstad, 1972). Prolonged steady sounds may diminish in loudness due to auditory fatigue, where the brain essentially diminishes attention to a prolonged sound because of irrelevance, or to habituation, a reduction in stimulated neural activity (Roederer, 1995, p. 96). The intensity-loudness relationship is confounded by frequency: The loudness a particular intensity elicits varies with frequency, as discussed below. The ear's variation in sensitivity with frequency is especially important for music; in general lower sounds may be played "louder" than higher sounds before they are judged as being too loud.

Volume and Density

Volume is the apparent size or extensity of a sound: The sound of a tuba usually is "larger" than the sound of a piccolo. *Density* is the apparent compactness of a sound; the piccolo sound generally is more focused or pinpointed than the tuba sound. Stevens (1934a; 1934b; 1975) believed that volume and density were basic tonal attributes and reported studies in which observers could make judgments independently of loudness. Both properties vary as functions of combinations of frequency and intensity: Both increase as intensity increases; with increasing frequency volume decreases and density increases (Guirao & Stevens, 1964; Stevens, 1975). There is question as to whether volume and density are separate properties, as Stevens claimed, or opposite poles of the same property, and the properties certainly are not given much attention in musical research. While the authors recommend that volume not be used as a synonym for loudness (as it often is), they generally believe that volume and density are now largely a psychoacoustic curiosity, with little relevance for musical perception, either at a tonal or a more global level.

Annoyance and Noisiness

Hellman (1982; 1985) had subjects listen to a series of tones embedded in varying degrees of background noise. In addition to estimating loudness, subjects estimated how much the sounds "bothered" them (*annoyance*) and the sounds' clarity or quality (*noisiness*). Besides identifying properties about which the subjects could agree, the research is important because it showed that the dominant of the three properties varied with overall intensity and with the ratio of tone to noise. Furthermore, annoyance corresponded more closely to loudness than to noisiness. Perhaps people who complain about "loud" music occasionally are reacting to something other than the perceived strength of the sounds: They may be "annoyed" by the style of music or find it to be "noise"!

Measurement of Loudness

Quantifying loudness is challenging, controversial, and, for some, impossible. One may quantify the stimulus with relative ease, although one then really is quantifying a physical aspect, not loudness. There are ways to quantify listeners' responses to stimuli.

Stimulus measures. Intensity is defined as an amount of power per unit area, and watts per square meter (w/m^2) are common units for sound intensity. Most sound intensities are rather small values. Just one w/m^2 is a rather intense sound that approaches the upper limit of hearing, sometimes called the threshold of pain. At 1000 Hz the threshold of hearing is around .000000000001 w/m^2, one-trillionth of a watt. Writers often use negative powers of ten to express such tiny decimal fractions; the above threshold of hearing is 10^{-12} w/m^2.

Sound intensity usually is expressed in terms of intensity *level* rather than pure intensity. Intensity level represents a comparison with a baseline value, just as a building's fourth floor is the fourth floor in comparison to the ground. Comparisons of particular intensities to baseline intensities are ratio comparisons which use the *decibel.*

Decibels, often abbreviated as dB, are measures of power ratios. They are not limited to sound; light and electric current also may be measured in decibels. Decibels are best defined by the computing formula. For sound intensity level,

$$D_{IL} = 10[\log(I/I_0)],$$

where D_{IL} is the number of decibels, I is the particular intensity being compared to a baseline and placed on the particular intensity level, and I_0 is the baseline value. The intensity at the threshold of hearing is often used; hence 10^{-12} w/m^2 is a common baseline.

Three consequences of a decibel value being a shorthand expression of a ratio are that (a) 0 db does not necessarily mean an absence of power or sound, (b) a relatively small range of decibels expresses a relatively large range of acoustical power, and (c) one can not simply add decibel values to obtain an intensity level for tonal combinations.

A comparison of a baseline with itself will yield an intensity level of 0 dB. This is not necessarily inaudible, depending on frequency; it is simply the result of the 1:1 ratio formed by identical intensity values. It is not a true zero, the genuine absence of a property in question.

An intensity level of 60 dB represents the comparison of an intensity of 10^{-6} w/m^2 (.000001 w/m^2) with a baseline of 10^{-12} w/m^2. Similarly, 70 dB represents 10^{-5} w/m^2 (.00001 w/m^2). The 10 dB difference represents a tenfold (10:1) difference in power—.00001 is ten times .000001. An intensity level of 80 dB represents .0001 w/m^2 (10^{-4}); the difference between 80 and 60 dB represents a one hundredfold (100:1) difference in power—.0001 is 100 times .000001. *Any* 10 dB difference in intensity level means that one sound has ten times the intensity of another. A 20 dB difference always represents one sound having 100 times the intensity of the other, a 30 dB difference represents 1000 times, 40 dB, 10,000 times, etc. The decibel scale is logarithmic; equal decibel amounts represent equal ratios.

Given what the individual values represent, two decibel values can not be summed directly in any meaningful way. Two intensity levels of 60 dB do not total 120 dB—they total approximately 63 dB. Each intensity corresponding to 60 dB is .000001 w/m^2; .000001 w/m^2 + .000001 w/m^2 is .000002 w/m^2, not .00001 w/m^2, represented by 70 dB, and *certainly not* 1.0 w/m^2, which is represented by 120 dB. Any intensity level increases by approximately 3 dB when combined with an equivalent level. (Even 0 dB + 0 dB = 3 dB.) If two summed values are not equivalent, the result will be something less than 3 dB added to the higher level; e.g., 60 dB + 59 dB = 62.2 dB.[11]

Although sound intensity level has become easier to measure in recent years, *sound pressure level* (SPL) remains a more common stimulus measure. SPL usually is easier to measure, and it relates logically to the concept of pressure variations being responsible for sound sensations. SPL decibels are computed differently, in relation to a different baseline, although the ratio comparison principle is the same. A common formula is

$$D_{SPL} = 20[\log P/P_0],$$

where D_{SPL} is the number of decibels, P is the particular pressure value of concern, and P_0 is the baseline pressure. A common baseline is .00002 newtons per square meter (n/m^2). With SPL decibels, a difference of 20 dB represents a tenfold difference; 40 dB represents a hundredfold difference, etc. Most dB values found in research reports are SPL values. Ideally, investigators would express dB values that clearly specify the baseline and the property. Usually they do not, so the reader generally assumes SPL, with a .00002 n/m^2 baseline.

Sound level meters can describe the sound pressure level at a particular location quite adequately. More sophisticated integrating sound level meters can provide other values of interest. The equivalent continuous sound level (L_{eq}) is the same amount of energy content as a varying sound pressure level over a designated time period; e.g., one hour of 100 dB SPL plus seven hours of 70 dB SPL yields an L_{eq} for the eight hours of 91 dB. The day-night level (L_{dn}) is also sound level spread over a period of time, except that readings from part of the time, often night time hours when many people wish to sleep, are biased upwards by 10 dB. Sound exposure level (SEL) is the constant sound pressure level of a one second sound which has the same amount of acoustic energy as the original sound; essentially, a sound spread over a longer time period is squeezed into one second. The sound pressure level which is exceeded a certain criterion percentage of the time may be recorded; e.g., L_{10} = 90 dB SPL would mean that ten percent of the time during a designated period the SPL equalled or exceeded 90 dB. In all cases, these are measures of a physical condition. While one may infer psychological consequences, they are not response measures.

Response measures. A conservative view of loudness measurement

---

[11]This assumes that the two underlying vibrations are in phase. If phase relationships change, the height of the superposed waveform changes, so the intensity level changes. Constantly alternating constructive and destructive interference, as in first order beating, will result in a constantly changing combined intensity level. Destructive interference may result in an intensity level which is less than that of any component singly; totally destructive interference will result in no intensity (but not necessarily 0 dB).

says that one can describe loudness but not measure it. A more liberal view says that one can make equivalency judgments, but direct measures of subjective loudness are impossible. A more radical view says that loudness can be measured directly if one does not insist on counting units. The present discussion will consider measurement of equivalencies, as exemplified by equal loudness contours, and the sone scale.

Equal loudness curves connect frequency-intensity combinations which judges deem to be equivalent in loudness. The fact that the curves indeed are *curved* shows the way frequency confounds the intensity-loudness relationship. If a particular intensity elicited an identical loudness across all frequencies, the "curves" would be straight lines. Fletcher and Munson (1933) made some of the first equal loudness contours by having eleven judges make 297 observations of comparative loudness; in their honor, the contours often are called "Fletcher-Munson curves" today. Figure 4-4 displays a set of curves. The curves are not exact; in addition to interpolation of data points, the curves are influenced by the standard frequency to which judgments are related (Molino, 1973) and whether one listens in a free field or through headphones (Scharf, 1978). The general shape is such that the curves "go down" as frequency increases to around 2000 Hz, thereby illustrating increasing auditory sensitivity. Beyond about 3000 Hz sensitivity decreases; the curves "go up." The amount of change in curvature is less at higher loudness levels.

Any two points on an equal loudness curve theoretically are equally loud (although there are individual differences), and they are equal in *phon* value. Phons are equivalent to decibels at 1000 Hz; e.g., a 1000 Hz tone of 60 dB is 60 phons: Any other frequency-intensity combination judged as equal to the 1000 Hz-60 dB combination also is 60 phons. Phons technically are measures of loudness *level*, not loudness. They enable loudness comparisons at the equal to, greater than, or less than level.

Various attempts to develop a measurement scale on the basis of how much louder one sound is than another have occurred over the years (Beck & Shaw, 1967; Stevens, 1975; Warren, 1970). The *sone* scale probably is best known. Originally, one sone was equivalent to 40 phons; a more contemporary definition (Stevens, 1972; 1975) is that one sone is the loudness of a third-of-an-octave band (frequency spread) of noise, centered on 3150 Hz, at an SPL of 32 dB. Sones are based on judgments of sensation ratios. On paper, they have a systematic relationship to decibels; a growth of 9dB SPL represents a doubling of sones. (Stevens (1975) presents a table of sone values.) While it may be tempting to belittle the sone scale, one must recognize that the loudness sensation, however measured, is a judgment, and any measure of sound not based

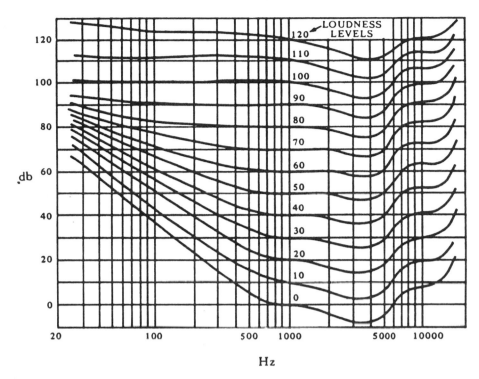

Figure 4-4. Sample equal loudness curves. The curves connect frequency-intensity level combinations which are judged to be equally loud as a 1000 Hz standard of a given intensity level.

on judgment can not measure a psychological sensation resulting from sound.

The Power Law

The first two editions of this text gave considerable attention to Stevens's power law, which essentially says that a lawful relationship exists between an increasing stimulus value and the rate of growth in some associated response. That relationship is expressed by a decimal exponent, a "power function," expressing the size of a response ratio as a function of a stimulus ratio. Equal stimulus ratios elicit equal sensation ratios. Under many conditions, the law seems to hold. Stevens's (1975) text, published posthumously with his widow's assistance, provides many details. Magnitude estimation, an important means for measurement that is based on stimulus matching rather than counting, is important in obtaining the response measures necessary for investigating power law relationships; it also is useful in many other areas. Stevens describes magnitude estimation in theory and in psychophysical applications; Boyle and Radocy (1987) describe it in the context of musical performance evaluation.

When loudness is measured in sones and the stimulus is a narrow band of noise centered on 3150 Hz, measured in SPL, the power function is .67. In actual practice, other power functions may occur. The power function will vary with the stimulus frequency range. Loudness generally grows more rapidly at lower frequencies, and individuals vary in their sensations and their abilities to express them with numbers. The authors have sacrificed detailed discussion of the power law in order to devote more attention to other areas. They ask the reader to take on faith that (a) loudness may grow systematically as a function of natural perceptual processes, and (b) individuals are capable of making more subtle loudness judgments than traditional musical dynamic markings suggest.

Masking

As is obvious from ordinary experience, one sound, normally perfectly audible by itself, may become inaudible in the presence of a louder sound. This phenomenon is simultaneous *masking*. The masked or covered sound is the masked tone (or noise); the sound that does the masking is the masker. Orchestral woodwind players sometimes will disregard certain passages because they are not "exposed." They feel that since other instruments will mask the "unexposed" passage in full orchestral performance anyway, there is no need to give special attention to the passages in practice sessions.

Studies of simultaneous masking generally show that a masker's most effective masking is for sounds near its frequency[12] (although recent evidence suggests that the masker may be more remote from the masked sound (Espinoza-Varas & Watson, 1989, p. 89)), the frequency area over which masking may occur may be greater for frequencies above the masking frequency (especially at higher intensity levels), and that a noise is more effective as a masker than a tone (Egan & Hake, 1950). Simultaneous masking has obvious musical importance. It also is exploited in environmental situations, as in providing background music or a systematic noise to mask undesirable sounds.

In addition to simultaneous masking, forward and backward masking are possible in the laboratory. In forward and backward masking, the masking sound respectively precedes or follows the masked sound by a very brief time period. Forward masking probably is a matter of reduced

---

[12]If both the masker and the masked sound are tones, first order beating may indicate the presence of the softer masked tone when the masked tone's frequency is close to that of the masking tone. Second order beating may reveal octave relationships.

auditory sensitivity or prolonged neural stimulation from the masker. Backward masking[13] is mysterious; it may result from listeners' confusion of the weaker masked signal with the following stronger masking signal (Moore, 1989, pp. 119–122).

Loudness Summation

Individual loudnesses sum to form combined loudness, but the summation is not a simple process of addition. Since sounds summate differently under different conditions, loudness summation has musical importance.

Fletcher (1946), using an early tone synthesizer, demonstrated that complex tones sound louder than pure tones. Stevens (1956) noted that separate noise bands (and, by analogy, groups of frequencies) are not simply additive. Even widely separated frequencies can have a mutually inhibitive effect.

In a classic and oft-cited study, Zwicker, Flottorp, and Stevens (1957) showed that loudness separation for pure tones depends on frequency separation in relation to the critical band width. When the frequency spacing (Δf) between simultaneous pure tones is increased to a critical point (Δf approximately equal to 100 Hz for a 500 Hz standard, to 180 Hz for a 1000 Hz standard, to 350 Hz for a 2000 Hz standard), the loudness sensation increases. A similar loudness increase was noted when the width of the noise band was increased beyond a certain point. At low SPLs, with wide frequency spacing, there is no summation; the total loudness is equivalent to the loudest individual tone. Loudness summation appears greatest for tones at a loudness level of 50 to 60 phons; uniform spacing of frequency components produces greater loudness than nonuniform spacing.

The three "cases" of loudness summation identified by Zwicker et al. may be stated in relation to the critical band width (Roederer, 1995, pp. 92–93). Components *within* a critical band width summate so that the total loudness is the loudness elicited by the sum of the original intensities. Components *beyond* a critical band width (but not greatly so) summate so that the total loudness is the sum of the individual loudnesses elicited by each intensity. Symbolically, using L_T to indicate total loudness, Σ to indicate summation, I_1 through I_n to indicate a group of individual intensities, and E to indicate an "eliciting operator" for converting an intensity or group of intensities to the elicited loudness, the first case (within the cbw) is

---

[13]In this context, backward masking refers to inability to hear a sound that occurred earlier in time. It is not the use of "backward masking" or "backmasking" to refer to incomprehensible or inaudible messages becoming clear when a tape is played backwards.

$$L_T = E[\Sigma(I_1 + I_2 + \cdots + I_n)].$$

The second case (beyond the cbw but not greatly so) is

$$L_T = \Sigma[E(I_1) + E(I_2) + \cdots + E(I_n)].$$

The third case, where the components are well beyond the cbw, is where the total loudness is equivalent to the loudest component; there is no summation.[14]

In writing and arranging music, composers and orchestrators may exploit the different cases of loudness summation. A fully scored "open spacing" chord usually sounds louder than a "close spacing" chord, even with an identical number of instruments. In addition to differing in timbre, octaves usually sound louder than unisons. Generally, unless the frequencies differ extensively, two well-spaced frequencies will sound louder than two frequencies quite near each other.

The critical frequency difference for loudness summation vanishes under conditions of dichotic presentation. For ear differences between the separate frequencies of 0 to "several thousand" Hz, Scharf (1969) noted that dichotic pairs remained equally loud. Dichotic summation occurred even when the tonal sensation was of two separate localized tones, one in each ear. This is logical in relation to studies showing ordinary loudness summation related to the basilar membrane's critical band width: Dichotic presentation prevents phenomena that depend on the cbw.

In one of his last published works, Stevens (1972) outlined a computational procedure, based on careful laboratory observations, for the perceived loudness of a noise divided into third-octave bands. By analogy, it may apply to mixtures of complex tones. The procedure uses a standard reference of a one-third-octave band of noise centered on 3150 Hz, the sone as defined earlier, the power law for loudness, equal loudness contours for noise, and the summation rule

$$S_t = S_m + F(\Sigma S - S_m),$$

where S_t is the total loudness, S_m is the loudness of the loudest sound, ΣS is the sum (in sones) of the loudness of all bands, and F is a tabled value which varies as a function of the loudest band.

Recently, Zwicker and Fastl (1990, pp. 213–214) proposed measuring loudness via a "loudness meter" which could measure specific loudnesses among the various critical bands encompassing the hearing range. Basically, the "meter" would be calibrated in third-octave frequency

---

[14]This all assumes an unchanging relative phase. In reality, as phase changes, the total amplitude of the superposed waveform, its combined intensity, and the resulting loudness will change as interference patterns change. Again, a combined (summated) loudness may be softer than any of its components, especially with two components in case one.

bands, with adjustments for low (< 280 Hz) frequencies. It would make readily apparent those parts of a complex sound that contribute most to overall loudness.

Dangers to Hearing

There is danger in exposure to loud sounds. That is true whether the sounds are industrial or traffic noise, irritating music, or the most delightful music imaginable. Exposure to sound at high intensity levels can cause a *temporary threshold shift* (TTS); i.e., a greater amount of intensity is necessary in order for the listener to just perceive a sound. Temporary threshold shifts may depend on the amount of SPL in the critical bands around the affected frequencies as well as the exposure time (Yamamoto et al., 1970). With prolonged exposure, as in working regularly in a noisy environment or listening to music at high loudness levels night after night, the threshold shifts may become permanent.

Given the loud percussive style of much rock music, investigators have studied rock musicians for hearing decrements. Jerger and Jerger (1970) measured the hearing sensitivity of nine rock performers just before a performance and within one hour of the performance's conclusion. Eight musicians showed a threshold shift of at least 15 dB for at least one frequency in the 200–8000 Hz range;[15] some losses were as high as 50 dB. Rintelmann, Lindberg, & Smitley (1972) exposed 20 women with normal hearing to recorded rock music at a SPL of 100 DB under two conditions: once as 60 minutes of continuous music, the other time as three-minute music segments alternating with one-minute segments of "background" (80 dB) disco noise. The TTS was less for the intermittent music condition, although recovery (return to normal hearing threshold) was about the same for both conditions. The investigators noted that 50 percent of the women in the intermittent condition and 80 percent in the continuous music condition were "endangered" in accordance with published standards restricting daily exposure to high sound levels.

Personal radio headsets provide individual listeners with ample opportunity to expose themselves to preferred sounds at excessively high SPL's. These devices are not protecting their wearers against outside sounds while they produce "inside" sounds; hearing protection is not provided in any significant way (Skrainar et al., 1985). While the desirable sounds indeed may mask undesirable sounds, if the desired sounds are at a sufficiently high level for sufficiently long, danger is present.

Music educators, who are obligated to teach individuals to listen to

---

[15]Some frequencies in this range may appear too high for musical purposes, but speech intelligibility suffers from a loss of high frequency sensitivity because consonants then sound blurred.

music in responsible and safe ways, may be at risk due to prolonged exposure to higher level sounds in rehearsal and performance situations. Cutietta et al. (1994) employed standard audiometric methods to test the hearing sensitivity of 104 music teachers, including 55 choral or general music teachers, 38 high school band directors, and 11 elementary band teachers. In order to allow for recovery of any temporary threshold shift, the investigators were careful to allow at least three and one-half hours between the end of any music activity and the beginning of testing. Comparisons of the resulting audiograms with typical patterns of noise-induced hearing loss and of presbycusis[16] showed that 14 percent of the subjects showed some degree of hearing loss, a percentage that was high in comparison with a population of similar age and gender (Willott, 1991). Nineteen percent showed a pattern typical of noise-induced hearing loss. Within the subjects with a type of hearing loss, band directors were effected the most adversely; their natural age-related declines in hearing sensitivity evidently were confounded by noise-induced hearing loss. The researchers caution that many of the band directors also were active performers, many in "loud" settings, and that considerable individual differences exist. Yet, previous work by Cutietta, Millin, and Royse (1989) suggested that about 41 percent of a sample of band directors showed some noise-induced hearing loss, as compared with an average of 7 percent in the general population of the United States.

Just as not everyone who smokes will develop lung cancer, not everyone who listens to music at high sound levels will destroy hair cells excessively, but loud sounds greatly increase the likelihood of such destruction, just as cigarette smoke increases the likelihood of disease. The danger to hearing is not just propaganda from people who dislike particular musical styles or are unduly bothered by noisy environments. Musicians who plan rehearsals of large groups in small rooms, stand near powerful speakers while they perform, or feel that they must be "totally bathed" in sound should acknowledge the risks they create for themselves and for others. Investment in a modern set of ear plugs, custom fitted and manufactured to attenuate sound without changing the relative relationships among dynamic levels, is wise for many performers and music students.

---

[16]Presbycusis is the "normal" loss of sensitivity to higher frequencies that accompanies aging. It usually is more pronounced in males than in females. One may question the extent to which such loss is "normal" as opposed to being a result of prolonged exposure to high intensity sounds.

Timbre Phenomena

Timbre or tone quality is the tonal attribute that distinguishes tones of identical pitch, loudness, and duration. An oboe and a viola can play an A of identical frequency and sound pressure level for an identical period of time, but they sound clearly different. Timbre is a highly multidimensional perceptual property, and it is difficult to control separate dimensions, so timbre perception lacks a research base comparable to that of pitch or loudness perception. However, in recent years researchers have exploited sophisticated mathematical analyses and the digital analysis and synthesis of tones to uncover additional aspects of timbre. We consider timbre's relationship to waveform, timbre recognition, and measurement.

Waveform-Timbre Relationship

Timbre is a psychological property. Its closest quasiparallel physical property is waveform, the pattern of displacements associated with a sound wave. A complex waveform depends on the particular component frequencies, the number of frequencies, the relative strengths of the frequencies, and the relative phases among the frequencies (Backus, 1977). A waveform is a dynamic, changing event—relationships among the components change with time. As Butler (1992) points out, component relationships vary with time and overall dynamic level. While musical instruments sound differently to a large extent due to differences in waveform, no static representation of a waveform accounts sufficiently for resulting timbre sensations.

Even static portrayals of waveforms require recognition of phase relationships. Authorities once believed that the ear is "phase deaf," in accordance with Ohm's acoustical law. Supposedly, sounds containing components identical in frequency and amplitudes but different in relative phase would look different in waveform but sound identical in timbre. Research later showed that although phase sensitivity is relatively weak, relative phase has subtle effects on timbre, particularly when changing phase relationships occur within a continuously sounding tone (Patterson, 1973; Plomp & Steeneken, 1969; Raiford & Schubert, 1971; Risset & Wessel, 1982).

Influences within Waveform

Within the dynamic waveform, the *onset* portion and other transient characteristics are especially important for the timbre sensation. The onset, also called the attack, initial frequency smear, rise time, and initial transient, is the opening portion of a tone, where the energy supplied exceeds the energy expended. In tones produced by continuous excitation of the vibrating source, such as with a bowed string, a blown reed or mouthpiece, or vibrating vocal folds, the onset is followed by a steady state section, where energy supplied and expended are roughly in balance. Tones produced by impulsive excitation of the vibrating source, such as piano tones and plucked string tones, have no steady state. The *offset* or decay, where energy expended exceeds any supplied, concludes a tone.

A vibrating system can not attain a reasonably steady vibration pattern instantaneously. The onset contains a certain amount of "noise" in the form of additional inharmonic frequency components that will not be part of the steady state sound. Individual frequency components differ in their "rise times," or times to attain their eventual amplitudes. Individual tones will differ in their degrees of inharmonicity and the time required to attain a steady state, if one indeed occurs.

Winckel (1967) discusses extensively onset effects from theoretical and experimental standpoints. Onset times vary with different instruments; the trumpet has a rapid onset of about 20 msec; the flute requires about 200 to 300 msec. Furthermore, any tonal attack includes a rapidly decaying initial "smear" of inharmonic and harmonic frequencies (the onset), and the frequency width (range) and time of the "smear" vary with the quality of attack. Staccato attacks have relatively wide "smears" and short onset times. Legato attacks have relatively narrow "smears" and long onset times. Onset behavior inherent in a musical performance medium is modified by performer idiosyncrasies and the acoustical environment. Winckel's work clearly shows that attempts to compare "good" and "bad" sounds via an oscilloscope or to imitate orchestral instruments with organs and synthesizers lacking sophisticated control of tonal portions are unlikely to be fruitful: They can not duplicate onset behavior.

A second contains 1000 msec; even the "long" onset time of 300 msec is less than half a second. The importance of such a brief time for the timbre sensation is illustrated dramatically by experiments where the initial tonal portion is physically removed, as in removing a portion of a recording tape. Elliott (1975), for example, demonstrated that even experienced musicians may have considerable difficulty in identifying common orchestral instruments when their tones' onset portions are missing.

Caution regarding effects of the onset and other transient aspects on timbre recognition is necessary. In a study comparing college students' abilities to match systematically altered digitally sampled instrument sounds with models, Kendall (1986) found that students were significantly more accurate in recognizing timbre in the context of realistic musical phrases than in that of isolated tones. Yet, context alone was not enough— when transient characteristics were replaced in the synthesized stimuli by steady state sections, contextual cues were not adequate. Nor were they adequate when reasonably steady-state areas were replaced by transients. Kendall concluded that how the entire spectrum varies across time is important in categorization of timbre.

The relative distribution of energy among the partials may vary with the overall sound pressure level. In general, higher partials have proportionately more energy at greater SPL's than they do at weaker levels (Hall, 1990; Risset & Wessel, 1982). This is particularly true for wind instruments. The band director who asks the band to play with exactly the same timbre in loud and soft passages may be asking for an impossibility.

To add a little more to the importance of variances in the waveform, one should recognize that in the free-field listening situation characteristic of a concert hall, reverberant sound dominates direct sound for a major part of the audience. The waveform differs from point to point, so even steady-state tones may have different timbres at different locations (Plomp & Steeneken, 1973).

Butler (1992, p. 141) concludes that timbre perception is complex and influenced by the steady state waveforms, transient characteristics (especially the onset), and slower spectral changes over a series of tones.

Tone Source Recognition

The basilar membrane stimulation pattern resulting from a particular complex waveform's characteristics probably is the physiological basis for timbre perception, at least in the static case of a steady-state waveform (Plomp, 1970).

Balzano (1986) questioned the importance of spectral characteristics regarding distribution of energy, number of partials, etc. He felt that time-based variation is responsible for recognition of particular instrumental sounds, a form of information which maintains relative constancy regardless of the waveform changes that come from changes in an instrument's particular fundamental frequency or overall intensity level.

Roederer (1995, p. 152) discusses dynamic ("in context") tone source recognition as a matter of timbre perception, resulting from neural processing of waveform information, storage in memory with a learned label, and comparison with prior information. Anyone with normal hearing may experience the sensation of a clarinet sound as opposed to a trumpet sound, but distinguishing between the two in terms of labels requires learning, which likely results in actual neural modification of cortical structures.

Measurement of Timbre

Timbre is multidimensional. As a result, there is not and cannot be a measurement unit analogous to the mel for pitch or the sone for loudness. Qualitative descriptions may employ many adjectives, similar to those found in orchestration texts, such as "rich," "mellow," "thin," "buzzy," "comical," "noble," etc. Quantification may occur through locating a particular tone along a set of dimensions.

Modern attempts to measure timbre may employ subjects' verbal descriptions or judgments of tonal similarity to uncover underlying dimensions along which timbre perceptions may be ordered. For example, von Bismarck (1974a; b) had eight musicians and eight nonmusicians classify twenty-five 200 Hz complex tones with varying waveforms, five steady-state vowel segments, and five noise bands along thirty seven-point scales formed by bipolar adjectives (semantic differentials). His statistical analysis yielded four factors, which collectively explained 91 percent of the subjects' variability in classifying timbres. The most important factor was *sharpness* (as in one pole of "dull-sharp," not high in pitch), which seemed to depend on the upper frequency in a complex sound and the comparative progressive reduction in upper partial strengths, i.e., the slope of the spectral envelope.[17] By demonstrating that sharpness may be doubled or halved, just as loudness, von Bismarck suggested another possible basic tonal property.

Grey (1977) synthesized tones to match natural oboe, clarinet, saxophone, English horn, French horn, flute, bassoon, trumpet, and string tones. Subjects judged the tones, equal in pitch, loudness, and duration, for perceived similarity. Using multidimensional scaling, Grey found that similarity ratings could be organized along three dimensions in geometric space. One dimension was the spectral energy distribution which resulted from the particular waveform. Another was related to low and high frequencies in the onset. The third dimension was related to spectral fluctuations.

Plomp (1970) showed that multidimensional analyses of the physical spectra of organ tones gave a similar dimensional configuration to analyses of subjects' similarity ratings. While dimensional research is complex, there is no way to order sounds on any unidimensional scale with respect to timbre (Rasch & Plomp, 1982), so quantitative measurement of timbre must employ multidimensional methodology.

---

[17]The "envelope" is a sound's "shape" across time, formed by connecting the peaks of amplitude in the complex waveform.

Summary

Chapter Four has presented considerable information related to music's psychoacoustical foundations. It is difficult to simplify that which is inherently complex, but the chapter's main points include the following:

1. Musical sounds depend on rapid atmospheric pressure fluctuations resulting from physical vibration, usually regularly recurring or periodic.
2. Pressure fluctuations are transmitted as mechanical vibrations to the inner ear, where they are processed and converted to electrochemical signals directed to the brain.
3. Tones have physical characteristics, which would exist independently of any human observer, and psychological characteristics, which require a human observer.
4. Pitch, a tone's apparent location on a high-low continuum, depends on the physical property of frequency, but the pitch-frequency relationship is not perfect.
5. In addition to its highness-lowness dimension, pitch includes dimensions of definity, which refers to how obvious the pitch sensation is, and similarity, intimacy, or circularity, which refers to how a particular pitch relates to other pitches.
6. Pitch assignment for a pure tone depends upon the area of basilar membrane stimulation.
7. A simultaneous combination of pure tones forms a sensation of unison, beating, roughness, or two tones in accordance with the frequency separation of the tones.
8. The amount by which a frequency must change in order to elicit a pitch difference varies with the individual, the occasion, and the frequency range.
9. A complex tone's pitch depends on the low pitch resulting from the waveform's spatial pattern and repetition frequency, detected through the central neural process of fundamental tracking.
10. Combination tones result from cochlear distortion; they are distinguished from low pitch in that they require more than minimal intensity level for perception and are peripheral rather than central effects.
11. Musicians usually consider consonance or dissonance as another label for various intervals, while nonmusicians evaluate intervals in accordance with the phenomenon.
12. Consonance and dissonance judgments depend heavily on training and experience, but there may be some physical basis for consonance due to basilar membrane alignment of tonal components.

13. Why complex tones from separate sound sources generally result in harmony while individual complex tones yield a unitary pitch sensation is unclear.

14. The apparent size of a musical interval of constant ratio may vary with frequency range and other conditions in an idiosyncratic manner.

15. First order beating, an apparent rise and fall in loudness of a mistuned unison, is a peripheral effect.

16. Second order beating, an apparent waxing and waning or fluttering of a mistuned nonunison interval, is a central pitch processing effect.

17. Absolute pitch, the ability to name a tone without reference to any external pitch standard, may be related to learning label-sensation connections at a critical age.

18. Attempts to measure pitch as distinct from frequency via the mel scale have been somewhat disappointing.

19. Loudness, the apparent strength or magnitude of a sound, depends largely on intensity, but the intensity-loudness relationship is not perfect.

20. Loudness is distinguished from volume, the apparent size or extensity of a tone, and density, the apparent compactness, but recognition of volume and density as separate tonal properties is inconsistent.

21. Decibels are measures of intensity level and sound pressure level (physical characteristics), not loudness.

22. Equal loudness curves connect frequency-intensity combinations which produce loudness levels equivalent in phons.

23. Equal loudness curves show how frequency confounds the intensity-loudness relationship; a given intensity does not elicit an equal loudness sensation across all frequencies.

24. Loudness may be measured via various techniques; the sone scale was derived from estimations of loudness.

25. The power law suggests that loudness grows in a lawful manner in relation to growth in sound intensity; the growth rate varies with stimulus conditions.

26. One sound may mask another.

27. Loudness summation depends on the particular component frequencies, their degrees of separation, and relative phase as well as individual loudnesses; there is no simple additive process.

28. Exposure to music at high intensity levels may reduce hearing sensitivity, perhaps permanently.

29. Timbre depends on the physical factors influencing waveform as well as onset and transient waveform characteristics.

30. Musical context may be important in recognition of timbre.

31. Tone source recognition depends on learning as well as timbre perception.
32. As timbre is a multidimensional property, its measurement beyond qualitative descriptions depends on uncovering dimensions along which perceptual judgments of timbre may be placed.

References

Bachem, A. (1984). Time factors in relative and absolute pitch discrimination. *Journal of the Acoustical Society of America, 26,* 751–753.

Backus, J. W. (1977). *The acoustical foundations of music* (2nd ed.). New York: W. W. Norton.

Balzano, G. (1986). What are musical pitch and timbre? *Music Perception, 3,* 297–314.

Beck, J., & Shaw, W. A. (1967). Ratio-estimations of loudness intervals. *American Journal of Psychology, 80,* 59–65.

Bharucha, J. J. (1984). Anchoring effects in music: The resolution of dissonance. *Cognitive Psychology, 16,* 485–518.

Boyle, J. D., & Radocy, R. E. (1987). *Measurement and evaluation of musical experiences.* New York: Schirmer Books.

Bugg, E. G. (1933). An experimental study of factors influencing consonance judgments. *Psychological Monographs, 45* (2). (Whole No. 201).

Butler, D. (1992). *The musician's guide to perception and cognition.* New York: Schirmer Books.

Corso, J. F. (1954). Unison tuning of musical instruments. *Journal of the Acoustical Society of America, 26,* 746–750.

Corso, J. F. (1957). Absolute judgments of musical tonality. *Journal of the Acoustical Society of America, 29,* 138–144.

Cuddy, L. L. (1968). Practice effects on the absolute judgment of pitch. *Journal of the Acoustical Society of America, 43,* 1069–1076.

Cutietta, R. A., Klich, R. J., Royse, D., & Rainbolt, H. (1994). The incidence of noise-induced hearing loss among music teachers. *Journal of Research in Music Education, 42,* 318–330.

Cutietta, R. A., Millin, J., & Royse, D. (1989). Noise-induced hearing loss among school band directors. *Council for Research in Music Education, 101,* 41–49.

Dallos, P. S., & Sweetman, R. H. (1969). Distribution patterns of cochlear harmonics. *Journal of the Acoustical Society of America, 45,* 37–45.

Dallos, P., Billone, M. C., Currant, J. D., Wang, C. Y., & Raynor, S. (1972). Cochlear inner and outer hair cells: Functional differences. *Science, 177,* 356–360.

Davis, H. (1962). Advances in the neurophysiology and neuroanatomy of the cochlea. *Journal of the Acoustical Society of America, 34,* 1377–1385.

DeGainza, V. H. (1970). Absolute and relative hearing as innate complementary functions of man's musical ear. *Council for Research in Music Education, 22,* 13–16.

Deutsch, D. (1982). Grouping mechanisms in music. In D. Deutsch (Ed.), *The psychology of music* (pp. 99–134). New York: Academic Press.

Egan, J. P., & Hake, H. W. (1950). On the masking pattern of a simple auditory stimulus. *Journal of the Acoustical Society of America, 22,* 622–630.

Elliott, C. A. (1975). Attacks and releases as factors in instrument identification. *Journal of Research in Music Education, 23,* 35–40.

Espinoza-Varas, B., & Watson, C. S. (1989). Perception of complex auditory patterns. In R. J. Dooling & S. H. Hulse (Eds.), *The comparative psychology of audition: Perceiving complex sounds* (pp. 67–94). Hillsdale, NJ: Lawrence Erlbaum Associates.

Farnsworth, P. R. (1938). The pitch of a combination of tones. *American Journal of Psychology, 51,* 536–539.

Farnsworth, P. R. (1969). *The social psychology of music* (2nd ed.). Ames: Iowa State University Press.

Fletcher, H. (1946). The pitch, loudness, and quality of musical tones. *American Journal of Physics, 14,* 215–225.

Fletcher, H., & Munson, W. A. (1933). Loudness. *Journal of the Acoustical Society of America, 5,* 82–108.

Gacek, R. R. (1972). Neuroanatomy of the auditory system. In J. V. Tobias (Ed.), *Foundations of modern auditory theory* (vol. 2) (pp. 241–262). New York: Academic Press.

Gjaevenes, K., & Rimstad, E. R. (1972). The influence of rise time on loudness. *Journal of the Acoustical Society of America, 51,* 1233–1239.

Goldstein, J. L. (1970). Aural combination tones. In R. Plomp & G. F. Smoorenburg (Eds.), *Frequency analysis and periodicity detection in hearing* (pp. 230–247). Leiden: Sijthoff.

Grey, J. M. (1977). Multidimensional perceptual scaling of musical timbres. *Journal of the Acoustical Society of America, 61,* 1270–1277.

Guirao, M., & Stevens, S. S. (1964). The measurement of auditory density. *Journal of the Acoustical Society of America, 36,* 1176–1182.

Hall, D. E. (1990). *Musical acoustics* (2nd ed.). Belmont, CA: Wadsworth.

Hellman, R. P. (1982). Loudness, annoyance, and noisiness produced by single-tone noise complexes. *Journal of the Society of the Acoustical Society of America, 72,* 62–73.

Hellman, R. P. (1985). Perceived magnitude of two-tone complexes: Loudness, annoyance, and noisiness. *Journal of the Acoustical Society of America, 77,* 1497–1504.

Houtsma, A. J. M., & Goldstein, J. L. (1972). The central origin of the pitch of complex tones. *Journal of the Acoustical Society of America, 51,* 5520–5529.

Jeffress, L. A. (1962). Absolute pitch. *Journal of the Acoustical Society of America, 34,* 987.

Jerger, J., & Jerger, S. (1970). Temporary threshold shift in rock-and-roll musicians. *Journal of Speech and Hearing Research, 13,* 221–224.

Kendall, R. A. (1986). The role of acoustic signal partitions in listener categorization of musical phrases. *Music Perception, 4,* 185–214.

Kock, W. E. (1935). On the principle of uncertainty in sound. *Journal of the Acoustical Society of America, 7,* 56–58.

Krumhansl, C. L. (1979). The psychological representation of musical pitch in a tonal context. *Cognitive Psychology, 11,* 346–374.

Lundin, R. W. (1947). Toward a cultural theory of consonance. *Journal of Psychology, 23*, 45–49.

Meyer, M. (1956). On memorizing absolute pitch. *Journal of the Acoustical Society of America, 28*, 718–719.

Molino, J. A. (1973). Pure-tone equal-loudness contours for standard tones of different frequencies. *Perception and Psychophysics, 14*, 1–4.

Moore, B. C. J. (1974). Relation between the critical bandwidth and the frequency difference limen. *Journal of the Acoustical Society of America, 55*, 359.

Moore, B. C. J. (1989). *An introduction to the psychology of hearing* (3rd ed.) London: Academic Press.

Moore, B. C. J., Glasberg, B. R., & Peters, R. W. (1985). Relative of individual partials in determining the pitch of complex tones. *Journal of the Acoustical Society of America, 77*, 1853–1860.

Nordmark, J. O. (1968). Mechanisms of frequency discrimination. *Journal of the Acoustical Society of America, 44*, 1533–1540.

Patterson, B. (1974). Musical dynamics. *Scientific American, 231* (5), 78–95.

Patterson, R. (1973). The effects of relative phase and the number of components on residue pitch. *Journal of the Acoustical Society of America, 53*, 1565–1572.

Perrott, D. R., & Nelson, M. A. (1969). Limits for the detection of binaural beats. *Journal of the Acoustical Society of America, 46*, 1477–1481.

Peterson, J., & Smith, F. W. (1930). The range and modifiability of consonance in certain musical intervals. *American Journal of Psychology, 42*, 561–572.

Pickles, J. O. (1982). *An introduction to the physiology of hearing.* London: Academic Press.

Plomp, R. (1965). Detectability threshold for combination tones. *Journal of the Acoustical Society of America, 37*, 1110–1123.

Plomp, R. (1967a). Beats of mistuned consonances. *Journal of the Acoustical Society of America, 42*, 462–474.

Plomp, R. (1967b). Pitch of complex tones. *Journal of the Acoustical Society of America, 41*, 1526–1533.

Plomp, R. (1970). Timbre as a multidimensional attribute of complex tones. In R. Plomp & G. Smoorenburg (Eds.), *Frequency analysis and periodicity in hearing* (pp. 397–411). Leiden: Sijthoff.

Plomp, R. (1976). *Aspects of tone sensation.* London: Academic Press.

Plomp, R., & Levelt, W. J. M. (1965). Tonal consonance and critical bandwidth. *Journal of the Acoustical Society of America, 38*, 548–560.

Plomp, R., & Steeneken, H. J. M. (1969). Effect of phase on the timbre of complex tones. *Journal of the Acoustical Society of America, 46*, 409–421.

Plomp, R., & Steeneken, H. J. M. (1973). Place dependence of timbre in reverberant sound fields. *Acustica, 28*, 50–59.

Radocy, R. E. (1977). Pitch judgments of selected successive intervals: Is twice as frequent twice as high? *Psychology of Music, 5* (2), 23–29.

Radocy, R. E. (1978). The influence of selected variables on the apparent size of successive pitch intervals. *Psychology of Music, 6* (2), 21–29.

Raiford, C. A., & Schubert, E. D. (1971). Recognition of phase changes in octave complexes. *Journal of the Acoustical Society of America, 50,* 559–567.

Rakowski, A. (1979). The magic number two: Seven examples of binary apposition in pitch theory. *Humanities Association Review, 30,* 24–45.

Rasch, R. A., & Plomp, R. (1982). The perception of musical tones. In D. Deutsch (Ed.), *The psychology of music* (pp. 1–24). New York: Academic Press.

Rhode, W. S., & Robles, L. (1974). Evidence from Mossbauer experiments for nonlinear vibration in the cochlea. *Journal of the Acoustical Society of America, 55,* 588–596.

Rintelmann, W. R., Lindberg, R. F., & Smitley, E. K. (1972). Temporary threshold shift and recovery patterns from two types of rock and roll music presentation. *Journal of the Acoustical Society of America, 51,* 1249–1254.

Risset, J. C., & Wessel, D. L. (1982). Explanation of timbre by analysis and synthesis. In D. Deutsch (Ed.), *The psychology of music* (pp. 26–58). New York: Academic Press.

Ritsma, R. J. (1970). Periodicity detection. In R. Plomp & G. Smoorenburg (Eds.), *Frequency analysis and periodicity detection in hearing* (pp. 250–263). Leiden: Sijthoff.

Roederer, J. G. (1995). *The physics and psychophysics of music: An introduction.* (3rd Ed.). New York: Springer-Verlag.

Scharf, G. (1969). Dichotic summation of loudness. *Journal of the Acoustical Society of America, 45,* 1193–1205.

Scharf, G. (1978). Loudness. In E. D. Carterette & M. P. Friedman (Eds.), *Handbook of perception* (vol. 4) (pp. 187–242). New York: Academic Press.

Sergeant, D. (1969). Experimental investigation of absolute pitch. *Journal of Research in Music Education, 17,* 135–143.

Shepard, R. N. (1964). Circularity in judgments of relative pitch. *Journal of the Acoustical Society of America, 36,* 2345–2353.

Shepard, R. N. (1982). Structural representations of musical pitch. In D. Deutsch (Ed.), *The psychology of music* (pp. 344–390). New York: Academic Press.

Sherbon, J. W. (1975). The association of hearing acuity, diplacusis, and discrimination with musical performance. *Journal of Research in Music Education, 23,* 249–257.

Siegel, J. A., & Siegel, W. (1977). Categorical perception of tonal intervals: Musicians can't tell *sharp* from *flat*. *Perception and Psychophysics, 21,* 399–407.

Skrainar, S. F., Royster, L. H., Berger, E. H., & Pearson, R. G. (1985). Do personal radio headsets provide hearing protection? *Sound and Vibration, 19* (5), 16–19.

Stevens, S. S. (1934a). Tonal density. *Journal of Experimental Psychology, 17,* 585–592.

Stevens, S. S. (1934b). The volume and intensity of tones. *American Journal of Psychology, 46,* 150–154.

Stevens, S. S. (1935). The relation of pitch to intensity. *Journal of the Acoustical Society of America, 6,* 150–154.

Stevens, S. S. (1956). Calculation of the loudness of complex noise. *Journal of the Acoustical Society of America, 28,* 807–832.

Stevens, S. S. (1972). Perceived level of noise by Mark VII and decibels (E). *Journal of the Acoustical Society of America, 51,* 575–601.

Stevens, S. S. (1975). *Psychophysics.* New York: Wiley.

Stevens, S. S., Davis, H., & Lurie, M. H. (1935). The localization of pitch perception on the basilar membrane. *Journal of General Psychology, 13,* 297–315.

Stevens, Volkmann, J., & Newman, E. B. (1937). A scale for the measurement of the psychological magnitude pitch. *Journal of the Acoustical Society of America, 8,* 185–190.

Stevens, S. S., & Warshofsky, F. (1965). *Sound and hearing.* New York: Time, Inc.

Strange, A. (1972). *Electronic music.* Dubuque, IA: W. C. Brown.

Terhardt, E. (1974a). Pitch, consonance, & harmony. *Journal of the Acoustical Society of America, 55,* 1061–1069.

Terhardt, E. (1974b). Pitch of pure tones: Its relation to intensity. In E. Zwicker & E. Terhardt (Eds.), *Facts and models in hearing* (pp. 353–360). New York: Springer-Verlag.

Van der Geer, J. P., Levelt, W. J. M., & Plomp, R. (1962). The connotation of musical consonance. *Acta Psychologica, 20,* 308–319.

Von Bekesy, G. (1960). *Experiments in hearing.* New York: McGraw-Hill.

Von Bismarck, G. (1974a). Timbre of steady sounds: A factorial investigation of its verbal attributes. *Acustica, 30,* 146–149.

Von Bismarck, G. (1974b). Sharpness as an attribute of the timbre of steady sounds. *Acustica, 30,* 159–172.

Wallin, N. I. (1991). *Biomusicology: Neurophysiological neuropsychological, and evolutionary perspectives on the origins and purposes of music.* Stuyvesant, NY: Pendragon Press.

Ward, W. D., & Burns, E. M. (1982). Absolute pitch. In D. Deutsch (Ed.), *The psychology of music* (pp. 431–452). New York: Academic Press.

Warren, R. M. (1970). Elimination of biases in loudness judgments for tones. *Journal of the Acoustical Society of America, 48,* 1397–1403.

Whitfield, I. C. (1967). *The auditory pathway.* London: Arnold.

Whittle, L. S., Collins, S. J., & Robinson, D. W. (1972). The audibility of low-frequency sounds. *Journal of Sound and Vibration, 21,* 431–448.

Willott, J. F. (1991). *Aging and the auditory system: Anatomy, physiology, and psychophysics.* San Diego, CA: Singular Publishing.

Winckel, F. (1967). *Music, sound and sensation.* (T. Binkley, trans.). New York: Dover.

Woodworth, R. S., & Schlosberg, H. (1965). *Experimental psychology* (rev. ed.). New York: Holt, Rinehart, and Winston.

Yamamoto, T., Takagi, K., Shoji, H., & Yoneada, H. (1970). Critical band width with respect to temporary threshold shift. *Journal of the Acoustical Society of America, 48,* 978–987.

Zwicker, E., & Fastl, H. (1990). *Psychoacoustics: Facts and models.* Berlin: Springer-Verlag.

Zwicker, E., Flottorp, G., & Stevens, S. S. (1957). Critical band width in loudness summation. *Journal of the Acoustical Society of America, 29,* 548–557.

CHAPTER FIVE

RHYTHMIC FOUNDATIONS

The foundations of musical behavior examined in Chapter Five contrast somewhat with those foundations or perspectives of Chapters Two, Three, and Four. Chapter Two examines musical behavior's social and cultural foundations. It considers music as a sociocultural phenomenon and suggests that music's social and cultural contexts strongly influence musical behavior. Any attempt to understand or account for musical behavior without adequate recognition of social and cultural influences is, in the authors' opinion, incomplete and inaccurate. *Musical behavior is socially and culturally dependent.*

Chapter Three examines music's functional applications in contemporary life. While most of the sociocultural *functions* discussed in Chapter Two remain applicable today, Chapter Three focuses on a variety of specific applications, some of which capitalize on music as a tool in contemporary media. Other applications examined include particular industrial, commercial, therapeutic, and educational functions.

Chapter Four focuses on human response to tonal stimuli; the basic concern is to understand response to various attributes of a tonal stimulus as a result of human psychophysiological makeup. Sloboda (1985, p. 239) terms this approach a *biological approach* to music psychology, because it tends to stress the physiological variables that underlie human interaction with music. The learning mechanism and basic neurological pathways for processing tonal stimuli appear to be biologically determined and as such reflect inherent human possibilities for processing tonal stimuli.

Chapters Five and Six, with due recognition of musical behavior's dependence on sociocultural and biological influences, examine the contributions of *cognitive psychology* to understanding musical behavior. A superficial dichotomy may appear between the study of musical *behavior* and music *cognition,* but the authors, as do many other educators and psychologists, recognize that behavior and cognition are integrally related and mutually interdependent. Reasons for various educators, psychologists, and other writers appearing to focus either on *behavior* or *cognition* to the neglect of the other often are deep-rooted, philosophical, complex, and perhaps irrelevant to the present discussion. Since research from both perspectives has made invaluable contributions to understanding musical behavior, the authors have drawn on research from both perspectives. However, because of the dramatic surge of interest in music cognition in the 1980s (e.g., Deutsch, 1982; Dowling & Harwood, 1986, Fiske, 1990; Hargreaves, 1986; Howell, Cross, & West, 1985; Serafine, 1988; Sloboda, 1985; Taylor, 1981), Chapters Five and Six seek to explicate such contributions to the understanding of musical behavior's rhythmic, melodic, and harmonic foundations.

Why Study Rhythm?

Rhythm is an essential component of all musics, whether of primitive societies, traditional Western art music, or contemporary popular styles. Despite its musical importance, Cooper and Meyer (1960, p. v) note that the study of rhythm in performance "has been almost totally neglected in the formal training of musicians since the Renaissance."

This is not to suggest, however, that rhythm as a phenomenon has not been studied. To the contrary, investigators have studied rhythm both intensively and extensively from many different perspectives. Winick's (1974) annotated bibliography of rhythm includes nearly 500 sources. Innumerable definitions and explanations of rhythm and its various attributes exist. Theorists have examined music's rhythmic structure, and through their analyses have developed and/or theorized underlying organizational schemata for Western music (e.g., Clarke, 1989; Cooper & Meyer, 1960; Johnson-Laird, 1991; Lerdahl & Jackendoff, 1983; Yeston, 1976). Philosophers have offered theories of rhythmic response. Rhythm has been studied both as a stimulus and response (Lundin, 1967), and recent years have seen increasing concern with examining the processes underlying the perception of rhythm. Other writers have been concerned with exploring developments in rhythm from the time of the ancient Greeks to the present, while still others have considered musical rhythms in relation to rhythms in nature. A smaller group of writers has been concerned with notational systems. Persons concerned with influencing human behavior through music have recognized and studied rhythm's role in music used to modify nonmusical behaviors. Performing musicians, in addition to depending on rhythm to lend structure and hold performances together, use rhythm as one means of enhancing expression or creativity. A recent research focus has been on rhythm's expressive attributes. Music teachers are concerned with rhythm from a pedagogical perspective.

Despite such interest, rhythm traditionally has been less studied than melody or harmony. Dowling and Harwood (1986, p. 179) argue that the neglect of rhythm has been especially unfortunate for the psychology of music because "rhythmic information is, if anything, more fundamental to music cognition that pitch information." Theorists, psychologists, and educators increasingly are devoting efforts to understanding its musical role and how people interact with rhythm in music. Obviously, diverse approaches to the study of rhythm and rhythmic behavior exist. Persons concerned with understanding rhythmic behavior's psychological foundations must scrutinize and synthesize a vast body of diverse literature into a conceptual framework that will provide a basis for understanding the rhythmic behaviors of performers, listeners, and students. Such a framework necessarily requires examining (a) rhythm's function in music, (b) rhythmic structures in music, (c) psychological processes underlying rhythmic behavior, (d) the development of rhythmic behaviors, (e) teaching and learning rhythmic behaviors, (f) analyses of rhythmic performance, and (g) evaluation of rhythmic behaviors.

Functions of Rhythm in Music

When the musics from all cultures of the world are considered, it is rhythm that stands out as most fundamental. *Rhythm is the organizer and the energizer.* Without rhythm, there would be no music, whereas there is much music that has neither melody nor harmony. (Gaston, 1968, p. 17)

Cooper and Meyer (1960, p. 1) also view rhythm as fundamental to music: "To study rhythm is to study all of music. Rhythm both organizes and is itself organized by all the elements which create and shape music processes." Mursell (1956, pp. 254–257), whose study and writing concerning rhythm spanned forty years, notes that rhythm (a) gives life, sparkle, reality, and expressiveness to musical performance; (b) adds immensely to the pleasure of listening; (c) greatly facilitates musical performance and music reading; and (d) is the best and most natural starting point for musical creation.

Benjamin (1984) recognizes three particular functions that musical meter serves in the perception of music. Meter's primary function is to provide a way for measuring time in terms of a specific work as it is heard. It also facilitates the perception of group structure by providing an underlying framework for the melodic phrase rhythm. Benjamin's third function of meter essentially is aesthetic: Music's metric hierarchy provides structural time-points which greatly expand the functional range of interplay between time and pitch.

Sloboda (1985, p. 188) also argues that rhythm provides an important organizational basis in music and maintains that rhythm and tonality are mutually interactive systems. He notes that "knowledge of the tonal structure can help determine the rhythmic structure, and *vice versa.*"

Clearly, rhythm's primary musical function is to give order. Music is a temporal art which must be organized in such a way that is comprehensible. Rhythm, in its broadest sense, *"is everything pertaining to the temporal quality (duration) of the musical sound"* (Apel, 1944, p. 640). It is the organization of sound's durational attributes which indeed allows sound to become music. When comprehensible organization is lacking, the listener does not perceive the sound as music.

Gabrielsson (1982a, pp. 159–163), however, maintains that rhythm in music involves more than the performed musical sound and proposes a general model for what is involved in musical rhythm. For Gabrielsson, musical rhythm involves *musical performance,* which produces *sound sequences,* which in turn may elicit psychological and physiological responses in the listeners. He notes that listeners' responses may be of three types: (a) *experiential,* including various perceptual, cognitive, and emotional variables; (b) *behavioral,* including more or less overt movements such as tapping the beat with one's foot, swaying of the body, or dancing; and (c) *physiological,* such as changes in breathing, heart rate, or muscular tension.

Rhythm provides music's forward movement, thus making music a dynamic (in the sense of motion and change), energizing force. Music with little rhythmic movement elicits lesser dynamic response than music in which rhythmic movement is active. Rhythm gives "life" to music, and a "feel" or "sense" of rhythm as the dynamic force within music facilitates a person's interactions with music, both as a performer and a respondent.

Whether as a performer or respondent, an individual's interaction with rhythm in music can result in aesthetic experience (Sachs, 1953, p. 18). Rhythm's increasing importance as an aesthetic device is readily apparent when one compares its prominence and complexity in twentieth century music with its role in renaissance, baroque, classical, and romantic music.

Most traditional definitions of rhythm allude in some way to rhythm as music's organizational and dynamic force.[1] Even with general agreement regarding rhythm's basic function in music, there is, as Creston (1964, p. v) notes, a need "to separate the chaff from the wheat." Discussions of rhythm and its attributes yield little consensus, but understanding the attributes of rhythm in music is essential to understanding the

---

[1]For discussions of various definitions of rhythm, see Creston (1964) and Behrens (1984).

psychological foundations of rhythmic behavior. The next section examines the various attributes of rhythmic structure in music.

Rhythmic Structure in Music

Descriptions of the attributes of musical rhythm are many and varied. The descriptions employ some commonality of terms, but the terms do not always have common meanings. Mursell (1937, p. 190), for example, recognizes two attributes of musical rhythm: (a) the underlying beat and (b) the phrase rhythm. Cooper and Meyer (1960, p. 3) recognize three basic modes of temporal organization: (a) pulse, (b) meter, and (c) rhythm. Gordon (1971, pp. 67–69), in a departure from traditional terminology, maintains that rhythm is comprised of three basic elements: (a) tempo beats, (b) meter beats, and (c) melodic rhythm. Relations resulting from combinations of these three basic elements comprise "rhythmic patterns" that "elicit music meaning . . . in the mind of the listener" (Gordon, 1971, p. 69). Creston (1964, pp. 1–44), writing from a composer's vantage point and considering rhythm in terms of "the organization of duration in ordered movement," a view consistent with the authors' perception of the function of rhythm in music, identifies four basic rhythmic aspects: (a) meter, (b) pace, (c) accent, and (d) pattern. Creston views the terms *time* and *tempo* as somewhat indefinite and inaccurate and replaces them with *meter* and *pace* respectively. Most current writers also use meter in place of time, but substitution of pace for tempo is less common. Tempo remains the prevalent term. *Accent* is used in the traditional sense (emphasizing a beat), while *pattern* refers to any subdivision of a pulse or beat into smaller units.

Benjamin (1984, p. 359), however, maintains that *accent* and *grouping* "are the basic, if not neatly separable, modes of partitioning musical time and that meter is a secondary construct, imposed on the interaction of group structure and accent, in response to certain practical and aesthetic needs." Gabrielsson (1973), based on analysis of data from several experiments, recognizes the following properties of rhythm: (a) meter, (b) the level of accent on the first beat, (c) the type of "basic pattern," (d) the prominence of a basic pattern, and (e) the "uniformity-variation" or "simplicity-complexity" of a rhythm.

As may be apparent, any examination of music's rhythmic structure is somewhat confounded by the fact that discussions of structure, particularly ones such as those by Benjamin (1984), Lerdahl and Jackendoff (1983), Gabrielsson (1973, 1982a), Clynes and Walker (1982), and Dowling and Harwood (1986), necessarily reflect *perceived structure*, albeit in as "objective" a manner as possible. To varying degrees, such discussions treat rhythmic structure both as a psychological phenomenon and as an objective physical (acoustical) phenomenon. Consequently, discussions of structure reflect various writers' personal and research-based experiences with both the physical structure of notated and performed rhythm and the perception of rhythm, a psychological phenomenon. More recently, Clarke (1987b, 1989) and Pressing (1993) have sought to clarify the differences in the structural (scientific) and psychological (musical) properties of rhythm.

Clarke (1987b) recognizes several levels of structure in the organization of time in music. He views the written symbols as the lowest level of a hierarchical structure "in which the most abstract higher levels embody the relationships between lower level events" (p. 212). Clarke notes that the temporal properties represented by notation include (a) tempo, (b) the relative durational properties of individual events and silences, (c) grouping relationships, and (d) meter. He points out that pitch, timbre, and dynamics also help to define some grouping boundaries, metrical structures at higher levels than the notated measure, and patterns of tension and relaxation ("directed motion"). He observes that articulation and other changes in durational proportions of notated rhythmic values during performance cause the "idealized durational proportions of a score [to lose] their small whole number property" (p. 213), but argues that these changes are perceived as stylistic interpretations and that durations between event onsets (i.e., the beginnings of individual notes) are not affected directly.

Clarke (1989) sees a gap between descriptions of music's formal structures and the approaches of cognitive psychology and cites three problems in indiscriminately intermixing the two approaches: (a) it assumes that formal structure and perceptual properties function in the same way, (b) psychological processes tend to be subjectively variable, and (c) there is a tendency to confuse cultural norms with perceptual norms. He recommends that scholars maintain a clear separation between the two approaches while at the same time trying to establish a rapport between them.

Recognizing that the same dichotomy also applies to the present discussion, the authors include a somewhat traditional overview of rhythmic structure for the interested reader. Discussion of the cognitive bases of rhythm follows.

The *beat,* often referred to as *pulse,* underlies rhythm's structural components. The beat is the basic unit of duration, and beats divide duration into equal segments. Beats are time points on a duration continuum (Lerdahl & Jackendoff, 1983, p. 18). Kramer (1988, p. 97) maintains that people "do not literally *hear* beats. [They] experience them, . . . feel them, and . . . extrapolate them." Beats are fundamental to music's metric structure, while pulses are significant in relation to its rhythmic context.

A problem arises in discussion of beat with respect to meter. Meter signatures ostensibly specify the unit of notation that receives a beat (i.e., fills the time-span from one beat to the next); in practice, however, the unit designated by a meter signature as receiving the beat is not always the same as the beat that is felt in response to the music (as in, for example, a ¾ "Viennese" waltz or a 6⁄8 march at a customary march tempo). Mursell (1937, pp. 189–198) uses the German term *Takt* to indicate the felt beat; Farnsworth (1969, p. 233) refers to it as the *true beat.* For this discussion, the *metric beat* is that which a meter signature indicates. The beat felt in response to music is the *true beat.* Instances in which the true beat coincides with the metric beat, as it does in much music, will simply be referred to as beat. Metric beat will be used only when referring to a beat indicated by a meter signature that does not coincide with the true beat.

Meter involves the grouping of beats, usually metric beats. Just as beats, meter is periodic in that its function is "to mark off the musical flow, insofar as possible, into equal time spans" (Lerdahl & Jackendoff, 1983, p. 19). Meter usually is considered in terms of notation and is commonly indicated by bar lines. The idea is that the first beat of each measure should receive an accent, thus delineating the meter. Obviously, music does not always conform mechanically to this pattern; departure from the norm allows music to be an expressive medium rather that confining it to being mechanical or arithmetical.

Most theories of meter recognize that more than one level of meter may operate within a musical work. Since meter involves grouping of beats, multiple levels of meter are more a matter of perception than structure, and therefore will be examined later in the discussion of meter perception. It is sufficient to note here that with rapid tempi, the effect on the listener often is to make the notated measure the felt unit of beat, rather than the metric beat. These true beats often are grouped in turn into several measures, thus creating the effect of a superimposed meter.

In other instances, neither the metric beat nor the measures are the same as the true beat; e.g., 6⁄8 meter in moderate or faster tempo is felt in twos, with the dotted-quarter note functioning as the unit of the true beat. Jaques-Dalcroze (1921, Musical Supplement, p. 1) suggested a plan to make meter signatures more meaningful and avoid the confusion between the metric beat and the true beat. The note that represents the beat unit would be substituted for the lower number in the meter signature (see Figure 5-1).

Tempo, or *pace* as Creston terms it, refers to the speed at which beats

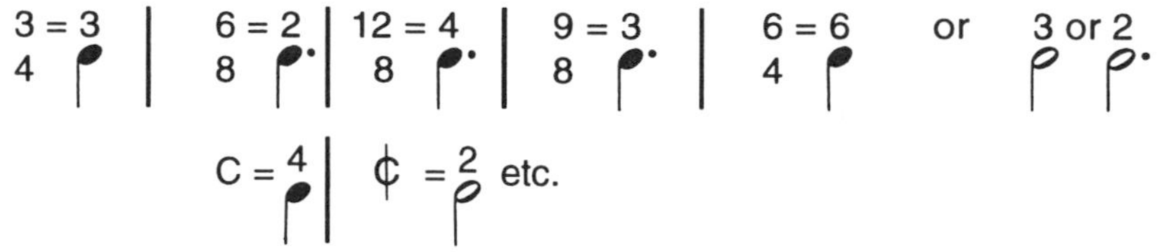

Figure 5-1. Jaques-Dalcroze's rationalized meter signatures. While Jaques-Dalcroze's suggestion has received some following in recent years, it is far from common practice, and musicians must continue to cope with distinguishing between the metrical beat and the true beat.

recur. Tempo in music notation is indicated in general terms by use of the traditional Italian terms, including (from slowest to quickest) *grave, largo, adagio, lento, andante, moderato, allegro,* and *presto.* More precise tempo indications are given in terms of metronome markings which indicate the number of times a given note value or unit of time recurs in one minute. The note value indicated may coincide with either the metric beat or the true beat. A typical metronome marking is ♩ = M.M.80.[2] This means that the quarter note is the beat unit, and the beat would recur at the rate of 80 per minute.

Accent is the aspect of rhythm which makes prominent or emphasizes a beat. Creston recognizes eight types of accents: dynamic, agogic, metric, harmonic, weight, pitch, pattern, and embellished. A *dynamic accent* emphasizes a beat by means of tone intensity; i.e., the tone is louder than others. An *agogic accent* emphasizes by means of duration, i.e., the tone is longer than those preceding or following it. A *metric accent* basically reflects the particular grouping of true beats or metric beats and often is a dynamic accent. A *harmonic accent* emphasizes a beat by use of dissonance or harmonic change on the beat. A *weight accent* expresses emphasis through change in texture. A *pitch accent* denotes emphasis on the highest or lowest tone of a group. *Pattern accents* occur on the initial tone of a melodic figure that is repeated. *Embellished accents* emphasize a beat through the use of melodic embellishments, e.g., mordents, trills, or grupetti. Creston views accent as the "very life of rhythm" without which meter becomes monotonous, pace (his term for tempo) has no sense of motion, and pattern becomes a nebulous elaboration.

Lerdahl and Jackendoff (1983, pp. 30–35) and Benjamin (1984) also provide in-depth discussions of types and functions of accents. They focus more on the role and function of various accents in *grouping* durational events within the total musical structure. They are careful, however, to delineate between *metric* accents, which reinforce groupings

---

[2]Maelzel constructed the metronome in 1816, and M.M. is a standard abbreviation for Maelzel Metronome.

of beats, and other types of accents, which facilitate other groupings within the musical context as well as serve various other musical and aesthetic functions.

Kramer (1988) maintains that there are really just three types of accents: stress, rhythmic, and metric. He argues that breakdowns into more than these three types simply call attention to factors that cause accents. Stress accents, which may be created by a sharp attack, a high loudness level, an embellishment, etc., are what musicians commonly call accents, and they operate independently of the metric downbeat. Metric accents, which may even occur on rests, essentially help define the regular grouping of beats. Rhythmic accents help define rhythmic groups and may serve to define rhythmic groups at several levels, e.g., a motive, phrase, period, section, or movement.

Beat, meter, tempo, and, to a degree, accent are the most agreed upon aspects of rhythmic structure. Phrase rhythm, melodic rhythm, rhythm pattern, or rhythm group are some names given to the rhythm of the melody and harmony parts that overlie and/or are entwined with beat, meter, tempo, and accent. These "overlying" aspects of rhythmic structure constitute an area in which it is quite difficult to separate discussion of physical structure from rhythm as a psychological phenomenon. Whereas beat and meter essentially provide reference points in musical time, tempo refers to the speed as which beats recur, and accent provides a means for emphasizing a beat, a listener may group phrase or melodic rhythm patterns at various levels. Because grouping is a function of both the musical structure and the perceiver's experience, most of the discussion regarding grouping is under the section below on the perception of rhythm. However, some descriptions of the basic structural units of melodic rhythm are included here.

Mursell (1937, pp. 176–185) and Cooper and Meyer (1960, p. 6) recognize some basic rhythmic groups called "units," which involve grouping unaccented pulses around an accented pulse as the basic structural level for melodic rhythms. Derived from ancient Greek poetic meter, the five basic units include *iamb* (U−), *anapest* (UU−), *trochee* (−U), *dactyl* (−U), and *amphibrach* (U−U); the dash indicates an accent. The theory is that these units underlie the melodic rhythms of music, but Yeston (1976, pp. 27–34) notes several problems in attempting to reduce rhythm to such basic units, particularly when laws of perception are considered. He maintains that attempts to analyze rhythm in these terms are overly reductive and not reflective of the realities of rhythmic variety.

Gordon (1971, pp. 67–71; 1980, pp. 31–58) and Creston (1964, pp. 34–43) view subdivisions of beats as the underlying structural units for melodic rhythms. Both Gordon and Creston agree that beats are subdivided into basically twos or threes. When the beat is divided into two equally spaced subdivisions (which he calls *meter beats*), Gordon labels this duple meter; when the beat is subdivided into three meter beats he labels it triple meter.[3] Creston refers to subdivisions as *patterns,* which may be classified as *regular* or *irregular* and *simple* or *compound.* Regular patterns reflect subdivisions suggested by meter signatures; irregular patterns are subdivisions not suggested by meter signatures. Repeated patterns are called simple patterns, and changing patterns are considered compound.

Regardless of how one labels or describes rhythm patterns, there is agreement that melodic rhythms overlay and entwine themselves in relation to the beat. Melodic rhythms may vary infinitely; they may be even, uneven, use subdivisions of beats, or involve durational values extending over many beats. It is the very freedom of melodic rhythm that provides a primary means for making music a dynamic energizing force.

While melodic rhythms with its free organization in relation to the substructure of beat, accent, and meter provides both variety and unity for musical structure, composers may employ many additional extensions of rhythmic structure to provide even greater interest. The potentials of polyrhythms, multimeters, changing meters, changing tempi, and nonmetrical rhythms, in combinations with the potential for rhythmic variety within conventional rhythmic structure, make rhythmic structure a truly dynamic, integral, and essential part of all music.

Cognitive Bases of Rhythmic Behavior

Until recent years, efforts to understand the perceptual bases of rhythmic behavior have been more a matter of speculation and theory than research. Traditional psychology of music literature recognized three classes of theories intended to account for human interaction with musical rhythm: (a) instinctive, (b) physiological, and (c) motor. Lundin (1967, pp. 116–122) proposed a fourth theory, which emphasized the role of learning in the development of rhythmic behaviors. The instinctive theory, of which Seashore (1938) was a major proponent, held that "there are two fundamental factors in the perception of rhythm: an instinctive tendency to group impressions in hearing and a capacity for doing this

---

[3]The reader should keep in mind that Gordon's "duple" and "triple" meter are based on groupings of *subdivisions of beats;* conventional references to duple and triple meter are based on whether accented beats are grouped in twos or threes. More recently, Gordon has modified his terminology, and he now uses the terms *macrobeats* and *microbeats* respectively in place of *tempo beats* (Gordon's older term for conventional beats) and *meter beats.*

with precision and stress" (p. 138). This theory reflects the position that rhythmic potential is an inherited trait, not a learned one. A number of studies, however, provide data suggesting that training can improve rhythmic potential (or "capacity" as Seashore preferred), thus disconfirming the theory (e.g., Coffman, 1949, p. 74; Lundin, 1967, p. 114; Nielson, 1930, p. 78).

Physiological theories suggest that rhythmic responses depend upon recurring physiological processes. Belief that the human heart rate is a basis for musical rhythm and tempo has been most prevalent; Jaques-Dalcroze (1921, pp. 79–82) was an avid supporter of this view. However, evidence to support the heart rate theory is entirely lacking. Mursell (1937, p. 155) criticizes the heart rate notion on the basis that there is no psychological mechanism by which the heart beat gives us our sense of time. Lund (1939) reported no significant relationships between college students' preferred tempi for selected popular songs and the rate of any of their objectively measured physiological processes. Recent research on tempo perception, discussed below, also offers little or no support for physiological theories. While the "natural" rhythms of human physiology, including the menstrual cycle and cyclic changes in body temperature, wakefulness, and biochemistry, may influence a person's *receptivity* to musical stimuli, they are too lengthy, complex, and variable to explain rhythmic responses to relatively short-term musical stimuli.

The motor theory holds that rhythm depends on the action of the voluntary muscles. Schoen (1940, p. 21) notes that nearly all investigations concerning the nature of rhythmic experiences find a motor or musical factor, thus lending support to motor theory advocates. Mursell (1937, p. 162) and Lundin (1967, p. 106) both recognize the motor theory as the most plausible of the traditional theories, but neither accepts it without reservation. Mursell argues that neuromuscular movement does not function in isolation from the human brain; rather, music functions in conjunction with the brain and central nervous system which control voluntary movements. Lundin, although essentially an S–R psychologist, views rhythmic behavior as both a perceptual and behavioral response.

Lundin's (1967, pp. 106–113) account of rhythmic response recognizes the importance of learning, which involves both perception and motor response. Perception of rhythm requires observation of rhythmic stimuli and may or may not involve overt behaviors. It involves both perceptual *organization* of rhythmic stimuli and *discrimination* among stimuli, and Lundin contends that the ability to organize and discriminate among rhythmic stimuli is dependent on learning. Hebb's (1949, pp. 22–37) classic discussion of the role of experience in perception strongly supports Lundin's position. Lundin goes on to argue that overt motor rhythmic responses have a perceptual base and that overt motor rhythmic responses reflect the *clarity* of an individual's perceptions. Anyone who has taught music recognizes that student's rhythmic behaviors can be modified. To say that rhythmic behaviors can be explained independently of learning, therefore, is to ignore the evidence.

Recent years have seen a growing body of research related to rhythmic behavior's cognitive bases. Much of the research has focused on perception of various aspects of rhythm. Although most rhythmic behavior involves interaction with music as a more or less holistic, integral part of musical behavior, the present discussion examines the research and related writings as they pertain to (a) the role of movement in the perception of rhythm, (b) tempo perception, (c) meter perception, (d) perception of rhythm groups, and (e) expressive timing in music.

Movement and Perception

Tradition and music teachers' conventional wisdom tend to support the view that movement somehow interacts with and facilitates rhythmic perception and performance, but Behrens (1984) questions this "long-assumed relationship between rhythm and movement." Examination of certain general theories that address the issues of mental/motor interactions may be relevant to the discussion.

Piaget, who devoted a lifetime to epistemology, places much importance upon early sensorimotor learning as the basis of intellectual development.[4]

> In his scheme of things, a sensorimotor intelligence, not perception, provides the foundation for later intellectual development (and, . . . it is the matrix from which and in which perception itself originates and evolves). (Flavell, 1963, p. 472)

Hebb's (1958, p. 116) studies of early sensorimotor experiences of chimpanzees corroborate Piaget's view. Chimpanzees whose sensorimotor experiences were limited greatly during infancy were much slower at learning simple tasks than were other chimpanzees who had been allowed normal sensorimotor experiences during infancy.

Views that motor activity aids in thinking are not new. Indeed, the motor theory served as an impetus from which modern views concerning the effect of movement on thinking have evolved. The motor theory of thought originally was devised in order to avoid postulating ideation to explain thinking. Hebb (1958, p. 58) states:

> It proposed that, when a man is thinking, what is really going on is that he is talking to himself, or making movements with his hands and fingers that are too small to be seen. Each word or movement of the hand produces feedback

---

[4]Piaget's views regarding learning are examined in Chapter Ten.

stimulation that produces the next one, in a chain reaction; instead of ideation, therefore, what we have is a series of S–R reactions. The theory is no longer entertained as a complete explanation . . . but the conceptions which it developed concerning sensory feedback remain valid and important for the understanding of serial behavior.

Sensory feedback is usually of two kinds: exteroceptive and proprioceptive. Exteroceptive sensory cells are excited by events external to the body. Proprioceptive sensory cells are excited by body *movements,* and proprioceptive feedback is of particular relevance in understanding rhythmic behavior.

Proprioceptive feedback usually is equated with kinesthetic feedback. Feedback from movement is now called proprioception rather than kinesthesis, because the concept of kinesthesis generally is associated with introspection, whereas proprioception emphasizes receptor and sensory nerve action which can be determined neurophysiologically (Osgood, 1953, p. 29).

That proprioceptive pathways to the thalamus, cerebellum, and cortex exists is an established fact (Morgan, 1965, p. 258). There are three types of neural receptor cells for proprioceptive sensations: (a) "spray type" cells at different positions in the joints, (b) Golgi and organs, and (c) Pancenian corpuscles. These cells are actually in the joints rather than in the muscles.

Proprioceptive stimuli may travel to the cortex via either of two routes. The direct route is through the thalamus. The other, more diffuse and indirect, is through the reticular activating system. Morgan (1965, p. 41) reports that the various sensory inputs and outputs are not clearly separated in the reticular system.

Thus, neurophysiological findings support the contentions that sensory feedback from movement is related to higher mental processes. However, the precise role that proprioceptive impulses play in higher mediating processes is not known. It is, though, subject to much speculation.

Osgood (1953, p. 651) says, "it may be that motor tone merely serves as a facilitative agent for mental activity in general." Hebb (1958, p. 69) maintains that thinking cannot be accounted for by central processes alone or by muscular feedback alone: Both mechanisms are involved.

At least two theories of perception have movement as one of their bases. These theories primarily are concerned with visual perception, but the principles involved also apply to perceptions through other sensory media.

Hebb maintains that eye movements are essential to visual perception. He does not, however, insist that perceptual integration is wholly the result of such motor activity. Eye movements "contribute, constantly and essentially, to perceptual integration, even though they are not the whole origin of it" (Hebb, 1949, p. 37).

The sensory-tonic field theory of perception postulates that both proprioceptive and exteroceptive feedback are essential to perceptual integration (Allport, 1955, pp. 183–207). This theory holds that it can be shown experimentally that sensory, i.e., exteroceptive, and tonic, i.e., proprioceptive, factors are equivalent with respect to their contributions to the dynamic outcome.

Perhaps the following statement best summarizes the status of the motor versus mental controversy:

> Actually the interrelation of motor and mental activity is one of cyclic and reciprocal interdependence. However, the nature of the problem and current trends in thinking make it necessary at this time to emphasize, particularly the dependence of the mental upon motor activity. (Sperry, 1964, p. 429)

In the last decades of the nineteenth century and the early decades of the twentieth century, the perception of rhythm was investigated frequently. Introspective analysis was the accepted experimental technique of the times; thus, when evaluating the findings concerning the value of movement (or kinesthesis as it was called) as an aid in the perception of rhythm, this factor requires consideration.

Ruckmick (1913, pp. 305–359) attempted to answer "once and for all" the question concerning the role of kinesthesis in the perception of rhythm. In his much quoted study, he presented subjects with both auditory and visual rhythm patterns. The subjects were to give their impressions of the groupings verbally. His conclusions were that (a) the perception of rhythm may occur without accompanying kinesthesis, (b) individual differences exist in the amount of kinesthesis involved in the perception of rhythm, and (c) kinesthesis generally is connected most prominently with the initial clear perception of the type and form of rhythm. Much later, Ruckmick (1945, p. 8) explained that the last conclusion meant that "kinaesthesis [sic] was essential for the establishment of a rhythm pattern." It was only after a rhythm pattern had been established that kinesthesis ceased to be necessary for the perception of a rhythm.

From the review of Ruckmick's and other early studies concerning rhythmic perception, Boring (1942, p. 587) concluded that many perceptions are grouped by concomitant kinesthesis and many are not. "Kinesthesis is not a *sine qua non* of rhythm."

Moog's (1979) comparison of rhythmic discrimination of physically handicapped, mentally handicapped, and normal children supports the contention that movement facilitates perception. He notes that both children who had limitations of movement due to physical handicaps and children of lower intelligence scored significantly lower than normal children on an investigator-constructed measure of rhythmic discrimination. He concluded that children with limitations of movement since early childhood do not develop their perception skills to the same extent as normal children.

Thackray's (1968) investigation of rhythmic abilities sought to clarify the distinction between rhythmic perception and rhythmic performance and to investigate the extent to which the two are related. A factor analysis of the correlation coefficients among the seven rhythmic perception subtests revealed a fundamental factor in rhythmic perception: *The ability to perceive and memorize a rhythmic structure as a whole, and to analyze it consciously* (Thackray, 1968, p. 15). Thackray's rhythmic perception test battery essentially involved *discrimination tasks*, and the responses required were symbolic, i.e. verbal, rather than instrumental, i.e. movement. Thackray concluded that three essentials for rhythmic perception exist: (a) ability to count, (2) time discrimination, and (3) loudness discrimination.

Researchers' use of terminology has not always been consistent with Thackray's distinction between perceptual behaviors and performance behaviors, but there appears to consensus that movement and perception of rhythm are integrally related. Gabrielsson (1973, 1982a) and Fraisse (1982), apparently in an effort to avoid such a dichotomy, suggest that it might be more appropriate to speak of rhythmic *experience* rather than rhythmic perception. Fraisse states that "it is necessary not to dissociate motor *behaviors* linked to rhythms from . . . perceptions" and that "the play of music is always based on movements" (p. 175). He goes on to note that because of the motor component rhythmic perception is in effect "plurisensorial."

Tempo Perception

Beats and meter provide the underlying structure upon which rhythm patterns are superimposed. Perception of tempo, the rate at which beats recur in music, is important, because beats divide time into a series of reference points around which the listeners and performers organize their rhythmic responses and performances. Dowling and Harwood (1986, p. 186) maintain that beats serve as "cognitive frameworks" for perception of rhythm. If listeners and performers cannot perceive the rate at which the beats are recurring, their perceptions (and behaviors) related to rhythmic patterns may be impaired.

Fraisse (1982, p. 149) also argues that rhythmic perception depends on tempo, "because the organization of succession into perceptible patterns is largely determined by the [Gestalt psychology] law of proximity." If a tempo becomes too slow, the forms of both rhythm and melody become difficult for a listener to discern. When a performer is unable to feel (i.e. perceive) the tempo of a piece, the performed rhythmic patterns become disjointed from the overall temporal structure. In short, it appears that rhythmic response and performance are seriously deficient for individuals who are unable to perceive an underlying tempo.

Sink's (1984) analysis of the psychological dimensions underlying the auditory processing of monotonic and melodic rhythmic patterns supports the contention that tempo perception is basic to rhythmic processing. Her analysis of data from 38 university students' rhythmic dissimilarity judgments revealed that duration and tempo were the underlying dimensions of rhythmic processing.

Perhaps because of the increased cognizance of tempo's importance to the rhythmic experience of music, research on tempo perception has increased in recent years. Kuhn (1974) observed that professional musicians could identify decreases in the tempo of beats produced by a metronome more easily and more quickly than increases in tempo. Subsequent studies by Geringer and Madsen (1984) and Wang (1984), which examined tempo perception in a musical context, yielded results that were consistent with Kuhn's finding that tempo decreases were easier to perceive than tempo increases. A surprising sidelight of both of these studies was that no significant differences existed between the responses of music majors and nonmusic majors.

Wapnick (1980) examined the perception of tempo change in terms of subjects' *magnitude estimations* of tempo deviation from given standards. He observed that 48 undergraduate music students' responses were systematically affected by the standard/repetition speed ratio. He observed an apparent propensity to estimate repetitions as either twice or half as fast as the standard.

Duke (1987) asked college music majors to tap the perceived beat of periodic monotonic stimuli presented at various speeds ranging from 40 to 200 tones per minute. His results revealed that rates above 120 beats per minute were apparently "too fast" to be perceived as beat notes; rates slower than 60 beats per minute appeared "too slow" to be perceived as beat notes. In response to stimuli presented at faster than 120 or slower than 60, subjects tended to tap rates that were half or double the rates of the respective stimulus tones. Duke concluded that there is a relatively narrow tempo range within which trained musicians perceive periodic stimulus tones as beats.

Several studies have examined the effects of selected variables on tempo perception and preference. Kuhn (1977) observed that, contrary to conventional wisdom, dynamic level during performance had no effect on the tempo of 20 university students' performance of a well-known Beethoven melody. However, subjects did tend to perform both the second half of the melody and the second performance of it faster than the tempo established for the initial performance. Kuhn concluded that musicians tend to increase tempo during solo performance of easy-to-perform melodies.

Wang (1983) examined the effects of rhythm pattern, texture, beat location of tempo change, and direction of tempo change on the amount of time college students need to perceive tempo change. Besides the result noted above that tempo decrease is easier to perceive than tempo increase, she observed that significantly more time was needed to perceive tempo change for uneven rhythms than for even rhythms and for melody alone than for melody with accompaniment. Her data also suggest that differential rhythmic groupings may influence tempo perception.

Wang and Salzburg (1984) examined the influence of music training and age of 116 string students' ability to perceive tempo change. Subjects were asked to identify the direction of tempo change or whether there was no change. Data revealed a statistically significant curvilinear relationship between tempo perception and music training and between tempo perception and age. Subsequent regression analysis indicated that musical style, initial tempo, and direction of change also contributed significantly to tempo perception, leading the investigators to conclude that tempo perception is a complex phenomenon, for which not all parameters are yet identified.

Killian (1985) sought to determine college music majors' (a) tempo performance accuracy across repeated trials under differing feedback conditions, (b) tempo perception accuracy after performing and hearing a recording of the performance, and (c) the relationship between verbal perception and tempo performance. The three feedback conditions included performance results only, performance plus a prerecorded metronome standard before the next trial, and control. Data revealed no statistically significant effects of condition on tempo performance, but significant results were observed for subjects' perceptions of accuracy. Subjects receiving feedback improved accuracy of tempo perception. The relationship between performance and perception accuracy was analyzed by examining frequency of agreements between performance and perception, and overall there was a low percentage of agreement between performance and perception scores (32.5%).

More recently, a series of studies has examined various influences on the perception of beat note change in modulating tempos (e.g., Duke, 1989; Geringer, Duke, & Madsen, 1992; Geringer, Madsen, & Duke,

1993/1994). The basic question seems to be whether other musical aspects influence respondents' perception of tempo changes. Duke (1990) reports that tempo judgments of "nonmusicians and novice musicians are greatly influenced by the rhythmic content of the excerpts about which the judgments are made" (p. 9), noting that their tempo responses are influenced by the rhythm of the most prominent melodic rhythm. The level of rhythmic activity (density) apparently has a great influence on children's and nonmusicians' tempo discrimination.

Geringer, Madsen, and Duke's 1993/1994 study, which was essentially a replication and extension of their 1992 study, sought to determine when the beat note pulse of musical tempo became too fast or too slow to be felt as a musical beat. Data from 85 graduate and undergraduate music majors revealed that the direction of the change and the timbre of the stimulus examples were significant influences on the subjects indications of changes in beat note pulse. Tempo decreases were more readily identified than tempo increases. The data also supported earlier research in which it was observed that musicians tend to perceive beat tempos within the approximate range of 60 to 120 beats per minute (65 to 115 for this particular study).

Sheldon (1994) examined the effects of three variables (tempo, musical experience, and listening mode) on tempo modulation perception. Comparing the Continuous Response Digital Interface[5] responses of 80 music majors and 80 nonmusic majors, she observed that music majors were significantly better at identifying tempo changes than nonmusic majors and that overall subjects were better at detecting tempo acceleration than tempo deceleration. Also, subjects were less efficient in identifying tempo changes when watching a conductor while listening than when listening alone or listening and moving.

To summarize, tempo perception is basic to rhythmic processing. The perception of regular recurring beats provides a cognitive framework for rhythmic perception and performance. However, perceptual accuracy does not guarantee performance accuracy. Tempo perception and performance are complex phenomena and are influenced by, or at least related to, a number of stimulus and perceptual variables. Tempo per se of listening examples has an influence on respondents' ability to identify tempo changes. Decreasing tempos are easier to detect than increasing tempos. The rhythmic density of the prominent melody in a musical

---

[5]The Continuous Response Digital Interface (CRDI) is a device with which observers can indicate perceived changes in a stimulus property (such as tempo) as they observe the stimulus (such as ongoing music).

excerpt has a particularly strong influence on children's and nonmusicians' detection of tempo changes.

Trained musicians appear to have a propensity for perceiving periodic rhythmic stimuli in terms of a limited range of tempi. The work of Geringer, Duke, and Madsen documents the propensity to double or halve rates of periodic stimuli so that they fall within 60 to 120 beats per minute. This tendency to group beats to fall within a perceptually manageable range, however, may be as much a matter of meter perception as tempo perception.

Meter Perception

Musicians, educators, and psychologists generally agree that meter perception involves grouping beats, usually in relation to an accented beat. In traditional Western music, meter is periodic, and while some may argue that the measured grouping of beats provides a rigidity leading to a metronomic, unmusical performance and response, Benjamin (1984) makes an eloquent case for just the opposite view. He argues that metric structure, especially when considered at multiple levels, in larger units, and in greater depth, "is at times supple and, far from being anti-musical, at all times enriches the musical experience by giving the listener a measured grip on the time in which music's events happen." Gabrielsson (1988) notes that musicians alter beat relationships in the interest of musical style and expression. Metric relationships provide a framework for alterations.

As noted in the discussion of rhythmic structure, notation creates some problems relative to meter perception in that beats and meter indicated by notation may not conform to the beats and meter that listeners perceive or "feel." Creston (1964, p. 3) suggests that tempo is a primary variable in determining whether a perceived or felt grouping of beats conforms to a notated grouping, i.e., the grouping indicated by the meter structure. Some of the research discussed in the preceding section supports Creston's contention.

Jones (1985) notes that while various definitions and accounts of meter frequently fail to distinguish clearly between notation and perception of meter, perhaps a more important concern is in the contradications regarding how metric patterns are perceived or subjectively organized. To provide at least a partial resolution to some of the contradictions, he conducted a dialectic analysis of five theories or approaches to defining meter. Theories examined include what he termed a traditional music theory definition and those offered by Cooper and Meyer (1960), Yeston (1976), Gordon (1971; 1980), and Serafine (1975). The traditional music theory definition tends to focus on groupings of beats in terms of notated measures, and as discussed above, inherent differences frequently exist between what is notated and what is perceived.

Cooper and Meyer (1960) and Yeston (1976) both recognize that metric groupings may occur at more than one level. Cooper and Meyer emphasize "architectonic" levels of meter and suggest that meter usually is present at three levels. Their "primary level" of meter is the level on which beats are felt and counted. Subdivisions of the primary level are considered lower level meter; units of the primary level are combined to form higher level meter. Jones views their theory as an elaboration and extension of the traditional definition. He criticizes the theory for not considering tempo's influence on the selection of levels. Also, the theory appears to focus more on visual than on aural perception and analysis.

Yeston's theory recognizes that meter is periodic and depends on at least two rates of rhythmic motion that interact relative to each other. The fastest level, termed *foreground,* is grouped by the slower motion, termed the *background.* Any intermediary levels are called *middlegrounds.* Yeston's complex system of analysis allows melody and harmony to play a major role in determining which level of meter is considered dominant. Jones notes that this allowance for pitch relationships to influence how meter is determined is a unique contribution of Yeston's theory. However, the system is essentially an analytic tool and as such offers only limited insight into the aural perception of meter.

Gordon's theory, aspects of which were outlined under the discussion of rhythmic structure, places primary emphasis on subdivisions of the traditional beat. The subdivisions, which are called *meter beats (micro beats),* are the primary basis for his hierarchy of meter and rhythm. The hierarchy, which is theoretically rather than empirically-based, has two main categories, *usual* and *unusual;* classifications into the categories depend on various groupings of *tempo beats (macro beats)* and *meter beats.* The system has value for those who follow Gordon's particular instructional system and are willing to disregard traditional terminology and concepts of meter. Many musicians, however, are unwilling to think of duple and triple meter primarily in terms of subdivisions of the basic beat that is felt or perceived. Jones (1985) and Brink (1983) criticize the theory from several other perspectives: its theoretical rather than empirically basis, its failure to accommodate adequately higher levels of metric groupings, and some inconsistencies of the theory with musical practice.

Serafine (1975, p. 32) defines meter as essentially the equivalent of beat, apparently in an effort to avoid cultural bias as reflected in the proclivity of traditional Western music to be grouped in two's or three's. Jones (1985) argues that in such a theory has little value for conceptualizing metric music and maintains that equating pulse with meter adds unnecessary semantic confusion to the research literature.

Jones's synthesis of his theoretical analyses is that general agreement exists that "metric groupings occur at the level of the basic beat, as well as at levels of subdivision and multiples of that beat" (p. 54). He notes virtually unanimous agreement about the frequent inconsistency of meter signatures with meter and rhythm perception and performance. He suggests that the relationship between tempo and meter perception should be explored.

Madsen, Duke, and Geringer (1986) examined 100 musicians' note preferences for excerpts of eight relatively familiar orchestra works in which dotted notes, which ordinarily are subdivided into three, were presented at original tempi and at tempi either 12 percent faster or slower. Excerpts were purposely ambiguous with whether they "could be felt, perceived, or conducted in either a 'slower one' or a 'faster three'" (p. 103). Generally, when tempi were faster, subjects tended to select the dotted note as the unit of the beat, and when tempi were slower, they tended to select the subdivision of the dotted note as the unit of the beat, suggesting that tempo is a primary variable in determining the units of the beat and metric groupings.

Boyle's (1987) exploratory investigation of meter perception also supports the contention that tempo is a primary variable in musician's categorizations of melodies into different meters. Twenty college musicians were asked, without more specific instructions, to classify 20 unfamiliar melodies into metric grouping of two's, three's, or four's. Tempi for beat notes ranged from 70 to 200 beats per minute. Although the computer generated melodies were constructed with no accents, they were designed to reflect idiomatic rhythm patterns in duple and triple meter and included only duple and triplet subdivisions of the beat. Subjects clearly categorized meter into two's, three's and four's according to the intended beat note rather than in terms of duple or triplet subdivisions. Furthermore, at faster tempi, melodies designed to reflect 4/4 meter tended to be categorized in two's rather than four's.

Data from both the Madsen, Duke, and Geringer study and the Boyle study raise questions regarding the tempo at which musicians begin to group periodic stimuli at higher levels. While neither theory nor research has yet provided definitive answers to the perception question, it appears that tempo is a basic structural variable in determining the level at which periodic stimuli are grouped. At faster tempi, listeners tend to do more grouping, while at slower tempi, they tend to respond to smaller metric units. Apparently the same perceptual phenomenon that has been observed for tempo perception operates for meter perception.

Butler's (1992) observations about how musicians tap polyrhythmic patterns such as two-against-three, three-against-four, or two-against-five-against-seven, which in effect are akin to cross-meter patterns, reflect a similar phenomenon. He notes that when respondents were faced with more complex patterns they tended to tap along with the slowest stream. He observes that respondents "are facile at shifting from one rhythmic level to another, possibly seeking the simplest pattern into which the others will nest. This might be a sensible way of viewing the aural identification of meter" (Butler, p. 160).

Windsor (1993), following Clarke's (1987a) work, suggests that meter perception is categorical and that there is an interdependence of dynamic accents and perceived metric structure. Based on the results of three experiments in which he varied the accents to suggest patterns ranging from clear metric patterns to ambiguous patterns to clear metric patterns, Windsor's data suggest that "metre [sic] is indeed perceived categorically" (p. 137). He concludes that "dynamic accents and their metrical interpretation are truly interdependent, regularity in the former leading to a metrical interpretation that guides the pick-up of further accents" (p. 138). He maintains that the clear perception of meter "allows for and supports the perception of non-metrical accentuation as syncopation and expression" (p. 139).

Both theory and research suggest that listeners may perceive meter at different levels, and tempo appears to be a particularly important influence on the level at which it is perceived. Dynamic accents also greatly influence the perception of meter. Perhaps even more important variables, which have been little explored by psychologists, are those related to the perceiver's musical experience and training.

Rhythm Groups

While grouping periodic beats into meter and lower levels of meter into higher levels appears to depend primarily on tempo, grouping nonperiodic musical duration events into rhythm patterns appears to be a function of many other variables, some of which relate to the musical structure and others of which relate to the listener's experiences. As Davies (1978, p. 197) puts it, rhythm groups "are properties of people, as well as musical sounds." While the musical stimuli may be grouped objectively in a given way, they are never really grouped until perceived as such, because perceptual grouping is ultimately a psychological phenomenon.

Sloboda (1985, pp. 28–30) maintains that perceptions of durational pattern are *categorical;* i.e., experienced listeners tend to perceive aurally presented rhythm patterns (as well as pitch patterns, which are discussed in Chapter Six) into *categories* consistent with previously experienced rhythmic (and pitch) groupings. He draws an analogy to the manner in which people, apparently universally, organize basic speech sound classes called "phonemes" into perceptual categories. Although a given phoneme's sounds may vary slightly across multiple hearings, people perceive the hearings as the same and as functionally equivalent. As with all cases of categorical perception, a certain flexibility in stimulus boundaries allows placement of slightly different stimuli within identical categorical boundaries.

To support this view, Sloboda cites data indicating that accurate perception of slight deviation from musical rhythms is quite difficult and notes that performers are rarely able to *exactly* imitate another's performance (p. 30). He cites data provided by Sternberg, Knoll, and Zukofsky (1982) showing that highly trained professional musicians were unable to reproduce nonstandard divisions of a beat accurately, although they were very accurate in reproducing traditional subdivisions of a beat. He goes on to suggest that while training will enable musicians to discriminate subtle rhythmic differences, most people do not experience them as such; they perceive the rhythms in terms of previously experienced categories and most likely subconsciously experience the subtle rhythm differences as difference in the quality or style of performance.

In ensemble performance situations, asynchronization (i.e., lack of exactly simultaneous onset times for simultaneously sounding tones) is inevitable, yet listeners may experience very precise attacks. According to Rasch (1988), people may overlook differences in onset times of up to 80 msec, even though they can detect 20 msec differences when judging whether a click, tone, or noise comes first. Of course, differences in rise times and intensity differences among tones may be partly responsible, in addition to categorical perception.

Clarke's (1987a) study of categorical rhythm perception lends strong support to Sloboda's assertion that the perception of rhythm groups is categorical. In his study he presented 10 music students with short melodic sequences in which the durations of the penultimate and antepenultimate tones were systematically varied between equal duration values (1:1 ratio) and a 2:1 ratio in duration, with seven intervening values, none of which conformed to either the 1:1 or 2:1 ratios. The subjects were asked to indicate whether the various randomly ordered sequences belonged to the 2:1 ratio class or the 1:1 ratio class and to discriminate between replications of paired sequences. Data from both identification and discrimination tasks provided strong evidence that subjects perceived a real categorical distinction between the two rhythm types. Clarke suggests that "we perceive duration relationships between notes as belonging to two basic classes: *even* and *uneven* divisions of a metrical timespan . . . [and that] the position of the categorical boundary between the two classes is dependent upon the metrical context" (Clarke, 1987a, p. 30). Clarke argues that categorical perception functions to separate essential structural units or events from nonstructural information. He considers the former to be *invariants of a perceptual context* and the latter to include the *expressive* information. He maintains that "the separation of temporal information into a domain of structure and a domain of expression resolves the apparent paradox that small whole number duration ratios are the simplest to perceive and reproduce, but that real human performances do not conform to the integer proportions" (p. 31).

Lerdahl and Jackendoff (1983, p. 13) note the importance of rhythmic grouping by stating that once a listener "has construed a grouping structure for a piece, he has gone a long way toward 'making sense' of the piece." They go on to argue that grouping is the "most basic component of musical understanding."

Rhythm groups, just as metrical groups, are hierarchical in that listeners may subsume "surface structures" or patterns into larger and more abstract "deep" structures, based on combinations of durational structures, as well as melodic, harmonic, textural, and extramusical information. (There are some similarities between this line of reasoning and the seminal work of Chomsky (1957, 1965, 1968) regarding deep structures in language and Schenker's (1935/79) theoretical system for conceiving musical structures as outgrowths of an underlying musical core or *Urtext*.) Sloboda's (1985) text is both an introduction to and a detailed treatment of the cognitive organization of music on the basis of abstracted structures.

Many attempts to model hierarchical perceptual structuring of music exist; West, Howell, and Cross (1985) provide an excellent review. No model yet appears completely adequate either from a practical or theoretical standpoint. West, Howell, and Cross (pp. 45–48) make five general observations and offer three specific principles for developing models of perceived structure. Their observations and principles are reviewed here because they provide an overview of what such models are trying to accomplish and demonstrate their relevance to perception and cognitive organization of music.

Their first observation is that anything in the music that can be perceived should be able to influence perceptual groupings. Neither pitch nor rhythm alone determines grouping and hierarchical organization; different sorts of musical information may conflict and interact. Second, listeners bring prior experiences to the musical encounter. Whatever organizational components emerge for listeners must be in terms of scales, idioms, rhythms, and other aspects that have meaning for the listeners. Third, not all music immediately will be perceived, organized, and classified in a detailed, well-ordered hierarchy, even by sophisticated listeners. A composition's distinctive features may change with repeated listening. West, Howell, and Cross's fourth observation is that the organizational structure resulting from applying a model to a particular piece should be verifiable in terms of the behavior of particular listeners. Particular structural preferences should be predictable. Finally, extramusical or historical context may influence structural grouping, as when lyrics demand linguistically sensible phrasing or when instrumental characteristics restrict possible performance options.

Their first specific principle is that models must account for both vertical and horizontal structures, because music often involves a string of concurrent events across time. Good continuation, proximity, similarity, regularity, symmetry, and common fate, grouping principles encompassed by Gestalt psychology, could be a significant part of a model. Grouping is suggested at various sounds' locations, repetitions, and sequential movements. Lastly, groups formed from Gestalt principles may form larger groups at higher hierarchical levels. "Dominant" events within a larger group, such as accents, dynamics, or prominent pitches, may subsume other events and be "dominant" or be subsumed by other events in a higher-order group. A lengthy sequence of sounds may be just one grouping at the highest level, while more and more subgroupings exist at increasingly lower hierarchical levels.

One of the most elaborate models, inspired in part by psycholinguistics and grammar, is that of Lerdahl and Jackendoff (1983). They propose four hierarchical components (rather like conceptual skeletons) in the structure of a musical composition. Essentially, the components differ in their organizational bases. Two components, *metrical structure* and *grouping structure,* are concerned primarily with durational structure, whereas the other two components, *time-span reduction* and *prolongational reduction,* focus on pitch structures. Of relevance to the present discussion, *grouping structure* suggests that the continuous stream of musical events is segmented, from three- or four-event (note) motives into phrases and into larger sections. Certain "rules" of the Lerdahl and Jackendoff theory, *well-formedness rules,* which specify possible structures, and *preference rules,* which designate the probable structures that are likely to conform to the way experienced listeners organize the music, govern grouping structures. The preference rules specify principles that appear to govern the establishment of group boundaries and include (a) principles of proximity and change; (b) a principle of parallelism, which states that musical segments construed as parallel should hold equivalent in the grouping structure; and (c) a principle of symmetry, which suggests preferred subdivisions and groupings of segments into two parts of equal length. In essence, Lerdahl and Jackendoff's rules recognize that both nondurational aspects of musical structure, such as attack, articulation, dynamics, and registration, and more global considerations, such as symmetry and motivic, thematic, rhythmic, and harmonic parallelism, may influence grouping structure (Lerdahl and Jackendoff, pp. 43–55).

Barela (1979) recognizes three elements of a rhythmic group: upbeat or anacrusis, accent, and afterbeat. Lerdahl and Jackendoff prefer the term anacrusis over upbeat and define it broadly to include the "span from the beginning of a group to the strongest beat in a group" (p. 30). An accent, often termed a structural accent because it results from some nonmetrical event such as pitch, dynamics, or texture, reflects the focal point of a rhythm group to which the events of the anacrusis point. Following the accent are the afterbeats of the rhythm group, which Lerdahl and Jackendoff prefer to call the extension of the group.

Empirical testing of theories of rhythmic grouping such as that offered by Lerdahl and Jackendoff is virtually nonexistent, and if the recent interest in cognitive theories of musical processing are to gain and maintain credibility, they must be validated empirically. Although the bulk of the research on cognitive processing of music has been concerned with melodic rather than rhythmic processing, a limited amount of research concerning perception of rhythm groups has been conducted, and studies providing data relevant to some of the variables underlying rhythmic grouping are examined here.

Povel and Essen (1985) examined university psychology students' perception and reproduction of temporal patterns in a nonmusic context. They sought to validate a theory of cognitive processing in which it is assumed that listeners attempt to generate an "internal clock" to facilitate accurate perceptions of given patterns. They maintain that the selection of the internal clock is based primarily on the distribution of accents perceived in the pattern, although it also might be influenced by another concurrent pattern or by the preservation of a clock induced through previously presented patterns. The investigators maintained that when no internal clock was induced, a temporal pattern was poorly reproduced or judged as complex.

The temporal order in which sounds occur may be overridden in perceptual organization of rhythm patterns. *Auditory stream segregation,* in which auditory input is organized into two simultaneous patterns on the basis of common elements rather than strict temporal order, and rhythmic or melodic *fission,* in which alternating tones form two separate melodic rhythms, are interesting cases of rhythm perception which are not uncommon in music.

When Bregman and Campbell (1971) presented a short cycle of six tones (three high and three low) at a rapid rate, their subjects invariably divided the sequences into two streams on the basis of frequency. The patterns actually perceived were only those which related elements in the same subjective stream. The perceptual split depended on the frequency difference and presentation rate; faster presentation rates required less difference between high and low tones in order to induce the streaming effect.

Auditory stream segregation on the basis of frequency differences is more likely when the tones are short and discrete. Frequency glides between the tones and longer tones result in a continuity which makes the temporal order easier to follow and discourages stream splitting (Bregman & Dannenbring, 1973).

Rhythmic fission was illustrated by Dowling (1968), who presented tone sequences, at about ten tones per second, which were constructed so that frequency differences between *successive* tones was *large* while the difference between *alternate* tones was *small.* Melody was detected among alternating tones of the same intensity and frequency range, especially when observers were directed in their listening. The rhythmic fission was intensified by intensity differences or stereophonic separation between the patterns.

In a later study, Dowling (1973) showed that two familiar melodies formed by alternating successive tones ("interleaved" melodies) are easily identified as the result of melodic fission when the two melodies' frequency range do not overlap. When frequency ranges do overlap, the task is more difficult, although listeners can track a familiar melody if it is prespecified, i.e., they know the melody in advance. All melodies were altered to a rhythm of alternating quarter notes and quarter rests, and the combined tonal sequences ("interleaved" melodies) were presented at a rate of eight tones per second.

The organization of auditory streams is context dependent; e.g., widely separated frequencies may be in one stream if other stimulus elements are noises. Two organizational principles, one of element similarity and one of temporal proximity, may conflict. Basically, auditory streams appear to form in such a manner that elements within a stream are maximally similar (McNally & Handel, 1977).

Whether rhythm patterns are more easily perceived in isolation or in a total musical context has been subject to much speculation and a limited amount of research. Individuals vary in other claims regarding which presentation mode is easier, and research apparently is inconclusive.

Sink's (1983) summary of research on the effect of context yields no clearcut conclusion regarding the effects of context. Petzold (1966) reported no significant differences in children's ability to perform rhythm patterns presented in melodic or monotonic contexts, but Gabrielsson (1973) and Moog (1979) both reported data suggesting that melodic information interfered with the processing of rhythmic information. Boisen (1981), however, reported no statistically significant effects of melodic context on 2,207 seventh, ninth, and eleventh graders' perceptual judgments of rhythmic completeness or incompleteness, while Schellenberg and Moore (1985) reported that memory for rhythm patterns by 57 music majors and 57 nonmusic majors was significantly better when patterns were presented in a melodic context.

Obviously, data could vary for many reasons, but it appears that the matter of context is not a simple one. In an effort to examine the issue systematically, Sink (1983) studied the effects of rhythmic and melodic alterations on rhythm dissimilarity judgments of university music students. The melodic alterations included monotony, M-shaped melodies, and V-shaped melodies; nine rhythmic alterations were used. Her results indicated that both melodic and rhythmic alterations affect dissimilarity judgments.

To gain further information regarding rhythmic judgments, Sink (1984) investigated the psychological dimensions underlying the auditory processing of monotonic melodic-rhythmic patterns and the influences of selected musical experiences on the dimensionality of 38 university music students' rhythmic processing. Rhythm was recognized as a multidimensional structure within music's broader multidimensional structure. Dimensions identified as possible organizers of rhythmic information in music included tempo, meter, rhythmic patterning, and melodic patterning. Subjects' experiential variables examined included ensemble experience, listening habits, and musical preferences.

Sink's data suggest that tempo, duration and pitch characteristics, melodic and rhythmic phrase patterning, and monotony are organizers of rhythmic processing. Major performing instrument and classification of major performing instrument also significantly affect the dimensionality. Analysis of variance data revealed a slight affect of "generic style" music listening preference, music course experience, and hours of music listening. Sink concluded that "the importance of each organizer for subjects depended in part on the objective ordering of rhythmic and tonal information, and in part on past music experiences, particularly instrumental training" (p. 190).

An earlier multidimensional analysis of the dimensionality of rhythmic patterning by Gabrielsson (1973a) also revealed that tempo was a primary dimension in similarity and dissimilarity ratings. His analysis also suggested that density of patterns, which he labeled "rapidity," was another underlying dimension for the processing of melodic-rhythmic patterns.

Recent research by Duke (1994) further supports the importance of tempo in similarity and dissimilarity judgments. Using 240 third-, fourth-, and fifth-grade children and 80 undergraduate nonmusic majors as subjects, Duke asked subjects to make same/not the same judgments for two performances of the same pattern, each of which was presented at a different tempo. For some control items in which the tempo of the pairs was held constant, subjects could discriminate between patterns that were the same and patterns that were not the same. Data from comparisons for items with patterns presented at different tempi, however, revealed that both tempo and direction of tempo change affected the same/not the same comparison. The mean number of correct responses was significantly lower for the slowest tempo than for the items presented at faster tempi, and subjects were better able to identify "same" patterns when the second presentation of the pattern was faster than the first presentation.[6]

To summarize, the perception of rhythm groups in music is both categorical and hierarchical. Rhythm groups contain three basic components: an anacrusis, a structural accent, and its extension. Theory suggests that certain perceptual laws, including Gestalt laws, operate in rhythmic processing. Multidimensional analysis and other research suggest that the extent to which rhythm groups are perceived as groups is a function of both the musical structure (particularly tempo but also all of its interacting rhythmic, melodic, harmonic, dynamic, textural, and articulation events) and the listener's experience. Theories such as that of Lerdahl and Jackendoff attempt to encompass the effects of such structural and experiential variables, but systematic, empirical validation of such theories is lacking, perhaps because isolating the effects of the myriad of variables that underlie how a listener groups rhythm patterns is difficult and complex.

Expressive Timing

Musicians long have recognized that "musical," "expressive," or "artistic" performance involves more than just playing the right notes at the right time. Such performance, referred to simply as expressive performance in the present discussion, necessarily involves deviations from metronomically or mechanically regular rhythmic performance. The work of

---

[6]If people indeed are more sensitive to tempo decreases than to increases, a faster performance of an otherwise identical pattern should be more similar than a slower performance.

Bengtsson and Gabrielsson, using their RHYTHMSYVARD computer program, provides clear documentation that professional musicians systematically vary their performances from the mechanical norm (Bengtsson & Gabrielsson, 1980, 1982; Gabrielsson, 1973b, 1982a, 1985, 1988). Their data support the hypothesis that "performance of musical rhythm is characterized by certain systematic variations (SYVAR) relative to some kind of norm" (Gabrielsson, 1985, p. 70). Their work provides empirical evidence that musicians vary performances by (a) changing the time ratios between notated note values, (b) placing notes before or after the underlying metric beat, and (c) elongating phrase endings. They argue that such variations enable both performers and listeners to experience musical rhythm beyond the structural level; these variations from the mechanical norm contribute to the experience of the *motional* and *emotional* dimensions of rhythm. In short, these variations contribute to music's expressiveness.

Research on expressive timing may be grouped into three broad categories: (a) placement, duration, and ratios of tones within a structural framework, (b) the effect of structure on expressive timing, and (c) the shaping of a *ritardando* or *accelerando*. The classical work of Bengtsson and Gabrielsson with the accompaniment to the "Viennese" waltz, which is usually performed with a "short first beat" and "early and elongated second beat" is a clear example of research in the first category. Gabrielsson maintains that the "too early second beat" is not meant to upset the three-part division of the measure; rather, it is to "contribute to the unmistakable motion character of a Viennese waltz" (1985, p. 79). Research examining musicians' and nonmusicians' preferences for versions of the accompaniment to the Viennese waltz (i.e., with various note placements and durations on beats one and two) revealed that experienced musicians clearly preferred the version that approximated the note placements and durations of the traditional "Viennese" waltz accompaniment (Bengtsson & Gabrielsson, 1983). Apparently, musicians learn through experience the stylistically appropriate or correct deviations from the notated norm.

Bengtsson and Gabrielsson's work with systematic variations in the performance of the theme from Mozart's Piano Sonata in A major revealed several deviations from the notated time values. In performances of the theme, which is in 6/8 meter, the dotted-eighth/sixteenth/eighth notes were consistently performed with elongated first and third notes and a shortened second note, and quarter/eighth patterns were usually performed at about a 1.75:1 ratio rather than the 2:1 ratio indicated by the notation. Performance profiles for the Mozart theme also revealed considerable lengthening of tones in the fourth and eighth measures of the theme, suggesting that musical phrasing concerns clearly override metronomic regularity in expressive musical performance.

Traditional rhythm performance in jazz idioms deviates from notated values. Perhaps the most common deviation is the dotted-eighth/sixteenth pattern. The notation implies a 3:1 ratio between the notes, but in practice the norm appears to be about a 2:1 ratio. Rose (1989) examined other aspects of the timing of a jazz rhythm section and observed that beat duration changed with the musical context. He also observed that individual onsets across the section varied in time but occurred in a similar order: The drums were usually first, then the piano, and finally the bass. Systematic variation from the notated norm is clearly an accepted part of jazz performance style.

Clarke (1982) used a Bechstein piano equipped with photocells measuring hammer movement linked to a computer to analyze the performance of Eric Satie's *Vexations* by two graduate music students. The music consisted of three measures played repeatedly with some variation in order. Individual repetitions could be performed at different tempos, but with the restriction that a steady tempo be maintained within the repetition. Clarke examined the relationships between tempo and rhythm. He observed that structure and grouping were indicated by phrase lengthening and acceleration away from boundaries. At slower tempi, the music was grouped into smaller divisions, and the effect of phrase lengthening became more pronounced. Clarke concluded that rhythmic grouping is partly dependent on tempo.

In analysis of performances of another work by Satie, the *Gnossienne no. 5,* Clarke (1985) sought to create a model of how expression changes the underlying structure of beats. After examining the performance of various subdivisions of a beat, he concluded that expression can alter a performance by (a) expanding or contracting the interval between beats or (b) by altering the length of individual notes or groups of notes.

Repp's (1990) statistically detailed analyses of 19 famous pianists' performances of a Beethoven minuet revealed patterns which support Clarke's work. Although Repp's intent was to obtain data to support the hypothesis that there was a "Beethoven pulse," which involved a systematic alteration in the durations of three even quarter notes and several other subdivisions of the beat, Repp's data revealed no underlying "Beethoven pulse" in the performances of the 19 pianists. However, the most prominent rhythmic deviation he observed was phrase lengthening, particularly at moments of harmonic and melodic tension, which clearly exemplified expressive timing. His analyses agreed with Clarke's findings that slower performances tend to emphasize phrase boundaries while faster performances tend to focus more on other expressive deviations.

Phrase lengthening is perhaps the most accepted method for expressive timing in musical performance. In practice, performances by music teachers and recordings of professional musicians provide models of expressive *ritardandos, rubato,* and *accelerandos* for students to emulate. Whether all models are equally expressive is doubtful; experts might agree that some timing changes are more expressive than others, and this assumption has given rise to a limited body of research regarding the shape of expressive timing changes in music. Several models for ritards have evolved from this line of research.

Sundberg and Verrillo (1980) examined the final ritards in 24 recordings of harpsichord music and found that final ritards generally could be divided into two phases, an initial irregular phase and a second phase that reflected essentially a linear profile. Further analysis revealed several relationships: (a) the length of the ritard is proportional to the length of the cadence, (b) the length of phase two is related to the length of the final motive, (c) the rate of tempo decrease depends upon the pre-ritard average tempo and the length of phase two, and (d) the last tempo measure correlates to the pre-ritard mean tempo.

Feldman, Epstein, and Richards (1992) compared examples of tempo changes in five music excerpts, including music of Stravinsky, Tchaikovsky, and the barter chant of the Yanomami Indians of Venezuela. The excerpts were chosen for their unusual length of tempo change and for their natural musical execution. Each of the excerpts was fitted to three mathematical equations relating rate of tempo change to time within the excerpt: linear, quadratic, and cubic.[7] The results indicated that all of the tempo changes could be modeled by equations accounted for by either a linear or parabolic force, resulting in a quadratic or cubic ritardando or accelerando. This suggests that there is a measurable and definable paradigm for beautiful, natural sounding tempo changes.

Expressive timing as a dimension of expressive performance is receiving increasing interest from both researchers and performers. Space precludes an exhaustive examination of the growing body of research on the topic, but readers are encouraged to examine studies by Todd (1985, 1989, 1992) and Repp (1992a, 1992b) as well as other work by the authors cited here.

---

[7]In a linear (straight line) relationship, one variable consistently increases (or decreases) as another increases (or decreases). In a quadratic (inverted U) relationship, one variable increases for a while and then decreases as another increases. In a cubic relationship, rather like sawteeth when graphed, one variable alternately increases and decreases systematically while another variable decreases.

Development of Rhythmic Behaviors

Rhythmic behaviors include a broad spectrum of behaviors, ranging from simply tapping the toe in time with the beat to sightreading intricate rhythms to the subtleties of expressive timing. The development of rhythmic behaviors has been the subject of much speculation, research, and trial and error. This section examines research finding and music teachers' views regarding the development of rhythmic behaviors. In addition, it reviews approaches to measuring rhythmic behaviors.

Research on the development of rhythmic behaviors basically is developmental or experiential. Developmental research can be either longitudinal or cross-sectional. Longitudinal studies investigate one group's rhythmic abilities (or whatever trait one wishes to study) over an extended period of time, whereas cross-sectional studies compare a trait in different groups at various age or developmental levels. Although longitudinal studies usually are the preferred methodology, nearly all studies of the development of rhythmic behavior are cross-sectional. Few involve the study of a given group for more than one year.

Developmental Research

Although there are some exceptions, nearly all developmental research regarding rhythmic behaviors examines one of the following two behaviors: (a) the ability to keep time with the beat of music and (b) the ability to repeat or perform a given rhythm pattern. The variables in the different studies are numerous, thus making it difficult to understand clearly the status of rhythmic behaviors at different age or developmental levels. Some studies also examine rhythmic behaviors in conjunction with behaviors related to pitch organization.

Studies of infants' rhythmic development, however, necessarily involve a research strategy different from the types just mentioned. The investigator must observe the infants' rhythmic behaviors, either freely emitted or in response to rhythmic stimuli.

Several studies (Allen, Walker, Symends, & Marcell, 1977; Chang & Trehub, 1977; Demany, McKenzie, & Vurpillot, 1977) indicate that infants respond to differences in rhythm patterns. Infants apparently tend to habituate to a recurring pattern, but when a change occurs, they respond. One study used eye movement as a measure of response to change; the other two used heart rate as a measure of change.

Moog (1976, pp. 39–40) observed that infants begin responding to music with overt movements between the ages of four and six months. He notes that the infants do not move in disorganized clumsy ways; rather, they use clear repetitive movements, related to the rhythmic aspects of the musical stimulus. As the child develops, the movements increasingly are coordinated with both the musical rhythm and dynamics. The movements of the four- to six-month-old infant often involve whole-body movements, but as the child develops the overt rhythmic responses also change, particularly to include more movements with individual body parts. Moog reports that by the age of eighteen months about 10 percent of children are able, for short stretches of time, to match their movements to the music's rhythm.

Sloboda (1985, p. 200), however, questions whether infants during the first year of life are actually able to demonstrate overt rhythmic behaviors. He particularly questions some of Moog's results and suggests that much of the alleged rhythmic behavior reflects a high degree of inference on the part of the adult observer. Before he would accept infant movements as "rhythmic behaviors" he would expect them to clearly reflect one or more of the following: (a) moving or beating in time to music, (b) imitating a given rhythm pattern, (c) subdividing a beat, or (d) omitting a beat and then resuming it in correct time after a pause (pp. 200–201).

Studies of rhythmic behavior in early childhood, childhood, and into adolescence show a general refinement in rhythmic skills with increasing age. Jersild and Bienstock (1935) examined two- to five-year-old children's ability to beat time to music. Seventy-four children's responses were analyzed, and a large increase in scores was evident between two- and five-year-olds. Of 400 possible beats (administered in smaller segments), the number of correct beats for the two-year-old was 84.5, three-year-olds, 109.4, four-year-olds, 159.9, and five-year-olds 192.8.

Rosenbusch and Gardner (1968, pp. 1271–1276) studied five- to thirteen-year-olds' abilities to reproduce four different rhythm patterns. Responses were compared for four age groups: five to seven, seven to nine, nine to eleven, and eleven to thirteen. Results showed a significant decrease in errors with increase in age.

Gardner (1971, pp. 335–360) studied first, third, and sixth graders' abilities to reproduce given rhythmic patterns. Each child was asked to duplicate twenty rhythm patterns, each of which included from four to eight taps. The mean numbers of correctly tapped patterns for the three groups were 7.35, 13.00, and 16.00, respectively. These differences were statistically significant at the .01 level.

Petzold (1966, pp. 184–251) asked elementary school children to reproduce common rhythm patterns found most frequently in seven elementary basal music series published between 1953 and 1959. Patterns were about two measures long and in three common meters: 2/4, 3/4, and 6/8. Petzold also asked children to respond to a "Periodic Beat Test," which involved a series of beats at four different tempi. Each beat was presented twice and arranged so that the respondent moved from a fast tempo through three successively slower tempi; the order was reversed for the second part of the test. Usable data were obtained for 331 children on the "Rhythmic Patterns Test" and for 241 on the "Periodic Beat Test." Petzold summarized his results with respect to differences in grade level responses:

> The ability to respond accurately to the aural presentation of rhythmic patterns does not change substantially after the child has attained third grade. The same plateau is reached by third grade when children are expected to maintain a steady tempo that is provided by a metronome.

Taylor's (1973, pp. 44–49) study of the musical development of children aged seven to eleven also revealed increases in rhythmic responsiveness for the younger children. He reports statistically significant differences between the mean rhythm scores of the younger groups but no significant difference between the means of his two oldest age groups.

An examination of norms for children on some standardized rhythm aptitude tests provides another perspective on the development of rhythmic behavior with age. Bentley (1966b, p. 116) reports a "fairly steady increase from year to year" on the rhythm memory portion of his *Measures of Musical Abilities* (1966a). The normative data for some 2,000 boys and girls aged seven through fourteen support his statement. There is a mean yearly increase from 3.9 for seven-year-olds to 8.8 for fourteen-year-olds. Normative data for the *Seashore Measures of Musical Talents* (1939, 1960) and Gordon's *Musical Aptitude Profile* (1965) also reflect increases in score with age level, even though both tests purport to measure factors that are little influenced by training.

A series of studies by Pflederer and Sechrest (1968, pp. 19–36) testing Piaget's theories of conservation[8] tend to support the position that rhythmic behaviors (meter and rhythm) are a function of development. Foley (1975), however, reports data suggesting that conservation can be expedited through training.

Bamberger (1982), who was primarily concerned with how children conceptualized a rhythm pattern, asked children ranging from four to ten years of age to draw a picture of a familiar nursery rhyme so that they could remember it or another child could clap it. The youngest children (four and five) tried to duplicate the clapping motion, resulting in swirling scribbles. The six- and seven-year-olds tended to draw figural representations of individualized claps, whereas the oldest children tended

---

[8]Conservation refers to the invariance of a particular dimension of empirical objects even though change occurs in other dimensions. Piaget partially views concept development in terms of conservation, which is nothing more than the stabilizing of a particular concept in the child's thinking (Zimmerman, 1971, pp. 16–17). More material on conservation appears in Chapter Ten.

to group the claps in metric fashion. The effects of learning were apparent in the oldest children's responses, but an important finding was how the young children tended to make the drawings as near like the clapping behavior as possible; they were not able to deal with the patterns as abstractions.

Grieshaber's (1987) critical review of research on children's rhythmic tapping also supports the view that rhythmic behaviors improve with age, but she notes many methodological problems in the research and observes that there are inherent problems in using clapping tasks as measures of rhythmic behavior for young children, who often lack the coordination to perform anything beyond the simplest tapping task.

In studying the development of rhythmic behaviors, it is apparent that developmental research does not provide clear-cut answers. The issues are confounded by variables in research design and the type of rhythmic behaviors studied, not to mention the validity and reliability of the various measures of rhythmic behavior. At best, we may conclude that rhythmic behaviors generally increase with age, although there tends to level in older children. To accept unquestioningly, however, that increases in rhythmic abilities are solely a function of age or developmental level is to disregard both the body of research concerning the development of rhythmic behaviors through experimental learning experiences and the empirical knowledge of music teachers who "know" that instruction can improve rhythmic behaviors. The next section examines the research literature regarding the development of rhythmic behaviors through learning experiences.

Experimental Research

Most of the research discussed herein is "experimental" because it seeks to examine the effects of some learning experience on the development of rhythmic behaviors. Much of it, however, lacks the rigorous control of the variables that would enable it to meet standards for research design in the behavioral sciences as delineated by Campbell and Stanley (1963), so interpretations must be made with caution.

The scope and variety of experimental research regarding the development of rhythmic behaviors also make it difficult to reach definitive conclusions. While some studies are concerned with behaviors reflecting discriminating among rhythmic stimuli, many others involve complex motor behaviors. Some investigators study the development of rhythmic behaviors in young children whereas others are concerned with older children, adolescents, or adults.

Jersild and Bienstock (1935) studied the effects of practice on young children's ability to keep time with music. Fourteen subjects, ranging in age from twenty-five to forty-four months, participated in a training program distributed over a ten-week period. The training program used a variety of means to direct their attention to the act of keeping time; these included bodily movements, vocalizations, and hand clapping. Although the fourteen children receiving practice obtained a mean score higher than a matched control group, the difference was not statistically significant. Neither were their posttest scores significantly higher than their pretest scores.

Coffman (1949), however, in a study of the effects of training on junior high and college students' scores on the Seashore rhythm discrimination test, found that trained subjects made statistically significant gains in rhythm discrimination scores while control group subjects did not. The training program involved a variety of rhythmic activities, including eurhythmics.

Dittemore (1970) examined the effects of a one-week rote teaching program of chanting and clapping melodic rhythm patterns on first through sixth graders' ability to chant melodic rhythm patterns. For two of the four criterion exercises, there were no significant differences among the six grade levels; for the two exercise involving more complex pattern, however, statistically significant differences were observed. Because of the study's nature, it is difficult to draw definitive conclusions regarding either the effects of the training or abilities at the different grade levels.

DeYarmin (1972) compared the effects of training in singing songs in usual, mixed, and unusual meters with the effects of training in singing songs only in usual meter on kindergarten and first-grade children's ability to chant melodic rhythm patterns. As in the Dittemore study, children were taught the songs by rote, and chanting and clapping were part of the learning activities. Five minutes of five successive music classes were used for instruction for each song; a sixth music period was used for recording each child's chanting of the song's melodic rhythm. Results showed no significant differences in the scores of children receiving instruction with songs in usual, mixed, and unusual meters. DeYarmin concluded that music programs for young children should include more songs in mixed and unusual meters.

Zimmerman's (1971) recognition that Piaget's developmental sequence applies to the development of musical behaviors has led to some research testing the hypothesis that conservation is a function of developmental level and cannot be influenced by training. Research by Foley (1975) and Perney (1976) suggests that training may facilitate conservation in certain musical tasks.

Foley's study dealt with improving conservation of (a) tonal patterns under the deformation of rhythm patterns and (b) rhythm patterns under the deformation of tonal patterns. Subjects included six intact second-grade classes, with three classes randomly designated as experimental and the others as control. The experimental training used varied musical activities to foster the development of conservation. The experimental group made a statistically significant increase in their scores on the test for conservation of tonal and rhythm patterns; the increase was significantly greater than that of the control group. The investigator concluded that improvements in the conservation of tonal and rhythm patterns can be accelerated through training. Further, the training program was believed to have much practical significance in that expenses, equipment needs, and training required of teachers were quite minimal.

Perney (1976) examined the relation of musical training, verbal ability, and the combination of sex and grade on second and third graders' development of conservation of metric time. Results indicated no difference in performances of children who played musical instruments and those who did not. The mean performance of the second graders was higher, though not significantly higher, than that of the third graders. The most important finding, however, was that the second graders had greater verbal ability than the third graders, and there was a statistically significant correlation between children's verbal ability and their ability to perform the musical tasks. Perney concluded that performance of the musical tasks is not determined by age alone; rather, it is related more closely to verbal ability.

Although more research clearly is necessary before one can draw definite conclusions regarding whether rhythmic development is a function of age or development or whether it can be fostered through training, there is sufficient reason to question the hypothesis that rhythmic development is solely a function of age.

Reading rhythms also is an important rhythmic behavior, and the balance of the research discussed in this section focuses on ways of developing such behaviors.

Palmer (1976) compared the approaches to rhythm advocated by Richards (1967) and Gordon (1971). Subjects were 136 fourth-grade children, forty-eight in the two Richards experimental classes, fifty in the two Gordon experimental classes, and thirty-eight in two control group classes. In addition to an investigator-constructed measure of rhythmic performance achievement, written achievement was measured via the rhythm portions of three standardized music achievement tests. Result showed a statistically significant difference between the control and aggregated experimental classes in terms of rhythm reading achievement. However, no clear-cut differences were found between the achievement of the classes using the Richards approach and the classes using the Gordon approach.

Skornicka (1958) compared two approaches to teaching instrumental music reading to beginners. The experimental approach emphasized time and rhythm by requiring playing quarter notes at the beginning of training (rather than the traditional whole notes), tapping the foot to mark the beat, and counting time mentally. The control group used conventional band method books and no bodily movements. At the conclusion of the study, the experimental group achieved significantly higher sight-reading scores on the *Watkins-Farnum Performance Scale* than did the control group.

In a study designed to examine the effects of bodily movement, notably foot tapping the beat and clapping the melodic rhythm, on junior high school band musicians' ability to sight read rhythms both in isolation and in context with other aspects of notation, Boyle (1968) observed that subjects using movement made significantly ($p < .01$) greater increases in both rhythm reading scores and music reading scores than did subjects who did not employ movement while reading rhythms. Results were based on individual performance tests given to 191 subjects representing a proportional random sample of the students in twenty-four junior high training bands. The *Watkins-Farnum Performance Scale* was the measure of music reading ability and the rhythm patterns of it, notated on a single pitch, served as the measure of rhythm reading ability. A high degree of relationship ($r = .81$) was found between the subjects' score on the two measures.

Elliott's (1982) multiple regression analysis of factors influencing university music students' instrumental sightreading supports the contention that rhythm reading is an important component of general music reading. Of seven predictor variables examined (technical proficiency, rhythm reading ability, sight-reading ability, cumulative grade-point average, grade-point average, and major instrument grade-point average), Elliot concluded that "rhythm-reading ability is the single best predictor of instrumentalists' sight-reading scores" (p. 13).

Researchers also have employed principles of programmed instruction as the experimental variable in teaching rhythm reading. An important aspect of this approach is providing the subjects with feedback regarding their performance. Ihrke (1969), the first to report research of this nature, developed a rhythm monitor which accepted tape recorded impulses and triggered an (error) light unless responses were properly timed. He compared the performance of university students in a course called "Music for the Classroom Teacher" who used the monitor with the performance of students who did not use it. Students using the rhythm monitor made significantly greater gains ($p < .001$) in their scores on a rhythm reading test than did students not using the system.

Shrader (1970) also developed a program for teaching rhythm reading. He utilized a stereotape teaching machine, with one channel activating a counter which indicated the number of correct responses made on a given exercise. He administered ten forty-five minute lessons to thirty-four high school students. Results showed that students using the teaching machine made significantly greater gains in rhythmic reading scores than did a control group. Shrader's teaching machine is now available commercially (TAP MASTER RHYTHMIC SIGHT READING SYSTEM) and has received acceptance as an important teaching tool.

The studies cited above represent the diverse experimental research related to teaching and learning rhythmic concepts and behaviors. As should be apparent, they reflect diverse purposes, hypotheses, samples, independent and dependent variables, and some contradictory results. As Sink (1983) contends, teaching and learning rhythmic concepts and behaviors are complex and controversial tasks. Clearly, a need exists for well-defined, systematic research on teaching and learning rhythmic concepts and behaviors. The following examination of teaching practices for rhythmic development further reflects the diversity of opinion and approach.

Teaching Practices for Rhythmic Development

Practitioners' views regarding ways to develop rhythmic behaviors are generally the result of trial and error techniques; "successful" approaches pass from teacher to student, and many now have become tradition. Most appear to work for their proponents, although, as Horner (1965, pp. 140–141) has noted and as the above review also suggests, experimental evidence to provide a basis for comparison of the various methods is rare. They are summarized here to provide the reader with an overview of teaching practices.

Jackson (1963) summarizes devices and technique commonly used in rhythm training. They are (a) counting aloud, (b) tapping the underlying beat, (c) the metronome, (d) tapping or clapping the phrase rhythm, (e) use of words, (f) ensemble experience, (g) conducting.

The advantage of counting aloud is that it clearly outlines the beat. Its danger, she contends, is that it emphasizes the beat's mathematical rather than rhythmic aspects. Tapping the underlying beat has two advantages over counting: (a) it involves more extensive muscular action and (b) it does not emphasize arithmetic.

The metronome is valuable for setting the tempo and preventing tempo vacillation. Because it is an entirely external criterion, its usefulness is limited. Obviously, the use of such a device while reading music with varying tempi is impractical.

Tapping or clapping the phrase rhythm and the use of words as a system or mnemonics are both helpful techniques in the learning of phrase rhythms. Conducting aids in making students aware of the underlying beat. Kelly (1993) found that beginning band students who received ten weeks of instruction in basic conducting techniques as part of their regular band classes made significantly greater improvements in reading rhythms than did students in control bands who rehearsed more but received no conducting instruction.

Ensemble experience is one method of making students conform to the underlying beat. However, Revelli (1955) maintains that ensemble experience has been a staff for students to lean upon, and that their ability to read suffers from the lack of systematic procedures for analyzing the various rhythm patterns.

Muscular movement is basic to most of the rhythm teaching devices mentioned above. That rhythm is best approached through bodily movement indeed has become the byword of elementary school music programs. Few references to elementary school music fail to support this view.

Jaques-Dalcroze (1921) was one of the first to explore the possibilities of bodily movement as an aid in developing a sense of rhythm. In his system, generally referred to as Dalcroze Eurhythmics, students learn specific movements for different rhythm patterns. After learning the movements, the students "realize," i.e., express by body movements, the rhythms of the music. Much stress is placed upon the ability to improvise rhythmic movements to music.

An especially pertinent aspect of the Jaques-Dalcroze (1915, p. 33) method is the use of separate limbs of the body to mark the underlying beat and the phrase rhythms. Coordinated movements to music constitute the essence of the system.

The use of rhythm syllables also has received much emphasis in recent years, perhaps because of the emphasis on the application of the various adaptations of the Kodaly approach (Bachman, 1969; Lewis, 1972; Richards, 1967). Each of these approaches makes extensive use of rhythm syllables in developing elementary aged children's rhythm reading skills.

Gordon (1971, pp. 72–75) also is an advocate of rhythm syllables in developing rhythm readiness as a prerequisite to rhythm reading, but he also recognizes that the development of rhythmic understanding has its basis in the feeling of rhythm patterns through movement.

In his final publication regarding teaching rhythm, Mursell (1956, pp.

265–278) summarized three essential approaches to the development of rhythmic behaviors. He believed the first and most essential approach to rhythm is by the way of bodily movement. Secondly, he believed that the rhythm instruments are extremely valuable tools. Their value is that they tend to sharpen rhythmic behaviors by requiring more precise, more definite, and more discriminating responses. Finally, he believed that the study of rhythm symbols allows children a new, deeper, more generalized understanding of rhythmic experience. His recommendations should not be taken lightly.

Hood's (1970) publication on the teaching of rhythm essentially reflects the types of activities advocated by Mursell. Moving to music, study of rhythm notation, and the use of rhythm instruments are used as approaches for teaching rhythm.

Teachers of instrumental music tend to focus on teaching rhythm reading. Magnell's (1968) summary of systems for reading rhythm at sight essentially parallels Jackson's. He does, however, elaborate on some approaches. He views foot tapping as basic to counting, chanting, clapping, and conducting. He also advocates the "down-up" principle as a mean for organizing rhythm patterns in relation to the beat. Another principle he notes is that of the "time unit." The eighth note is usually the time unit maintained throughout the piece being counted. The student must mark the beat with hand movements (it could be with the foot) and count the number of time units in each note. Many other teachers also advocate the use of foot tapping, e.g., Hoffer (1973, p. 377), Kohut (1973, pp. 19–23), and Pizer (1969).

In summary, commonalities exist among the approaches to rhythmic development advocated by practitioners. Most teachers advocate more than one approach. The relative merits of the respective approaches, however, have not all been verified under controlled conditions. Perhaps the most important issue is, as Palmer (1976) notes, that teachers at least employ some systematic approach to rhythmic development rather than leaving it to incidental learning as part of the total curriculum.

Evaluation of Rhythmic Behaviors

Evaluation of rhythmic behaviors generally involves one of three types of behavior: (a) behaviors reflecting discriminations between aurally presented stimuli, (b) movement behaviors demonstrating an ability to keep time with the beat or to reproduce an aurally presented rhythm pattern, and (c) behaviors reflecting an ability to discriminate between or associate visual rhythm symbols with aurally presented rhythm patterns.

The last category includes all music reading behaviors, although one patterns constitutes a fourth type of behavior. In addition, several rhythm tests require behaviors which at best relate only peripherally to the three basic types of behaviors. This discussion, however, will be limited primaily to the rhythm tests employing aspects of the three basic types of behaviors.

Several issues are involved in the evaluation of rhythmic behaviors. One noted previously in this chapter was whether *reproduction* of patterns or steady beats is a legitimate indication of rhythmic perception. Research has provided no clear-cut answers regarding the question, although it probably is prudent for teachers to recognize that failure to reproduce or perform a pattern does not necessarily indicate failure to perceive the pattern. Researchers and test designers usually select the response mode on some philosophical basis or else they follow precedents in test design.

In selecting or developing a test of rhythm perception or ability, the primary concern is to select a response modality which best demonstrates what one is concerned with measuring. Pilot testing always should be done to ascertain the test's validity and reliability, as well as its appropriateness for the group being tested. If the concern is for measuring discrimination, the response mode should not require movements that may introduce problems for some respondents. If the concern is for aural-visual discrimination, musical performance should not be involved, but if the concern is for reading music, performance most likely should be involved.

Andrews and Deihl (1967) found that several response modes might be necessary for gaining a clear understanding of children's musical abilities. Their *Battery of Musical Concept Measures,* which unfortunately is not generally available, employed two written group measures (verbal and listening) and two nonwritten individual measures (manipulative and overt).

Rainbow (1981) notes an issue in the evaluation of preschool children's rhythmic abilities. Traditionally, investigators have made inferences regarding young children's rhythmic perceptions on the basis of their movements, e.g., tapping, clapping, or marching. Rainbow's data, however, suggest that vocal chanting is a much better response mode than movement tasks because three- and four-year-old children in his three-year longitudinal study had much more difficulty reproducing patterns through movement than through vocal chanting. Schleuter and Schleuter (1985) made similar observations for kindergarten and first-grade children's rhythmic responses. Grieshaber's (1987) review of the literature on children's rhythmic tapping yielded the same conclusion.

The question of group versus individual measurement is of practical significance to both researchers and music teachers. While individual testing may be desirable, it is often prohibitive in terms of time and cost. Group measures often must serve as a compromise, although certain performance situations necessarily cannot be so assessed.

The issue of whether to evaluate rhythmic behaviors in isolation from a total music context has concerned music psychologists since testing became an interest. Seashore's (1938) view, reflecting what has been termed the "theory of specifics" approach, was that given traits or abilities should be isolated for evaluation under highly controlled conditions. Mursell's (1937) view, termed the "omnibus" approach, reflected the view that musical behavior should be evaluated as a totality rather than breaking it into subparts. Most contemporary approaches to evaluating rhythmic behaviors attempt to incorporate at least some rhythmic behavior in a total music context, although many measures also include some breakdown of rhythmic behaviors. Older tests usually reflect one or more approaches, depending on the purpose for which the evaluation is made. The purpose of the evaluation and the nature of the data sought should determine the nature of the chosen evaluation approach.

Several particularly interesting approaches to evaluating rhythmic behaviors have come about as a result of technological developments, including computer analysis of performance, e.g., Shrader (1970), Petzold (1966), Ihrke (1969), Thackray (1968), Bengtsson and Gabrielsson (1980, 1983). Such technological advances have greatly facilitated precision in analysis of rhythmic behaviors, but, as Grieshaber (1987) has noted, such developments pose their own types of problems. Most computer or other electronic analysis programs do not have the flexibility to allow for variability in performance.

Following is a brief overview of the approaches to assessing rhythmic behaviors in published standardized tests. Many tests are designed for children above the age of eight, adolescents, and adults, although two tests are designed primarily for young children.

Test Four of Bentley's (1966a) *Measures of Musical Abilities* is a ten-item rhythm test that requires subjects to indicate on which of four beats a second rhythm pattern differs from the first. The rhythm test is an aural discrimination task and is designed for children aged seven to eleven. Although normative data are available for the rhythm test, reliability and validity data are available only for the four tests as a whole.

The *Seashore Measures of Musical Talents*[9] (Seashore, Lewis, & Saetveit, 1939, 1960) include two tests related to rhythm, both of which are aural

---

[9]As of this writing (1995) the Seashore battery is out of print, despite its long history of use. The battery nevertheless is described here because it exemplifies a particular approach.

discrimination tasks. The "rhythm test" presents two tapped rhythm patterns and asks the respondent to indicate whether they are the *same* or *different;* the other, called the "time test," presents two tones and asks the respondent to indicate whether the second is of *longer* or *shorter* duration than the first. Although Mursell and other proponents of the omnibus theory question whether these are valid measures of "musical" talent, there seems little question that they are valid measures of the two particular discrimination tasks. Their reliability coefficients range from .63 to .72.

The "rhythm test" of the *Drake Musical Aptitude Tests* (Drake, 1957), which is really a measure of the ability to silently maintain a given tempo, has two nonequivalent forms. Reliabilities range from .83 to .95 for form A and .69 to .96 for form B. Validity coefficients, based on comparisons with teachers' ratings of rhythm aptitude, range from .31 to .85.

Gordon's (1965) *Musical Aptitude Profile* include a "rhythm imagery" test as one of its three basic parts. This test has two subtests, each of which requires respondents to discriminate between two hearings of a musical example performed on a violin. The tempo test requires indicating whether the ending of a second presentation of a melody has the same tempo as the ending of the first or whether it was changed. The meter test asks whether a second statement of a melody is like the first or whether it differs from it with respect to *accents* which determine the meter. Split-halves reliabilities for the subtests range from .66 to .85; for the "rhythm imagery" portion as a whole they range from .82 to .91. Validity coefficients, based on teachers' estimates of musical talent, range from .64 to .74.

Gordon developed two additional music aptitude tests for use with children: The *Primary Measures of Music Audition* (1979) and the *Intermediate Measures of Music Audition* (1982). The primary measures are for children in kindergarten through grade three and the intermediate measures are for children in grade one through four. Each test has a tonal and a rhythm portion, and the tasks are essentially the same on both portions of the tests. On the rhythm portion, the child must indicate whether the second of two short rhythm patterns is the same as or different from the first pattern. The reliability coefficients are satisfactory for both measures, ranging from .60 to .92 for the various grade levels.

The *Iowa Tests of Musical Literacy* (Gordon, 1991) include two divisions, "Tonal Concepts" and "Rhythmic Concepts." Each division has three subtests, (a) "Audiation/Listening," (b) "Audiation/Reading," and (c) "Audiation/Writing." The subtests of the Rhythmic Concepts division require the following types of responses:

Audiation/Listening: differentiation between rhythmic patterns in which beats essentially are subdivided into duplets and triplets.

Audiation/Reading: determining whether given aural patterns match given notated patterns.

Audiation/Writing: filling in noteheads, flags, and rests to make a notated pattern match an aurally presented pattern. Reliability coefficients for the subtests generally range from about .70 to .80. The author maintains that the test has rational and content validity. Concurrent validity coefficients, based on comparisons with sight singing and dictation scores, range from .44 to .52 for the Rhythmic Concepts division. The tests have six levels and provide normative data for grades four through twelve.

Colwell's (1969–1970) *Music Achievement Tests* provide measures of rhythm behaviors in a musical context. A "meter discrimination" subtest asks respondents to indicate whether a musical example moves in two's or three's, i.e., is it in duple or triple meter. An "auditory-visual discrimination" subtest asks respondents to indicate measures in which the rhythm of notated melodies differs from the rhythm presented aurally. The test-retest reliability coefficient for the rhythm items is .80. The tests claim content validity because they reflect the objectives common to most basal music series at the time of their construction.

Several measures of aural-visual discrimination also include rhythm as part of a total test, but most do not include separate scores for the rhythmic portions, e.g., Knuth, 1966; Farnum, 1953. Rhythm also is one of the criteria for scoring the *Watkins-Farnum Performance Scale* (Watkins & Farnum, 1954), but neither does it provide a separate rhythm score.

Researchers and teachers concerned with selecting or developing measures of rhythmic behaviors should first and foremost consider the nature of the rhythmic task they wish to evaluate and be certain that any measure selected or developed indeed measures that task in a manner appropriate for the level of student being evaluated.

Summary

The major points of this chapter include the following:
1. Rhythm provides structure to music and serves as its dynamic, energizing force.
2. Rhythm structure in music has several basic aspects: (a) tempo, (b) beat, (c) meter, and (d) melodic or phrase patterns.
3. Traditional theories regarding human response to rhythm are of four basic types: (a) instinctive, (b) physiological, (c) motor, and (d) learning.

4. Initial development of rhythmic behaviors is inextricably related to movement.
5. Research related to rhythm may be categorized as it relates to (a) movement and perception, (b) tempo and beat perception, (c) meter perception, (d) rhythmic grouping, and (e) expressive timing.
6. Although developmental research is inconclusive, rhythmic behaviors generally increase with age for younger children but level out for older children.
7. The development of rhythmic behaviors can be expedited through training.
8. Although the development of rhythm reading skills is a major concern to both researchers and teachers, neither research nor practice yields any consensus regarding a "best" way to facilitate rhythm reading.
9. Evaluation of rhythmic behaviors usually involves assessment of one of three basic types of behavior: (a) behaviors requiring discriminations between aurally presented stimuli, (b) movement behaviors demonstrating an ability to keep time with the beat or to reproduce an aurally presented rhythm pattern, and (c) behaviors reflecting an ability to associate visual rhythm symbols with aurally presented rhythm patterns.

References

Allen, T.W., Walker, K., Symends, L., & Marcell, M. (1977). Intrasensory and intersensory perception of temporal sequences during infancy. *Developmental Psychology, 13,* 225–229.

Allport, F.H. (1955). *Theories of perception and the concept of structure.* New York: Wiley.

Andrews, F.M., & Deihl, N.C. (1967). *Development of a techniques for identifying elementary school children's musical concepts.* Cooperative Research Project 5-0233, The Pennsylvania State University.

Apel, W. (1944). *Harvard dictionary of music.* Cambridge: Harvard University Press.

Bachman, T. (1969). *Reading and writing music* (Books 1 & 2). Elizabethtown, PA: The Continental Press.

Bamberger, J. (1982). Revisiting children's drawings of simple rhythms: A function of reflection-in-action. In S. Strauss (Ed.), *U-shaped behavioral growth.* New York: Academic Press.

Barela, M.M. (1979). Motion in musical time and rhythm. *College Music Symposium, 19* (1), 78–92.

Behrens, G.A. (1984). In search of the long assumed relationship between rhythm and movement. *Contributions to Music Education, 11,* 33–54.

Bengtsson, I., & Gabrielsson, A. (1980). Methods for analyzing performance of musical rhythm. *Scandinavian Journal of Psychology, 21,* 257–268.

Bengtsson, I., & Gabrielsson, A. (1982). Analysis and synthesis of musical rhythm.

In J. Sundberg (Ed.), *Studies of Music Performance (pp. 27–60)*. Stockholm: Royal Swedish Academy of Music, Publication No. 39.

Bengtsson, I., & Gabrielsson, A. (1983). Performance of musical rhythm in 3/4 and 6/8 meter. *Scandinavian Journal of Psychology, 21*, 257–268.

Benjamin, W.E. (1984). A theory of musical meter. *Music Perception, 1*, 355–413.

Bentley, A. (1966a). *Measures of musical abilities.* New York: October House.

Bentley, A. (1966b). *Musical ability in children and its measurement.* London: George G. Harrap.

Boisen, R. (1981). The effect of melodic context on students' aural perception of rhythm. *Journal of Research in Music Education, 29*, 165–172.

Boring, E.G. (1942). *Sensation and perception in the history of experimental psychology.* New York: Appleton-Century.

Boyle, J.D. (1968). The effects of prescribed rhythmical movements on the ability to sight read music (Doctoral dissertation, University of Kansas, 1968). *Dissertation Abstracts, 29*, 2290–2291.

Boyle, J.D. (1987). An exploratory investigation of meter perception. *Council for Research in Music Education, 91*, 10–14.

Bregman, A.S., & Campbell, J. (1971). Primary auditory stream segregation and perception of order in rapid sequences of tones. *Journal of Experimental Psychology, 89*, 244–249.

Bregman, A.S., & Dannenbring, G.L. (1973). The effect of continuity on auditory stream segregation. *Perception and Psychophysics, 13*, 308–312.

Brink, E. (1983). A look at E. Gordon's theories. *Council for Research in Music Education, 75*, 2–14.

Butler, D. (1992). *The musician's guide to perception and cognition.* New York: Schirmer.

Campbell, D.T., & Stanley, J.C. (1963). *Experimental and quasiexperimental designs for research.* Chicago: Rand McNally.

Chang, H., & Trehub, S.E. (1977). Infant's perception of temporal grouping of auditory patterns. *Child Development, 48*, 1666–1670.

Chomsky, N. (1957). *Syntactic structures.* The Hague: Mouton.

Chomsky, N. (1965). *Aspects of the theory of syntax.* Cambridge: MIT Press.

Chomsky, N. (1968). *Language and mind.* New York: Harcourt Brace Jovanovitch.

Clarke, E.F. (1982). Timing in the performance of Erik Satie's "Vexations." *Acta Psychologica, 50*, 1–19.

Clarke, E.F. (1985). Some aspects of rhythm and expression in performances of Erik Satie's "Gnossienne No. 5." *Music Perception, 2*, 299–328.

Clarke, E.F. (1987a). Categorical rhythm perception: An ecological perspective. In A. Gabrielsson (Ed.), *Action and perception in rhythm and music* (pp. 19–33). Stockholm: Royal Swedish Academy of Music, Publication No. 55.

Clarke, E.F. (1987b). Levels of structure in the organization of musical time. *Contemporary Music Review, 2*, 211–238.

Clarke, E.F. (1989). Mind the gap: Formal structures and psychological processes in music. *Contemporary Music Review, 3*, 1–13.

Clynes, M., & Walker, J. (1982). Neurobiological functions of rhythm, time, and pulse in music. In M. Clynes (Ed.), *Music, mind, and brain* (pp. 171–216). New York: Plenum Press.

Coffman, A.R. (1949). *The effects of training on rhythm discrimination and rhythmic action.* Unpublished doctoral dissertation, Northwestern University.

Colwell, R. (1969–70). *Music achievement tests.* Chicago: Follett.

Cooper, G., & Meyer, L.B. (1960). *The rhythmic structure of music.* Chicago: The University of Chicago Press.

Creston, P. (1964). *Principles of rhythm.* New York: Franco Columbo.

Davies, J.B. (1978). *The psychology of music.* London: Hutchinson & Co.

Demany, L., McKenzie, B., & Vurpillot, E. (1977). Rhythm perception in early infancy. *Nature, 266,* 718–719.

Deutsch, D. (Ed.) (1982). *The psychology of music.* New York: Academic Press.

DeYarmin, R.M. (1972). An experimental analysis of the development of rhythmic and tonal capabilities of kindergarten and first grade children. In E. Gordon (Ed.), *Experimental research in the psychology of music* (Vol. 8, pp. 1–44). Iowa City: University of Iowa Press.

Dittemore, E.E. (1970). An investigation of some musical capabilities of elementary school students. In E. Gordon (Ed.), *Experimental research in the psychology of music* (Vol. 6, pp. 1–44). Iowa City: University of Iowa Press.

Dowling, W.J. (1968). Rhythmic fission and perceptual organization. *Journal of the Acoustical Society of America, 44,* 369.

Dowling, W.J. (1973). The perception of interleaved melodies. *Cognitive Psychology, 5,* 322–337.

Dowling, W.J., & Harwood, D.L. (1986). *Music cognition.* Orlando, FL: Academic Press.

Drake, R.M. (1957). *Drake musical aptitude tests.* Chicago: Science Research Associates.

Duke, R.A. (1987). *Musicians' perception of beat in monotonic stimuli.* Unpublished research paper, MENC Southern Division Conference, Orlando, FL, May 1987.

Duke, R.A. (1989). Effect of melodic rhythm on elementary students' and college undergraduates' perception of relative tempo. *Journal of Research in Music Education, 37,* 246–257.

Duke, R.A. (1990). Beat and tempo in music: Differences in teachers' and students' perceptions. *UPDATE, Applications of Research in Music Education, 9* (1), 8–12.

Duke, R.A. (1994). When tempo changes rhythm: The effect of tempo on nonmusicians' perception of rhythm. *Journal of Research in Music Education, 42,* 27–35.

Elliott, C.A. (1982). The relationships among instrumental sight-reading ability and seven predictor variables. *Journal of Research in Music Education, 30,* 5–14.

Farnsworth, P.R. (1969). *The social psychology of music* (2nd ed.). Ames: The Iowa State University Press.

Farnum, S.E. (1953) *Farnum music notation tests.* New York: The Psychological Corporation.

Feldman, J., Epstein, D., & Richards, W. (1992). Force dynamics of tempo change in music. *Music Perception, 10,* 185–204.

Fiske, H. (1990). *Music and mind.* Lewiston, NY: The Edwin Mellen Press.

Flavell, J.H. (1963). *The developmental psychology of Jean Piaget.* Princeton: Van Nostrand.

Foley, E.A. (1975). Effects of training in conservation of tonal and rhythmic patterns on second grade children. *Journal of Research in Music Education, 23,* 240–248.

Fraisse, P. (1982). Rhythm and tempo. In D. Deutsch (Ed.), *The psychology of music* (pp. 149–180). New York: Academic Press.

Gabrielsson, A. (1973a). Similarity ratings and dimension analyses of auditory rhythm patterns, II. *Scandinavian Journal of Psychology, 14,* 161–176.

Gabrielsson, A. (1973b). Studies in rhythm. *Acta Universitatis Upsaliensis, 7,* 3–19.

Gabrielsson, A. (1982a). Perception and performance of musical rhythm. In M. Clynes (Ed.), *Music, mind, and brain* (pp. 159–169). New York: Plenum Press.

Gabrielsson, A. (1982b). Performance and training of musical rhythm. *Psychology of Music, Special Issue,* 42–46.

Gabrielsson, A. (1985). Interplay between analysis and synthesis in studies of music performance and music experience. *Music Perception, 3,* 59–86.

Gabrielsson, A. (1988). Timing in music performance and its relations to music experience. In J.A. Sloboda (Ed.), *Generative processes in music: The psychology of performance, improvisation, and composition* (pp. 27–51). Oxford: Clarendon Press.

Gardner, H. (1971). Children's duplication of rhythm patterns. *Journal of Research in Music Education, 19,* 355–360.

Gaston, E.T. (1968). Music and man. In E.T. Gaston (Ed.), *Music in therapy* (pp. 7–29). New York: Macmillan.

Geringer, J.M., & Madsen, C.K. (1984). Pitch and tempo discrimination in recorded orchestral music among musicians and nonmusicians. *Journal of Research in Music Education, 32,* 195–204.

Geringer, J.M., Duke, R.A., & Madsen, C.K. (1992). Musician's perception of beat note: Regions of beat change in modulating tempos. *Council for Research in Music Education, 114,* 21–33.

Geringer, J.M., Madsen, C.K., & Duke, R.A. (1993/1994). Perception of beat note change in modulating tempos. *Council for Research in Music Education, 119,* 49–57.

Gordon, E. (1965). *Musical aptitude profile.* Boston: Houghton Mifflin.

Gordon, E. (1971). *The psychology of music teaching.* Englewood Cliffs, NJ: Prentice-Hall.

Gordon, E. (1979). *Primary measures of music audiation.* Chicago: G.I.A. Publications.

Gordon, E. (1980). *Learning sequences in music: Skill, content, and patterns.* Chicago: G.I.A. Publications.

Gordon, E. (1982). *Intermediate measures of music audiation.* Chicago: G.I.A. Publications.

Gordon, E. (1991). *Iowa tests of music literacy* (2nd ed.). Chicago: G.I.A. Publications.

Grieshaber, K. (1987). Children's rhythmic tapping: A critical review of research. *Council for Research in Music Education, 90,* 73–82.

Hargreaves, D.J. (1986). *The developmental psychology of music.* Cambridge: Cambridge University Press.

Hebb, D.O. (1949). *Organization of behavior.* New York: Wiley.

Hebb, D.O. (1958). *A textbook of psychology.* Philadelphia: Saunders.

Hoffer, C.R. (1973). *Teaching music in secondary schools* (2nd ed.). Belmont, CA: Wadsworth.

Hood, M.V. (1970). *Teaching rhythm and using classroom instruments.* Englewood Cliffs, NJ: Prentice-Hall.

Horner, V. (1965). *Music education, the background of research and opinion.* Hawthorne, Victoria, Australia: Australian Council for Educational Research.

Howell, P., Cross, I., & West, R. (Eds.) (1985). *Musical structure and cognition.* London: Academic Press.

Ihrke, W.R. (1969). *An experimental study of the effectiveness and validity of an automated rhythm training program.* Storrs: University of Connecticut. (ERIC Document Reproduction Service No. ED 032 790)

Jackson, S.L. (1963). Ear and rhythm training. *Music Educators Journal, 50* (1), 133–135.

Jaques-Dalcroze, E. (1915). *The eurhythmics of Jaques-Dalcroze.* Boston: Small Maynard.

Jaques-Dalcroze, E. (1921). *Rhythm, music, and education.* London: Chatto and Windus.

Jersild, A.T., & Bienstock, S.F. (1935). *Development of rhythm in young children.* New York: Bureau of Publications, Teachers College, Columbia University.

Johnson-Laird, P.N. (1991). Rhythm and meter: A theory at the computational level. *Psychomusicology, 10,* 88–106.

Jones, R. (1985). A dialectic analysis of selected contradictions among definitions of meter in music. *Council for Research in Music Education, 83,* 43–56.

Kelly, S.N. (1993). *An investigation of the effects of conducting instruction on the musical performance of beginning band students.* Unpublished doctoral dissertation, University of Kansas, Lawrence.

Killian, J.N. (1985). The effect of differential feedback on tempo performance and perception. *Contributions to Music Education, 12,* 22–29.

Knuth, W.E. (1966). *Knuth achievement tests in music.* San Francisco: Creative Arts Research Associates.

Kohut, D.L. (1973). *Instrumental music pedagogy.* Englewood Cliffs: Prentice-Hall.

Kramer, J.D. (1988). *The time of music.* New York: Schirmer Books.

Kuhn, T.L. (1974). Discrimination of modulated beat tempo by professional musicians. *Journal of Research in Music Education, 22,* 270–277.

Kuhn, T.L. (1977). Effects of dynamics, halves of exercise, and trial sequences on tempo accuracy. *Journal of Research in Music Education, 25,* 222–227.

Lerdahl, F. & Jackendoff, R. (1983). *A generative theory of tonal music.* Cambridge: MIT Press.

Lewis, A.G. (1972). *Listen, look, and sing.* Morristown, NJ: Silver Burdett.

Lund, M.W. (1939). *An analysis of the "true beat" in music.* Unpublished doctoral dissertation, Stanford University.

Lundin, R.W. (1967). *An objective psychology of music* (2nd ed.). New York: Ronald Press.

Madsen, C.K., Duke, R.A., & Geringer, J.M. (1986). The effects of speed alterations on tempo note selection. *Journal of Research in Music Education, 34,* 101–110.

Magnell, E. (1968). Systems for reading rhythms at sight. *The Instrumentalist, 23* (2) 68–70.

McNally, K.A., & Handel, S. (1977). Effect of elemental composition on streaming and the ordering of repeating sequences. *Journal of Experimental Psychology: Human Perception and Performance, 3,* 451–460.

Moog, H. (1976). The development of musical experience in children of pre-school age. *Psychology of Music, 4* (2), 38–47.

Moog, H. (1979). On the perception of rhythmic forms by physically handicapped children and those of low intelligence in comparison with non-handicapped children. *Council for Research in Music Education, 59,* 73–78.

Morgan, C.T. (1965). *Physiological psychology* (3rd ed.). New York: McGraw-Hill.

Mursell, J.L. (1937). *Psychology of music.* New York: W.W. Norton.

Mursell, J.L. (1956). *Music education, principles and programs,* Morristown, NJ: Silver Burdett.

Nielson, J.F. (1930). A study of the Seashore motor-rhythm test. *Psychological Monographs, 40,* 74–84.

Osgood, C.E. (1953). *Method and theory in experimental psychology.* New York: Oxford University Press.

Palmer, M. (1976). Relative effectiveness of two approaches to rhythm reading for fourth-grade students. *Journal of Research in Music Education, 24,* 159–168.

Perney, J. (1976). Musical tasks related to the development of the conservation of metric time. *Journal of Research in Music Education, 24,* 159–168.

Petzold, R.G. (1966). *Auditory perception of musical sounds by children in the first six grades.* Madison: University of Wisconsin. (ERIC Document Reproduction Service No. ED 010 297)

Pflederer, M., & Sechrest, L. (1968). Conservation-type responses of children to musical stimuli. *Council for Research in Music Education, 13,* 19–36.

Pizer, R. (1969). Toward more accurate rhythm. *The Instrumentalist, 23* (2) 75–76.

Povel, D., & Essens, P. (1985). Perception of temporal patterns. *Music Perception, 2,* 411–440.

Pressing, J. (1993). Relations between musical and scientific properties of time. *Contemporary Music Review, 7,* 105–122.

Rainbow, E. (1981). A final report on a three-year investigation of rhythmic abilities of preschool aged children. *Council for Research in Music Education, 66/67,* 69–73.

Rasch, R.A. (1988). Timing and synchronization in ensemble performance. In J.A. Sloboda (Ed.), *Generative processes in music: The psychology of performance, improvisation, and composition.* Oxford: Clarendon.

Revelli, W.D. (1955). To beat or not to beat? *Etude, 73* (6), 19, 48.

Repp, B. (1990). Patterns of expressive timing in performances of a Beethoven minuet by nineteen famous pianists. *Journal of the Acoustical Society of America, 88,* 622–641.

Repp, B. (1992a). A constraint on the expressive timing of a melodic gesture: Evidence from performance and aesthetic judgment. *Music Perception, 10,* 221–242.

Repp, B. (1992b). Diversity and commonality in music performance: An analysis of timing microstructure in Schumann's "Traumerei." *Journal of the Acoustical Society of America, 92,* 2546–2568.

Richards, M.H. (1967). *Threshold to music.* New York: Harper and Row.

Rose, R.F. (1989). An analysis of timing in jazz rhythm section performance. *Dissertation Abstracts International, 50,* 3509A.

Rosenbusch, M.H., & Gardner, D.B. (1968). Reproduction of auditory and visual rhythmic patterns by children. *Perceptual and Motor Skills, 26,* 1271–1276.

Ruckmick, C.A. (1913). The role of kinaesthesis in the perception of rhythm. *The American Journal of Psychology, 24,* 305–359.

Ruckmick, C.A. (1945). The nature of the rhythmic experience. *Proceedings of the Music Teachers National Association, 39,* 79–89.

Sachs, C. (1953). *Rhythm and tempo.* New York: W.W. Norton.

Schellenberg, S., & Moore, R.S. (1985). The effect of tonalrhythmic context on short-term memory of rhythmic and melodic sequences. *Council for Research in Music Education, 85,* 207–217.

Schleuter, S.L., & Schleuter, L.J. (1985). The relationship of grade level and sex differences to certain rhythmic responses of primary grade children. *Journal of Research in Music Education, 33,* 23–30.

Schenker, H. (1935). *Der freie satz.* (E. Oster, trans., 1979). New York: Longman.

Schoen, M. (1940). *The psychology of music.* New York: Ronald Press.

Seashore, C.E. (1938). *Psychology of music.* New York: McGraw-Hill.

Seashore, C.E., Lewis, D.L., & Saetveit, J.G. (1939; 1960). *Seashore measures of musical talents* (revised). New York: The Psychological Corporation.

Serafine, M.L. (1975). *A measure of meter conservation, based on Piaget's theory.* Unpublished doctoral dissertation, University of Florida.

Serafine, M.L. (1988). *Music as cognition.* New York: Columbia University Press.

Sheldon, D.A. (1994). Effects of tempo, musical experience, and listening modes on tempo modulation perception. *Journal of Research in Music Education, 42,* 190–202.

Shrader, D.L. (1970). An aural approach to rhythmic sight-reading, based upon principles of programmed learning, utilizing a stereo-tape teaching machine. (Doctoral dissertation, University of Oregon, 1970). *Dissertation Abstracts International, 31,* 2426.

Sink, P.E. (1983). Effects of rhythmic and melodic alterations on rhythmic perception. *Journal of Research in Music Education, 31,* 101–114.

Sink, P.E. (1984). Effects of rhythmic and melodic alterations and selected musical experiences on rhythmic processing. *Journal of Research in Music Education, 32,* 177–194.

Skornicka, J.E. (1958). *The function of time and rhythm in instrumental music reading competency.* Unpublished doctoral dissertation, Oregon State College.

Sloboda, J.A. (1985). *The musical mind.* Oxford: Clarendon Press.

Sperry, R.W. (1964). Neurology and the mind-brain problem. In R. Issacson (Ed.), *Basic readings in neuropsychology.* New York: Harper and Row.

Sternberg, S., Knoll, R.L., & Zukofsky, P. (1982). Timing by skilled musicians. In D. Deutsch (Ed.), *The psychology of music* (pp. 182–240). New York: Academic Press.

Sundberg, J., & Verillo, V. (1980). On the anatomy of the ritard: A study of timing in music. *Journal of the Acoustical Society of America, 68,* 772–779.

Taylor, R.G. (Ed.) (1981). *Documentary report of the Ann Arbor Symposium.* Reston, VA: Music Educators National Conference.

Taylor, S. (1973). Musical development of children aged seven to eleven. *Psychology of Music, 1* (1), 44–49.

Thackray, R. (1968). *An investigation into rhythmic abilities.* London: Novello & Company Limited.

Todd, N. (1985). A model of expressive timing in tonal music. *Music Perception, 3,* 33–57.

Todd, N. (1989). A computational model of rubato. *Contemporary Music Review, 3,* 69–88.

Todd, N. (1992). The dynamics of dynamics: A model of musical expression. *Journal of the Acoustical Society of America, 91,* 3540–3550.

Wang, C.C. (1983). Discrimination of modulated music tempo by music majors. *Journal of Research in Music Education, 31,* 49–55.

Wang, C.C. (1984). Effects of some aspects of rhythm on tempo perception. *Journal of Research in Music Education, 32,* 169–176.

Wang, C.C., & Salzburg, R.S. (1984). Discrimination of modulated music tempo by string students. *Journal of Research in Music Education, 32,* 123–132.

Wapnick, J. (1980). Pitch, tempo, and timbral preferences in recorded piano music. *Journal of Research in Music Education, 28,* 43–58.

Watkins, J.G., & Farnum, S.E. (1954). *The Watkins-Farnum performance scale.* Winona, MN: Hal Leonard Music.

West, R., Howell, P., & Cross, I. (1985). Modelling perceived musical structure. In P. Howell, I. Cross, & R. West (Eds.), *Musical structure and cognition* (pp. 21–52). London: Academic Press.

Whitson, T.C. (1951). *A study of rhythm perception at the junior high school level.* Unpublished master's thesis, University of Texas.

Windsor, L. (1993). Dynamic accents and the categorical perception of metre. *Psychology of Music, 21* (2), 127–140.

Winick, S. (1974). *Rhythm: An annotated bibliography.* Metuchen, NJ: Scarecrow Press.

Yeston, M. (1976). *The stratification of musical rhythm.* New Haven, CT: Yale University Press.

Zimmerman, M.P. (1971). *Musical characteristics of children.* Washington: Music Educators National Conference.

CHAPTER SIX

MELODIC AND HARMONIC FOUNDATIONS

An understanding of music's pitch structure has interested people since the beginning of recorded history, and Weber (1958) maintains that the drive to rationalize pitch structure has shaped Western musical development to a large degree. Pitch structure in Western music has both horizontal and vertical dimensions. While other musics have evolved with elaborate developments of the horizontal dimension, none has approached the sophistication of Western music's vertical dimension, harmony.

The horizontal dimension involves pitch sequences, while the vertical dimension involves structuring simultaneous pitches. Music theorists primarily have been concerned with deriving systems for codifying and explaining practices with respect to these structures. Systems of scales and harmony are outgrowths of theorists' efforts.

Because music is a social and therefore a changing phenomenon, theorists' work is never complete. Scales and harmonic systems based on eighteenth and nineteenth century melodic and harmonic practices are inadequate for explaining all pitch structures of twentieth-century music; no doubt they will be even less adequate for twenty-first century music.

While theorists traditionally have focused on melodic and harmonic structures per se, theorists in recent years have become increasingly interested in understanding how people perceptually and cognitively organize melodic and harmonic structures and larger musical forms. Much of the research base for this "cognitive science" approach lies in psychology, linguistics, neurophysiology, philosophy, computer science, and music theory (Lerdahl & Jackendoff, 1983, p. 332). This concern for understanding music perception and cognition has stimulated theoretical and empirical research regarding the nature of the cognitive processes or structures involved in interactions with musical stimuli.

This chapter examines the nature of melody and harmony in Western music in terms of both its tonal structure and people's interactions with and responses to tonal structure. For convenience, the discussion is organized under several broad headings: (a) definitions of melody, harmony, and tonality, (b) scale, modal, and other pitch structures, (c) cognitive processes underlying pitch-related behaviors, (d) development of melodic and harmonic behaviors, and (e) evaluating melodic and harmonic behaviors.

Extended Definitions

For most listeners to Western music, melody is inseparable from harmony and rhythm, although people usually tend to remember melodies rather than rhythms or harmonies. The overwhelming majority of common melodies exist in tonal harmonic frameworks, utilizing chord structures built in thirds and progressing toward somewhat predictable "resolutions."

Melody

Whether constructed within a tonal harmonic framework or not, two factors contribute to each melody's individuality: *pitch relationships* and *durational relationships* among the tones. As noted in Chapter Four, pitch is a relative phenomenon concerning the placement of tones on a high-low continuum. Pitch's circularity, similarity, or intimacy dimension, which involves tonal relationships, also is crucial to melody.

Constructing a melody involves selecting tones from the pitch continuum and placing them in temporal sequence. Because pitch is a continuous variable, any pitch conceivably can occur in a melody. *Portamenti* and *glissandi* are examples of melodies using minute pitch differences. Electronic music frequently uses these "sliding" pitches, but most melodies, Western and non-Western, utilize fixed pitches.

Sloboda (1985, pp. 24–28) suggests that the use of fixed pitches in music may be related to the "categorical nature of pitch perception."[1] He draws some analogies between the structures of language and music, noting that basic speech-sound classes of language (*phonemes*), which reflect a *range* of sounds along a continuum, actually are perceived as given sound units. Similarly, he views the use of fixed pitches in music as a "phonology" of pitch, noting that pitches are perceived categorically, particularly by musicians. In Western music we are accustomed to hearing musical tones within given scale and tonal harmonic frameworks. Individual tones may be mistuned yet still be perceived as a certain

---

[1]According to Burns and Ward (1982, pp. 250–251), the term *categorical perception* was coined about 1970 by a speech-perception group to describe the results of their experiments in the perception of some speech tokens that varied along a single acoustic continuum. Burns and Ward cite a number of studies demonstrating that the concept of categorical pitch is also appropriate for nonspeech stimuli, especially musical intervals. With musical stimuli, the effect is more easily demonstrated with musically trained individuals who are able to readily label stimuli than with individuals without musical training (p. 252).

pitch. Apparently there are "categorical boundaries," which may vary from listener to listener, and as long as these are not exceeded the tone is perceived as having the pitch of that category.

Particular fixed pitches for use in melodies usually are selected from within conventions and traditions of a given musical culture. In non-Western cultures, many of which have not developed a tonal system based on a tertian harmonic framework, the octave is divided in various ways. Some cultures use *microtonic* scales, dividing the octave into a greater number of pitches than the seven tones of the Western diatonic scale. Other cultures utilize fewer pitches per octave, and their scales are classified as *macrotonic* scales. Most Western melodies utilize tones within the diatonic scale system and have an implied, if not always accompanying, harmonic framework.[2] Regardless of the scale system used in selecting pitches for a melody or whether the melody uses sliding or fixed pitches, the sequence of pitch relationships contributes to a given melody's individuality.

As long as the tonal sequence's relative pitch positions and rhythm remain constant, the melody remains the same. Changing either the relative pitch positions or the rhythm, therefore, changes the melody *structurally* and may or may not change it *perceptually*. The melody notated in Figure 6-1 has the pitch relationships of "America" (also "God Save the Queen"), but the rhythm makes it an entirely different melody.

Figure 6-1. "America."

Composers and some performers change tones and pitches of melodies for aesthetic or artistic purposes. The degree to which the melody's tonal or rhythmic structure can change while still eliciting a response of "sameness" naturally is subject to many variables. Farnsworth (1969, p.

---

[2]Twelve-tone, or serial, melodies are a notable exception to this practice. Such melodies essentially involve a sequence of each of the twelve tones of the chromatic scale in any order chosen by the composer, and each tone must be used before another can be repeated.

49) believes that once a melody is learned it can be changed considerably and still be recognized. The degree to which it can be changed and still be recognized appears to be a function of the listener's familiarity with the melody, particularly any *expectations* developed regarding it. Dowling's (1973) comparisons of listeners' responses to simultaneous pairs of familiar "interleaved" melodies supports the contention regarding expectations. When subjects knew which tunes to listen for, they were able to recognize them, but when they had no such expectations, they were not able to recognize them.

Melody may be defined either in terms of its structural characteristics or people's responses to it. Music theorists traditionally have examined melodies in terms of structural characteristics, while psychologists have been more interested in people's responses to or perceptions of melody. Melody also has been examined from a philosophical perspective, although Hickman (1976) questions whether "aesthetics of melody" has any meaning today. The present discussion of melody is divided into two broad sections: structure of melody and perceptual organization of melody. Farnsworth (1969, p. 48) classifies descriptions of melody in terms of structural characteristics as *formalistic* and those involving perceptual or psychological variables as *relativistic*.

Structural characteristics of melody. In its broadest sense, melody means any succession of single tones (Ortmann, 1926), and, as noted above, both pitch and durational relationships contribute to each melody's individuality. The particular patterns of ups and downs of pitches in a series of tones provides its *melodic contour*. The uniqueness of a melodic contour is strengthened by its particular rhythmic configuration. As demonstrated in Figure 6-1, a radical change in rhythmic configuration may change a melodic contour perceptually. Thus, a melodic contour, together with its unique rhythmic configuration, serves as a *Gestalt* or holistic pattern to which a listener responds. A melody may be performed at different tempi and at different pitch levels, but unless the tempo is changed radically, there is a "sameness" about it and people tend to perceive it as the same melody. More will be said later of the variables affecting melodic recognition.

Most discussions of melody's structural attributes focus primarily on its pitch attributes. Lundin (1967, pp. 77–79), for example, sees three particular melodic attributes: (a) *propinquity,* (b) *repetition,* and (c) *finality.* The tones of most Western melodies are propinquous, that is, close together. Analyses of intervals of melodies by Ortmann (1937) and Radocy (1977) both reveals a preponderance of smaller successive intervals (conjunct) over larger intervals (disjunct).

Melodies are repetitious in that certain tones tend to repeat with considerable frequency. Radocy's examination of randomly selected melodies from *The Norton Scores* (Kamien, 1972) and from *357 Songs We Love to Sing* (1938) supports Lundin's view. In the Norton example, the tones *do, mi,* and *so* accounted for 45 percent of all the tones; when *ti* and *re* were added the percentage increased to 69. The corresponding songbook percentages were 67 and 81. Clearly there is a tendency in most Western melodies to return to certain notes with great frequency.

Lundin's third attribute, finality, refers to a tendency for melodies to end according to certain conventions of *cadence,* which convey an impression of momentary or permanent conclusion. Cadences in melodies constructed within a Western tonal harmonic framework often have an implied harmonic accompaniment, although not necessarily. Final tones of melodies often are ones which have been repeated frequently or emphasized in the body of the melody.

Ortmann (1926) believed that a melody's structural characteristics could be understood best by examining the pitch relationships of the melodic contour in isolation from the harmony and rhythm. His analysis revealed several *static* (his term) attributes of melody that are inherent in all melodies and that tend to attract a listener's attention. They include (a) *first and last tones,* (b) *highest and lowest tones,* (c) *repeated tones,* (d) *interval size,* (e) *pitch direction,* (f) *pitch proximity,* (g) *emphasis in tone groups,* (h) *interval relationship,* and (i) *degree of emphasis.* The first three attributes are termed *absolute,* while the balance are considered *relative.* Ortmann maintains that the relative attributes are more important than the absolute attributes. Melodic memory, which involves *relative pitch* recall, is common among listeners to Western music, while *tone memory,* i.e., absolute pitch, is relatively rare.

As may be apparent, the above discussion does little to limit the type of tone sequences that may be called melody. It is consistent with Mursell's (1937, p. 103) view that "melody need have not unified structure." It does, however, reveal that Western tonal melodies frequently use small intervals between tones, repeat some tones with great frequency, and incorporate some type of convention to establish finality. (A more-or-less random sequence of tones, as one might obtain by throwing darts at mounted staff paper, is atypical of tonal melodies.) Further, it suggests that the emphasis a tone receives within a melody depends on its structural relationship to other melodies.

The answer to "What constitutes a melody?" is not solely a function of its structural characteristics; the answer also must be considered in terms of the listener.

Perceptual organization of melody. Perhaps Mursell's (1937, p. 104) statement best answers the question "What constitutes a melody?": *"A sequence of tones constitutes a melody when it is apprehended in terms of a unified and single response,"* but then a more important question arises: "What psychological factors influence an individual's perception and apprehension of a sequence of tones as a melody?"

A traditional (and still generally accepted) explanation of melodic perception invokes the laws of Gestalt psychology. A melody is perceived as a Gestalt according to fundamental organizational laws derived from the study of visual perception, the laws of *proximity, similarity, common direction,* and *simplicity* (Bower & Hilgard, 1981, pp. 302–310). Tones that are close together in time or space are more likely to be perceived as a melodic unit than tones that are not close together. Similar (repeated) tones also tend to be perceived as a unit. Melodic perceptions proceed in a common direction toward completion, and the tendency is to perceive the Gestalt (tonal contour or pattern) in its simplest form.

The organizational laws of Gestalt psychology are reflected in the structural characteristics discussed above. People tend to organize a series of tones as a melody more readily if most tones are close in frequency, involve a certain amount of repetition, and proceed toward a finish in a somewhat direct manner. Relations among the tonal elements themselves define the Gestalt-like experience of melody (Espinoza-Varas & Watson, 1989).

The authors do not, however, intend to suggest, as do some proponents of Gestalt psychology, that capacity to perceive contour or pattern in melody is an inborn capacity that requires no learning. As Hebb (1949, pp. 17–59) both argues and carefully documents, the perception of *relative* phenomena, of which melody is one, involves the ability to perceive patterns and develops only as result of prolonged experience (learning), whether formal or informal, with the particular phenomenon. To recognize a given tonal sequence as a melody requires experience with tonal sequences of a similar style.

Thus, familiarity with a melody or melodic style is an important variable in influencing what an individual perceives as melody. As an individual interacts with music of his or her culture, he or she learns and comes to accept its melodic conventions. Experience with melodies in a given scale system enables an individual to develop certain *expectations.* When new tonal sequences in similar style are encountered, the individual recognizes the new sequence as conforming or not conforming to expectations for that which he or she has learned as melody.

More recent accounts of melodic perception have examined it in terms of cognitive processes and structures.[3] Indeed, the burgeoning research literature in the "cognitive psychology of music," as research in the field is termed, focuses primarily on the perception of pitch and melody.

Dowling and Harwood (1986, pp. 124–144) describe the pattern of expectations a listener has regarding a melody as a *melodic schema*. (*Schemata* are "knowledge structures," developed from prior experience, with which an observer may organize perceptions into cognitions.) Such schemata are developed through immersion in one's musical culture from early childhood. Employing context-dependent information beyond the specific pitches, melodic schemata apparently reflect melodic contour, interval relationships, pitch chroma (the circular dimension of pitch), and tonality. Carterette and Kendall (1989, p. 147) view "unconscious" schemata as an implicit musical knowledge that guides musical expectancies.

Music psychologists find a theoretical base in Chomsky's (1957, 1965, 1968) seminal work regarding deep structures of language and Schenker's (1935/1979) theoretical system for conceiving surface musical structures as outgrowths of an underlying musical core or *Urtext*. Drawing analogies between hierarchical cognitive structures underlying music and language behaviors, music psychologists suggest that music's surface structures (notes and rests) are subsumable into larger and more abstract "deep" hierarchical structures, based on combinations of melodic, harmonic, rhythmic, and extramusical information. Sloboda's (1985) excellent text is both an introduction to and a detailed treatment of the cognitive organization of music on the basis of abstracted structures.

The "deep" or "abstracted" structures serve as a means of organization. Their degree of "reality" in any conscious sense is questionable. Cook (1990, pp. 3–4) points out that people do not actually hear large-scale Schenkerian analysis. Even traditional musical forms lack perceptual reality for many listeners. As Cook states,

> unless they have both the training and the inclination to track the form of a piece of music in theoretical terms as they listen, people experience recurrence without actually observing what it is that recurs; they experience coherence but not the unitary organization in terms of which a theorist or analyst would explain that coherence. People enjoy musical compositions . . . without really perceiving them at all. (p. 68)

Many attempts to model hierarchical perceptual structuring exist; West, Howell, and Cross (1985) provide an excellent review. (More will

---

[3]The reader should remember that *structures* discussed in research in cognitive psychology refer to theoretical cognitive constructs rather than tonal structures *per se*.

be said of hierarchical structures later in this chapter.) Common to development of many of the models are examinations of melody's *phonology, syntax,* and *grammar.* Sloboda (1985, pp. 11–52) provides clear, authoritative definitions and descriptions of these constructs. Essentially, phonology concerns the way in which pitch sounds (*phonemes*) are divided into discrete sound (perceptual) categories. Syntax is concerned with the combination of sound units into sequences, and grammar is concerned with the "rules" for using, or processing, syntactical sequences.

Many model tonal hierarchies are built, either explicitly or implicitly, upon *generative grammars,* organizational rules that underlie musical structures. This approach is similar to that exemplified by Chomsky's work with language. Sloboda (1985, pp. 34–47) argues that "the *structures* embodied in such grammars have psychological reality" (p. 34). He uses Sundberg and Lindblom's (1976) generative grammar for eight-bar nursery tunes to demonstrate how a musical grammar resembles the generative phonology of language grammars. Lerdahl (1988, p. 233) distinguishes between *compositional* grammars, which generate musical stimuli, and *listening* grammars, which generate mental representations of sonic events. Of particular importance to the present discussion is the fact that many accounts of perception and cognition of melody are couched in terminology reflecting grammatical structures as psychological reality.

Whether one speaks of schemata, rules of generative grammar, or expectations regarding melody, general agreement exists that the Gestalt laws of perceptual organization noted earlier in this discussion remain valid. The melodic expectations, or schemata, of an individual growing up in a Western culture most likely are for tonal Gestalts, probably couched in a tonal harmonic framework, that utilize diatonic scale tones, generally have small intervals between tones, return with considerable frequency to certain tones, and usually end with some implied conventional cadence.

When an individual is confronted with a melody in an unfamiliar style, and hence has no particular expectations, the probability of responding to it as a melodic entity is lessened considerably (Meyer, 1967, p. 277). The failure of total serial music to achieve wide acceptance is partly because listeners have not learned the style's structural premises. Meyer also maintains that the nature of serial melodies, which requires each chromatic tone within the octave to appear before another may be repeated, does not allow sufficient repetition or *redundancy* for listeners to perceive them as a whole. The melodic pattern, while structurally *logical,* lacks sufficient *psychological* unity for perception by the casual listener. Further, Meyer suggests that there is no homogeneous core of style to serve as a reference point for serial music; the stylistic diversity

within the idiom is too great. In terms of Lerdahl's (1988, p. 235) generative grammars, the compositional grammar has "lost touch" with the
listening grammar.

In conclusion, Lundin's (1967, p. 84) position that melody is a function
of both a listener's previous experience and certain sequential characteristics appears to provide the most viable basis for defining melody. An
individual learns his or her culture's melodic idioms. Some musical
knowledge is explicit and verbalizable, but much is implicit, the result of
unconscious schemata guiding musical expectations (Carterette & Kendall,
1989, p. 147). Familiarity with cultural melodic idioms provides a basis
for developing expectations (or for formulating schemata) regarding
unfamiliar tonal sequences, thus enabling response to a new sequence as
a melodic entity. However, a culture's melodic idioms are the product of
a musical development which recognizes that melodies must incorporate
some unifying structural attributes that will enable listeners to perceive
and remember them. Tonal series that provide bases for perceptual
organization in accordance with the Gestalt laws of organization appear
to be the most readily accepted and therefore are most likely to be
perceived as melodies. Ultimately, only the perceiver can judge whether
a tonal sequence functions as a melody: If it does, it *is* a melody.

Harmony

Harmony is such an important aspect of Western music that people
often respond to isolated melodies in terms of harmonic expectations as
much as in terms of melodic expectations. As Sloboda (1985, p. 52) notes,
"when listeners hear a melody, their processing of it normally involves
the attempt to retrieve implicit harmonic and rhythmic structure." Apel
(1969, p. 372) maintains that "from the beginning of the eighteenth
century on, the beauty of melodic lines depended largely on the effective
arrangement of the harmonies underlying them."

In its broadest sense, harmony refers to music's vertical pitch structures
as opposed to its horizontal pitch structure, melody. Apel (1969, pp.
371–374) summarizes its development. Early combinations of melodies,
organum, generally involved parallel motion between two or three
melodies, but as judgments developed that certain intervals between
melodies "sounded better" simultaneously than others, there was increased
concern for the resultant sounds of the multiple voices. It was not until
about the mid-sixteenth century that harmony gained acceptance as a
primary structural concern in music. Apel categorizes the era between
900 and 1450 as the period of *pretertian harmony.* (Music prior to this era
was essentially melodic.) Harmony of this era is characterized by much

parallel motion, open spacing among voices, and some use of triads at the beginning and ending of phrases.

The years between 1450 and 1900 are considered the era of *tertian harmony*.[4] Western music of this era resulted in the development of triadic harmony from triad movement in an essentially modal sequence, through strong tonic, subdominant, and dominant triads in music of the late baroque and classical periods, to harmonies of the romantic period that exploited the triadic system to its extremes with extensive use of chromatic alterations and distant modulations.

While the preponderance of twentieth-century music still is constructed within a tertian harmonic framework, Apel considers the era beginning in 1900 through the present as the period of *posttertian harmony* because of the development of vertical structures that deliberately violate the triadic harmony system. Debussy's "parallel chords," Scriabin's quartal harmony, Schoenberg's serial techniques, aleatoric music, *musique concrete,* and many of the developments in electronic and avant garde music reflect efforts to organize the vertical dimension of pitch in manners different than tertian harmony.

Because harmony in its various forms is such an integral component of most Western music, and therefore a factor for consideration in examining musical behavior, it will be examined in terms of both its structural and perceptual characteristics.

Structural characteristics of harmony. Simultaneous pitch combinations generally are one of two basic textures, *polyphonic* or *homophonic.* (Melody alone is *monophonic,* i.e., it involves only a single pitch at a time.) Polyphonic texture combines two or more simultaneously sounding melodies. Concern with "how good" (the consonance-dissonance character) the resulting simultaneous pitches sound varies to a large degree with the era in which the music was composed. Generally, polyphonic music of the pre- and posttertian eras reflects less concern for the character of the simultaneous sounds than polyphonic music of the tertian harmony era. Homophonic texture features one melody supported by a tertian harmonic framework and considers *both* the resultant horizontal and vertical dimensions of the musical sound.

Most references to harmony in music are to homophonic music constructed in a tertian harmonic framework. Harmony in this narrower and more common sense refers to the highly developed system of chords

---

[4]"Tonal harmonic framework" as used in the previous section refers to the tertian harmony system. As will be noted in the discussion of tonality, the tertian harmony system elicits a strong feeling for a tonal center; hence, the expression "tonal harmonic framework" applies to music constructed according to the practices of tertian harmony.

and relations between chords that characterize most Western music, particularly that of the baroque, classical, and romantic periods. While differences in harmonic practices of the three periods exist, harmony of the three periods has a common structural base.

Music of these periods, which comprises the predominant styles of "classical" music performed today, is constructed around a key, center, or tonic. Music constructed around a key center possesses *tonality,* or "loyalty to the tonic." (The next section provides a more detailed discussion of tonality.) The triads or chords constructed on the first, fourth, and fifth degrees of the scale, respectively called the tonic, subdominant, and dominant, serve as the primary structural mechanism for maintaining emphasis on the tonal center. Once this mechanism became firmly established as the vehicle for focusing attention on the tonal center, thus providing harmonic unity or repetition, composers could depart from the harmonic framework and then return to the tonic. Harmonic conventions were developed through which functional chord progressions, structured around the tonic, subdominant, and dominant but also extending through chords built on other scale tones as well as through modulations into other keys, served as the primary unifying force. Harmonic practices of the romantic period carried this system to its extremes.

Twentieth-century developments of ways for combining pitches simultaneously have resulted in varied techniques and styles. This is not to suggest, however, that tertian harmony is no longer used as a compositional device. To the contrary, it is still the primary structural mechanism for combining pitches simultaneously, particularly in popular music.

Perceptual organization of harmony. Theorists have studied and analyzed music's harmonic structure since its inception, and harmony continues to be a major area of study for students preparing for careers in music. Until recently, however, there has been relatively little study of harmony in terms of people's responses to it or their ability to comprehend it.

Traditional attempts to explain response to harmony were in terms of mathematics. Beginning with the work of the Greek philosopher Pythagoras in the sixth century B.C., promulgated by medieval church scholars, responses to the predominantly melodic music of those times were examined and explained in terms of simple mathematical ratios. With the development of music constructed in a tonal harmonic framework, mathematical explanations continued, but because of the compromises of equal temperament,[5] convenient explanations in terms of simple mathematical ratios no longer applied. Consequently, attempts to explain harmony

---

[5]The equal tempered scale is discussed later in this chapter.

in terms of psychological characteristics must look beyond music's "scientific" or mathematical aspect.

Both Farnsworth (1969, pp. 37–41) and Lundin (1967, pp. 88–89) believe that response to harmony is a *cultural phenomenon.* Just as individuals' experiences with their culture's music enable them to develop melodic expectations, the experiences also foster harmonic expectations. Music in which the harmony does not conform in a general way to the harmonic practices with which a listener is familiar sounds "strange" or "different." Even though most listeners cannot verbalize *what* sounds strange or different, the effect is disturbing because the listener's general expectations are unfulfilled.

Harmony, just as melody and rhythm, also is comprised of patterns and is perceived in terms of "wholes" (Mainwaring, 1951). Individuals respond to harmony in terms of its totality rather than its individual tones or chords. (It is only during formal musical training that most individuals attempt to analyze harmony into its constituent parts.)

There are three primary "holistic" attributes of harmonic structure toward which individuals respond and develop expectations: (a) tonality, (b) harmonic movement, and (c) finality. The laws of perceptual organization noted under the discussion of melody also appear basic for perceiving harmonic attributes. Tonality, with its tonal center, provides an underlying repetition or redundancy which helps a listener respond to a complex sequential series of multiple sounds bombarding the central nervous system via the auditory sensory mechanisms. As Meyer (1967, pp. 288–293) has noted, experience with music constructed in a tonal harmonic framework provides the basis for perceiving redundancy, in this case tonality, which enables a listener to "make sense" of music heard in relation to expectations.

Response to harmonic movement appears to occur in a manner similar to the response to melodic contour. Harmonic movement or progression is a *relative* phenomenon, as is melody. We respond to harmonic movement in *relation* to tonality. Practices in functional harmony become a standard or model for listeners' harmonic expectations. As harmonic practices change, listeners learn the new harmonic styles and develop expectations accordingly.

Meyer (1967, p. 292) believes that a primary difficulty composers face in having a large number of listeners accept contemporary music, particularly serial music and other music not constructed within a tonal harmonic framework, is that it lacks the unifying harmonic attributes that provide the redundancy necessary for meaningful perception. As Krumhansl (1990, p. 270) puts it, "a basic mismatch may exist between this style's ([12-tone serial] treatment of all chromatic scale pitches equally, and the [learned] psychological tendency to relate all pitches to a few stable and unchanging reference pitches." Music constructed in a tonal harmonic framework has an inherent redundancy through its tonal center and harmonic movement in relation to that center.

The direction of the melody line at cadence points is readily predictable for melodies constructed in relation to a tonal harmonic framework, and the conventions of cadence used during the eighteenth and nineteenth centuries still provide the basis for most Westerners' finality expectations. Few listeners would not expect a dominant-seventh chord to resolve to a tonic chord, even though most of them could not label the chords. Experience in hearing harmony provides the basis for such expectations, even without any formal musical training, just as experience in hearing melody builds melodic expectations.

Contemporary music psychologists have not studied harmonic perception nearly as much as they have studied melody. Articles on aspects of rhythmic and melodic perception abound in edited volumes of research and writings on music psychology (e.g., Clynes, 1982; Deutsch, 1982; Howell, Cross, and West, 1985), but there is a virtual void of information on harmonic perception in these volumes. Nevertheless, there appears to be at least a tacit acceptance that, just as for melodic perception, experienced listeners develop internalized cognitive structures or schemata of musical keys, key relationships, and functions of chords within keys. Theory and research to support such assumptions is limited, although some recent research especially related to harmonic perception offers principles suggesting how experienced listeners organize harmonic information.

Krumhansl, Bharucha, and Castellano (1982) identified three *context-dependent* principles of harmonic organization, all of which are supported by experimental evidence. One principle is *contextual identity:* When a chord occurs in an established key context, it is heard as more closely related to *itself* than when it is out of the context of key. This means that the chord will be recognized more easily in the context key or a closely related key than in a distant key.

A second principle is *contextual distance:* Two different chords are more closely related (perceptually similar) when they are in the same key than when they are not both in the same key. The closer the keys, the less extreme is the difference. For example, the C and G major triads, which contain tones found in both the C major and G major diatonic scales, are quite closely related. The C major and D major triads are not so closely related, although since D major is the dominant of G major, a closely related key to C major, the C–D relationship is closer than, say, the relationship between the C major and Db major triads.

The third principle, related to the order in which chords occur in a particular musical example, is *contextual asymmetry:* Two successive chords are more closely related when the first chord is out of context and the second chord is in context than when the first chord is in and the second chord is out. The strength of contextual asymmetry is a function of the context key and the keys of which the chords could be a part. Perceptual distance decreases as the second chord moves closer to the context key and the first chord moves further from it. As an example, in C major, movement of a D major triad to a G major triad results in a greater perceptual similarity between the two triads than the opposite movement, G to D. If, in the second case, the chords are made parallel *minor* chords so that a G–Bb–D chord moves to a D–F–A chord, the distance decreases.

Krumhansl, Bharucha, and Kessler (1982) identified a "core" of eight chords on the basis of how well the chords from the keys of C major, G major, and A minor seemed to follow each other in paired combinations. The "core" included the I (tonic), II (supertonic), IV (subdominant), V (dominant), and VI (mediant) chords from C major, the I, II, IV, V, and VI chords from G major, and the I, IV, V, and VI chords from A minor. Those chords reduce to eight triads: C major (C E–G), D minor (D–F–A), E minor (E–G–B), F major (F–A–C), G major (G–B–D), A minor (A–C–E), D major (D–F#–A), and E major (E–G#–B). The I, IV, and V chords were particularly close in each key. Chords unique to G major or A minor were relatively remote. Subjects perceived C major as the dominant tonality; they had a strong preference for sequences ending on the C chord. There was a lesser preference for sequences ending on the G chord; no regular pattern existed for A minor.

Bharucha and Krumhansl (1983) gathered further evidence that the principles of contextual identity, contextual distance, and contextual asymmetry governed harmonic organization in tonal contexts. On the basis of their experimental data obtained from musically experienced subjects who evaluated how "well" one chord seemed to follow another or how "well" a chordal sequence differed from another due to one altered chord, the investigators reconfirmed the "context" principles and identified three additional "key" principles that govern harmonic organization *independently* of context: *key membership, intrakey distance,* and *intrakey asymmetry.*

The "key" principles are not surprising in view of the traditions of Western music theory, but the investigators helped give the principles a research basis. According to the key membership principle, chords from the same key are more related than chords from different keys. For example, the G major and E minor triads, I and VI from G major, are more related than the G major and Eb major triads. The intrakey distance principle says that a key's I, IV, and V chords (the key's "harmonic core") are related more closely than the key's "non-core" chords. In D major, for example, the relationships among the D, G, and A major triads are stronger than the relationships among the triads built on the remaining scale degrees, E, F#, B, and C#. Intrakey asymmetry means that paired chords from the same key are more closely related if the first chord is not in the "harmonic core" and the second is than they are if the first chord is in the "core" but the second is not. The II–V relationship, exemplified in C major by a D minor chord moving to a G major chord, is closer than the V–II relationship, exemplified in C major by the G–D chordal movement.

Together the "key" principles and the "context" principles summarize the organization of harmonic information, according to Bharucha and Krumhansl. The "key" and "context" principles reflect how experienced listeners abstract underlying structures from complex musical stimuli. The principles also suggest that harmonic perception involves the perception of *relationships* among patterns, particularly those related to chordal sequences and keys. It can also be argued that the principles provide further support that the perceptual organization laws of Gestalt psychology are operating during music perception; they certainly do not refute them.

Krumhansl (1990, pp. 211) points out the "strong interdependencies between the three levels of musical structure: tones, chords, and keys" and notes that empirical studies support the view that "structures applicable to tones, chords, and keys are strongly tied to one another." Further, she notes that the correspondence between psychological data and the frequencies of tones and chords in tonal harmonic music suggests that the "internal representation of tonal and harmonic relations is acquired through experience" (p. 212).

Tonality

Implicit in the discussion of both melody and harmony is the recognition that tonality unifies the perception of music constructed within a tonal harmonic framework. Much twentieth-century music, however, does not have a tonal harmonic framework; some music is structured specifically to be atonal. Yet Temko's (1972, p. 33) study of pitch predominance in twenty avant-garde compositions revealed agreement among subjects concerning a predominant pitch in each of the compositions. Apparently even atonal and electronic music not designed with an *a priori* tonality may evoke listener response in terms of some central or focal pitch. Considering tonality from this perspective, most music could be said to reflect a "loyalty to the tonic" (Apel, 1969, p. 855), perhaps the most generally accepted broad definition of tonality.

This tonic is the *tonal center* and serves as the tone to which other tones ultimately return; the tonal center is the basic musical expectation to which most other expectations relative to melodic and harmonic perception are related. Such relationships are an extension of the intimacy, similarity, and circularity dimension of the psychological tonal property of pitch, discussed in Chapter Four.

Implicit in most discussions of tonality in Western music is the application (and limitation) of the term to music constructed in a tonal harmonic framework, using essentially tones of either a major or minor diatonic scale. As is noted in the next section, Western tertian harmony is built with the scale and chord tones of diatonic scales, and references to tonal music and tonality usually refer to music constructed of scale and chord tones from diatonic scales.

Melodic movement in tonal music includes both conjunct and disjunct motion. Conjunct motion is essentially scalar, although chromatic and/or altered scale tones may be used. Disjunct motion involves skips or leaps, usually on tones outlining chords underlying the implied harmonic framework. Melodies of the baroque and classical periods tend to outline scale and chord patterns more clearly than music of the romantic period, much of which involves chromaticism and frequent key modulations.

Taylor (1976) reports that pitch structure of melodies is one determinant of tonality. The more the melodic movement conforms to the scale and chord structure of the key in which a melody is constructed, the greater the tonal strength, or tonality, of the melody. Melodies not using the scale and chord tones of the key have less tonal strength, and melodic contour alone does not appear to be a significant factor in the determination of the tonal strength of a melody.

Tonal strength may be quantified in terms of ambiguity by using an adaptation of information theory (Attneave, 1959; Taylor, 1971, 1976). Individuals sing what they hear as a melody's tonal center; the proportions of singers singing any particular tone from twelve chromatic scale tones are placed in the formula,

$$TS = \Sigma\, p\, (\log_2 1/p)$$

where

$\qquad$ TS = tonal strength obtained by consensus,

and

p = proportion of observers selecting any particular tone.

If all sing the same tone, there is no ambiguity regarding the tonal strength, and the quantified value is 0.00. The upper limit of the TS value depends on the number of singers; if there were twelve singers and each one sang a different chromatic scale tone, the TS would be 3.58.

Cuddy's (1982) research on the perception of tonality yielded similar results. Subjects in her study rated melodies which ended on the tonic and whose structures used diatonic scale tones in patterns based on tertian harmony traditions as having a higher degree of tonality than melodies whose structures did not closely follow the diatonic scale and chord patterns of tertian harmony. Subjects for Cuddy's study included both trained musicians and people without formal training in music; the results were virtually the same for both groups.

Melodies of the baroque and classical periods tend to have greater tonal strength than romantic melodies. In turn, romantic melodies elicit a stronger feeling for tonality than melodies that are not written within a tonal harmonic framework.

Krumhansl and Bharucha's "context" and "key" principles suggest that the perception of harmonic movement in tonal music also is intertwined with and dependent upon the chord patterns of tertian harmony. With the development of functional harmony in the seventeenth and eighteenth centuries, the basic patterns of harmonic movement and relationships among chords were established. The consistency of harmonic progressions in eighteenth-century music provides sufficient redundancy for listeners to develop and maintain strong feelings for tonality. Music of the romantic period, which also is constructed essentially within a tonal harmonic framework, extends harmonic practices far beyond those of the baroque and classical periods. It would be interesting to see the extent to which Krumhansl and Bharucha's context and key principles, which were derived under carefully controlled (perhaps "stereotypical") conditions, apply to music reflecting harmonic practices of the romantic period.

To date, most examinations of the psychological structures and processes related to perception of tonality have been in terms of Western music constructed within a tonal harmonic framework. Erickson (1982), however, suggests the need to expand the definition to the "tonal" music of all times and places. The particular definition he recommends "has the additional merit of leaving the relation between system and perception ready for research" (p. 522). The recommended definition:

> Tonality may be broadly conceived as a *formal structure in which pitch content is perceived as functionally related to a specific pitch-class or pitch-class-complex of*

resolution, often preestablished and preconditioned, as a basis for structure at some understood level of perception. . . . (The terms *pitch class* and *pitch-class-complex* are used to denote pitch independent of specific registral occurrence, or a complex of such pitches generically understood.) (Berry, 1976, p. 27)

Scales and Modes

Definitions of *scale* and *mode* are many and varied. In a narrow sense each has a particular meaning, but in a broad sense they both refer to the same phenomenon: the basic tones of a composition arranged in order of pitch from lowest to highest (or highest to lowest). Most Western music divides the octave into a basic number of discrete fixed pitches, which psychologists now recognize as being perceived as members of *pitch classes* or *categories,* hence the increasing number of references to fixed pitches as *categorical pitch.* The number and particular arrangement of pitches in a scale or mode may vary, although convention suggests that only a limited number of pitch arrangements have gained widespread acceptance.

Usage implies acceptance. Particular pitch arrangements that continue to be used by at least some cultural or subcultural group apparently have gained a certain acceptance; pitch arrangements that are not used apparently are not acceptable.

Conventional practice in today's Western music divides the octave into twelve equal semitones, i.e., a *chromatic* scale. Virtually all standard musical instruments have the capability for producing the chromatic scale. However, the chromatic scale is not the predominant scale; the *diatonic* scale, a designated order of tones and semitones which preceded the chromatic scale historically, remains the predominant pattern. Even though ancient Greek and medieval church scholars recognized chromaticism, dividing the octave into twelve *equal* semitones did not occur until the development of equal temperament, which is discussed later in this chapter. Chromaticism is very much evident in romantic and some contemporary music, but the chromatic scale *per se* has not become the predominant scale of Western music, even though virtually all musical instruments can produce it.

Essentially, a scale is diatonic if the octave includes seven fixed pitches, usually creating five whole-tone intervals and two semitone intervals, with an eighth pitch doubling the lowest at the octave and eliciting a response of functional equivalence with the lowest tone. (The term *mode* often refers to a particular sequence of intervals, as in a major mode being two whole-tones, a semitone, three whole-tones, and a semitone.)

The phenomenon of the functional equivalence of octaves, sometimes referred to as octave generalization or examined in terms of perceptual similarity, intrigues many persons concerned with understanding music perception. It appears to be related to a property of pitch termed *tone chroma,* which is an outgrowth of a "two-component theory" of pitch that recognizes two dimensions, *tone height* and *tone chroma* (Revesz, 1953, pp. 59–65). For Western music, generally, tones of different pitches (and usually pitch names), i.e., tones other than at the octave, are said to differ in pitch height; tones at the octave (and usually having the same pitch name) are said to have the same tone chroma.

The phenomenon of tone chroma is complex and often is represented graphically by a helix or torus in which tone chroma is represented as a circular dimension and tone height is represented as the vertical dimension. Additional dimensions may exist in other geometrical configurations. Several excellent accounts of the phenomenon are available (Deutsch, 1982; Sergeant, 1983; Shepard, 1982), and readers interested in examining the perceptual bases of tone chroma may want to consult them. Deutsch (p. 272) notes that contemporary music theorists make an analogous distinction between *pitch* and *pitch class.* Tones at the octave, the functional equivalents, are considered members of the same pitch class.

In common usage, the arrangement of tone and semitones within the octave determines whether the pitch arrangement is considered a scale or mode. The two predominant pitch arrangements for Western tonal music are called major and minor scales, although many consider those scales to be particular modes. Following is a discussion of the functions of scales, scale tuning systems, major and minor scales, and other modal and scale structures.

Functions of Scales

According to Mursell (1937, p. 107), musical scales are social phenomena that allow for exploitation of tonal relationships. He maintains that scales are *not* manifestations of some mathematical idea. Neither, he says, are there *natural* scales; if there were, all cultures would use the same scales.

Musical systems are created by people. As a system develops, changes are made in terms of human feelings and perceptions rather than to fulfill any order of goodness in terms of frequency ratios. Evolved scale systems reflect attempts to codify and make the systems available for use by others. If music were not a sociocultural phenomenon, there would be no need for musical scales; each person could develop a private scale system.

The tempered diatonic scale system is probably the most far-reaching and authoritative standardization of music for social purposes the world has ever known (Mursell, p. 107). Musical instruments, notation, and practices of Western cultures are so integrally bound to this system that new systems which are incompatible with the diatonic scale system appear unlikely to gain widespread acceptance. Even in electronic music, the compositions that generally meet with greatest acceptance usually involve the use of some traditional instruments or timbres and melodies and harmonies based on the diatonic scale.

Musical scales also provide a basis for establishing definite tonal relationships. Together with rhythm they provide the consistency which people need to deal with the infinite range of sounds from which music is comprised. Without a predominant scale system, it is unlikely that music ever would have become the potent force it is today. Scales make it possible for people to create and organize from sounds a construct (music) that has functional and aesthetic value for significant proportions of most cultural groups.

Scale Tuning Systems

Throughout music history, changes have occurred in both the frequency standard, an absolute phenomenon, and the tuning of scales, a relative phenomenon. Backus (1977, pp. 150–151) notes that the frequency of A_4 (second space on the treble clef staff, the present A 440) has varied from somewhere in the range of 415 to 428 Hz during the mid-eighteenth century to as high as 461 Hz in the late nineteenth century. Standards also have varied from country to country. It was not until 1953 that the International Standards Organization officially recognized A = 440 HZ as the frequency standard for music.

Scale tuning systems have been subject to much debate by mathematicians, acousticians, and music theorists since the time of the ancient Greeks. While the tempered diatonic scale is today's standard for Western music, there is still much controversy regarding performance practices with respect to it and other tuning systems (Barbour, 1951, pp. 196–201; Farnsworth, 1969, pp. 26–27; Ostling, 1974).

Tempered means that the scale tones have been changed so that, except for the octave, intervals resulting from simultaneous combinations of tones within the scale are not in simple, i.e., whole number, mathematical ratios among the frequencies of the respective tones, as are the intervals in some other tuning systems. *Equal temperament* is the name given to the tuning system which divides the octave into twelve equal semitones.

Equal temperament developed along with, and indeed made possible, the development of Western tonal harmony. Earlier tuning systems were adequate for monophonic music and to a degree for polyphonic music, but as polyphony developed with increased emphasis on the sonorities resulting from the music's vertical structure, previous tuning systems proved inadequate. While detailed discussion of the various tuning systems is more appropriately a concern of musical acoustics or history books, a brief discussion of the most prominent systems is necessary here, particularly since controversy remains regarding tunings used in performance today. Readers interested in studying tuning system in greater depth should consult the excellent presentations by Barbour (1951), Backus (1977), Blackwood (1985), and Wilkinson (1988). Blackwood provides an authoritative and detailed mathematical basis for the recognizable diatonic scales. Wilkinson provides a basic guide to alternative scales, temperaments, and microtunings using synthesizers, with particular focus on microtonality and microtuning in twentieth-century electronic music. Wilkinson also includes descriptions of several contemporary tunings, including the 19-, 24- (quarter-tone), 31-, and 53-tone scales.

The diatonic scale has its roots in the tetrachords which were the basis of the Greek "Greater Perfect System." Tetrachords were series of four descending tones, the range of which was a perfect fourth. Depending on the arrangement of the two inner tones, the tetrachords were one of three *genera: diatonic* (two whole tones and one semitone), *chromatic* (a minor third and two semitones, or *enharmonic* (a major third and two quarter tones). The diatonic genus apparently was the most popular among theorists at the time. Combinations of tetrachords, primarily in conjunct arrangement and with an added tone at the bottom, formed the Greek Greater Perfect System from which the present day diatonic system evolved. The pattern *do, re, mi, fa, so, la, ti, do,* although originally conceived in inverse order, has been basic to much Western music ever since.

Tuning of Greek scale intervals apparently was based on the system developed by Pythagoras (*c.* 550 B.C.). His tuning system, now called the Pythagorean scale, derived frequencies of all tones from the interval of a pure, i.e., beatless, fifth, which has the simple ratio of 3:2 between the respective frequencies of the upper and lower tones.[6] Theoretically, the Pythagorean diatonic scale frequencies are obtained by forming a series of successive ascending fifths which then are lowered to the correct octave to form the scale. In practice, as Backus (1977, pp. 137–139) and Roederer (1995, p. 173) have described, the tuning of the scale is derived by tuning a beatless ascending fifth, a beatless descending fourth, a beatless descending fifth, etc. The result is the same, a scale that has beatless perfect fourths, fifths, and octaves (see Table 6-1).

---

[6]The perfect fourth (ratio = 4:3) also may be the basis for deriving a Pythagorean scale.

Table 6-1

RATIOS AMONG INTERVALS OF THE PYTHAGOREAN DIATONIC SCALE ON C

	do		re	mi	fa	so	la	ti	do
Freq. ratios from do			$\frac{9}{8}$	$\frac{81}{64}$	$\frac{4}{3}$	$\frac{3}{2}$	$\frac{27}{16}$	$\frac{243}{128}$	$\frac{2}{1}$
Freq. ratios adjacent tones		$\frac{9}{8}$		$\frac{9}{8}$	$\frac{256}{243}$	$\frac{9}{8}$	$\frac{9}{8}$	$\frac{9}{8}$	$\frac{256}{243}$
Frequency*	256		288	324	341.3	384	432	486	512
Pitch name	do		re	mi	fa	so	la	ti	do

*Scientific pitch, which has middle C = 256 Hz, as opposed to standard pitch, which has middle C = 261.3 Hz, is used for convenience.

As long as melodic music is performed without transposing, modulating, or using chromatic tones, the Pythagorean scale works well. However, its small semitone is a problem for instrument makers. Further, when the tuning system is extended to include chromatic tones, it results in nonequivalent enharmonic tones, thereby yielding different sizes of semitones. Also, since a Pythagorean scale must be formed in relation to a given starting tone, identical letter names may have different frequencies in different keys; e.g., F will be slightly different in the keys of C, Eb, and A. Clearly, the Pythagorean scale is inadequate for Western tonal harmony.

Just intonation, according to Barbour (pp. 89, 105), appears to have evolved during the fifteenth and sixteenth centuries as theorists sought to improve upon Pythagorean tuning. Just intonation has some advantages over Pythagorean tuning in that it uses more simple ratios between tones and accommodates building triads from simple ratios among major and minor thirds. Just intonation is so named because its intervals conform to the ratios between the tones of the overtone series;[7] i.e., the fifth has a 3:2 ratio, the fourth a 4:3, the major third a 5:4, and the minor third a 6:5. Table 6-2 shows the ratios among adjacent frequencies and in relation to do.

Although having the advantage of simple ratios, just intonation also has a number of disadvantages which for all practical purposes render it useless in most Western tonal music: (a) the scale has two different ratios for whole tones (8:9 and 9:10), (b) the fifth, D–A (in reference to the key of C), is not the same as the other fifths (27:40 versus 2:3), and (c) it does not accommodate modulation to other keys. The farther away from the

---

[7]The "overtone," "harmonic," or "partial" series is the sequential order of theoretical components of a complex tone with no missing harmonics. It has considerable practical value in deriving fingerings for wind instruments, especially brass instruments.

Table 6-2

RATIOS AMONG INTERVALS IN JUST INTONATION

Freq. ratios from *do*		$\frac{9}{8}$		$\frac{5}{4}$		$\frac{4}{3}$		$\frac{3}{2}$		$\frac{5}{3}$		$\frac{15}{8}$		$\frac{2}{1}$
Freq. ratios adjacent tones	$\frac{9}{8}$		$\frac{10}{9}$		$\frac{16}{15}$		$\frac{9}{8}$		$\frac{10}{9}$		$\frac{9}{8}$		$\frac{16}{15}$	
Frequency	256		288		320		341.3		384		426.6		480		512
Pitch name	*do*		*re*		*mi*		*fa*		*so*		*la*		*ti*		*do*

reference key and the more use of accidentals, the more untenable the system becomes. Just as the Pythagorean scale, just scales have tones which require different frequencies in different keys. In short, it is of little value for instruments of fixed pitch such as keyboard and wind instruments, which must accommodate chromaticism and modulation or transposition to all keys. It has been claimed, however, that instruments of variable pitch (string and voice) can accommodate the difficulties of modulation by adjustment and hence play thirds "better in tune," i.e., with "purer" or beatless intervals.

As efforts were made to accommodate harmony and modulation in Western music, two other systems evolved: *meantone* and *equal temperament*. Both involved altering or tempering some scale tones. It is not clear when meantone temperament was first used, but Barbour (p. 25) suggests that it was as early as the beginning of the sixteenth century. Several variations of meantone tuning exist, but the system's essential aspect is that it alters (flattens) some of the fifths of the Pythagorean scale, thus allowing a limited degree of modulation. Its name was derived from the fact that the whole tone C–D was half the size of the major third resulting from the alterations of the fifth. Meantone temperament was used extensively in Europe throughout the seventeenth century and well into the eighteenth century until the acceptance of equal temperament.

Equal temperament is so named because it divides the octave into twelve equal semitones. (Other divisions are possible; technically, division of the octave into any number of equivalent units is "equal temperament.") Each adjacent pair of tones has the same ratio of frequencies, 1:1.05946. Although the octave is the only simple ratio (2:1), there is a consistency among each of the other intervals regardless of key. Equal temperament overcomes the limitations on transposition, modulation, and use of chromaticism that are inherent with Pythagorean, just, and meantone tunings.

The equal tempered semitone is divided into 100 equal parts called *cents.* A semitone therefore equals 100 cents, a whole tone 200 cents. An equal tempered fifth is 700 cents, i.e., it encompasses seven semitones, while the octave, made up of twelve semitones, equals 1200 cents. Cents for a given interval may be computed with the formula $n = 3986.31[\log (f_2/f_1)]$ in which n = number of cents, f_1 = lower tone frequency, and f_2 = upper tone frequency.

Cents are a convenient way for comparing the size of intervals in the various tuning systems. Table 6-3, adapted from Farnsworth (p. 25), compares the size of intervals in the four tuning systems discussed above. As is apparent, the equal tempered fifth is slightly (two one-hundredths of a semitone) smaller than the beatless Pythagorean and just fifths; conversely, the equal tempered fourth is slightly larger than the Pythagorean and just fourths.

Table 6-3

COMPARISON OF PYTHAGOREAN, JUST, MEANTONE, AND EQUAL
TEMPERED TUNINGS

	do	*re*	*mi*	*fa*	*so*	*la*	*ti*	*do*
Pythagorean	0	204	408	498	702	906	1110	1200
Just	0	204	386	498	702	884	1088	1200
Meantone*	0	204	386	503	697	890	1083	1200
Equal	0	200	400	500	700	900	1100	1200

*This is the tuning used by Pietro Aron around 1523.

The major discussions regarding tuning tendencies in contemporary performances, however, center on tuning the major third, *do-mi,* and the size of the interval between the leading tone (*ti*) and *do.* Although equal temperament is recognized as the standard, some performers insist that triads are "better in tune" if they approximate the tuning of the just triad, which has a major third 14 cents lower than the equal tempered major third. This would be possible for performances of a cappella choirs and string quartets, which are not bound by the constraints of keyboard or many wind instruments. Some research (Greene, 1937; Nickerson, 1949) suggests that soloists on string instruments that can adjust intonation tend to approximate Pythagorean tuning when performing leading tones. Backus (1977, p. 150) notes that musicians tend to make adjustments in accordance with what "sounds best."

Barbour (1951, pp. 191–202) and Ostling (1974) review much of the rhetoric regarding the issue and cite the limited research on the matter. Apparently no research has been conducted regarding choirs' tuning tendencies, but Barbour suggests that even if choirs did attempt to adjust to just intonation, the overall pitch would probably fall if the harmonic progressions are traditional diatonic progressions. He does concede, though, that such adjustments might be possible in modal progressions such as those used by Palestrina. He maintains, however, that choirs singing with wind instruments quickly adapt to the intonation of the accompanying instruments.

Perhaps the classic study of intonation tendencies in performance is by Nickerson (1949), who analyzed performances of individual members of string quartets, both in isolation and in ensemble. He concluded that (a) performances do not conform completely to just, Pythagorean, or equal temperament, (b) performances of melodies both in solo and ensemble approach Pythagorean tuning, and (c) factors that cause this pattern appear to dominate both ensemble demands and presumed experience with equal temperament.

Roederer (1995, p. 177), however, cautions against concluding that soloists have a particular preference for Pythagorean intonation. He notes that other studies (Terhardt & Zick, 1975) have shown a tendency for performers to play or sing sharp the upper tone of all successive intervals.

While research is inconclusive regarding intonation practices in contemporary performances, it is apparent that much deviation from equal temperament does occur and is still perceived as "acceptable." Perhaps Ostling (1974, p. 18) best summarizes the current state of the matter:

> Research agrees that good intonation is not any one basic tuning system used exclusively. Beyond that, it seems to this writer that a basic minimum standard of at least equal temperament should be expected—the norm—from which artist-performers will depart for melodic gravitation and/or harmonic reinforcement, as the situation requires, and that is about all one can conclude, at least to date.

Meanwhile, we still have directors of a cappella choirs who insist that their choirs are able to sing in just intonation. Some string players consistently report that they must adjust their intonation differently when playing in a string quartet and when playing with (an equal tempered) piano accompaniment. Clearly, more research is needed.

Major and Minor Modes

Major and *minor* are terms used to describe interval size and type of scales, triads, or keys. With intervals the term simply denotes differences in intervals of a second, third, sixth, or seventh; minor intervals in each class contain one less semitone than the major interval in each class.

When used to distinguish between types of scales, triads, and keys, the basic distinction between major and minor is in the size of the third: the third of the major scale (key, triad) is four semitones, while the third of the minor scale (key, triad) contains only three semitones.

The pattern of tones and semitones within a scale constitute the mode.[8] The basic interval pattern of the major scale or mode is TTSTTTS, where T stands for a whole tone and S stands for a semitone. The minor mode has three variations: natural, melodic, and harmonic. All three forms have the lowered third, thus beginning TS for the intervals between the first three tones, but vary in the intervals between the highest three tones. The interval patterns for the three forms, respectively, are natural—TSTTSTT, melodic—TSTTTTS (ascending) and TSTTSTT (descending), and harmonic—TSTTSAS, with A standing for an augmented second.

The establishment of major and minor as the tonal bases of Western music appeared to evolve with the establishment of equal temperament and the development of harmony. In equal temperament, major and minor scales may be constructed on each of the twelve tones of the chromatic octave, and the interval and chordal relationships within a scale built on a given degree of the octave, i.e., in a given key, are functionally identical to those built in other keys. The fact that music built on major and minor scales (and their harmonic patterns) has dominated Western music of the past three hundred and fifty years so completely suggests that major and minor scales and their concomitant systems of tonality and harmony provide an intelligible tonal harmonic framework for Western music.

Other Modes

While major and minor scales are the predominant scale modes for Western music, many other scale patterns have developed, both within Western cultures and in other cultures. No other pattern, however, has developed into a harmonic system that in any way approaches that of Western tonal harmony based on the major and minor scales, although some scales are in many respects compatible with Western tonal harmony.

The traditional narrow sense of the term *mode* refers to the *church modes* devised by scholars of the medieval church. They consist of eight diatonic scales, using the names of earlier Greek modes but differing in organization and structure, that are the tonal basis of Gregorian chant. Apel (1969, p. 165) describes the system as follows:

> Each [consists] of the tones of the C-major scale (White keys) but starting and closing on d, e, f, or g and limited to the range of an octave. For each of these

---

[8]The mode is determined by the interval pattern within the scale, not by the scale tuning system. One may construct a major, minor, or another mode within a just, Pythagorean, tempered, or any other system.

four notes, called a final (*finalis*), there exists two modes distinguished by the different position of the octave range (*ambitus*) and called respectively authentic and plagal. In the *authentic modes* the ambitus extends from the final to the upper octave; in the *plagal* modes from the fourth below the final to the fifth above it.

In the sixteenth century two scales on A and two on C, which essentially were the natural minor and major scales, were added to the system, bringing the total to twelve. The four authentic modes are the Dorian, Phrygian, Lydian, and Mixolydian. The plagal modes use the same four names but with the prefix "hypo," and the added minor and major modes are called the Aeolian and Ionian respectively. Some also recognize a Locrian mode. Following are the church modes, their ranges, and final notes, in reference to the white keys. (In actuality, each mode is determined by its characteristic interval relationships; a modal scale could start on any tone.)

Mode	Final	Range
Dorian	D	D–D
Hypodorian	D	A–A
Phrygian	E	E–E
Hypophrygian	E	B–B
Lydian	F	F–F
Hypolydian	F	C–C
Mixolydian	G	G–G
Hypomixolydian	G	D–D
Aeolian	A	A–A
Hypoaeolian	A	E–E
Locrian	B	B–B
Hypolocrian	B	F–F
Ionian	C	C–C
Hypoionian	C	G–G

Some of the church modes still are used in the traditional chants in the liturgy of the Catholic Church. Some also are found in folk and contemporary popular music, reflecting considerable rejuvenation of interest in them in the latter half of the twentieth century.

Many other modes have been developed in Western cultures, but only a few have gained much lasting acceptance. Perhaps Debussy's *whole-tone* scale is one of the most successful. It divides the octave into six whole tones, and there are only two basic scales: (a) C,D,E,F#,G#,A#,C and (b) C#,D#,F,G,A,B,C#. The purpose of the whole-tone scale was to break away from the strong feeling for the tonic which traditional tonal harmony elicits. The omission of the three fundamental intervals of tonal harmony—perfect fourth, perfect fifth, and leading tone—was the strategy for accomplishing this.

Pentatonic scales have five tones to the octave and have developed in other cultures as well as Western cultures. The pentatonic scale commonly used in Western cultures has no semitones and in the key of C uses the following tones: C, D, E, G, A, C. Pentatonic scales can be built on any tone of the chromatic scale; within each pattern they also can use any of the five tones as a tonic, thus having five different modes in a manner similar to the church modes. In practice, however, only two modes are used to any extent: the authentic mode, using C as the tonic, and the plagal mode, using G as the tonic.

The *chromatic* scale represents another modal system that has received a certain amount of use in Western cultures. It has been most used in terms of serial music. *Quarter-tone* scales, dividing the octave into twenty-four parts by halving the semitone, also exist.

Backus (1977, pp. 148–149) notes three other suggested scales, which divide the octave into nineteen, thirty-one, and fifty-three parts respectively. He notes that some combinations of the resulting small intervals closely approximate the semitones, thirds, and fifths of just intervals. Von Hoerner (1975) has developed an elaborate scheme of chords, intervals, and chromatic properties of the nineteen and thirty-one tone scales.[9] Perceptually, tiny adjacent intervals become difficult to distinguish.

With developments in computers, synthesizers, and other electronic equipment, it is possible to construct many other varieties of scales. Such scales, sometimes called *synthetic* scales, however, are intended to be unique and therefore of little general interest other than in relation to the particular compositions in which they are used.

Modal organization in music of other cultures offers a great variety of additional modal patterns. Descriptions of even the most common of these is beyond the scope of this discussion, although some are mentioned as examples.

Equally tempered scales also have been developed in the Orient (Farnsworth, 1969, pp. 23–25). The Siamese divided the octave into seven equal parts. Pentatonic scales, somewhat approximating the authentic mode of the Western pentatonic, have been used in nearly all ancient cultures—China, Polynesia, Africa, and Native American (Apel, 1969, p. 653). Chinese music also uses six-tone (sexatonic) and seven-tone (hepta-

---

[9]Theoretically, a person may divide the octave into any number of equal intervals. A division into n intervals uses the nth root of 2 as a multiplier or ratio symbol. With a division into 12 steps, 1.05946 ($\sqrt[12]{2}$) : 1 is the ratio between any two adjacent scale steps. With a division into n steps, $\sqrt[n]{2}{:}1$ is the ratio between any two adjacent scale steps. (The 2 is due to the 2:1 octave relationship.)

tonic) scales, while scales of India and the Middle East are characterized by the use of microtones, i.e., intervals smaller than a semitone.

The possibilities of modal organization in music are infinite, but it is apparent that only a few modal systems have gained any wide-spread acceptance. Reasons for this are primarily cultural, although the compatibility of a scale structure with laws and principles of perceptual organization also appears to be a factor.

Other Types of Pitch Organization

Earlier in this chapter it was mentioned that the twentieth century has given rise to new ways for organizing pitch structure. Lest other discussions in this chapter suggest that pitch organization is possible only within certain conventional frameworks, the present discussion briefly overviews selected twentieth-century Western developments in pitch organization.

The use of chromaticism and the resultant dissonance of the late romantic composers, particularly Wagner, led to a search for pitch organization beyond that which could be provided by triadic harmony. Chromaticism and modulation had evolved to the point that many composers no longer ended compositions in the original tonic key as had been the practice during the baroque, classical, and early romantic periods.

Three distinct developments regarding harmonic practices evolved during the late nineteenth and early twentieth centuries. Some composers continued to compose within the broad outline of a tonal harmonic framework, while at the same time utilizing chords of far greater complexity than traditional triads. A second group of composers continued to use chords from earlier harmonic practices, but sequenced them in such ways that expected progressions and resolutions were not forthcoming. Whole-tone music and polytonality were two results of this development. The third development was abandoning tonality for Schoenberg's serial techniques, which are intended to disrupt any feeling for tonality. Serial techniques, often called twelve-tone techniques because each of the twelve semitones in the octave must be used before another may be repeated, have aroused new interest in structuring the vertical dimension of pitch polyphonically, i.e., in terms of combinations of independent melodic lines. Twentieth-century polyphony, however, differs from contrapuntal writing of the baroque, classical, and romantic periods in that there is little or no concern for the vertical sonorities of traditional tertian harmony.

Three other developments of twentieth-century pitch organization also deviate from the practices of tertian harmony. *Aleatoric* or *chance* music introduces an unpredictability regarding either its composition or performance. Such music leaves some of the pitch, duration, and loudness structure to chance, thus making it very difficult for listeners to develop any melodic or harmonic expectations other than uncertainty itself.

In *musique concrete* traditional sound sources (instruments and voices) are replaced by sounds of various kinds—environmental noises, sounds of nature, or most any other conceivable sound source. These sounds can be recorded, combined, and modified at the composer's will. It may utilize fixed or changing pitches as well as sounds of indefinite pitches to create a collage of sounds. As might be expected, the pitch structure need have no confining framework such as tertian harmony, although it may be assumed that most composers creating music of this type do have some underlying organizational structure in mind.[10]

A final and perhaps most important development in pitch organization of twentieth-century music is electronic music, which with computers, synthesizers, and sound samples has given composers a new vista not only for organizing pitches, but also for creating and modifying new timbres and textures. Composers using an electronic medium can generate and combine pitches in an infinite variety of ways. No longer are the fixed divisions of an octave the basis for all music. The implications of electronic developments are staggering from a music perception standpoint, not only because of possible stimulus arrangements but also because of possible limitations in human respondents.

Developments in serial music, aleatoric music, *musique concrete*, and electronic music have created ambiguities for listeners accustomed to hearing only music constructed in a tonal harmonic framework. At present, the acceptance of such developments in "classical" music appears to be only among a relatively small musical subculture of composers, theorists, musicians, and other listeners. Electronically generated, modified, and/or reproduced sounds are a part of virtually all popular music of the 1990s. The general population of Western cultures, including many people who profess to have "considerable interest" in music, however, are not flocking to the concert halls or buying recordings of music that deviate too radically from tonal harmony. Whether this is just a normal slowness to accept new musical styles or whether it is because the music of these new developments lacks an organizational structure that allows listeners to perceive and cognitively organize the tonal structures is subject to conjecture.

---

[10]Pitch, of course, is not the only basis for musical organization. Rhythm patterns or timbral similarities may provide order to widely diverse pitch structures.

Psychological Processes

Chapter Four examined the processing of individual pure and complex tones; this section examines the psychological processes related to pitch structures in *music*. Much theory and research has sought to determine the internal higher level cognitive representations and strategies for processing musical stimuli. Most of this theory and research has been in relation to melodic organization of Western tonal music, although some work has extended to rhythmic and harmonic structures. Also, several attempts have been made to establish extended, elaborate hierarchical models of musical perception.

The impetus for this surge of interest in the cognitive structures of music is an outgrowth of a major shift in psychology toward focus on "higher level, more cognitive aspects of human behavior" (Krumhansl, 1983, p. 29) and several other developments. According to Krumhansl, the primary influences were Chomsky's (1965, 1975) linguistic theory, with its insistence that language behavior depends on abstract mental representations of linguistic structures, and developments in computer technology, which allowed the development of models and terminology for characterizing complex mental behavior as well as greatly facilitating precision in controlling research variables and analyzing data. Other influences, also noted by Krumhansl, are that two seemingly contradictory approaches for examining music perception provide important bases for research on cognitive processes. These include (a) the "reductionistic approach," reflected in the early work of Helmholtz (1863/1954) and Seashore (1919, 1938), which broke down complex auditory perceptual stimuli for examination in terms of sensory response to basic stimulus units, and (b) the work of Gestalt psychologists (Wertheimer, 1923/1955; Koffka, 1935) in developing laws of perceptual organization. Other important influences cited by Krumhansl were from music theory, which had (a) identified principles of organization for tonal music, (b) developed a terminology for characterization of pitch development, and (c) identified a number of music-theoretic accounts of the nature of the psychological processes in music perception.

Psychological processes are examined here as they relate to (a) hierarchical perceptual structures, (b) empirical studies of perception and memory, (c) melodic and harmonic expectations and information theory, and (d) pitch related behaviors.

Hierarchical Perceptual Structures

A number of hierarchical perceptual models for music exist; West, Howell, and Cross (1985) provide excellent reviews of some of the more influential ones. They also remind us that models are *analogues* that attempt to portray the psychological processes of music perception, and as such involve making inferences about how subjective experiences of musical sound stimuli in our senses and imagination may affect musical judgments and other behavior. Essentially, *models are descriptions of inferred psychological events.* They also are generalized, usually not accommodating individual differences. Nevertheless, most of them offer valuable insights into music perception, cognition, and behavior.

West, Howell, and Cross's (1985) observations and principles regarding hierarchical cognitive structures in music, noted previously in Chapter Five, are briefly reiterated here, because of the important perspective they provide regarding hierarchical perceptual structures. Essentially, they observed that persons developing models should recognize that (a) all perceptual dimensions of musical experience are reflected and accommodated; (b) each listener brings a unique history of music experience to each new music experience; (c) not all music is immediately perceived, organized, and classified in a well-ordered hierarchy, even by sophisticated listeners; (d) the theory should be verifiable in terms of behavior of particular listeners; and (e) extramusical or historical context may influence structural grouping. Their three modelling principles are that (a) models must account for both vertical and horizontal structures, because music involves patterning over time; (b) grouping principles of Gestalt psychology—good continuation, proximity, similarity, regularity, symmetry, and common fate—reflect global perceptual factors that operate in the context of cultural expectations; and (c) groups formed from Gestalt principles may form larger groups at higher hierarchical levels.

It is beyond the scope of this discussion to review the various perceptual hierarchies that have been proposed; however, for illustrative purposes two are briefly examined here: (a) Krumhansl's (1979, 1990) *tonal hierarchy* for Western tonal music and (b) two aspects of Lerdahl and Jackendoff's (1983) model that pertain to pitch structure, *time-span reduction* and *prolongation reduction.* (The aspects of Lerdahl and Jackendoff's model related to rhythmic structures were examined in Chapter Five.) Readers interested in examining these models in detail are referred to the original sources.

Krumhansl's theory evolved from a series of experiments on the processing of pitch patterns in a tonal context. In one experiment, musical subjects listened to a C major scale or triad, followed by paired tones. Subjects rated the tonal similarity within each pair on a 1–7 scale. Generally, tones from the C triad were rated as quite similar, other tones from the C major scale were as rated somewhat less similar, and nondiatonic tones (tones other than the scale tones) were rated as less similar yet. The second tones tended to have larger similarity effects; i.e., the pair was rated as more similar when the second tone was related more closely to the tonal context than the first tone.

In the second experiment, subjects heard patterns comprised of a standard tone, followed by eight interpolated tones and a final comparison tone, which either was the same as the standard or differed by a semitone. The task was to indicate on a 1–6 scale the certainty that the comparison tone matched the standard. Interpolated tones were either tonal, i.e., the standard was in the tonal context suggested by the interpolated tones, or atonal, i.e., the standard was nondiatonic in relation to the interpolated tones. In general, it was easier for subjects to remember diatonic standard tones when the "interference" was caused by diatonic interpolated tones. It was easier to remember nondiatonic tones when the interpolated tones were also nondiatonic. A similar third experiment in which the interpolated tones were free of test tones gave similar results. In a fourth experiment, subjects judged tonal sequences to be more "musical" than atonal sequences.

Krumhansl applied multidimensional scaling techniques to the similarity ratings and described a *tonal hierarchy*. The multidimensionality is represented by a three-dimensional cone, with the components of the tonic triad lying close together near the vertex. The next level, farther from the vertex, is a less closely related subset consisting of the remaining diatonic scale tones. Still farther from the vertex is a widely dispersed grouping of the nondiatonic tones which remain from the chromatic octave. In other words, in a tonal context the tonic triad (e.g., C–E–G in C major) has perceptual similarity among its components which is greater than any other similarity; the similarity among remaining scale tones (D, F, A, B in C major) is greater than that among nondiatonic tones (e.g., Bb, Db, G#). Perceptual similarities arising from experience with tonal contexts may be critical in guiding the perceptual tracking of a melody.

Butler (1989, 1990a, 1990b) takes issue with Krumhansl's tonal hierarchy theory, arguing that the theory "does not describe how listeners perceive those relationships as they unfold during the music listening act" (1990a, p. 7), and proposes an alternative theory as a basis for explaining listeners' ability to recognize the tonic. Butler maintains that listeners' choices of the most plausible tonic for a given musical excerpt are based on clear statements of *rare intervals* (minor seconds and tritones) within the excerpt. "The dominant-tonic succession that these temporal arrangements of rare intervals represent are characteristic to harmonic cadences in tonal music, and are seldom encountered in atonal music" (p. 9).

In response to Butler's criticism of the tonal hierarchy theory, Cuddy (1991) devised two studies which she claims reaffirm the privileged position of the ascending major triad, which is the core of Krumhansl's tonal hierarchy, thus strengthening the tonal hierarchy theory. Her first experiment asked subjects to judge the suitability of each of the twelve tones of the chromatic scale as a tonic for eight melodic test patterns: ascending and descending major triads, fifth patterns, minor triads, and diminished triads. Her results revealed that of the responses to the eight melodic patterns, responses to the ascending major triad most clearly defined the tonic as the key tone. In her second experiment, Cuddy asked a different group of subjects to rate the same eight melodic patterns for their "structural goodness." Again, respondents rated the ascending major as eliciting the highest level of structural goodness.

Without having any data to substantiate it, the present authors surmise that the tonal hierarchy theory and Butler's rare interval theory may be two sides of the same coin, and the side that one sees may be determined by the nature of the experimental methodology employed to test the theory. Musicians experienced with music constructed within the Western tonal harmonic framework most likely would find either the tonal hierarchy data or the rare interval data convincing when considered in isolation from the other; both positions have an intuitive "correctness" about them. The tonal relationships of Krumhansl's hierarchy appear to be congruent with musicians' experiences, but the strong dominant-tonic pull evoked by the rare intervals also are consistent with musician's experiences. Undoubtedly, there will be more research and discussion relative to the matter. Whatever subsequent research is forthcoming relative to the two positions, the reader must remember that both theories are dealing with inferred cognitive processes based on perceptions of musical events rather than the actual acoustical structure of the music.

Lerdahl and Jackendoff's (1983) elaborate hierarchical model of tonal structure is based more on theory than research. Two of its hierarchical components, *time-span reduction* and *prolongation reduction*, concern pitch structures. As the name implies, the time-span reduction hierarchy seeks to formalize the way in which pitch events are perceived at different levels of structural importance within a given time span. It involves examination of pitch within various levels of the hierarchical "tree" for that time-span, seeking to determine which pitch is most stable. That pitch is called the "head" of the time-span. The process is repeated hierarchically for groupings of time-spans, until the deepest, most abstract level of grouping is reached.

Two types of rules are applied in forming structures according to Lerdahl and Jackendoff: *well-formedness* rules, which specify possible structures, and *preference* rules, which designate the probable structures that are likely to conform to the way experienced listeners organize the music. Well-formedness rules may answer the question "What's possible?" Preference rules may answer the question "What corresponds to expectancies?" Well-formedness rules for time-span reduction are concerned with specifying the nature of time-span heads; preference rules for time-span reduction specify principles according to which time-span head is chosen.

Essentially, time-span reduction "is intended to account for the distribution of structural and ornamental [pitch] events in a piece, and to give a clear picture of the network of interconnected regions governed by these events" (Clarke, 1986, p. 6). Clarke notes that time-span reduction presents an essentially static and primarily spatial perspective on pitch organization in tonal music and that it ignores the dynamic properties operating within and beyond the boundaries of the time-span units.

Prolongation reduction attempts to overcome this problem. Whereas time-span reduction works from small groupings to larger, more abstract groupings (from surface to depth), prolongation reduction works in the opposite direction (from depth to surface). Showing some Schenkerian influences, prolongation reduction begins with a simple pitch event, perhaps representing an entire piece or section, and "elaborates this single event until a level of detail close to the musical surface is reached" (Clarke, p. 6). Prolongation reduction essentially assigns pitches hierarchical positions based on tension-relaxation and continuity. Prolongation reduction also has a hierarchical tree structure, and well-formedness rules for prolongation reduction are similar to those for time-span reduction. Preference rules select a hierarchy in term of melodic and harmonic stability and principles of harmonic progression derived from music-theoretic considerations.

As West, Howell, and Cross (1985, p. 39) state, the "model attempts to provide a symbolic representation of music that elucidates its structure as perceived by a listener." Lerdahl and Jackendoff suggest that the model provides a musical "grammar," which includes innate aspects arising from inherent cognitive organization. Just as people are "naturally" predisposed to acquire language, although the particular language they acquire is a function of learning, people may be "naturally" predisposed to acquire musical cognition, although the cognitized musical idioms and forms will depend on cultural experience and learning. Variation is possible in language and music, but there are limits to that variation.

Empirical Studies of Perception and Memory

Most of the recent research on music cognition has focused on perception and/or processing of melodic patterns, primarily ones presented in a tonal context. Serafine (1983) notes that this focus contrasts with earlier traditional research in music psychology that tended to dwell on response to single pitches, durations, or chords. Contemporary concerns in music cognition "focus on the structure and relationships *among* elements" (Serafine, p. 5).

Serafine sees three categories of cognitive processes for music: (a) *global, field-defining processes* that facilitate characterization of the general nature of a piece of music; (b) *temporal processes* that involve groupings of both successive, horizontal events and simultaneous, vertical events into units and groups of units; and (c) *nontemporal processes* that include more abstract processes such as *motivic* or *rhythmic abstraction, transformation, closure,* and *hierarchical structuring.* The research examined herein generally fits into the third category.

Examining hierarchical structuring of compound melody, Serafine (1983) tested the assumption that, in certain types of melodic passages, listeners abstract "an underlying structure that embodies two or more simplified or more basic melodies" (p. 9) from a single melody line. Subjects were presented three musical examples: (a) a short piece of music; (b) a *reduction* of the piece to its "more basic structural tones;" and (c) a similar but "wrong" reduction, i.e., with tones not basic and structural. Both the "correct" and "wrong" were presented at different levels of structure, i.e., at *foreground* and *middleground* levels. Subjects (adult nonmusicians) were able to select the "correct" over the wrong reduction at the foreground level, but not at the middleground level. Serafine concluded that her data provide evidence of an initial level of structuring for untrained listeners and that, perhaps even more importantly, the data provide evidence that hierarchical structurings are legitimate cognitive processes rather than just theoretical constructs.

Dowling and Harwood (1986, pp. 130–144) summarize a series of studies suggesting that contour, interval size, and tonal scale system are important features in adults' perception of and memory for melodies and that these features may have different importance, depending on the task's demands. Contour is a particularly important feature for short-term memory tasks, but for long-term memory, where many melodies may share similar contours, interval size plays a much more important role in helping adults differentiate among melodies. Dowling and

Harwood also recognize the importance of individual differences in musical experience for music cognition, particularly with respect to employing learned melodic features, such as the tonal scale system, for processing melody.

Idson and Massaro (1978) conducted a series of experiments involving structural transformations of melodies to evaluate the effects of interval size, contour, tone height, and tone chroma on melodic recognition. In two transformations, a melody's component tones were displaced by octave intervals, either preserving or violating the patterns of change in pitch direction (melodic contour). When contour was violated, perception of the melody was severely disrupted, but when contour was preserved, the melodies were identified as accurately as the untransformed melodies, suggesting that contour, as well as interval size, provides essential information for melodic perception.

Cuddy, Cohen, and Miller (1979) provide evidence that diatonic conditions and cadential relationships are important information for maintaining melodic structures and recognizing deviations from those structures. Forty-eight subjects with "general interest in music" indicated which one of two transpositions of standard melodies was correct. Each transposition was either to the dominant (e.g., G in relation to C) or tritone (e.g., F# in relation to C) tonality in relation to the particular standard's diatonic context. Altered tones, which made particular melodies "wrong" in relation to their standards, were a semitone up or down from where they would have been in a totally accurate transposition. Subjects' performance deteriorated when the "core" of three tones containing the alteration were embedded in a nondiatonic context; it improved when a cadence was provided. The most accurate recognition occurred when (a) there was a diatonic and cadential context, (b) the altered tone was nondiatonic, and (c) the transposition was to the dominant level. The worst recognitions occurred under nondiatonic conditions. Essentially, the investigators provided important evidence that musical structures provide aids which people who are sensitive to those structures may employ in recognizing alterations in a tonal sequence.

Cuddy, Cohen, and Mewhort (1981) asked 120 undergraduates to rate short melodic sequences in terms of tonality or tone structure, with highest ratings for sequences with "musical keyness" or "completeness" and lowest ratings for sequences that contained "unexpected" or "jarring" tones. The seven-tone melodic sequences reflected five levels of harmonic structure; in addition, they varied in two other dimensions, contour and excursion. Essentially contours were simple and complex, depending on the number of direction changes, and excursion was either zero or nonzero, depending on whether the final tone of the sequence was the same as the first or whether it differed from the first. In a second experiment, 60 students were asked to select the position of the correct transposition of the test sequence. A third experiment employed procedures similar to the second, but used on-line computer generated sequences. Results of experiment one revealed that as the rules of diatonicism were violated, i.e., as the harmonic structure changed from the highest level of tonal structures to sequences that deviated radically from diatonic tonal structure, there was a dramatic change in ratings. Both highly trained musicians and subjects with little formal training rated the sequences consistently according to the harmonic structure. Experiments two and three revealed that subjects were able to identify correct transpositions of melodies with greatest accuracy for melodic sequences with the highest level of harmonic structure and with the simplest contour and excursion. In a subsequent experiment using a similar but more difficult task, Cuddy (1982) confirmed that the variables of structure, contour, and excursion held even when mistunings were introduced in the melodic sequences.

Implicit if not directly suggested in each of the above studies is the dependence of perception and memory on the tonal harmonic framework of the melodic pattern. Apparently, people most easily recognize and remember melodies that conform most closely to the rules and grammar of Western tonality. Such findings are consistent with Krumhansl's tonal hierarchy, discussed in the previous section.

The dependence of Western music and the Western listener on harmonic structure and tonality for remembering melodies apparently affects performance. Sterling (1985) examined the effects of stylistically diverse harmonizations on 25 college singers' performances of an unfamiliar tonal melody that had been learned to a specific criterion level. The harmonizations included traditional tonal, chromatic, dissonant, quartal, and chords with extensions. Results revealed a higher degree of vocal accuracy when the melody was accompanied by traditional tonal harmonic accompaniment, suggesting that the structure provided by the tonal harmony affects singers' reproductions of melodies.

The potential of research on music perception and cognition for understanding and facilitating musical behavior appears to be great, although few efforts have been made to "apply" the results as part of a structured pedagogy of music. Perhaps the research base is as yet insufficient for such application, but the challenge remains for both psychologists and educators to interpret and apply such findings.

Expectations and Information Theory

The vast array of musical stimuli comprising melody and harmony, with their inherent attributes of tonal and rhythmic structure, timbral variations, and dynamic change, presents listeners with a stimulus complexity that, without some mechanism for creating perceptual order, would appear as unintelligible cacophony. Indeed, to some individuals, much of what others call *music* is unintelligible cacophony! The question under consideration here, therefore, is "How do individuals create musical meaning out of the mass of sounds called melody and harmony?"

From a psychological perspective, melody and harmony are highly complex, but it appears that most individuals can derive a certain amount of musical *meaning* from them.[11] Many individuals who appear to gain meaning from music, however, have no extensive or intensive formal musical training. On the other hand, even some highly trained musicians apparently perceive little meaning from some avant-garde music. Members of Western culture also can listen to a given Oriental melody and have great difficulty in recognizing any semblance of organizational structure. Still, some individuals within a Western culture can listen to Brahms' *D Major Symphony* and marvel at its structure while others perceive it as unintelligible cacophony. Such observations beg the question, "Why does music hold meaning for some individuals and not for others?"

One approach to the question involved information theory (e.g., Broadbent, 1958; Moles, 1966; Meyer, 1956, 1967). This approach recognizes that a central problem in dealing with complexity is an individual's *capacity* for such. Capacity for perception and cognition of complex stimuli is limited for everyone, although each individual limits vary. We do not know how to assess the limits of perceptual capacity except under somewhat artificial conditions for some isolated tasks. Information theory provides a construct for examining perceptual capacity for music.

Information theory basically is a system for quantifying the amount of *uncertainty* involved in a sensory stimulus or *message*. "A message is a finite, ordered set of elements of perception drawn from a repertoire and assembled in a structure" (Moles, 1966, p. 9). Messages may be spatial or temporal; music, like dance, is a time-based art and provides largely temporal messages, whereas painting, sculpture, and photography provide largely spatial messages.

> If the circumstances surrounding the reception of a particular sensory event are such that only one possible symbol *could* have been transmitted, the

---

[11]As used in the present discussion musical meaning refers to perceptual and conceptual meaning; Chapter Eight examines musical meaning as aesthetic meaning.

amount of information conveyed by the correct identification of that symbol (or message) is zero. If the message is one chosen from two equally likely alternatives then the amount of information acquired through a correct reception of it is one *bit*, or one binary decision's worth. (Watson, 1973, p. 293)

The greater the amount of *information* conveyed via the sensory *message*, the less the *redundancy*, and the greater the *uncertainty of meaning or response*.[12] In theory, a mathematical formula can predict the probability of a response, but the complex nature of melody and harmony, coupled with the human variable in terms of previous experience with melody and harmony, makes absolute accuracy of prediction virtually impossible.[13] The authors concur with Meyer (1967, p. 20) that our inability to measure precisely the amount of information in a musical message does not weaken or invalidate information theory as a basis for examining musical meaning; the theory still provides a useful construct for examining musical expectation as well as a framework for studying musical perception.

The amount of *information* an individual receives when listening to melody or harmony, and hence an individual's *expectations* regarding them, is a function of two basic variables: (a) the extent to which the *structural* characteristics of melody and harmony conform to fundamental laws of perceptual organization and (b) the individual's previous experience with the given style of melody and harmony. As should be apparent from previous discussion, melodies and harmonies that conform most closely to the rules and grammar of Western tonal harmonic structure generally conform to the fundamental laws of perceptual organization; the tonal harmonic framework provides the structural unity, and the melody or harmony is received as a Gestalt or holistic pattern.

The expectations an individual develops from melody and harmony are related to their *perceptual redundancy*. While information theory per se holds that a message's redundancy is characteristic of the stimulus alone, Meyer (1967, pp. 277–279) maintains that redundancy in a musical message depends on both the extent to which structural characteristics conform to the laws of perceptual organization (structural redundancy) and the degree to which the individual has learned the syntactical-formal premises of the musical style (cultural redundancy).

---

[12]This may seem puzzling if one thinks of "information" only as clarification or repetition. In information theory, information is nonredundant or new. In a simple visual comparison, the message A A A A A A A contains less information and less uncertainty than A B C B C because the shorter string of letters has less redundancy.

[13]Specific quantification of information in music is also complicated considerably by conflicts regarding what the basic *unit* of musical information is. Is it the individual tone, a chord, a phrase, or a period? It probably varies with the music and the listener.

Redundancy is never total, even in a musical style with which an individual is familiar; melody and harmony in Western tonal music have some disorder, ambiguity, and unpredictability.

> Were a composition totally redundant, the result would be completely pre-dictable, and consequently, total tedium.... The relative disorder or randomness that necessarily complements redundancy may be called *perceptual information.* (Meyer, 1967, p. 278)

Perceptual redundancy, which varies with the individual listener, relies heavily on memory of previous experiences (long-term memory) with the style and allows the individual listener to create psychological order out of the melody or harmony, thus developing expectations and mean-ing or understanding. If redundancy is too low, the perceptual informa-tion is too great for the melody or harmony to be understood. If the redundancy is too high, the music will be so predictable as to become quickly boring.

As may be apparent to the reader, the harmonic framework of Western music, with its melodies and harmonies using a familiar scale system and constructed in such ways that tonality and melodic and harmonic move-ment are built in, gives the musical stimulus redundancy. Regardless of the historical period and its stylistic peculiarities, tonality and scales provide strong *structural redundancy.*

When an individual with his or her lifetime of experience with Western tonal music, which Meyer calls *cultural redundancy,* listens to unfamiliar tonal music which has *structural redundancy* due to its tonal harmonic framework, the *perceptual redundancy* is high, thus limiting the amount of new or extraneous *information* in the music. Hence, the individual more readily can "make sense" of the unfamiliar music than he or she could if it were in a style which did not have structural redundancy and for which he or she had developed no cultural redundancy.

This does not mean, however, that everyone maturing in a Western culture automatically will understand all tonal music, because within Western culture the variety of musical style is great; further, the range of experiences individuals within a Western culture have with music also is great. It does suggest, however, that if given adequate experiences with tonal harmonic music, an individual should have a strong psychological basis for interacting with it.

To recapitulate, perceptual redundancy limits the amount of informa-tion a listener receives in a musical message. The greater the redundancy, the more accurate the listener's expectations. Perceptual redundancy enables a listener to conceive melody and harmony as patterns or *Gestalten* even though he or she obviously may not perceive and remember each constituent tone or chord of the pattern. The expectations complement the tones and chords actually perceived to create the musical pattern.

When a listener encounters melodies or harmonies which have little structural redundancy and for which he or she has not developed cultural redundancy, there is increased information. With the increased information, the accuracy of the individual's expectations decreases. When information is so great that the individual cannot develop expectations regarding the melodic or harmonic patterns, the music holds little meaning. Meyer (1967, pp. 283–293) suggests that the *lack* of perceptual redundancy, with its constituent aspects of structural and cultural redundancy, is most likely the reason serialism has failed to gain widespread acceptance. The authors submit that some avant-garde electronic music that does not provide structural redundancy also will be unlikely to gain wide-spread acceptance, particularly since few individuals are developing any cultural redundancy for such music.

Research on Musical Expectancy

Interest in how people develop musical expectancies has given rise to both theory and research. Jones (1981, 1982) developed an expectancy model which suggests that musical expectancies result from an interplay between *ideal prototypes* and *ordinary patterns*. Ideal prototypes are the simple perfect symmetries that underlie a particular style; they are abstract representations of melodic, harmonic, and rhythm patterns that probably exist only in laboratory settings as ideal standards of the given style. Jones's ordinary patterns are more complex and reflect interesting deviations from the ideal patterns. She suggests that expectancies are formulated when ordinary patterns deviate from the idealized symmetries of the ideal prototypes. The discrepancies between the two types of patterns results in an element of surprise which in turn facilitates perception and retention of the musical sequence. The theory presumes a musical system with built-in order and consistency, such as the tonal harmonic framework of Western tonal music.

Carlsen and his colleagues have conducted a number of studies concerned with melodic expectation. Carlsen, Divenyi, and Taylor (1970) examined the effects of two-tone melodic intervals (or "contexts"), which they considered to be *expectancy-generating stimuli*, on music students' melodic continuations of the patterns. While the study was essentially exploratory, the results revealed that subjects' responses for certain intervals tended to cluster and that it was possible to develop *melodic expectancy profiles* for certain intervals.

A subsequent study using the same technique (Carlsen, 1981) sought to develop expectancy profiles for various intervals. This study revealed that different intervals not only generated different expectancy profiles, they also yielded different expectancy-generating strength. Ascending major and minor seconds, the descending minor second, the ascending minor sixth, and the ascending and descending minor seventh all generated strong expectancies. Carlsen also observed that subjects from different cultures tended to generate different continuations, supporting the view that music expectancies depend on previous experiences with music.

Unyk and Carlsen (1987) gathered data on listeners' melodic expectancies and then developed short melodies based on each individual's expectancy profile. Thus, a unique set of 24 melodies was developed for each subject. The 24 melodies, which were used in a melodic dictation task, represented two levels of expectancy strength at each of three levels of expectancy: (a) fulfilled, (b) fulfilled contour but with violated interval size, and (c) both unfulfilled contour and interval size. The results revealed that each melodic pattern produced distinct patterns of response which were similar to the expectancies of Carlsen's 1981 study. Melodies with strong expectancy generators yielded significantly fewer dictation errors for melodies with fulfilled contours and interval size than for the other two levels of expectancy. However, for melodies with weak expectancy generators, violated expectancies did not result in significantly more dictation errors than for melodies with fulfilled expectancies. Unyk and Carlsen suggest that their results support the theories of Meyer (1956, 1967) and Jones (1981, 1982) that listening to music involves formulating expectancies about future events in the unfolding music pattern. For melodies with strong expectancies, violations of expectancy lead to reduced ability to identify and recall the music events.

Schmuckler's (1988) four-part study examined factors underlying the formation of (a) melodic expectations, (b) harmonic expectations, (c) expectancies for a full musical context, and (d) skilled pianists' performances of music expectations. Using a modified version of the probe tone technique devised by Krumhansl and Shepard (1979) and stimuli derived from the vocal line of a Robert Schumann song, Schmuckler asked musically trained subjects to rate how well each of ten continuations, each of which presented a different stopping point or probe position of a stimulus, fit the context or their expectations of what was going to come next. Schmuckler averaged the subjects' data for the various continuations; he referred to these averages as *melodic expectancy profiles.*

Schmuckler's melodic expectancy profiles confirmed that some continuations are more expected than others. To determine the influence of tonality on these profiles, Schmuckler correlated the average ratings for the 10 probe positions with previously obtained data on the perceived stability of the tones of the chromatic scale in reference to a tonal context (Krumhansl & Kessler, 1982). These ratings, which Schmuckler referred to as *ideal key profiles,* then were used to assess the effects of tonality on melodic expectations. Schmuckler suggests that by defining a certain key space from which the expected tones are drawn, tonality does influence expectations: It increases the probability of certain continuations while simultaneously decreasing the probability of others (p. 69).

Schmuckler's second experiment sought to test whether harmonic sequences generated specific expectations for an upcoming chord (p. 94). In brief, Schmuckler found that listeners generally anticipated the chords typically found in common chord sequences in Western tonal compositions. He notes that "global features of a harmonic passage, such as larger context, or the general musical form, also guide expectancy formation" (p. 96). Also, he observed that listeners were generally more accurate in their anticipations for harmonic events than for melodic events.

Schmuckler's third experiment examined expectations in a full musical context, apparently combining the melodic and harmonic stimuli from experiments one and two. As might be expected, listeners' expectations about upcoming musical events were very accurate, perhaps an additive effective of their melodic and harmonic expectations. Schmuckler suggests that the "predictability of the harmonic context makes the melodic implications clearer" (p. 119).

Schmuckler's fourth experiment examined performances of six experienced pianists' expectations; specifically, it sought to determine whether expectancy profiles generated by performers were similar to the expectancy profiles generated in the earlier experiments. The pianists were asked to complete the performance of the musical stimuli used in experiments one, two, and three. There was considerable variation in the length of the six subjects' melodic continuations, but the performers' first tones "tended to agree with the ratings of different melodic expectations from Experiment 1" (p. 126); however, there was only moderate agreement among the six performers' balance of the melodic continuations. Harmonic continuations were weaker than the melodic continuations, but "there was reasonable correspondence between the harmonic expectancy profiles and the performed chords" (p. 129). The strongest correspondences between performer-produced continuations and the expectancy profiles were for the full-context condition. Schmuckler cautions that the results of experiment four are tentative yet very suggestive, noting that "the relatively strong correlations between the expectancy profiles of Experiments 1–3 and the initial performer-produced events provide evidence that the ratings gathered in the first three Experiments did accurately reflect what listeners expect to happen" (p. 134).

From this brief discussion of research on musical expectations, it is apparent that Meyer's theory of expectation can be verified empirically. Extensions and refinements of expectation theory have been developed (e.g., Jones, 1990; Unyk, 1990) and will undoubtedly provide a bases for much subsequent research in musical expectation.

Pitch-Related Behaviors

Expectations are fundamental to both receptive and production behaviors. While their role in receptive behaviors should be apparent from the preceding discussion, their role is perhaps less clear regarding production behaviors. In reception of melody and harmony, expectations are essentially a function of memory of previous experiences with melody and harmony which in turn facilitate perception of new melodies and harmonies. Woodruff (1970) calls these memories of previous experiences *concepts* (see also Chapter Ten) and suggests that they provide the basis for musical behavior. Regelski (1975, p. 11) has elaborated on the view that concepts are general thought tendencies and suggests that they result from (a) perception and cognition of many particular personal experiences with the learning or skill to be mastered, (b) the transfer of certain learnings from these particular personal experiences to other particular but somewhat different situations, and (c) a gradually evolving tendency toward increased frequency of the particular musical behavior.

Expectations, therefore, are basic to the conceptualization of music. Musical concepts, recognized as cumulative tendencies toward response resulting from cognitive musical organizations, are the product of memories and classifications of previous experiences with musical stimuli. While musical concepts involve covert cognitive activity, they form the basis for both receptive and production behaviors. Receptive behaviors are essentially perceptual and therefore covert in nature; production behaviors involve production or reproduction of music.

Receptive behaviors. The basic problem in studying receptive behaviors is that they are essentially covert, and to gain some understanding of them, investigators must devise some overt manifestation of them, a task which often creates as many questions as the investigator answers. Investigators do not always agree regarding the appropriateness of certain overt behaviors as valid reflections of certain covert perceptual or conceptual activity. For example, investigators studying "perception of melodies" might devise musical tasks to serve as evidence of melodic perception; these tasks might range from simply recognizing a melody or discriminating between two melodies to singing or notating an aurally presented melody. Some "melodies" used in research are limited, contrived tonal sequences that may or may not be representative of melodies in Western music. While some investigators operationally define their terms and limit their generalizations, others apply vague labels to their studies and sometimes generalize far beyond what the data warrant, thereby leaving the reader with a mass of seemingly contradictory information regarding receptive musical behaviors. The situation is compounded when theoretical considerations are intermixed with presentations and discussions of empirical data. Unfortunately, there appears to be no neat and tidy solution to the problem.

The reader should keep in mind, however, that receptive behaviors are essentially perceptual and involve *recognition of* and *discrimination between* musical stimuli. Both processes are fundamental to reception of melody and harmony. While listening to music an individual, usually without any particular awareness, constantly separates the familiar from the unfamiliar and compares new patterns with memories of previously learned patterns. The better the new melodies and harmonies match the expectations based on memories of previous experiences, the more comprehensible they are.

Fiske's (1990, 1993) theory of music cognition holds that music listening essentially can be reduced to a series of such decisions. He describes the central premises of his theory as follows:

> (a) music cognition is unique to human brains, (b) identification of musical patterns is limited to tonal and rhythmic (T–R) relationships, (c) music cognition requires time and effort, (d) realized T–R patterns are limited to three kinds: a given pattern P, patterns derived from P (called P'), and patterns which are distinctly different from P (called Pn), (e) pattern comparisons, a major function of music cognition and musical thinking, between say two T–R patterns, are limited to three conclusions: (1) the patterns are identical, (2) the second pattern is a derivation of the first, and (3) the second is distinctly different from the first. (1993, p. 2)

Two additional classes of receptive musical behaviors are *analytical* and *aural-visual discrimination.* Essentially, these are extensions of recognition and discrimination, but each goes beyond the basic receptive processes. Analytical behaviors reflect efforts to consciously categorize melodic and harmonic patterns into their constituent parts. Aural-visual discrimination involves associating aural stimuli, including melodic and harmonic patterns, with their symbolic (notational) representations.

As may be apparent to the reader, receptive behaviors are difficult to isolate entirely from performance behaviors; an element of "performance" exists in any overt manifestation of receptive behaviors. Also, failure to produce does not necessarily mean failure to perceive or receive. A person may be unable to sing because of a vocal production problem rather than a reception or perception problem.

Production behaviors. While research related to production behaviors is examined in Chapter Seven, a brief discussion of the basic types of production behaviors is included here. They include singing, performing with an instrument, and creating music. Most musicians believe that the ability to make musical discriminations underlies all production behaviors. Without an ability to discriminate among pitches and pitch patterns, an individual would be unable to produce his or her musical intentions in any tonal manner. While the present discussion concerns production of melodies and harmonies, the principle is the same for all musical aspects, be they dynamics, rhythms, or timbres. If the individual can not discriminate among the tonal attributes, the production efforts are hindered.

Each of the three types of production behaviors is subdivided according to whether the behavior is a *re*production or *pro*duction of music. Singing and instrumental performance may involve production of melodies and harmonies not previously produced, i.e., improvisation. In improvisation, the performer combines new melodic and harmonic patterns within a given conceptual framework. Most improvising today, be it by the jazz musician or the church organist, is conceived within a tonal harmonic framework.

Singers and instrumentalists also are involved in the reproduction of melodies and harmonies. They may produce pitch patterns learned "by ear," i.e., by rote procedures, and patterns read or memorized from notation. At the risk of overgeneralization, it appears that most music performed in Western cultures involves reproduction rather than production.

Creative behaviors also can involve either production or reproduction of musical patterns. The apparent favorite pastime of music theory teachers, melodic and harmonic dictation, requires music students to reproduce in notation aurally given melodic, harmonic, and rhythm patterns. Production of notation, however, involves what some consider to be the ultimate musical behavior, composition.

Development of Melodic and Harmonic Behaviors

As may be apparent, the types of receptive and production behaviors are sufficiently broad that they could be divided into many sublevels or categories of musical behavior. While it may appear that a developmental taxonomy of melodic and harmonic behaviors could be developed, the uniqueness of each child's musical experiences is such that any attempt to set forth such a taxonomy would immediately encounter difficulties. Each child's development sequence, while subject to general laws of maturation, is necessarily unique, because musical development is greatly influenced by environment (Phillips, 1976; Sergeant & Thatcher, 1974). Nevertheless, some generalizations can be made regarding musical development and this section will examine them from two particular perspectives: research-based studies of musical development and music teachers' views.

Research-Based Findings

Research related to development of melodic and harmonic behaviors is primarily developmental research, i.e., studies of children's abilities to accomplish certain musical tasks at various age or developmental levels. A major problem with this approach is the gap between the various musical tasks children are asked to perform and the implications drawn from the performance of the tasks. Many varieties of tasks, including ones requiring musical performance, loosely are labeled as melodic perception, even though it is obvious that performance tasks involve production behaviors in addition to receptive behaviors. Loose application of labels to assessment of receptive and production tasks tends to confound the study of musical development, and the reader is cautioned to consider the nature of the behavioral task required in any given study and to draw conclusions only with due consideration of the nature of the tasks.

Another difficulty in drawing conclusions from studies of young children is the notorious *un*reliability of measuring instruments. Often conclusions are drawn on the basis of the investigators' observations of a very limited number of cases or on the basis of responses to tests of questionable validity and reliability. These difficulties, coupled with the uniqueness of each child's musical experiences, make sweeping generalizations about children's musical development extremely hazardous. Nevertheless, there is a growing body of research that reveals an increasing consensus regarding the development of melodic and harmonic behaviors, and some of the more significant studies are noted here.[14]

A series of studies by Trehub and her colleagues (Chang & Trehub, 1977; Trehub, Bull, & Thorpe, 1984; Trehub, Thorpe, & Morrongiello, 1987) indicates that response to melody begins in infancy. Chang and Trehub monitored five-month-old babies' "startle" response to changes in six-tone melodic patterns and observed changes of heart rate (deceleration) when a pattern with a different contour was played after the infants

---

[14]Some of the information regarding development appears in a condensed and general way in Chapter Ten.

had become habituated to another pattern. Such response, however, was not evident when contour was maintained but transposed up or down a minor third. The 1984 study (Trehub, Bull, & Thorpe) examined the effects of additional melodic transformations (transpositions to other keys, altering intervals while preserving contour, altering octaves with accompanying contour changes) on six- to eleven-month-old infants. Using the "operant head turn procedure" as the response measure, the investigators observed that the subjects responded to new melodies or tone sequences as *familiar* if the sequences had the same melodic contour and frequency range as a previously heard sequence, while sequences with either different contour or range were responded to as *novel.* The 1987 study (Trehub, Thorpe, & Morrongiello) tested nine- to eleven-month-old infants for their discrimination of changes in melodic contour in the context of variations in key or interval size. Results revealed that infants could detect changes in both variable contexts, lending further support to conclusions from previous studies that infants categorize sequences of sounds on the basis of global, relational properties such as melodic contour. The investigators noted that the absence of response to differences of key and key-plus-interval conditions suggests that infants encode contour, rather than interval, information. In a summative article, Trehub (1993) notes that infants are sensitive to contour and can discriminate between ascending and descending patterns, but they are insensitive to individual pitches and intervals.

Nearly all research on infants' and young children's development of melodic discrimination reveals an increase in skills with an increase in age; however, various studies do not agree regarding the exact ages at which given skills are developed. According to Hargreaves (1986, pp. 68–69), "vocal play," the precursor of spontaneous song, begins during the first year, suggesting that even six-month-old infants possess the prerequisites of music making: the ability to vocalize, vary and imitate pitch, and detect changes in melodic contour.

Sloboda (1985) observes that the first striking change in overt musical behavior after the first birthday comes at about 18 months of ages when spontaneous song singing begins to occur. "The main characteristic of spontaneous singing is the use of discrete stable pitches (rather than the microtonal glides of the earlier 'song babbling')" (p. 202). Such singing usually does not include words, leading Sloboda to suggest that musical development at this age occurs along a separate "stream" from speech. Spontaneous singing at this level does not appear to reflect efforts to imitate particular songs, although the singing begins to include short melodic patterns using intervals that approximate the seconds and thirds of tonal music.

Most accounts of children's singing during the latter half of the second year suggest a gradual change toward use of melodic patterns reflecting tonal, or culturally "correct," structures in spontaneous singing, as well as an "emerging ability to select melodic fragments from an increasingly large repertoire [of standard songs], and to match these with increasing accuracy to the components of standard models" (Hargreaves, 1986, p. 72). Apparently children begin to borrow certain aspects of songs they have heard and assimilate them more and more into their own spontaneous songs.

During the third year, children's spontaneous songs appear to become longer and reflect a definite trend toward use of diatonic scale intervals. Davidson, McKernon, and Gardner (1981, p. 305) suggest that children appear to develop a set of song-related expectations that in essence provide a "song frame" which structures their performances of songs. As Sloboda (1985, p. 204) notes, "by two-and-a-half, the child seems to have assimilated the notions that music is constructed around a small fixed set of pitch intervals, and that repetition of intervallic and rhythmic patterns is a cornerstone of music." However, the child as yet seems to lack any grasp of hierarchical structures governing groups of patterns that might prescribe direction and closure. Sloboda observes that songs of children of this age usually have an "aimless" quality, with little or no sense of "finishing."

Toward the end of the third year, children's singing begins to reflect less spontaneous song and more imitation of songs they hear in their environment. Moog's (1976) extensive study of children's musical development revealed that children in the early phases of this stage are able to imitate melodic contour more easily than they imitate exact pitch. However, during the third and fourth years, many children's capacity to imitate songs develops greatly, to the point that "most children can accurately reproduce the familiar songs and nursery rhymes of their culture by the age of five" (Sloboda, p. 205). Spontaneous song is no longer the predominant song style for the five year old. Apparently, children at about age five become much more concerned with accuracy of imitation, reflecting a general developmental trend toward precision and mastery of detail. Five year olds usually are able to maintain the key of a song much better than four year olds, apparently reflecting some higher order "knowledge" of key and tonal center that most four year olds have not yet developed.

The ability to maintain a key or tonal center is not necessarily the same as the ability to learn a song at a given pitch level. Sergeant and Roche's (1973) study of children's ability to learn to sing songs at specific pitch levels suggests that younger children may focus more on the absolute pitch when learning a melody than do older children. Over a three-week period they taught 36 children (13 three to four year olds, 10 five year olds, and 13 six year olds) to sing three melodies. Each melody was taught on an invariant pitch level. One week after the completion of the study, each child's singing of the melodies was recorded. Results revealed an inverse relationship between accuracy of pitch level and accuracy of the melodic pattern. The youngest group sang at the most accurate pitch level, but the oldest group sang the melodic patterns most accurately. The results support the investigators' hypothesis that younger children tend to focus on pitch *per se,* while with increased age and conceptual development they focus more on the attributes of melodic pattern. Sergeant and Roche suggest that absolute pitch skills could be developed if children were given training on fixed pitch instruments during a critical period, common to all children, before their preconceptual perception of pitch has been transcended by higher-order conceptual thinking. Michel (1973) also recognizes a critical period in musical development, but suggests that the critical period is between the ages of five and six, whereas Sergeant and Roche's data suggest that it might come earlier.

McDonald and Ramsey (1979) sought to replicate Sergeant and Roche's study with American preschool children. Seventy-six two through five year olds were taught to sing four songs of invariant pitch levels in six 30-minute training sessions over a three-week period. Their data partially supported Sergeant and Roche's results: There was a positive relationship between age and conceptualization of melody; however, their data did not yield the inverse relationship between age and pitch level, perhaps due to a more stringent scoring system for pitch level than that used by Sergeant and Roche.

A subsequent study by Ramsey (1983) examined the effects of age, singing ability, and instrumental experience on three, four, and five year olds' perception of melody as indicated by song vocalization. Five aspects of melody were evaluated: (a) absolute pitching, (b) melodic rhythm, (c) melodic contour, (d) tonal center, and (e) melodic interval. Her data revealed (a) significant differences in the performance of three, four, and five year olds on melodic rhythm, melodic contour, and melodic interval; (b) high ability singers scored higher than low ability singers on perception of melodic rhythm, melodic contour, tonal center, and melodic interval; and (c) instrumental and noninstrumental treatment groups did not differ significantly in perception of the melodic components. Surprisingly, the data yielded no significant age level effects on either absolute pitch or tonal center.

Zimmerman (1971, p. 28) notes that the ages of six to eight are marked by rapid development of melodic perception. Petzold (1966, p. 254) and some other researchers, however, report a leveling effect following the third grade, or around the age of nine.

Taylor (1973) notes that there is a marked development of harmonic awareness around the age of nine, but Thackray (1973) maintains that results of his harmonic perception test provide positive evidence that many children develop a considerable degree of harmonic awareness well before the age of nine. Bridges' (1965) study of harmonic discrimination ability of children in kindergarten through grade three also suggests a gradual development in harmonic discrimination ability. Moog (1976), however, maintains that his research show unequivocally that preschool-aged children do not experience any sort of harmony at all. Shuter-Dyson and Gabriel's (1981, pp. 147–149) review of several studies examining children's harmonic discrimination in terms of consonance and dissonance (essentially requiring the selection of which version sounded "better" or "correct" in paired comparisons) revealed great improvement between the ages of five and ten in selecting "better" or "correct" versions. Such findings lend support to the view that basic harmonic awareness is developed as part of children's enculturation with Western music.

Imberty's (1981, pp. 108–115) comprehensive study of the development of tonality reveals four age-related stages of tonal enculturation: (a) below age six, a period of perceptual *undifferentiation* regarding cadence; (b) from six and one-half to seven years, a *cadential perceptive scheme,* i.e., the child considers a musical phrase without a cadence as unfinished, but makes no clear differentiation among differing cadential movements; (c) around eight years, where the child can differentiate between a perfect cadence and absence of cadence and responds to interrupted cadences less clearly; the primary characteristic of this stage is the beginning of *perceptive decentration* which enables the subject "to connect what precedes the cadential formula with the formula itself" (p. 113); and (d) around ten years, characterized by the establishment of a *relation of order;* the perception of the dominant leads to anticipation of the tonic; *reversibility* is evident in the perception of tonal functions, and the syntactic elements of the musical phrase makes possible the precedence of order and logical anticipation. Imberty's research with older children did not reveal continued development, leading him to recognize a sort of "ceiling effect" that apparently can not be forced higher. Imberty's ceiling effect for tonality occurs at about the same age level as the plateaus for melody and rhythmic development observed by Petzold (1966).

In summary, melodic discrimination skills are apparent in infancy and continue to develop through about the age of eight, with a critical period for development somewhere around the age of five or six. Perhaps this critical period is reflected in the child's shift from the use of spontaneous song to imitation of songs heard in the child's cultural environment. Harmonic discrimination skills appear to develop later, with earliest awareness of harmony usually appearing around the age of five or six and with a marked increase in harmonic discrimination occurring about the age of nine. Whether the leveling in melodic skills around the age of nine is due to increased harmonic awareness, however, is subject to conjecture.

Music Teachers' Views

The research-based findings discussed above primarily reflect attempts to study children's melodic and harmonic development as a part of their enculturation process with Western music. As children reach school age, musical development becomes much more dependent on formal instructional experiences.

While music teachers naturally are concerned with more than developing melodic and harmonic behaviors, the present discussion examines some commonly used methods for developing melodic and harmonic behaviors. A general instructional sequence at the various levels of the elementary school emphasizes rhythm in the earliest levels, nursery school, kindergarten, and early primary grades. Melody receives greater attention in grades two through four, and harmony begins receiving greater attention in grades four through six. Nye and Nye (1985, p. 272) note that this is the general order in which children develop musical concepts.

The major musical activities for developing melodic and harmonic behaviors include singing, listening, and playing instruments. While movement sometimes is used to reinforce melodic behavior, it primarily is used to develop rhythmic behaviors.

Music teachers also recognize that much musical development occurs outside of school, but for many children school music represents their first formal learning experiences with music. The initial pitch-related concept that teachers try to develop in children is that of *high* and *low* pitch, or more properly, *higher* and *lower* pitch, since pitch is a relative phenomenon.

Aronoff (1969, p. 42) notes that young children should develop behaviors related to melodic direction and shape, which may be developed and reinforced through various musical activities—singing, listening, and playing instruments. Children learn that melodies move up, move down, or repeat tones; once direction is established, children's discrimination can progress to the point that they can describe how a melody moves—by steps or skips, repeated tones, sequences, etc.

While teachers recognize music reading as a developmental process ranging from following simple line notation to reading actual notation, they do not agree as to how best to teach it. Many music educators, of whom Mursell is a particularly strong advocate, maintain that reading is best facilitated through instrumental experiences in which the visual symbols stand for particular sounds and sets of movements. Others advocate a system to foster *relative* pitch reading within a scale or key. The predominant system of this type is the *movable do* syllables, although some teachers use a number system for the eight tones of the major scale. A *fixed do* system is used primarily in Europe. Gordon (1971, pp. 100–103) reviews the advantages and disadvantages of syllable and numbers and concludes that the *movable do* system is best.

Just as research shows that harmonic behaviors develop following melodic behaviors, music teachers have determined empirically that teaching harmony should follow teaching melody. Whether there is any cause and effect relationship here is unclear. Nye and Nye (1985, pp. 353–377) provide an extensive discussion of strategies for developing children's harmonic behaviors.

While this brief sketch of music teachers' views on the development of melodic and harmonic behaviors is limited both in scope and depth, it does indicate that the customary teaching sequence basically recognizes and follows the developmental sequence observed by researchers.

Evaluating Melodies and Harmonies

While an examination of the "goodness" of melody or the "appropriateness" of harmony perhaps is more appropriate in a discussion of aesthetics, it also is relevant to the psychological foundations of melodic and harmonic behaviors. The present discussion, while recognizing that "good" and "appropriate" can reflect value judgments and therefore are legitimate concerns from an aesthetic perspective, focuses on "goodness" and "appropriateness" from a perceptual standpoint.

What Is "Good" Melody?

The fundamental problem in determining goodness of a melody rests with the relative emphasis one places on its structural and psychological characteristics. If one evaluates only structure, such characteristics as propinquity, repetition, and finality might be important evaluative criteria. On the other hand, explanations in terms of psychological characteristics might concern the extent to which melodies are perceived as patterns or the degree to which a given melody is perceived as being within a familiar style.

Mursell (1937, pp. 105–106) notes that essentially all that is needed for an authentic melodic experience is "a tonal sequence held together and unified by a unity of response." He notes that "inferior" melodies lack unity in both structure and response.

Hickman (1976) reviewed a number of accounts of melody, including ones which variously treated a melody from technical, educational, musicological, and sociological perspectives among others, and concluded that order and pattern are essential constituents of good melodies. He then offered a four-criterion model for evaluating melodies: (a) the melody must manifest a pattern of elements, (b) the melody must be a product of a person or persons, (c) the melody must do more than adhere to specifications previously laid down, and (d) the melody must be worth having in itself apart from any purpose it may serve.

Lundin (1967, pp. 85–85) offers a behavioral or cultural interpretation of melody in which melody is viewed as a function of both the listener's previous experience and certain structural characteristics. He maintains that what have come to be perceived as melodies are a result of many centuries of musical development. New patterns were accepted gradually as people became familiar with them.

Sloboda (1985, pp. 52–55) views a melody's goodness in terms of the extent to which it conforms to the rules of its underlying generative grammar. If the melody conforms totally to the structural rules of Western tonal music, he suggests that the melody is likely to be dull; on the other hand, if the melody excessively violates basic structural rules, it may be unintelligible to listeners. Sloboda's view presupposes that listeners are enculturated in the grammatical rules of Western tonal music.

Smith and Cuddy (1986) examined the effects of repetition and rule familiarity on the "pleasingness" of 20 melodic sequences which varied in complexity of contour and harmonic structure. (The more complex the melodic sequence, the more it violated the rules of tonal harmonic structure.) Their data indicated that the more complex the underlying harmonic structure of the melody, the *less* pleasing the subjects rated it. Whether such *affective* responses reflect a measure of perceptual "goodness" may be debatable, but it certainly seems to support Sloboda's contention that as a melody deviates from the basic grammatical structures of tonal harmony, listeners respond to it differently.

Reimer (1989, pp. 133–138), while concerned with musical goodness rather than just melodic goodness, cites two aspects of goodness: *excellence,* which has to do with the syntactic or structural refinement in the music, and *greatness,* which has to do with the level of profundity of the music's expressive content. The two aspects are based respectively on Leonard Meyer's (1967, pp. 22–41) theories of value and greatness in music, which are discussed in Chapter Seven. While the *greatness* criterion is more properly discussed under aesthetics, the *excellence* criterion has its roots in the meanings of musical messages an individual receives while listening to music.

The meaning an individual receives when listening to a melody is a function of the uncertainty reflected in the information present in the melody. The amount of information an individual receives depends on both the structural and cultural redundancy of the melody, i.e., the extent to which the melody reflects a particular melody style and the degree to which the individual is familiar with and has developed expectations within that style. The greater the perceptual redundancy, the combined effect of structural and cultural redundancy, the more likely the melody is meaningful, and hence "good" for the individual.[15]

Goodness of a melody may vary from individual to individual. A good melody for kindergarten children is different from what is good for an adolescent. Similarly, a good melody for the musically sophisticated is different from that which is good for an untrained listener. A melody in unfamiliar style also would most likely lack goodness for a listener. However, the greater the number of individuals who find meaning in a melody, the more it would appear that the goodness status of the melody should be elevated in some manner.

What Is "Acceptable" Harmony?

"Acceptableness" of harmony has received considerably less attention than either melody or music as a whole. What attention there has been is related to one of two basic approaches: (a) studies of the age at which children become cognizant of harmony (e.g., Bridges, 1965) and (b) individuals' preferences for harmony of traditional tonal compositions (Wing, 1961; Long, 1968). Wing has a separate test for harmony, whereas Long asks individuals to select the "better of two musical renditions and tell whether it was better in terms of melody, harmony, or rhythm.)

The latter approach is particularly relevant to our discussion because in essence it seeks to assess individuals' preferences in terms of harmonic appropriateness for given examples of Western tonal music in "classical" style. To the extent that an individual's preferences conform to what musically trained judges agree is appropriate, the individual exhibits knowledge of harmonic style for Western music. While the "agreement with the experts" approach can be criticized a somewhat snobbish, the particular mode for evaluating has merit and offers many possibilities for examining views of "acceptable" harmony.

---

[15] Of course, the "good" melody may seem trite and boring due to excessive perceptual redundancy.

Ultimately the acceptableness of harmony, just as the goodness of melody, is an individual matter and is a function of an individual's experience with harmonic styles. The meaning an individual receives from harmony is related to the expectancies he or she has developed for the given style. The information theory framework noted in the discussion of goodness of melody also may apply to harmony. Appropriateness of harmony, therefore, also is an individual matter; the degree to which groups of individuals find given harmonies acceptable reflects a cultural or subcultural acceptance.

Evaluation of Melodic and Harmonic Behaviors

Evaluations of melodic and harmonic behaviors generally involve one or more of several basic types of behavior: (a) behaviors reflecting recognition of tonal patterns, (b) behaviors reflecting discriminations between aurally presented tonal patterns, (c) behaviors associating aural and visual stimuli, and (d) production behaviors. The preference test mentioned above conceivably could be considered a fifth type of behavior, although the authors view them as essentially requiring discriminations between tonal patterns. Also, production behaviors possibly could be subdivided into notation and performance behaviors.

Some of the same concerns noted under the discussion of the evaluation of rhythmic behaviors also are apparent in the evaluation of melodic and harmonic behaviors. The nature of the response mode selected for measuring discrimination could affect the assessment; group versus individual measurement also is an important consideration, both in terms of economy and accuracy. Failure to perform does not necessarily indicate failure to perceive. Finally, the specifics versus global measurement question is reflected in the approaches used in some of the tests. The value of a particular approach depends ultimately on the purpose of the evaluation and the nature of the data sought.

While the bulk of this discussion is devoted to selected published standardized music tests, it should be recognized that the most commonly used measures of melodic and harmonic behavior involve performance, usually from notation. Performance of both prepared and sightread pieces is used for evaluative purposes from primary school through professional levels. Melodic and harmonic dictation also are much used for evaluative purposes, particularly in high school and college music theory classes. The evaluative criteria for performances are usually in terms of a teacher's or panel of judges' perceptions of what is "correct" and "artistic" performance. While the pitfalls of this are many, the system apparently works to the satisfaction of many musicians; otherwise, there would be greater demands for refinements in the system.

Common to many published music tests is a *tonal memory* test, of which there are two basic approaches. One presents a model melody or series of tones. In subsequent hearings, which may range from two to six, the testee indicates *how* the melody was changed, usually from options such as key, rhythm, or pitch of some individual tone. The *Test of Musicality* (Gaston, 1957) and the *Drake Musical Aptitude Tests* (1957) use this type of tonal memory test.

The other type of tonal memory test also presents a model, but in subsequent hearings the testee must indicate *which tone* has been changed. The number of subsequent hearings also varies, usually from two to seven. Tests using this type of tonal memory test include the *Seashore Measures of Musical Talents* (Seashore, Lewis, & Saetveit, 1939, 1960), *Standardised Tests of Musical Intelligence* (Wing, 1961), and *Measures of Musical Abilities* (Bentley, 1966).

Gordon's (1965) *Musical Aptitude Profile* also measures tonal memory, or imagery as it is labeled in the test, by presenting a model melody and then a second melody which is either an embellished rendition of the model or an entirely different melody. This approach appears to assess the respondent's ability to discriminate tonal patterns at different structural levels, since the testees must determine whether the second melody would be like the model if the embellishing tones were not present. The "harmony" portion of the Gordon test also is unique. It involves essentially the same process, although the changes are in a bass line. The upper voice remains the same for both the model and second version.

Gordon (1979, 1982) developed three additional tests that include measures of tonal aptitude. The tonal subtest of the *Primary Measures of Music Audiation* is designed to assess the ability of children in kindergarten through grade three to discriminate between pairs of two- to five-tone aural patterns. One tone in the second of each pair is changed. The *Intermediate Measures of Music Audiation* has a similar subtest that follows the same format, but is designed for children in grades one through four.

Gordon's (1989) more recent *Advanced Measures of Music Audiation* is designed to assess tonal and rhythm aptitude scores for high school and college students. Based on Gordon's concept of "audiation," where a person mentally hears and comprehends musical patterns without immediate aural stimulation, the 30-item measure requires students to decide whether "answers" to musical "questions" are the same as the "questions," differ tonally, or differ rhythmically. Tonal differences may involve changes in individual pitch, mode, tonal center, or combinations thereof.

Rhythm changes may include altered durations, meters, tempi, or combinations thereof.

Thackray (1973, 1976) devised useful measures of tonality and harmonic perception. The tonality test measures tonality in melodies and has four subtests. Part I introduces modulations in some melodies and asks respondents to indicate whether the melodies sound "right" or "wrong." Part II uses short unfamiliar melodies, some of which are diatonic and clearly adhere to tonality while others do not. Testees are asked to determine whether each melody is "ordinary" or "peculiar." Part III asks testees to determine whether the melodies sound "finished" or "not finished," and Part IV asks testees to determine whether the concluding tone is the same as the beginning tone of a melody. Although the test is not standardized, it appears to be potentially very useful in assessing children's perceptions of tonality.

Thackray's harmonic perception test, also not standardized, has three parts. Part I presents a series of sounds played on the piano, some of which are single tones and some of which are chords. The testee is asked to indicate which are chords. Part II presents three- and four-tone harmonized melodies. The testee is asked to indicate which tone (if any) in a second hearing is harmonized differently. Part III presents a chord followed by a pause and then a progression of three, four, or five chords, and the respondent is asked to indicate where the given chord appears in the progression.

Colwell's (1969–1970) *Music Achievement Tests* measure a variety of behaviors related to melody and harmony. Some of the behaviors measured include determination of whether a pattern or phrase moves scalewise or in leaps, whether chords and phrases are in major or minor mode, whether notated melodies match aurally presented melodies, which among three tones following a cadence or phrase is the keytone, and what is the style period of aurally presented musical excerpts.

The *Iowa Tests of Music Literacy* (Gordon, 1991) measure three aspects of tonal concepts: aural discrimination, aural-visual discrimination, and notational skills. Essentially the aural discrimination tests (called "Audiation/Listening") measure the ability to discriminate between major and minor tonality and some additional modal patterns. The aural-visual discriminations tests ("Audiation/Reading") ask testees whether given notated melodies match aurally given melodies, and the notational tests ("Audiation/Writing") are quasi-dictation tests.

Several aural-visual discrimination tests measure melodic aural-visual discrimination, but separate scores are not provided for melody and rhythm, e.g., Knuth (1966) and Farnum (1953). Melodic performance also is a major criterion in the scoring of the *Watkins-Farnum Performance*

Scale (Watkins & Farnum, 1954), but neither does it provide a separate score for melody.

The same recommendations offered at the conclusion of the discussion of rhythm tests apply here. Researchers and teachers concerned with selecting and developing measures of melodic and harmonic behaviors should first and foremost consider the nature of the behaviors they wish to evaluate and be certain that any measures selected or developed indeed measure those behaviors in a manner appropriate for the level of student being evaluated.

Summary

Following are the major points discussed in the chapter:

1. The vertical structure of Western music is considerably more highly developed than that of other cultures.
2. Most Western music is constructed within a tonal harmonic framework.
3. Changing either the relative pitch positions or tones or the rhythm of a tonal sequence changes the melody structurally, although not always perceptually.
4. Melodies can be defined as both structural and psychological entities.
5. Recent accounts of melodic perception are inferred descriptions of the cognitive processes and structures developed from experience with melodies.
6. Model tonal hierarchies are based either explicitly or implicitly on generative grammars, the organizational rules that underlie musical structure.
7. Most models of melodic perception acknowledge the perceptual laws of Gestalt psychology.
8. Harmony in Western music is primarily tertian harmony.
9. There are three basic "holistic" attributes of harmony: tonality, harmonic movement, and finality.
10. Melodic and harmonic movement are relative phenomena.
11. Perceptual organization of harmony is context dependent.
12. Tonality is an underlying unifying device in the perception of Western tonal music.
13. The diatonic scale is the basic scale for Western music.
14. Scale systems are codifications of musical practices.
15. The tempered diatonic scale is the most far-reaching standardization of music in the world.
16. The diatonic scale evolved from the Greek "Greater Perfect System."
17. Equal temperament is the most satisfactory tuning system for Western music.

18. Major and minor scales comprise the basic tonal patterns or modes for most Western music.
19. Other modes include the church modes, the whole-tone scale, the pentatonic scale, the chromatic scale, the quarter-tone scale, synthetic scales, and scales of other cultures.
20. While most music uses fixed pitches in a tonal harmonic framework, some contemporary music uses sliding and indefinite pitches and may be designed without an intended tonality.
21. Hierarchical perceptual models essentially are descriptions of inferred psychological events.
22. Important hierarchical models regarding the perceptual organization of pitch structures are Krumhansl's tonal hierarchy for melodic patterns and Lerdahl and Jackendoff's time-span reduction and prolongation-reduction models.
23. Recent research in melodic perception confirms dependency of perception and memory on the tonal harmonic framework of a melody.
24. Musical meaning is a product of expectations a listener has developed.
25. Expectations are a function of the information a musical example provides.
26. Redundancy increases as information decreases.
27. Redundancy is a function of the structural characteristics of the music and a listener's previous experiences with music of that style.
28. Research confirms that there is a general consistency in musicians' expectations regarding melodic continuations of for given melodic fragments or contexts.
29. Basic receptive behaviors include recognition and discrimination.
30. Production behaviors are of three basic types: singing, performing music with an instrument, and creating music.
31. Children develop melodic behaviors before harmonic behaviors.
32. Practices of music teachers generally reflect the sequence in which melodic and harmonic behaviors develop.
33. The "goodness" of a melody and "acceptableness" of harmony in the psychological sense are functions of an individual's previous experience with melodies and harmony in given styles.
34. Evaluation of melodic and harmonic behaviors involves one or more of several types of behavior: (a) recognition of tonal patterns, (b) discrimination between aurally presented tonal patterns, (c) associations between aurally presented and visually presented patterns, and (d) production behaviors.

References

Apel, W. (1969). *Harvard dictionary of music* (2nd ed.). Cambridge, MA: Belknap Press.

Aronoff, F.W. (1969). *Music and young children.* New York: Holt, Rinehart and Winston.

Attneave, P. (1959) *Applications of information theory to psychology: A summary of basic concepts, methods, and results.* New York: Henry Holt.

Backus, J. (1977). *The acoustical foundations of music* (2nd ed.). New York: W.W. Norton.

Barbour, J.M. (1951). *Tuning and temperament.* East Lansing: Michigan State Press.

Bentley, A. (1966). *Measures of musical abilities.* New York: October House.

Berry, W. (1976). *Structural functions in music.* Englewood Cliffs, NJ: Prentice-Hall.

Bharucha, J.J., & Krumhansl, C.L. (1983). The representation of harmonic structure in music: Hierarchies of stability as a function of context. *Cognition, 13,* 63–102.

Blackwood, E. (1985). *The structure of recognizable diatonic tunings.* Princeton, NJ: Princeton University Press.

Bower, G.H., & Hilgard, E.R. (1981). *Theories of learning* (5th ed.). Englewood Cliffs, NJ: Prentice-Hall.

Bridges, V.A. (1965) An exploratory study of the harmonic discrimination ability of children in kindergarten through grade three in two selected schools (Doctoral dissertation, The Ohio State University, 1965) *Dissertation Abstracts, 26,* 3692.

Broadbent, D.E. (1958). *Perception and communication.* New York: Macmillan.

Burns, E.M., & Ward, W.D. (1982). Intervals, scales and tuning. In D. Deutsch (Ed.), *The psychology of music* (pp. 241–269). New York: Academic Press.

Butler, D. (1989). Describing the perception of tonality in music: A critique of the tonal hierarchy theory and a proposal for a theory of intervallic rivalry. *Music Perception, 6,* 219–242.

Butler, D. (1990a). A study of event hierarchies in tonal and post-tonal music. *Psychology of Music, 18,* 4–17.

Butler, D. (1990b). Response to Carol Krumhansl. *Music Perception, 7,* 325–338.

Carlsen, J.C. (1981). Some factors which influence melodic expectancy. *Psychomusicology, 1* (1), 12–29.

Carlsen, J.C., Divenyi, P.I., & Taylor, J.A. A preliminary study of perceptual expectancy in melodic configurations. *Bulletin of the Council for Research in Music Education, 22,* 4–12.

Carterette, E.C., & Kendall, R.A. (1989). Human music perception. In R.J. Dowling & S.H. Hulse (Eds.), *The comparative psychology of audition: Processing complex sounds* (pp. 131–172). Hillsdale, NJ: Lawrence Erlbaum Associates.

Chang, H.W., & Trehub, S.E. (1977). Auditory processing of relational information by young infants. *Journal of Experimental Psychology, 24,* 324–331.

Chomsky, N. (1957). *Syntactic structures.* The Hague: Mouton.

Chomsky, N. (1965). *Aspects of the theory of syntax.* Cambridge: MIT Press.

Chomsky, N. (1968). *Language and mind.* New York: Harcourt Brace Jovanovitch.

Chomsky, N. (1975). *Reflections on language.* New York: Pantheon.

Clarke, E.F. (1986). Theory, analysis and the psychology of music: A critical evalua-tion of Lerdahl, F. and Jackendoff, R., *A Generative Theory of Tonal Music, Psychology of Music, 14,* 3–16.

Clynes, M. (Ed.) (1982). *Music, mind, and brain.* New York: Plenum Press.

Colwell, R. (1969–70). *Music achievement tests.* Chicago: Follett.

Cook, N. (1990). *Music, imagination, and culture.* Oxford: Clarendon Press.

Cuddy, L.L. (1982). On hearing pattern in melody. *Psychology of Music, 10,* 3–10.

Cuddy, L.L. (1991). Melodic patterns and tonal structure: Converging evidence. *Psychomusicology, 10,* 107–126.

Cuddy, L.L., Cohen, A.J., & Mewhort, D.J.K. (1981). Perception of structure in short melodic sequences. *Journal of Experimental Psychology: Human Perception and Performance, 7,* 869–883.

Cuddy, L.L., Cohen, A.J., & Miller, J. (1979). Melody recognition: The experimental application of musical rules. *Canadian Journal of Psychology, 33,* 255–270.

Davidson, L., McKernon, P., & Gardner, H. (1981). The acquisition of song: A developmental approach. In R.G. Taylor (Ed.), *Documentary report of the Ann Arbor Symposium* (pp. 301–315). Reston, VA: Music Educators National Conference.

Deutsch, D. (Ed.) (1982). *The psychology of music.* New York: Academic Press.

Dowling, W.J. (1973). The perception of interleaved melodies. *Cognitive Psychology, 5,* 322–337.

Dowling, W.J., & Harwood, D.L. (1986). *Music cognition.* Orlando, FL: Academic Press.

Drake, R.M. (1957). *Drake musical aptitude tests.* Chicago: Science Research Associates.

Erickson, R. (1982). New music and psychology. In D. Deutsch (Ed.), *The psychology of music* (pp. 517–536). New York: Academic Press.

Espinoza-Varas, B., & Watson, C.S. (1989). Perception of complex auditory patterns by humans. In R.J. Dowling & S.H. Hulse (Eds.), *The comparative psychology of audition: Perceiving complex sounds* (pp. 67–94). Hillsdale, NJ: Laurence Erlbaum Associates.

Farnsworth, P.R. (1969). *The social psychology of music* (2nd ed.). Ames: The Iowa State University Press.

Farnum, S.E. (1953). *Farnum music notation tests.* New York: The Psychological Corporation.

Fiske, H.E. (1990). *Music and mind: Philosophical essays on the cognition and meaning of music.* Lewiston, NY: The Edwin Mellen Press.

Fiske, H.E. (1993). *Music cognition and aesthetic attitudes.* Lewiston, NY: The Edwin Mellen Press.

Gaston, E.T. (1957). *Test of musicality.* Lawrence, KS: O'Dell's Instrumental Service.

Gordon, E. (1965). *Musical aptitude profile.* Boston: Houghton Mifflin.

Gordon, E. (1971). *The psychology of music teaching.* Englewood Cliffs, NJ: Prentice-Hall.

Gordon, E. (1979). *Primary measures of music audiation.* Chicago: G.I.A. Publications.

Gordon, E. (1982). *Intermediate measures of music audiation* Chicago: G.I.A. Publications.

Gordon, E. (1989). *Advanced measures of music audiation.* Chicago: G.I.A. Publications.

Gordon, E. (1991). *Iowa tests of music literacy* (2nd ed.). Chicago: G.I.A. Publications.

Greene, P.C. (1937). Violin intonation. *Journal of the Acoustical Society of American, 9*, 43–44.

Hargreaves, D.J. (1986). *The developmental psychology of music.* Cambridge: Cambridge University Press.

Hebb, D.O. (1949). *The organization of behavior.* New York: Wiley.

Helmholtz, H. von. (1954). *On the sensations of tone as a physiological basis for the theory of music.* (A.J. Ellis, ed. and trans.). New York: Dover. (Originally published, 1863).

Hickman, A. (1976). Some philosophical problems of melody. *Psychology of Music, 4* (1), 2–11.

Howell, P., Cross, I., & West, R. (Eds.) (1985). *Musical structure and cognition.* London: Academic Press.

Idson, W., & Massaro, D. (1978). A bidimensional model of pitch in the recognition of melodies. *Perception and Psychophysics, 24*, 551–565.

Imberty, M. (1981). Tonal acculturation and perceptual structuring of musical time in children (trans. from original French). In *Basic musical functions and musical ability,* Publication No. 32 (pp. 107–130). Stockholm: Royal Swedish Academy of Music.

Jones, M.R. (1981). Music as a stimulus for psychological motion: Part I. Some determinants of expectancies. *Psychomusicology, 1* (2), 34–51.

Jones, M.R. (1982). Music as a stimulus for psychological motion: Part II. An expectancy model. *Psychomusicology, 2* (1), 1–13.

Jones, M.R. (1990). Learning and the development of expectancies: An interactionist approach. *Psychomusicology, 9* (2), 193–228.

Kamien, R. (Ed.) (1972). *The Norton scores* (rev. ed.). New York: W.W. Norton.

Knuth, W.E. (1966). *Knuth achievement tests in music.* San Francisco: Creative Arts Research Associates.

Koffka, K. (1935). *Principles of Gestalt psychology.* New York: Harcourt, Brace & World.

Krumhansl, C.L. (1979). The psychological representation of pitch in a musical context. *Cognitive Psychology, 11*, 346–374.

Krumhansl, C.L. (1983). Perceptual structures for tonal music. *Music Perception, 1,* 28–62.

Krumhansl, C.L. (1990). *Cognitive foundations of musical pitch.* New York: Oxford University Press.

Krumhansl, C.L., & Kessler, E.J. (1982). Tracing the dynamic changes in perceived tonal organization in a spatial representation of musical keys. *Psychological Review, 89*, 334–368.

Krumhansl, C.L., & Shepard, R.N. (1979). Quantification of the hierarchy of tonal functions within a diatonic context. *Journal of Experimental Psychology: Human Perception and Performance, 5*, 579–594.

Krumhansl, C.L., Bharucha, J.J., & Castellano, M.A. (1982). Key distance effects on perceived harmonic structure in music. *Perception & Psychophysics, 32*, 96–108.

Krumhansl, C.L., Bharucha, J.J., & Kessler, E.J. (1982). Perceived harmonic structure of chords in three related musical keys. *Journal of Experimental Psychology: Human Perception and Performance, 8,* 24–36.

Lerdahl, F. (1988). Cognitive constraints on compositional systems. In J.A. Sloboda (Ed.), *Generative processes in music: The psychology of performance, improvisation, and composition* (pp. 231–259). Oxford: Clarendon Press.

Lerdahl, F., & Jackendoff, R. (1983). *A generative theory of tonal music.* Cambridge: MIT Press.

Long, N.H. (1968). *The Indiana-Oregon music discrimination test.* Bloomington, IN: N.H. Long. (Originally published as the *Oregon Music Discrimination Test* by K. Hevner in 1935)

Lundin, R.W. (1967). *An objective psychology of music* (2nd ed.). New York: Ronald Press.

Mainwaring, J. (1951). Psychological factors in the teaching of music. *British Journal of Educational Psychology, 21,* 105–121, 199–213.

McDonald, D.T., & Ramsey, J.H. (1979). A study of musical auditory information processing of preschool children. *Contributions to Music Education, 7,* 2–11.

Meyer, L.B. (1956). *Emotion and meaning in music.* Chicago: The University of Chicago Press.

Meyer, L.B. (1967). *Music, the arts and ideas.* Chicago: The University of Chicago Press.

Michel, P. (1973). Optimum development of musical abilities in the first years of life. *Psychology of Music, 1*(2), 14–20.

Moles, A. (1966). *Information theory and esthetic perception.* (J.E. Cohen, trans.). Urbana: University of Illinois Press.

Moog, H. (1976). *The musical experience of the pre-school child* (C. Clarke, trans.). London: Schott.

Mursell, J.L. (1937). *Psychology of music.* New York: W.W. Norton.

Nickerson, J.F. (1949). Intonation of solo and ensemble performances of the same melody. *Journal of the Acoustical Society of America, 21,* 593–595.

Nye, R.E., & Nye, V.T. (1985). *Music in the elementary schools* (5th ed.). Englewood Cliffs: Prentice-Hall.

Ortmann, O. (1926). On the melodic relativity of tones. *Psychological Monographs, 35,* 1–35.

Ortmann, O. (1937). Interval frequency as a determinant of melodic style. *Peabody Bulletin,* 3–10.

Ostling, A., Jr. (1974). Research in Pythagorean, just, and equal-tempered tunings in performance. *The Journal of Band Research, 10* (2), 13–20.

Petzold, R.B. (1966). *Auditory perception of musical sounds by children in the first six grades.* Madison: University of Wisconsin. (ERIC Document Reproduction Service No. ED 101 297)

Phillips, D. (1976). An investigation of the relationship between musicality and intelligence. *Psychology of Music, 4* (2), 16–31.

Radocy, R.E. (1977). *Analyses of three melodic properties in randomly selected melodies.* Unpublished research report, The University of Kansas.

Ramsey, J.H. (1983). The effects of age, singing ability, and instrumental experiences on preschool children's melodic perception. *Journal of Research in Music Education, 31,* 133–145.

Regelski, T.A. (1975). *Principles and problems of music education.* Englewood Cliffs: Prentice-Hall.

Reimer, B. (1989). *A philosophy of music education* (2nd ed.). Englewood Cliffs, NJ: Prentice-Hall.

Revesz, G. (1953). *Introduction to the psychology of music* (G.I. C. de Courcy, trans.). London: Longmans, Green.

Roederer, J.G. (1995). *The physics and psychophysics of music, an introduction* (3rd ed.). New York: Springer-Verlag.

Schenker, H. (1979). *Free composition* (E. Oster, ed. and trans.). New York: Longman. (Originally published, 1935)

Schmuckler, M.A. (1988). *Expectation in music: Additivity of melodic and harmonic processes.* Doctoral dissertation, Cornell University.

Seashore, C.E. (1919). *The psychology of musical talent.* New York: Silver Burdett.

Seashore, C.E. (1938). *Psychology of music.* New York: McGraw-Hill.

Seashore, C.E., Lewis, D.L., & Saetveit, J.G. (1939; 1960). *Seashore measures of musical talents* (rev.). New York: The Psychological Corporation.

Serafine, M.L. (1983). Cognitive processes in music: Discoveries and definitions. *Council for Research in Music Education, 73,* 1–14.

Sergeant, D. (1983). The octave—percept or concept? *Psychology of Music, 11,* 3–18.

Sergeant, D., & Roche, S. (1973). Perceptual shifts in the auditory information processing of young children. *Psychology of Music, 1* (2), 39–48.

Sergeant, D., & Thatcher, G. (1974). Intelligence, social status and musical abilities. *Psychology of Music, 2* (2), 32–57.

Shepard, R.N. (1982). Structural representations of musical pitch. In D. Deutsch (Ed.), *The psychology of music* (pp. 344–390). New York: Academic Press.

Shuter-Dyson, R., & Gabriel, C. (1981). *The psychology of musical ability* (2nd ed.). London: Methuen.

Sloboda, J.A. (1985). *The musical mind.* Oxford: Clarendon Press.

Smith, K.C., & Cuddy, L.L. (1986). The pleasingness of melodic sequences: Contrasting effects of repetition and rule-familiarity. *Psychology of Music, 14,* 17–32.

Sterling, P. (1985). The effects of accompanying harmonic context on vocal pitch accuracy of a melody. *Psychology of Music, 13,* 72–80.

Sundberg, J., & Lindblom, B. (1976). Generative theories in language and music descriptions. *Cognition, 4,* 99–122.

Taylor, J.A. (1971). Perception of melodic intervals within melodic content (Doctoral dissertation, University of Washington, 1971). *Dissertation Abstracts International, 32,* 6481A.

Taylor, J.A. (1976). Perception of tonality in short melodies. *Journal of Research in Music Education, 24,* 197–208.

Taylor, S. (1973). Musical development in children aged seven to eleven. *Psychology of Music, 1* (1), 44–49.

Temko, P.M. (1972). The perception of pitch predominance in selected musical examples of avant-garde composers, 1945–1961 (Doctoral dissertation, Florida State University, 1971). *Dissertation Abstracts International, 32,* 5275.

Terhardt, E., & Zick, M. (1975). Evaluation of tempered tone scale in normal, stretched, and contracted intonation. *Acustica, 32,* 268–274.

Thackray, R. (1973). Tests of harmonic perception. *Psychology of Music, 1* (2), 49–57.

Thackray, R. (1976). Measurement of the perception of tonality. *Psychology of Music, 4* (2), 32–37.

357 songs we love to sing. (1938). Minneapolis: Schmitt, Hall, and McCreary.

Trehub, S.E. (1993). The music listening skills of infants and young children. In T.J. Tighe & W.J. Dowling (Eds.), *Psychology and music: The understanding of melody and rhythm* (pp. 161–176). Hillsdale, NJ: Lawrence Erlbaum Associates.

Trehub, S.E., Bull, D., & Thorpe, L. (1984). Infants' perception of melodies: The role of contour. *Journal of Experimental Psychology: Human Perception and Performance, 12,* 295–301.

Trehub, S.E., Thorpe, L.A., & Morrongiello, B.A. (1987). Organizational processes in infants' perception of auditory patterns. *Child Development, 58,* 741–849.

Unyk, A.M. (1990). Expectancy in music cognition. *Psychomusicology, 9* (2), 229–240.

Unyk, A.M., & Carlsen, J.C. (1987). The influence of expectancy on melodic perception. *Psychomusicology, 7* (1), 3–23.

Von Hoerner, S. (1975). The definition of major scales, for chromatic scales of 12, 19, and 31 divisions per octave. *Psychology of Music, 4* (1), 12–23.

Watkins, J.G., & Farnum, S.E. (1954). *The Watkins-Farnum Performance Scale.* Winona, MN: Hal Leonard Music.

Watson, C.S. (1973). Psychophysics. In B.B. Wolman (Ed.), *Handbook of general psychology* (pp. 275–306). Englewood Cliffs: Prentice-Hall.

Weber, M. (1958). *The rational and social foundations of music* (D. Martindale, J. Reidel, & G. Neuwirth, eds. and trans.). [n.p.]: Southern Illinois University Press.

Wertheimer, M. (1955). Laws of organization in perceptual forms. In W.D. Ellis (Ed.), *A source book of Gestalt psychology.* London: Routledge & Kegan Paul. (Originally published in German, 1923)

West, R., Howell, P., & Cross, I. (1985). Modelling perceived musical structure. In P. Howell, I. Cross, & R. West (Eds.), *Musical structure and cognition* (pp. 21–52). London: Academic Press.

Wilkinson, S.R. (1988). *Tuning in, Microtonality in electronic music.* Milwaukee: Hal Leonard Books.

Wing, H.D. (1961). *Standardised tests of musical intelligence.* The Mere, England: National Foundation for Educational Research.

Woodruff, A.D. (1970). How music concepts are developed. *Music Educators Journal, 56* (6), 51–54.

Zimmerman, M.P. (1971). *Musical characteristics of children.* Washington: Music Educators National Conference.

CHAPTER SEVEN

FOUNDATIONS OF PERFORMANCE, IMPROVISATION, AND COMPOSITION

People have intellectual and emotional listening experiences with music. Listening may have profound aesthetic significance, or be rather trite. Musicologists and psychologists may analyze music in terms of its theoretical construction, both in the sense of traditional music theory and psychological "deep" structures. Casual listeners may relegate music to being a commodity, or part of auditory decor. In an age of sophisticated recording and broadcast technology, it is especially easy for listeners to not consider that someone created the physical sounds that humans organize into music. While one might argue philosophically that "true" music is contained in a score, which may be realized only imperfectly, or exists in some metaphysical or spiritual state that temporal civilizations may imitate only approximately, the sonic musical experience requires actual creation of sounds. Until recently, music psychology traditionally neglected performance; the first two editions of this text were no exception.

Much of the world's music, especially in the Western classic tradition, is composed—someone provided the performer with a guide, often with particular expectations regarding the conversion of written symbols to sounds. Composition is a creative act, an essential part of comprehensive music education. Unfortunately, composition may be viewed as a gift unavailable to the ordinary person. Certainly, not everyone is a Mozart or an Andrew Lloyd Webber, but arranging sounds and silences and providing instructions for their realization is not an alien skill.

Many forms of music combine creation with recreation as performers improvise the music as they play or sing. Jazz is an obvious example, as are some folk styles. Improvisation proceeds within certain frameworks; it balances creativity with expectations.

Consequently, this chapter considers performance as a psychomotor behavior, the quality of performance expertise, performance anxiety, improvisation, and composition.

233

Performance as Psychomotor Behavior

Educational objectives occasionally are classified and organized hierarchically within three "domains": cognitive, affective, and psychomotor. Cognitive objectives usually require primarily intellectual behaviors, as in solving an equation or writing a novel. Affective objectives usually involve feelings and emotions; as the next chapter indicates, the affective response is one where the stimulus "acts" on the organism. Psychomotor objectives require considerable physical effort; musical performance and athletic skills are obvious examples. Readers who are interested in details of the various taxonomic structures may consult Bloom's (1956) cognitive taxonomy, the affective taxonomy of Krathwohl, Bloom, and Masia (1964), and the psychomotor taxonomies of Simpson (presented in Colwell (1970)) and Harrow (1972). The important point here is that musical performance is a set of psychomotor behaviors in which the brain (or "mind")[1] guides the body.

Practice techniques are important for developing skillful execution of the psychomotor behaviors requisite in musical performance. "How to practice" is a time-honored area of investigation in music psychology. During the 1930s, Rubin-Rabson conducted numerous studies regarding the memorization of piano music. Essentially, she found that the superiority of whole over part learning (i.e., memorizing relatively long sections versus short subsections) varies with the learner and the music (1940a), that "overlearning" (practicing well beyond what is necessary to meet a criterion) is of dubious value (1941a; b), that mental rehearsal[2] may benefit performance when it is incorporated into the practice routine, and that distributed practice over a longer time period is superior to massed practice in a marathon session, although there are individual differences (1937; 1940b).

Coffman (1990) contrasted practice conditions of mental rehearsal (which may be construed as a cognitive enhancement of psychomotor skills), alternating mental and physical rehearsal, strict physical rehearsal, and a control condition in which subjects read about sightreading. The subjects "practiced" under their designated conditions between a pre-test and a post-test involving keyboard performance of a simple composition.

---

[1]The brain is a physical entity; one could hold a brain removed from a cadaver in one's hands. The mind is a metaphysical construct, a summation of what the brain does (Restak, 1984, p. 201). Neural signals regarding performance emanate from the brain; the performer's decisions regarding what signals to send are a function of the mind.

[2]Mental rehearsal occasionally is compared humorously to the "think system," featured in Meredith Willson's musical comedy and movie *The Music Man,* where students were implored to "think" of Beethoven's "Minuet in G" as a means of practice, but mentally running over what must be done in a performance is a legitimate technique for an experienced performer.

Comparisons of times required to perform the criterion composition, pitch errors, and rhythm errors showed that (a) subjects who actually played during their practice condition had a significantly shorter performance time than control subjects, (b) strict physical and alternating mental/physical rehearsal practice resulted in a shorter performance time than mental rehearsal alone, and (c) the combination practice condition was not significantly different from the physical rehearsal alone. Mental rehearsal clearly is no substitute for physical practice.

Gruson (1988) studied the practice strategies of forty-three pianists, ranging from novice to advanced levels. The pianists practiced three unfamiliar (and unidentified) compositions—one Baroque piece, one contemporary piece, and one sonatina. The particular pieces were assigned to individual pianists in accordance with skill levels. Analyses of differences in practice time allocation among pianists of different skill levels showed significant positive correlations between skill level and repeating sections longer than a measure ($r = .72$), practicing the hands separately ($r = .49$), practicing each assigned composition rather than playing other music or stopping[3] ($r = .40$), making selfguiding statements (as in "better slow down") ($r = .39$), and making overt verbalizations, as in "I made a mistake!" ($r = .37$). Significant negative correlations (all $r = -.31$) existed between skill level and playing wrong tones, repetition of single tones, and stopping for at least two seconds within a five-second interval. An increase in pianistic skill apparently included an increase in the likelihood of employing longer and more systematic practice strategies and engaging in fewer sporadic stabs at the keyboard and less hesitation and off-task behavior. Gruson found that, in particular, the tendency to practice repeated intact sections increased with pianistic proficiency.

Gruson had some pianists continue to practice the assigned pieces for additional sessions; they generally did not change their practice strategies as they gained increasing familiarity with the music. Despite improvements in performance, the pianists largely maintained their practice routines. Gruson (p. 104) indicates "The most salient finding was the impressive consistency across sections of the importance of a number of variables, particularly repeating sections, as discriminators of different musical levels."

The particular practice techniques that benefit a performer depend on an interaction of the performer's skill, the performer's motivation, the performance medium, and the music. Music educators employ diverse

---

[3]Continually practicing the assigned music may be considered as "time on task;" more colloquially, the relationship suggests a tendency for the advanced pianists to not soosie-moosie around.

techniques with students, often without any particular research base. Many techniques are a function of underlying aspects of learning and musical development, discussed elsewhere in this text. In general, practice should be purposeful rather than happenstance, aimed toward specific musical and technical goals, engaged in regularly, and, for novice performers, under the guidance of an experienced performer. Time is important, but so is how the time is spent. In a broad sense, time spent listening to model performances, studying music silently, and relating a particular composition to other examples of the musical style are beneficial as well as actual psychomotor activity. After all, the mind guides the body in psychomotor behavior.

Performance Expertise

The expert performer exemplifies a person who has "mastered" many skills, all of which he or she may marshal in service of a musical goal. Practice strategies and time allocations are part of the total picture, but expertise involves more than efficient and beneficial practice.

Dreyfus and Dreyfus (1986) identified five stages through which learners in diverse fields pass as they acquire expertise: novice, advanced beginner, competence, proficiency, and expertise. Commenting on the final stage, Trotter (1986, p. 36) noted that "Experts don't apply rules, make decisions or solve problems. They do what comes naturally, and it almost always works."

Writing in the context of spatial intelligence, Gardner (1993, pp. 193–195) synthesizes research and commentary regarding the expertise of chess masters. The master has an abstract plan for a game. While chess masters may have a strong visual memory, they do not operate from a concrete picture of the chess board or simply memorize an intricate series of moves. Chess masters mentally can reconstruct a board which they have seen for only a very short time, provided that the chess pieces are arranged in a meaningful way, in accordance with the rules of the game. This arouses a set of patterned movements, based in experience and game contingencies, synthesized into an abstract game plan.

Sloboda (1985, p. 101) presents three general principles of expert performance, related to the execution of abstract *performance* plans for musical compositions. First, the expert is aware of large musical groupings within the composition. Such "groupings" are meaningful combinations of tonal and rhythmic material, grouped in accordance with hierarchical organizational principles. Where relatively inexpert performers give inordinate attention to local aspects of the musical surface structure, expert performers plan and execute in accordance with longer range goals. Second, the expert performer employs flexible unconscious procedures for solving local performance problems; conscious attention is devoted to the longer range plan. Inexpert performers must give full conscious attention to local problems, such as a difficult technical passage. Third, the expert monitors the performance as it evolves and takes corrective action when necessary to prevent inappropriate deviation from the performance plan: Sloboda likens this to knowing what to listen for more than simply listening. Even the monitoring stage is largely unconscious: A characteristic of highly developed psychomotor behavior is that a person can operate successfully without much conscious feedback. Clearly, the expert musical performer has mastered sufficient detail so that he or she can devote attention to a musical rendition of a large scale work.

The expert performer may be capable of extensive use of well developed knowledge structures or schemata. Clarke (1988) suggests that generative processes are involved in musical performance, including sightreading, prepared performance, and improvisation. Such processes may include representation of musical structure in an input form to the motor system, as well as the production and control of musical expression. He indicates that the cognitive structures involved in an abstract musical understanding and those involved in execution of a motor sequence in service of performance are hard to distinguish. In turn, those performance-related structures differ for the type of musical task.

The structures involved in playing music from memory theoretically are the most deeply embedded, although only part of them probably are involved at any one time within the performance. Reading relatively unfamiliar music requires coping with uncertainties, regardless of the performer's familiarity with the musical style. Such uncertainties arise from the performer considering different musical projections and combinations of notated patterns, an imperfect and incomplete stylistic knowledge, and musical creativity demanding a departure from stylistic norms. Clarke indicates (p. 6) that fully adequate generative structures require complete information; the performer who must play unfamiliar music has a limited structural representation of that music, one which must undergo continuous modification as the music develops.

With improvisation, the performer's structural representation is usually quite incomplete. The structural hierarchy may be rather ambiguous, and structures may be organized associatively (in a linear way, one musical event leading to another) or by repertoire selection (borrowing fragments from other musical sources and joining them).

A performance in many musical styles is more than a technically accurate rendition of properly sequenced sounds, important though that aspect is. Musical *expression* is necessary. Clarke believes that the performer derives expression from information found in musical structure, rather than from fixed patterns found in all music. The expressive parameters for pianists are tempo, dynamics, and articulation; other performance media may provide additional parameters. Interestingly, expression may be obvious *from* the musical structure, or expression may *clarify* the structure. When the structure is clear and the audience is composed of persons who are experienced in the musical style, the music's expressive characteristics are in response to or refinements of the music's inherent properties. Strong coherent musical structures arouse clear expectations in a knowledgeable audience, and that audience probably will hear unusual expressive features as a type of mistake. However, when the musical structure is weak or obtuse, the performer's expressions may impose a particular structure on the music. In a weak structure, deficient in musical organizational reference points, the audience must accept what the performer does. Music lacking in obvious tonality and formal structure provides the performer with an opportunity to educate the audience and shape their musical understandings through his or her expressive interpretations.[4] The expert performer balances structure and individual expression, as two quotes from Clarke (p. 24) suggest: "Clearly a performer must not contradict the structure to such an extent that the music becomes incomprehensible to a listener, but a performer must also avoid playing music in a trite and obvious way" and "At a more subtle level, an individual interpretation can be regarded as a personally selected patterning of the expressive principles that may persist over a long period of time."

In reporting her study of practice techniques and time allocations, discussed above, Gruson (1988) contrasts performers' differing levels of expertise in terms of contrasting strategies. She states (p. 108) "Musical practising [sic] may be viewed as a sequence of transactions from controlled to automatic processing in which larger and larger chunks of musical information are built up from more basic subcomponents." When a beginning student makes a mistake, he or she is likely to repeat the erroneous tone or measure. The piece basically exists as a linear sequence of independent notes, each of which functions as a small segment in a larger work. While the beginner thus builds from the bottom up, the expert builds from the top down: The expert decomposes the music into independent but musically linked, hierarchically organized patterns.

---

[4]Of course, as Chapter Six mentions, an audience may reject music which goes too far beyond its musical expectancies before they become sufficiently "educated."

The expert performer is more likely to follow an error with repetition of an entire musical structural unit rather than only a notational unit.

Thus, the expert performer has a considerable array of cognitive, affective, and psychomotor skills which he or she employs in the service of carefully planned musical goals. Expression and structural awareness are critical, and particular performance problems are resolved by following a carefully conceived and executed performance plan. In addition to developing technical skills, the performer needs to develop detailed conceptions of music in the styles which he or she hopes to perform.

Performance Anxiety

One problem afflicting many performers, even highly experienced ones, is anxiety. Anxiety, "a state of acute subjective distress that simultaneously motivates behavior aimed at reducing the distress" (Salmon & Meyer, 1992, p. 15), is an inevitable part of being human. Stressful situations, such as tests, auditions, public performances, and other situations in which a person is exposed to critical evaluation, normally will arouse some anxiety. Excessive anxiety is counterproductive. Test anxiety, a very real phenomenon that students of all ages experience, leads the individual to focus on personal inadequacy and real or imagined consequences (Krohne & Schaffner, 1983). According to Raynor (1981), about 25 percent of students are "failure-threatened"; i.e., they are motivated primarily to avoid failure. While clear standards and explanation of the importance of a particular performance may be beneficial for students who are "success-oriented" (how Raynor classifies another 25 percent of students), the "failure-threatened" student's future should not be linked to a present task. Musical performance is a type of "test," so concerns for test anxiety and individuals motivated mainly by avoiding failure are related intimately.

LeBlanc (1994) developed an eleven-level hierarchical model of sources of variation in music performance anxiety. Organized across time from planning for a public performance to receiving feedback following it, the model categorizes sources contributing to anxiety that arise from within the performer and from circumstances surrounding him or her. We briefly summarize each level here; we encourage interested readers to study the model and the underlying theory in LeBlanc's own presentation.

The beginning level of the hierarchy, numbered eleven (LeBlanc numbers the levels inversely), includes certain personal characteristics and experiences of the performer. Among these are age, musical ability, musical training, personality, amount and quality of performing experience, memory, and circadian rhythm. LeBlanc notes that adolescent performers may be especially vulnerable to anxiety, as are people who are basically pessimists, that musical ability and experience facilitate easing anxiety, and that, when possible, performers should perform at the time of day when they feel their best.

The difficulty and appropriateness of the music for performance comprise the tenth level. Obviously, some music is more difficult to play or sing than other music, and music that is appropriate for one performance situation may be quite inappropriate for another. Excessive difficulty and impropriety abet anxiety.

The ninth level of LeBlanc's hierarchy involves adequacy of the musical instrument (or voice) for the performance task, adequacy of preparation to perform, and adequacy of physical conditioning. An inadequate string or reed, fatigue, and just plain lack of practice contribute to anxiety.

The performer's emotional and physical health constitute the eighth level; performing under conditions of emotional or physical duress certainly can increase anxiety.

LeBlanc's seventh level is the performer's current affective state or mood. Regardless of what has or has not happened previously, when it is almost time to play or sing, the performer may be happy, sad, pensive, exhilarated, frightened, or in some other mood state.

Variables of the performing environment comprise the sixth level. LeBlanc notes measurement devices and procedures (these could include microphones, cameras, and adjudication procedures), physical comfort, whether one is required to perform from memory, distractions, and time of day. In addition, LeBlanc stresses the importance of the presence and behavior of the audience, authority figures (such as adjudicators), educators, family members (who may be supportive or overly critical), the media, and peers (such as fellow students or fellow professionals). Anxiety varies as a function of who one performs before and the environment in which the performance occurs.

The fifth level is one of self-perceptions immediately prior to the performance. Regardless of what actually is occurring, has occurred, or may occur, the performer's beliefs about various conditions, including the music's difficulty and appropriateness, how adequately he or she is prepared, personal appearance, amount of individual exposure (a solo passage draws attention), the performance's importance, and how supportive the audience is.

Arousal, physical and psychological, comprises the fourth level. As the performer is ready to begin, biological and cognitive processes are underway.

The actual performance begins at the third level; all of the previous levels represent prior points in time. LeBlanc indicates that this level is a focus of attention; presumably, the more the performer focuses on the performance itself, the less he or she will focus on anxiety-producing aspects.

The second level involves the self-perceptions of the fifth level during the performance. The performer receives immediate feedback through his or her own ears and may be encouraged or discouraged by the sound.

LeBlanc's first level includes subsequent feedback, as in audience comments, reviews, teacher evaluations, and performance ratings. Favorable feedback may alleviate anxiety in future performances.

Salmon and Meyer (1992) discuss comprehensively preparing for performance and alleviating anxiety. Much of the following discussion is based on their work, which readers who are especially concerned with performance anxiety are encouraged to read in detail.

As discussed earlier in this text, music has many social functions, and one can divorce social aspects from musical aspects only with difficulty. Many young performers are accustomed to receiving praise from parents, friends, and teachers in exchange for their public performances; they grow to link their self-esteem to the reactions of other people to their efforts. Motivation thus largely is extrinsic. With maturity, motivation becomes more intrinsic, but there still is a connection with reactions of other persons, including teachers, audition committees, critics, and audience members. Excessive focus on what others may think may induce stress as a performance is anticipated as well as while it is presented. Salmon and Meyer indicate (p. 25) "stress has more to do with how you evaluate and react to events than it does with the events themselves."

Many therapeutic aids for anxiety and stress exist; in extreme cases, pharmacological treatments are available, in accordance with a physician's guidance. Certainly, the promising performer who experiences debilitating episodes of stage fright or can not prepare adequately for performance because of associated anxiety should seek assistance. Yet, much of what is involved in coping with anxiety comes down to a sense of personal control, coupled with adequate planning. The performer should imagine a successful performance; practice sessions should involve more than learning music—they should include anticipation of feelings. Some anxiety is to be expected. Performer preparation includes selection of music, actively learning it, and the important few days and hours before the performance, when a wise performer may occupy time by engaging in activities over which he or she has considerable control. Physical manifestations of anxiety, such as accelerated heart rate and perspiration, will occur—they are normal and may be anticipated as such. Criticism of a performance will occur—yet the performer should be his or her own worst critic. There is no substitute for practice, but practice encompasses all phases of preparation, not only "learning the notes."

The belief that a little anxiety is a good thing may grow from a demonstrated curvilinear relationship between motivation and measures of efficiency: As motivation increases, performance efficiency increases to a certain point; after that, further increases in motivation lead to a decrement in performance (Atkinson, 1983). While one cannot pretend that an event which is important for one's career and musical advancement is trivial, one still may reflect on just what any individual performance means in life. Motivation to do one's best while recognizing that life is filled with diverse opportunities may be a healthy condition in approaching performance.

In discussing preparation for auditions, which may be quite stressful and critical for performers' professional advancement, Dunkel (1989) notes that the audition process is filled with risks to a person's self-esteem; again, separation of the social from the purely musical is difficult. The risk taken by undergoing a rigorous audition may be devastating, *but* it may build further esteem. Dunkel comments (p. 4) on the inevitable competitive aspect:

> All forms of competition are hostile. They may seem friendly on the surface but the prime motivation is to be or do "better than" anyone else. Although it may appear that the world is a competitive place, it is only competitive to those who feel the need to compete.

So, the person who elects to enter the competitive world of professional performance has chosen the anxiety and stress that accompany it. Dunkel presents a potpourri of advice, to which the interested reader is referred. Basically, one should focus carefully on goals, separate one's self from one's performance, and yet maintain a close relationship with music.

Improvisation

Musical performance may involve performances of (a) particular compositions, which may be learned either by rote and performed from memory or learned from notation and performed either from memory or from notation, or (b) improvisations, which involve extemporaneous performance of newly created music. Historically, improvisation and composition were more closely related than they generally are today. Many great composers were excellent improvisers, e.g., Bach, Handel, Mozart, Beethoven, and Schubert. Performances from the Baroque figured-bass tradition were essentially improvisations, allowing the performer to create music extemporaneously, but within the context of the tonal harmonic framework suggested by the figured bass.

Many compositions, particularly from the Baroque era, are called "improvisations," the intent being for the performer to embellish upon the provided melodic, harmonic, and rhythmic structures. The embellishments, which usually reflect the performer's musical expertise and technical virtuosity, constitute the improvisatory aspect of the musical rendition.

Pressing (1984a) indicates that improvisation in Western music had its roots in early monophonic vocal music, which during the first millennium was "primarily a mixture of Greek, Arabic, Jewish, Oriental, and Christian influences" (p. 65). Passed on by the oral tradition, performers had ample opportunity to be creative in their musical renditions. Pressing notes that improvisation was certainly important in solo passages, and perhaps even in choral passages. Melismatic flourishes in certain alleluias of the early Christian liturgy were continuations of the improvisatory practices of early vocal music. With the beginning of *organum* came improvised polyphony, and Pressing notes that *melismatic organum,* which involved the singing of florid phrases above the plainsong chant, began to occur in about the twelfth century (Pressing, 1984a, p. 65). As organum became passe around the middle of the thirteenth century, the motet with its *cantus firmus* became a predominant form. The other parts of motets were either improvised, composed, or embellishments of composed parts. In the fifteenth century, *faburden* allowed singers to improvise over a *cantus firmus,* using a system of "sights" in which each improvising singer read the cantus firmus but added a new part above or below the melody. Pressing notes that thirds and sixths above the bass were the preferred intervals, except at the beginning and endings of phrases, where octaves and fifths were preferred. Slightly later, *fauxbourdon* developed, and here the outer voices were usually notated, but the inner voices were improvised by the singers.

With developments in instrumental music in the early Renaissance era, particularly for keyboard instruments such as the clavichord and the harpsichord, came the development of *intablatures,* relatively plain transcriptions of vocal music, which seemed to serve as frameworks for improvisations on the keyboard instruments. By the beginning of the sixteenth century, there was a virtually explosion of improvisatory techniques and treatises about improvisation, which was considered a required skill for performers of the time. Pressing notes that there were four main improvisation procedures found in the sixteenth century: "ornamentation of a given line, addition of one or more contrapuntal parts to a cantus firmus (including imitation based on given or invented motives), themes and variations, and free improvisations" (1984a, p. 67). Improvisation's importance continued to develop and reached its peak in Western art music during the Baroque era; however, the Baroque also saw the beginning of the decline of improvisation in Western art music.

While embellishments and variations on composed melodies continued to be important modes of improvisation during the Baroque, keyboardists' realizations of a *figured bass* became the predominant mode of improvisation during the Baroque (Pressing, 1984b, p. 60). "The *cadenza* was the last distinctive [improvisational] device pertinent to the Baroque," (1984b, p. 66), and it remains a continuing part of solo performances even today. However, "the traditions of improvisation dramatically declined into virtual extinction" (1984b, p. 66) during the Classical and Romantic eras. There are many reasons for the decline of improvisations in Western classical music, and Pressing (1984b, pp. 66) suggests that the change of emphasis to composed music was perhaps a reflection of the "*Zeitgeist* of scientific method, economic centralization, rationality, and the upsurge of machinery technology." He also notes that the rise of musical amateurism with performers who lacked the skills of improvisation increased the demand for composed music rather than improvised music. Western classical music since the Baroque has been predominantly composed music.

Improvisation has remained an important aspect of the Western church organ playing tradition. While much of an organist's improvisation is functional, i.e., to accommodate the uncertain timing of particular parts of the ritual and to provide bridges between various musical portions of the church service, improvisational skill remains today an important part of the church organist's repertoire of performance skills.

Today, however, most people associate improvisation with jazz. To be a jazz musician, one must be able to improvise: One can not demonstrate true expertise in jazz performance without demonstrating expertise in improvisation. This is not to imply that improvisation is the sole property of jazz musicians. Many pop and folk musicians' performances include improvisations. Music educators consider improvisation (and composition) as important modes for "knowing music" (Stubley, 1992, p. 13). The new national standards for music education in the United States include the development of improvisational and compositional skills as two of the nine broad *content standards* for elementary and secondary school music (MENC, 1994).

Obviously, a musician may manifest improvisational skills, just as other musical skills, in varied ways and at many different levels. Whether all seemingly extemporaneous music performances are actually improvisations is not clear; it may simply be a matter of how one defines improvisation.

Apel's (1944, p. 351) fifty-year-old definition of improvisation as "the art of performing music as an immediate reproduction of simultaneous mental processes, that is, without the aid of manuscript, sketches, or memory" is a good starting point and is particularly apropos for contemporary music psychologists concerned with understanding the underpinnings of musical improvisation. Apel's definition calls attention to the importance of the cognitive processes underlying overt performance behaviors. As is apparent to most readers, high level performance skill alone does not necessarily enable one to be a high level improviser. *Performance expertise does not ensure expertise as an improviser, but expertise as an improviser requires expertise as a performer.*[5]

Although it usually will not be apparent to listeners, true improvisations are not rehearsed; people who "prepare" improvisations by creating, revising, (in some cases writing them out), memorizing, and then performing a given set of patterns for a piece are really engaged in something more akin to composition than improvisation, even though the "composition" may never be notated. Pieces learned by rote or by ear and performed from memory do not meet Apel's criteria for improvisation. True improvisers do not have the luxury of rehearsing their improvisations. As Sloboda (1985, p. 138) notes, an improviser's *first* idea must work.

Obviously, improvisation, particularly beyond the simplest levels, involves creative thinking about the organization and structure of the musical performance. Even people who appear to "naturally" play by ear or improvise have engaged in extended learning, albeit in most cases informally through the enculturation process. Indeed, good improvisers *learn* to improvise, but except for jazz musicians and organists, relatively few musicians understand much about the processes involved in improvisation or how to go about learning to improvise.

Pressing (1988, p. 130) notes that improvisation, as all music performance, involves continuing series of highly complex instantaneous neurological processes, including (a) the passing of complex electrochemical signals between the nervous, endocrine, and muscle systems; (b) the execution of complex physical actions; (c) rapid monitoring of the actions via visual, tactile, and proprioceptive feedback systems; (d) producing musical sounds and monitoring them via auditory feedback; (e)

---

[5]Readers should not infer that performance expertise necessarily requires expertise in music reading; many expert performers either improvise their performances or learn their music by rote, i.e., through use of imitation procedures and concomitant trial and error procedures.

cognitive evaluations of these sounds as music; and (f) further cognitive processing to generate the design of the next action sequence and trigger it. Pressing notes that the last two steps are more critical to the improviser than to musicians performing specific composed works and observes that the given steps

> are often collapsed into a three-component information-processing model of human behavior which has ready physiological analogies: input (sense organs), processing and decision-making (central nervous system . . .), and motor output (muscle systems and glands). (p. 130)

An examination of the complexities of the motor control system is far beyond the scope of the present discussion, and readers are encouraged to examine Pressing's succinct and highly readable account of the system and how the system facilitates error correction and motor refinement.

Based on his examination of the model and motor control system, Pressing speculates that skilled improvisers develop through practice "general patterns of neural connections specific to improvised motor control" (p. 131) and notes that these are akin to "motor action units," which may be combined into long chains to develop more complex movements" (p. 131). In summary, skilled improvisers develop a "repertoire" of neurological connections that may be triggered during the improvisational process. Because the processing of these connections is so rapid, the improviser's performance may appear to be "automatic" or "natural." The major difference among expert, not-so-expert, and non-skilled improvisers appears to be, at least from a psychoneurological perspective, (a) in the extent of their repertoire of general patterns of neural connections specific to improvisation motor control and (b) their ability to automatically call them into action. Individuals who must consciously think out subsequent steps in their improvisations obviously will lack the fluency, fluidity, and flexibility of expert improvisers.

Concomitant with the development of the repertoire of general patterns specific to motor control is the development of the movement patterns for overt realization of the improvisation. Psychomotor behaviors depend both cognitive processing and motor skills. The development of performance skills is essential to improvisers; they must have sufficient performance skill to do what they wish to do musically in their improvisation. To the extent that performance skills are inadequate, the quality of the improvisation, regardless the sophistication of the musical idea, is undermined. Therefore, practice to develop performance skills remains important for improvisers, although their practice is not necessarily to learn to perform particular pieces.

Sloboda (1985) and his colleagues (Sloboda, 1988) have taken the lead in examining the psychological underpinnings of the processes of improvisation and composition, and much of the material in this and the following section of this chapter is drawn from their insightful work. Following the lead of Sloboda (1985), the balance of this section will focus mostly on the type of improvisation that is most visible and has developed into the art par excellence for improvisation: jazz improvisation.[6]

Many music stores and music libraries abound in books and methods for potential jazz musicians regarding "how to improvise," and interest in such materials is high. This discussion will not examine such sources, but persons interested in lists or reviews of such materials should consult one of several excellent overviews of the materials (Doerschuk, 1984; Greennagel, 1994; Pressing, 1988). Doerschuk notes that a survey of extant literature might suggest that improvisation skill can be realized by memorizing scales, modes, and exercises, but he questions this, noting that such systems reflect only a limited perspective on improvisation. Doerschuk recommends that persons interested in a method for learning improvisation examine the work of Emile Jaques-Dalcroze (1921, 1930), whose tripartite approach to musicianship involved eurhythmics, solfege, and music improvisation.

Greennagel reviews both methods and research on improvisation and concludes that "most jazz improvisation methods are based on a traditional theoretical approach with variations appearing in terms of suggested listening, drill, or writing exercises, or in combination with play-along practice (1994, p. 35). He notes, however, that the approaches of two authors, Liebman (1988) and Sudnow (1978), focus much more on the creative aspects of improvisation than other approaches. Greennagel's review revealed that most of the research on jazz improvisation were of the "methods development" variety.

Pressing's (1988) review suggests that approaches to teaching jazz improvisation appear to reflect one or more of five broad perspectives: (a) the historical view that improvisation is essentially the equivalent of real-time composition; (b) the view that improvisation involves the establishment of patterns, models, and procedures specific to the improvisational situation, "which, if followed by those possessing a solid enough level of musicianship, will produce stylistically appropriate music" (p. 142); (c) the view that improvisation is best developed by setting a series of improvisational problems or constraints as in the Jaques-Dalcroze approach; (d) the view that improvisation involves the "presentation of multiple versions of important entities by the teacher . . ., leaving the student to infer completely on his or her own the ways in which improvi-

---

[6]Apologies are extended to organists, for whom improvisation is an important and necessary tool.

sation or variation may occur by an appreciation of the 'fuzziness' of the musical concept," (p. 143) which Pressing labels an "imitative, self-discovery approach", and (e) the view that creative musical performance is "allied to the self-realization ideas of humanistic psychology" (p. 144).

Based on his comprehensive review of the history, theory, and approaches to improvisation, Pressing offers a cognitive model of improvisation. He argues that such a model should explain "how people improvise; how people learn improvisational skill; and the origin of novel behaviour" (1988, p. 152). Pressing summarizes the central features of his model as follows:

> It is reductionist, in that cognitive structures of processing and control are considered to be broken down into aspects (acoustic, musical, movements, etc.), each of these into types of analytical representation (objects, features, processes), and each of these into characterizing elements (array components). At the same time the model is synergistic and capable of behavioural novelty, due to the extensive redundancy of the cognitive representations and the distributed and non-linear character of the outlined control processes. The extensive presence of feedback and feedforward contribute to this. The fundamental nature of the improvisation process is considered to be the stringing together of a series of "event clusters" during each of which a continuation is chosen, based upon either the continuing of some stream by the choosing of a new set of array entries that act as constraints in the generation of a new stream (new event-cluster class). (Pressing, 1988, p. 168)

While Pressing's complex and insightful model needs to be studied, understood, and examined empirically, it undoubtedly will be refined before it is accepted as "truth" by all who are interested in understanding the nature of the psychological processes underlying improvisation.

Meanwhile, Sloboda's (1985) characterization of some of the attributes of the jazz improvisation process may be useful. What seems to make improvisation manageable for jazz musicians is the fact that their improvisation takes place within a large set of formal constraints which provide the blueprint or skeleton for improvisation. The jazz improviser "uses a model which is, in most cases, externally supplied by culture, and which he embellishes and 'fills in' in various ways" (p. 139). Sloboda notes, for example, that jazz ensemble pieces often have a fairly invariant "chorus" played by the group in alternation with solo sections in which various individuals may improvise for a more-or-less fixed number of measures until the next chorus; the soloist must be knowledgeable of the underlying structure and how to get from his or her musical excursions back to the next chorus in a novel and musical way (Sloboda, p. 141).

In discussing the 12-bar blues and 32-bar song forms, Sloboda notes that the melody often is a "standard" initially played in a fairly straightforward manner and that the subsequent improvisations usually retain the basic harmonic sequence, but the *"essence* of improvisation, both here [32-bar song] and in the 12-bar blues, is in the melodic line" (p. 143). Sloboda maintains that jazz solo performance is necessarily melodic and that jazz piano came later, with the left hand providing rhythm and chords and the right hand "playing the solo."

What makes an improvisation a jazz improvisation is the musical vocabulary a performer draws on for the improvisation—the types of melodic, rhythmic, and harmonic devices used to build larger sequences. This vocabulary, however, is not just a memorized set of scale, chord, and rhythmic patterns. It is developed "through listening intently to other musicians and performing with them" (Sloboda, p. 143). Sloboda maintains that books and notation are not really necessary and notes that "many great jazz performers could not read a note of music" (p. 143).

The mention of "great" jazz performers immediately begs the questions, "What makes a jazz performance " 'great'?" and, more specific to the present discussion, "How does one evaluate the quality of an improvisation?" This discussion purposely will avoid the first question because the variables that may influence judgments of greatness are many, complex, highly subjective, and often go beyond an assessment of the performance per se, e.g., the "halo" effect regarding who is performing influences many people's judgments about the quality of the performance, improvised or otherwise. Attempts to evaluate the quality of an improvisation also are fraught with many problems, but several researchers have sought to develop objective criteria or guidelines for making such judgments more objective. To the extent that different judges agree in their assessments of the quality of an improvisation, the subjective component is minimalized.

Potter (1990) notes that "many factors may contribute toward making an improvised solo 'good' or 'great' " (p. 69) and that these reasons often are diverse and even contradictory. Solos may be valued for their technical virtuosity, beautiful tone quality, rhythmic characteristics, novelty, restraint and classical balance, use of quotations, and even "expressive use of growls, honks, squeaks, and split tones" (p. 69). While Potter is most concerned with analyses of improvisations, his recommendation that analyses of improvised jazz "be eclectic, holistic, using whatever approaches help explain the solo's effectiveness" (p. 69) holds implications for evaluation of improvisations.

Partchey's (1973) carefully controlled study of children's improvisations offers insights both into strategies for evaluating the quality of improvisations and for developing improvisational skills. Specifically, the study sought to develop a valid and reliable method of evaluating improvisation and to compare the effects of feedback, models, and repetition (i.e., trial and error) on the ability to improvise melodies. Eighty-six sixth-grade children were divided into three treatment groups, and each child was given three individual sessions in which to practice respectively improvising blues, whole-tone, and diatonic melodies with given tape-recorded accompaniments for each. Pre- and post-treatment evaluations involved pentatonic improvisations. Children in the feedback group got to hear immediate recordings of their efforts, the models group heard several examples of pre-recorded melodic improvisations, and the repetition group was given no specific instructions. Improvisations were performed on an alto-tenor xylophone, and specific pitch bars were set up for the particular scale to be used in the improvisation. Improvisations were evaluated on a nine-point scale according to two performance and three creative criteria: The performance criteria included pulse accuracy and rhythmic clarity; creative criteria included tonal variety, rhythmic variety, and unity (subcategories: repetition, imitation, pitch direction, and phrasing). Interjudge reliability for evaluations of improvisations using Partchey's criteria ranged from .92 to .95. There were significant pre-post treatment effects within each group, and pre-post changes in ratings for students receiving feedback were significantly greater than for the other two groups. Pre-post changes for creative criteria were statistically significant for the feedback and models groups, but pre-post changes for performance criteria were not.

Greennagel's (1994) study of predictors of jazz vocal improvisation skill required the development of a tool for evaluating jazz vocal improvisation skill. His basic criteria for evaluation somewhat paralleled Partchey's two broad categories (musicality and technical appropriateness), but he added two criteria specifically appropriate for the type of improvisations he was evaluating vocal improvisations over 12-bar blues choruses. Musicality refers to "how well the improvisation succeeds in making a musical statement" (p. 40), and technical appropriateness refers to "how well the improvisation fits the chord changes and anticipates those changes; also time feel" (p. 40). The additional criteria, articulation and relationship to blues, refer respectively to the use of "vowel and consonant articulation to verbalize intended sounds," and "how well the improvisation fits the traditional structure of the Blues" (pp. 40–41). Greennagel's criteria suggest that the evaluative criteria must be appropriate to the type, style, and general nature of the improvisation. The interjudge reliability coefficient for experience jazz musicians using Greennagel's criteria was $r = .86$.

The high interjudge reliability coefficients for Partchey's and Greennagel's evaluative tools suggest that reliable evaluations of improvisations in relation to particular criteria are possible. Evaluation of improvisations is more than just a subjective matter.

Composition

Sloboda (1985, p. 103) suggests that "composition is the least studied and least well understood of all musical processes, and [notes that] . . . there is no substantial psychological literature to review." Nevertheless, most colleges, conservatories, and universities teach music composition, and an examination of generative processes related to composition may be relevant to persons involved in such teaching.

While improvisation and composition share many commonalities, the differences between the two processes warrant separate discussions. As Sloboda (1985, p. 103) notes, the "constraints of improvisation—immediacy and fluency—make it likely that there are processes which improvisation and composition do not share." He is particularly concerned with examining two aspects of psychological activity that seem to be a part of the generative process of composition: "the occurrence of superordinate structures or plans which seem to guide and determine the detailed note-by-note working out . . . [and] the degree to which these plans can . . . be rather provisional. They can, for instance, be changed in light of the way a particular passage 'turns out'" (Sloboda, p. 103). In short, "the composer rejects possible solutions until he finds one which seems to be best for his purposes. The improviser must accept the first solution that comes to hand" (p. 149).

Sloboda (1985, pp. 102–103) suggests four possible approaches to gaining insights into composers' compositional processes: (a) examination of composers' sketches and notebooks, (b) examination of what composers say about their own compositional processes, (c) "live" observations of composers as they compose, and (d) observation and description of improvisatory performance. Sloboda recognizes several limitations of the first two approaches, noting that composers' sketchbooks and notebooks are particularly unsatisfactory for cognitive psychology because they cannot explain the unconscious processes a composer may use in bringing to consciousness a highly structured composition (p. 114). Besides the inherent concerns contemporary psychologists hold with respect to verbal reports, composers' writings about their compositional processes may be limited by the accuracy of a composer's memory for his or her thoughts experienced while composing a particular piece. Sloboda suggests that the most detailed and accurate description of a compositional process is to be gained "by examining verbalizations made *concurrent with* the act" (p. 123).

Sloboda also (1985, pp. 123–138) discusses two composers' protocols for compositions, one for a fugue by an unidentified composer and an account of his own composition for choir and organ. He notes that the fugue's composer began with certain constraints. As additional constraints emerged over the course of the composition, it became impossible to honor all of the constraints. The composer appeared to resolve this dilemma by either (a) temporarily dropping some constraints, (b) changing the constraints, or (c) modifying the new material to bring it back in line with earlier constraints.

In his own highly insightful compositional protocol, Sloboda also began with several constraints, citing particularly his compositional style, which he characterized as "twentieth-century English church" that emphasizes melody, counterpoint, and a strong tonal harmonic framework (p. 125), and that the work should be for four voice parts and organ. His protocol essentially presents a number of questions he posed during the process and the rationale for and nature of the decisions he made in order to satisfy his constraints and other self-imposed criteria for making the work as cohesive and musical (aesthetically satisfying) as possible. He notes that he eventually reached a point (about measure 50) where he feared that stopping to record his thoughts in words would cause him to lose some momentum, and he subsequently composed 35 measures without interruption. He maintains that his compositional strategy for the uninterrupted measures differed from that for the previous 50 measures for which he had provided a protocol, and concludes that "the requirement to provide a protocol may well alter, even disrupt entirely, the process one is trying to describe" (Sloboda, p. 136).

Sloboda draws three additional conclusions from his experience of providing a protocol for the composition. First, despite the detail he provided, his protocol still left much unsaid regarding the compositional choices made. Second, he reported that throughout the process, he tended to use previously written material as starting points for continuations, trying to make the continuations "fit" the earlier material. Finally, he suggests that "an important component of compositional skill is a degree of 'trust' in one's medium—a certainty that the habitual processes of generation will yield material which is richer than one first sees" (p. 138). Nevertheless, Sloboda views protocol description as "an essential first step in understanding any complex mental process" (p. 138).

A Theoretical Perspective

Sloboda (p. 116) recognizes two stages of composition: the "inspiration" stage, "where a skeletal idea or theme appears in consciousness," and the "execution" stage, "where the idea is subject to a series of more conscious and deliberate processes of extension and transformation." He finds it useful to divide a "typical" composer's compositional resources and processes into two broad categories: "unconscious" and "conscious." He suggests that a composer brings certain long-term knowledge, which includes a general tonal and stylistic knowledge and a set of "superordinate constraints on form and direction," to the compositional process. This long-term knowledge, which Sloboda classifies as unconscious knowledge, is brought into play as the composer works with his idea for a composition and develops it into a thematic kernel for the composition. As the composition develops, the composer applies certain techniques from his repertoire of compositional devices to develop the work into an intermediate form which may, through a series of goal alterations and subsequent judgments regarding the "rightness" of the intermediate form, eventually be molded into its final form. The allowance for goal alterations is important, because it allows "discovered properties of intermediate themes . . . [to] actually overwrite originally held goals, so that the composition can appear to the composer to generate its own momentum or 'life,' almost independently of his will" (Sloboda, p. 119). Determining the sources of, and the unconscious processes underlying, a composer's inspirations is quite difficult; consequently, most composers' accounts of their compositional processes are essentially accounts of what they consciously recall.

Emmerson (1989), who also recognizes "conscious" and "unconscious" dimensions of composers' compositional strategies, suggests that understanding a composer's strategies can be useful in composition pedagogy. He notes differences between traditional written composition and electroacoustical composition, where the composer works with taped sounds or from computers and can immediately obtain aural results, which provides material about which judgments can be made and decisions acted upon (p. 136). He offers two compositional models based on his experience with composing electroacoustical music, and suggests that they hold inferences for all genres of contemporary music. His "simple" model of composition has three aspects: (a) ACTION (create/combine the sounds), (b) TEST (listen and determine whether they *sound right together*), and (c) ACCEPT (store) or REJECT (modify as new ACTION). He notes that the notion of TEST has both local and more general aspects, the former relating to the composer's previous experiences and the latter to "groups of like minded people . . . and conceivably to audience participation also" (p. 137). Emmerson notes that a limitation of compositions using the simple model is that they are "embedded within the social psychology of . . . real time" (p. 137); that is, what sounds right is in essence dependent upon the extent to which the sounds conform to existing practice and preference rules.

Emmerson's elaboration of the model incorporates three new aspects: NEW ACTION, an ACTION REPERTOIRE, and REINFORCEMENT. Essentially, the elaborated model allows composers to incorporate either rule-based (conscious, learned) or intuitive (unconscious) bases for decisions made as a result of the TEST phase of the model. If the TEST phase results in a decision to REINFORCE the action, even though it might violate some rule-based system, the composer's ACTION REPERTOIRE is extended and available for use in NEW ACTIONS. Emmerson suggests that the consequences of NEW ACTIONS need research and that music psychologists may wish to analyze what makes a particular action or strategy sound "right." He cautions that the TEST phase is critical—"the sole arbiter of taste remains human" (p. 143).

Lerdahl's (1988, pp. 231–233) discussion of Boulez's *Le Marteau sans Maitre,* which was "widely hailed as a masterpiece of post-war serialism" (p. 231), exemplifies a composition that reflects Emmerson's elaborated model. Lerdahl observes that experienced listeners seem to find a certain comprehensibility in *Le Marteau* that is not always found when listening to serial works. Ostensibly, the work is serial, constructed according to the rules of serial composition, but, according to Lerdahl, Boulez also "shaped his material more or less intuitively, using both his 'ear' and various unacknowledged constraints" (p. 232). Lerdahl contends that "the degree to which *Le Marteau* is comprehensible, then, depends not on its serial organization but on what the composer added to that organization" (pp. 232–233).

Lerdahl suggests that Boulez actually employed two kinds of *musical grammars* in composing *Le Marteau:* a *compositional grammar,* "consciously employed by Boulez, that generated both the events of the piece and their serial organization . . . [and a] "*listening grammar,* more or less unconsciously employed by auditors, that generates mental representations of the music" (p. 233). Thus, Boulez relied on both the rules of serial composition and his experience as a listener in creating *Le Marteau.*

A fundamental problem of contemporary composition is that some rules of contemporary composition (compositional grammars), which Lerdahl terms "input organization," may bear little relation to rules of listening grammars and other intuitive constraints, which he terms "heard structures" (Lerdahl, p. 234). He contends that this "gap" between the two grammars "divorces method from intuition," leading composers to either to create and work with their own "private code" or with "no compositional grammar at all" (p. 235).

Lerdahl notes that "with the exhaustion of tonality at the turn of the century, anything became possible . . . , [and] composers reacted by inventing their own compositional grammars" (p. 235). He suggests that such an "avant-garde aesthetic" allowed composers to believe their own new systems were the wave of the future. These systems now appear to be merely arbitrary. "The avant-garde has withered away and all methods and styles are available to a point of confusion" (p. 236). He cautions young composers against giving up on compositional grammars and depending solely on "intuitive constraints"—ear and habit. He argues that compositional grammars are necessary for composers, but that they should take into account musical perception and cognition, which are critical variables in the development of listening grammars: Compositions must be comprehensible to knowledgeable listeners. For Lerdahl, comprehensibility "is a necessary if not sufficient condition for value" (p. 255). He goes on to make two claims regarding the aesthetic of composition:

1. The best music utilizes the full potential of our cognitive resources.
2. The best music arises from an alliance of a compositional grammar with the listening grammar. (p. 256).

Compositional Approaches of Selected Composers

Even given the limitations of verbal accounts of compositional processes, a recent review (Fulmer, 1995) of twelve contemporary composers' reported approaches to composition offers some insights into the psychology of composition, particularly with respect to how composers plan and structure their works. This section relies heavily on Fulmer's review, which is based on several sources: (a) his personal interviews with two composers—Dennis Kam and Sherwood Shaffer, (b) articles about composers—Andrzej Panufnik (Osborne, 1984; Truscott, (1987)) and Sir Michael Tippett (Bowen, 1981), (c) composers' own published accounts of their compositional strategies—Steve Reich (1968) and Robert Erickson (1994), and (d) published accounts of interviews with composers—Glenn Branca (Gagne, 1993), Elliott Carter (Edwards, 1971; Restagno, 1989), David Del Tredici (Canarroe, 1989; Moravec, 1992), Witold Lutoslawski (Varga, 1975), Karlheinz Stockhausen (Tannenbaum, 1987), and Iannis Xenakis (Zaplitny, 1975).

As might be expected, Fulmer's review reveals that different composers use different strategies and some composers use more than one strategy. For example, Andrzej Panufnik often begins by creating geometric shapes or designs which provide a skeletal framework for the his melodic, harmonic, and rhythmic concepts. Iannis Xenakis, trained as an engineer and architect, plans his compositions using mathematical processes derived from theories of probability, calculus, game theory, mathematical logic, and set theory.

New York composer Glenn Branca conceptualizes an entire work before starting a composition, thus enabling him to maintain a "Gestalt" of the work throughout the compositional process. Karheinz Stockhausen also plans the overall structure of a composition prior to beginning actual composition, and he remains faithful to his plans until the work is completed. Sir Michael Tippett states that he usually begins by "mapping out" an entire composition, including the length and formal structure. In the actual composition process, Tippett becomes involved physically by singing many of the sounds as he composes.

Elliott Carter begins with a general plan for the overall work, but indicates that he has "many of the details of the local events only very generally in mind" (Edwards, 1971, p. 104). Carter also assigns instruments a "character type," with each reflecting its own personality. This use of instruments to suggest character or personality usually evolves after a work is underway. Carter also notes that he sometimes sketches out possible solutions to problematic situations until he comes to a solution that satisfies him.

The late Polish composer Withold Lutoslawski begins with an overall conception of a work and develops what he calls "key ideas," which are the bases for the overall composition. Key ideas may include melodic themes, formal ideas, a particular order, some technical procedure, or a particular sonority or harmonic entity. Both the overall conception and the key ideas are necessary before Lotoslawski begins a work.

Dennis Kam initially plans the formal structure of a composition, which usually is considered in relation to previous and/or forthcoming compositions in order to create a larger structure. He tries to maintain the integrity of the initial formal structure, but occasionally alters it during the compositional process. Kam uses colors, visual images, and titles as unifying ideas for many of his compositions. Certain aspects of his compositions are "modular" and may appear in more than one composition. Fulmer notes that Kam reports that the pre-planning stage of a composition is often more exciting than the actual composing of a work and suggests that because Kam's compositions are usually interconnected with other compositions, "his music is a continual generative process" (p. 8).

David Del Tredici collects notebooks of musical ideas, themes, and patterns that come to mind periodically, which he then goes back through in search of ideas for a new work. He notes that the process is analogous to having a group of non-related words that require organization into sentences to make sense of them. Similarly, he must organize his musical fragments to make sense of them, a process somewhat akin to fitting together pieces of a puzzle. Del Tredici composes at the piano: Only after the work is completed does he orchestrate it.

Robert Erickson's compositional process is based primarily upon his remembrance of nonmusical sounds, which he collects, combines, and then combines in a musical context. Once a sound captures his interest, he imagines how it can be used in a variety of musical contexts. The new sounds suggest other sounds, creating a "snowball of sounds," which may form the basis of a new composition. He translates the nonmusical sounds into musical sounds via some subconscious process and indicates that intuition is critical to his entire process. He believes that "there are cognitive sides of his psyche that make logical and practical decisions for notation, but it is the intuition that is of most importance" (Fulmer, 1995, p. 7).

Sherwood Shaffer may use one of three bases for pre-compositional planning: (a) a program, such as a story line or picture; (b) shapes, which help outline the overall drama and formal structure; and (c) "figure themes," which are essentially motives or other thematic material.

American minimalist Steve Reich appears to be more concerned with a composition as a process in and of itself; consequently, extensive pre-planning appears to be less important than for other composers. As Fulmer states,

> In understanding Reich's compositional process, it is important to understand that his musical language derives from repetitive, cyclic, and rhythmic themes. . . . Reich looks for a simple motive or germ that can start the process and run all the way through it, gradually changing and manipulating the piece as it travels. Once the process is set, the piece works itself out. For Reich, compositional process and the sounding music are the same thing. (Fulmer, p. 9)

Fulmer notes that all of the composers report using some type of pre-compositional strategy as an idea and/or organizing basis for their compositions. These may include shapes, stories/texts, key themes/ideas, planned formal structures, and/or other non-musical ideas or abstractions. Several composers (Carter, Del Tredici, Erickson, Kam, Reich, and Shaffer) appear to make changes and work out solutions to composition problems as their works unfold. Stockhausen, Tippett, and Xenakis, however, appear to develop an overall plan for their compositions and strictly follow their plans until their works are completed.

This brief overview of the approaches of several composers' approaches to composition reveals that one may approach the creative process from a variety of perspectives. While composers may give somewhat similar accounts of the ways in which they approach a composition, Fulmer maintains that each composer's cognitive processes and aesthetic experience are unique (p. 10).

Composition Theory

The authors would be remiss if they failed to mention a relatively new approach to understanding the cognitive processes underlying music composition. The approach, *artificial intelligence and music* (AI and music), uses computer technology to develop models of human cognitive processes when engaged in musical activity. Models exist for a variety of cognitive processes related to music (e.g., listening, analyzing, performing, perceiving, improvising, and composing), but the present discussion is limited to applications related to music composition. Readers interested in pursuing research on AI and music processing other than composition should consult one of the following excellent sources (Balaban, Ebcioglu, & Laske, 1992; Clarke & Emmerson, 1989; Pressing, 1988; Smith, Smaill, & Wiggins, 1994).

Balaban, Ebcioglu, and Laske (1992) suggest that major differences exist between traditional AI research and AI and music. They note that modeling musical cognition is fraught with difficulties, particularly given that the reference domain of music is difficult to define. Even if one focuses on the processes of music composition, the context for the processes remains elusive. For example, what is being modeled: Creative processes? Or problem solving processes? How does the aesthetic enter into the model? Are we concerned with modeling cognitive processes underlying composition of traditional Western tonal music, various contemporary musics, other musics of the world, music of popular cultures, or all of the above?

Obviously, parameters were necessary in initial efforts to model compositional processes via AI and music technology and theory. Balaban, Ebcioglu, and Laske (1992) use the term *compositional theory* to "designate a new discipline of music research oriented toward an empirical theory of compositional processes in music" (p. 182). An outgrowth of computer applications in music over the past 35 years, the theory is empirical because it is based on empirical data regarding the mental processes of composition as indicated in composers' think-aloud protocols, retrospective reports, and other documents monitoring and reporting action sequences of musicians engaged computer-aided composition. Traditional composers' personal statements, as reported in the preceding section, are considered anecdotal and thus inadequate as a foundation for a scientific discipline such as compositional theory (p. 183). Most AI models for music composition also are limited not only by the mulitfaceted constraints with which composers must deal, but also with the limitations of the compositional processes for and the nature of the musical style a given model seeks to emulate and the capacity of the particular computer system and programs. Also, some models appear to be developed for gaining insight into the processes underlying the compositional process, whereas other appear to be developed for use in generating computer-assisted music compositions. Regardless the model's motivation, each model offers insights into the process of music composition. A few models are noted briefly here to provide an indication of the directions and extent of work in the area.

Ramalho and Ganascia's (1994) emphasis on the role of musical memory in their model of compositional tasks revealed two basic problems: (1) the problem of defining and building "musical memory" and (2) gaining information from experts regarding how to retrieve, modify, and fit events from musical memory into a given musical context. Working within the framework of jazz improvisation, they noted that musicians have great difficulty in expressing the rules they supposedly use and that the rules provided by the musicians "cannot be directly interpreted in a computational formalism" (p. 145). Their model also recognized that musical context is a major consideration in trying to develop a model.

Jones (1989) notes that models of music composition have been developed for both stochastic and non-stochastic contexts. Essentially, *stochastic* contexts involve statistical bases for some "decision-making" while *non-stochastic* contexts involve algorithms or sets of rules as guidelines for decision-making. He describes the use of *fractal models* in composing melodies; the essential property of a fractal model is self-similarity (Jones, p. 180). He also describes two "recursive techniques," *space grammars* and *L-techniques,* which he considers powerful tools for generating self-similar models.

Ames and Domino's (1992) *cybernetic composer* "is an example of music-theoretic empiricism" (p. 186). Able to compose in four genres—"standard" jazz, Latin jazz, rock, and ragtime, the cybernetic composer can access several different models for each genre regarding how pieces can be structured. Ensembles for each genre have four layers: solo part, background chords, bass lines, and drums, and because the instrumental roles for jazz, rock, and ragtime are well defined, "the program often gives the illusion of true interplay when the layers are actually going their separate ways (p. 187).

Another program, *Wolfgang,* was "designed to guide its compositional process biased by a cultural grammar of music, as well as by a *disposition* for crafting musical phrases such that they express a specific emotional characteristic" (Riecken, 1992, p. 210). Essentially, for a given compositional decision to be made within a given grammatical context, Wolfgang defines a set of possible solutions from its domain knowledge of music that satisfy the cultural grammar and then selects the solution that best satisfies Wolfgang's current disposition in order to embed a specific emotive potential into a given musical phrase.

Obviously, the variables underlying the development of valid models of composition are many and complex. Marsella and Schmidt (1992) and Laske (1992) discuss many of these problems. Certainly, many problems must be resolved before compositional theory yields any explanation that is sufficiently multifaceted, broad, and inclusive to convince nonbelievers in AI that the models developed via AI and music offer any final truth regarding the diverse and complex processes that musicians go through when creating a new composition. The authors speculate that research on the matter will continue well into the next century.

Summary

The major points in this section include the following:
1. Musical creation and performance provide essential stimuli for all other musical behaviors.
2. Musical performance is psychomotor behavior, where the mind guides the muscles.
3. Practice techniques vary with the performer, performance medium, and musical situation.
4. Mental rehearsal may be beneficial in conjunction with physical practice.
5. Expert performers are more likely than novices to practice intact meaningful musical segments in response to an error.
6. Practice is more than simply going over the music; it entails purposeful planning for musical goals.
7. Performance expertise is beyond just playing or singing well.
8. Expert performers may employ abstractions, based on meaningful musical groupings.
9. Execution of a musical performance involves cognitive structures, which vary among memorized performance, sightreading, and improvisation.
10. Musical expression may arise from musical structure or may shape it.
11. Performers' practice patterns may suggest their structural conceptions.
12. Performance anxiety is normal; many variables influence it.

13. Careful preparation, anticipation, and goal setting may help control performance anxiety.
14. Performers need to place the importance of any one performance in perspective in relation to their overall lives.
15. Improvisation involves extemporaneous performance of newly created music.
16. Improvisation in Western art music reached its peak during the Baroque era.
17. Today, most people associate improvisation with jazz.
18. Improvisation involves continuing series of highly complex instantaneous neurological processes.
19. Skilled improvisers develop a vast "repertoire" of neurological connections that may be triggered during the improvisation process.
20. Concomitant with the development of this repertoire is the development of movement patterns for overt realization of one's improvisations.
21. Pressing maintains that any model of improvisation should explain how people improvise, how they develop improvisational skills, and the origin of novel behavior.
22. The essence of most jazz improvisation is in the melodic line.
23. Studies show that it is possible to get reliable evaluations of improvisations in relation to particular criteria.
24. Improvisation and composition differ; an improviser has the constraints of immediacy and fluency and must accept the first solution that comes to hand, whereas a composer may reject solutions until he or she finds one that seems best for a given purpose.
25. There are four approaches to studying composers' compositional processes: (a) examining sketchbooks, (b) examining what composers say about their compositions, (c) observing composers' in-process composition, and (d) observation of improvisatory performance.
26. Examination of protocol descriptions seems to be an important step in understanding the complexities of composition.
27. There are two broad stages of composition: inspiration and execution.
28. There are unconscious and conscious dimensions to most composers' compositional strategies.
29. Theorists suggest that composers must employ both compositional grammars and listening grammars.
30. According to Lerdahl, the best music utilizes a listener's full cognitive potential.
31. A review of composers' descriptions of their compositional strategies suggests that composition may be approached from varied perspectives.

32. Compositional theory, an outgrowth of work in music and AI, offers a promising new direction for studying compositional processes.

References

Atkinson, J. W. (1983). Motivational psychology and educational measurement. In S. B. Anderson & J. S. Helmick (Eds.), *On educational testing* (pp. 29–44). San Francisco: Jossey-Bass.

Ames, C., & Domino, M. (1992). Cybernetic composer: An overview. In M. Balaban, K. Ebcioglu, & O. Laske (Eds.), *Understanding music with AI: Perspectives on music cognition* (pp. 186–205). Menlo Park, CA: The AAAI Press.

Apel, W. (1944). *Harvard dictionary of music.* Cambridge, MA: Harvard University Press.

Balaban, M., Ebcioglu, K., & Laske, O. (Eds.) (1992). *Understanding music with AI: Perspectives on music cognition.* Menlo Park, CA: The AAAI Press.

Bloom, B. (1956). *Taxonomy of educational objectives: The classification of educational goals, handbook I: Cognitive domain.* New York: David McKay.

Bowen, M. (1981). *Michael Tippett* (N. Snowman, Ed.). London: Robson Books.

Canarroe, J. (1991). Conversation: David Del Tredici interviewed by Joel Conarroe. *Contemporary Music Review, 5,* 239–256.

Clarke, E. F. (1988). Generative principles in music performance. In J. A. Sloboda (Ed.), *Generative processes in music: The psychology of performance, improvisation, and composition* (pp. 1–26). Oxford: Clarendon Press.

Clarke, E., & Emmerson, S. (Eds.) (1989). *Music, mind and structure: Vol. 3, Pt. 1, Contemporary Music Review* (N. Osbourne, Ed.-in-Chief). London: Harwood Academic Publishers.

Coffman, D. D. (1990). Effects of mental practice, physical practice, and knowledge of results on piano performance. *Journal of Research in Music Education, 38,* 187–196.

Colwell, R. (1970). *The evaluation of music teaching and learning.* Englewood Cliffs, NJ: Prentice-Hall.

Doerschuk, B. (1984). The literature of improvisation: How effective are current teaching materials? *Keyboard, 10* (10), 48, 49, 50.

Dreyfus, H. L., & Dreyfus, S. E. (1986). *Mind over machine: The power of human intuition and expertise in the era of the computer.* New York: Macmillan.

Dunkel, S. E. (1989). *The audition process: Anxiety management and coping strategies.* Stuyvesant, NY: Pendragon Press.

Edwards, A. (1971). *Flawed words and stubborn sounds.* New York: W.W. Norton and Company.

Emmerson, S. (1989). Composing strategies and pedagogy. *Contemporary Music Review, 3* (1), 133–144.

Erickson, R. (1994). Composing music. In J. Rahn (Ed.), *Perspectives on musical aesthetics* (pp. 165–174). New York: W.W. Norton.

Fulmer, D. (1995). *Composition as a generative process.* Unpublished paper, University of Miami.

Gagne, C. (1993). *Soundpieces 2: Interviews with American composers.* Metuchen, NJ: The Scarecrow Press.

Gardner, H. (1993). *Frames of mind* (2nd ed.). New York: Basic Books.

Greennagel, D. J. (1994). A study of selected predictors of jazz vocal improvisation skills. Unpublished doctoral dissertation, University of Miami.

Gruson, L. M. (1988). Rehearsal skill and musical competence: Does practice make perfect? In J. A. Sloboda (Ed.), *Generative processes in music: The psychology of performance, improvisation, and composition* (pp. 91–112). Oxford: Clarendon Press.

Harrow, A. J. (1972). *A taxonomy of the psychomotor domain.* New York: David McKay.

Krathwohl, D., Bloom, B. S., & Masia, B. B. (1964). *Taxonomy of educational objectives: The classification of educational goals, handbook II: Affective domain.* New York: David McKay.

Jaques-Dalcroze, E. (1921). *Rhythm, music, and education.* London: Chatto and Windus.

Jaques-Dalcroze, E. (1930). *The eurhythmics of Jaques-Dalcroze.* Boston: Small Maynard.

Jones, K. (1989). Generative models in computer-assisted musical composition. *Contemporary Music Review, 3* (1), 177–196.

Krohne, H. W., & Schaffner, P. (1983). Anxiety, coping strategies, and performance. In S. B. Anderson & J. S. Helmick (Eds.), *On educational testing* (pp. 150–174). San Francisco: Jossey-Bass.

Laske, O. (1992). The Observer tradition of knowledge acquisition. In M. Balaban, K. Ebcioglu, & O. Laske (Eds.), *Understanding music with AI: Perspectives on music cognition* (pp. 258–289). Menlo Park, CA: The AAAI Press.

LeBlanc, A. (1994). A theory of music performance anxiety. *Quarterly Journal of Music Teaching and Learning, 5* (4), 60–68.

Lerdahl, F. (1988). Cognitive constraints on compositional systems. In J.A. Sloboda (Ed.), *Generative processes in music* (pp. 231–259). Oxford: Clarendon Press.

Liebman, D. (1988). *Self-portrait of a jazz artist: Music thoughts and realities.* Rottenburg, Germany: Advance Music.

Marsella, S.C., & Schmidt, C.F. (1992). On the application of problem reduction search to automated composition. In M. Balaban, K. Ebcioglu, & O. Laske (Eds.), *Understanding music with AI: Perspectives on music cognition* (pp. 238–257). Menlo Park, CA: The AAAI Press.

Moravec, P. (1992). An interview with David Del Tredici. *Contemporary Music Review, 6,* 11–22.

Music Educators National Conference. (1994). *The school music program: A new vision.* Reston, VA: Music Educators National Conference.

Osbourne, N. (1984). Panufnik at 70. *Tempo, 150* (September), 1–10.

Partchey, K.C. (1973). The effects of feedback, models, and repetition on the ability to improvise melodies. Unpublished doctoral dissertation, The Pennsylvania State University.

Potter, G. (1990). Analyzing improvised jazz. *College music symposium, 30* (1), 64–74.

Pressing, J. (1984a). The history of classical improvisation, Part 1 (to 1600). *Keyboard, 10* (11), 64–68.

Pressing, J. (1984b). The history of classical improvisation, Part 2 (1600–1900). *Keyboard, 10* (12), 59–60, 65–67.

Pressing, J. (1988). Improvisation: Methods and models. In J.A. Sloboda (Ed.), *Generative processes in music* (pp. 129–178). New York: Oxford University Press.

Ramhalho, G., & Ganascia, J. G. (1994). The role of musical memory and learning: A study of jazz performance. In M. Smith, A. Smaill, & G. A. Wiggins (Eds.), *Music education: An artificial intelligence approach* (pp. 143–156). London: Springer-Verlag.

Raynor, J. O. (1981). Motivational determinants of music-related behavior: Psychological careers of student, teacher, performer, and listener. In R. G. Taylor (Ed.), *Documentary report of the Ann Arbor Symposium* (pp. 332–351). Reston, VA: Music Educators National Conference.

Reich, S. (1968). *Music as a gradual process.* New York: Anti-Illusion Catalog of the Whitney Museum.

Restagno, E. (1989). *Elliott Carter: In conversation with Enzo Restagno for Settembre Musica 1989* (K.S. Wolfthal, trans.). New York: Institute for Studies in American Music.

Restak, R. M. (1984). *The brain.* Toronto: Bantam Books.

Rieken, R.D. (1992). Wolfgang: A system for using emoting potentials to manage musical design. In M. Balaban, K. Ebcioglu, & O. Laske (Eds.), *Understanding music with AI: Perspectives on music cognition* (pp. 206–237). Menlo Park, CA: The AAAI Press.

Rubin-Rabson, G. (1937). The influence of analytic prestudy in memorizing piano music. *Archives of Psychology, 31* (220), 153.

Rubin-Rabson, G. (1940a). Studies in the psychology of memorizing piano music, II: A comparison of massed and distributed practice. *Journal of Educational Psychology, 31,* 270–284.

Rubin-Rabson, G. (1940b). Studies in the psychology of memorizing piano music, III: A comparison of the whole and part approach. *Journal of Educational Psychology, 31,* 460–476.

Rubin-Rabson, G. (1941a). Studies in the psychology of memorizing piano music, V: A comparison of prestudy periods of varied lengths. *Journal of Educational Psychology, 32,* 101–112.

Rubin-Rabson, G. (1941b). Studies in the psychology of memorizing piano music, VI: A comparison of two forms of mental rehearsal and keyboard overlearning. *Journal of Educational Psychology, 32,* 593–602.

Salmon, P. G., & Meyer, R. G. (1992). *Notes from the green room: Coping with stress and anxiety in musical performance.* New York: Lexington Books.

Sloboda, J. A. (1985). *The musical mind: The cognitive psychology of music.* Oxford: Clarendon Press.

Sloboda, J. A. (Ed.) (1988). *Generative processes in music: The psychology of performance, improvisation, and composition.* Oxford: Clarendon Press.

Smith, M., Smaill, A., & Wiggins, G.A. (Eds.) (1994). *Music Education: An artificial intelligence approach.* London: Springer-Verlag.

Stubley, E.V. (1992). Philosophical foundations. In R. Colwell (Ed.), *Handbook of research on music teaching and learning* (pp. 3–20). New York: Schirmer Books.

Sudnow, D. (1978). *Ways of the hand: The organization of improvised conduct.* Cambridge, MA: Harvard University Press.

Tannenbaum, M. (1987). *Conversations with Stockhausen* (D. Butchart, trans.). Oxford: Clarendon Press.

Trotter, R. J. (1986). The mystery of mastery. *Psychology Today, 20* (7), 32–38.

Truscott, H. (1987). The achievement of Andrzej Panufnik. *Tempo, 163* (December), 7–12.

Varga, B.A. (1975). *Lutoslawski profile: Witold Lutoslawski in conversation with Balint Andras Varga* (V.B. Andrassal, trans.). London: Chester Music.

Zaplitny, M. (1975). Conversation with Iannis Xanakis. *Perspectives of New Music, 14* (Fall–Winter), 86–101.

CHAPTER EIGHT

AFFECTIVE BEHAVIORS AND MUSIC

Psychologists increasingly have become concerned with affective behavior in its various manifestations, and with this increased interest several issues have surfaced. For example: What is meant by *affect* and *emotion?* Is *aesthetic* behavior the same as *affective* behavior? Are changes in physiological rates affective responses? Can the affective and aesthetic be examined from a behavioral perspective? Or, are philosophical explanations of aesthetic experience sufficient?

This chapter examines some of these basic questions. The discussion is organized according to four broad topics: (a) extended definitions of central terms, (b) the range of behaviors that may be considered affective, (c) some approaches to the study of affective responses to music, and (d) musical meaning and the variables that contribute to musical meaning.

Extended Definitions

Affective responses to music are largely covert, and researchers encounter many of the difficulties inherent in studying music cognition in their study of affective responses. Terms used to describe affective response essentially reflect psychological constructs inferred from observable behavior. Also, the terms and various implied constructs used to denote affective response to music are not discrete; discussions of them are confounded further by seemingly loose and indiscriminate application of the terms.

Three terms central to this discussion are *affect, emotion,* and *aesthetic.* While the terms perhaps are encountered more often in philosophical discussions, the intent here is to examine them from a psychological perspective. The distinction between psychological and philosophical use of the terms is not clear cut, although traditional usage does recognize their subjective and personal connotations. Other terms defined briefly include *attitude, interest, taste, preference, appreciation,* and *sensitivity.*

Affect

Observers of human behavior long have recognized three basic categories: thinking, feeling, and doing. Psychologists today refer to these respectively as cognitive, affective, and psychomotor behaviors. Affective behaviors include those which have a significant *feeling* dimension.

As used in everyday life, feeling has varied meanings, e.g., tactual perception (to *feel* a piece of cloth), cognitive belief (he or she *feels* something to be true), emotion, or simply whether an experience is pleasant or unpleasant. Psychologists do not use the term in a consistent way. To clarify matters, Young (1973) summarized eight classes of affective processes: (a) *simple feelings* of pleasantness or unpleasantness in response to sensory stimuli; (b) negative and positive *organic feelings* such as hunger, thirst, dietary satisfaction, or physical well-being; (c) *activity feelings,* including appetitive states of hunger, sexual desire, or other activity feelings such as enthusiasm or aversion; (d) moral, *aesthetic,* religious, or social sentiments and attitudes based upon previous experiences, education, and training; (e) persisting *moods* such as cheerfulness, elation, anxiety, or grief; (f) pathological *affects* of deep depression, apathy, or hostility; (g) *emotions* such as fear, anger, laughing, agony, or embarrassment, and (h) *temperaments* such as vivaciousness, cheerfulness, or moodiness.

As should be apparent, affect is a broad term applied to a wide variety of human feeling behaviors. The problem is exacerbated by the fact that affective processes are related to virtually everything that is psychological—perception, memory, learning, reasoning, and action. Therefore, any discussion of affective behavior in relation to music must be defined in terms more definitive than just whether or not it has an affective dimension, since Reimer and Wright (1992, p. 197) maintain that there is an affective dimension to all musical experience.

Emotion

One school of thought regarding music's import is that it conveys or expresses emotion. Proponents of this position, however, appear to use the term *emotion* in a broader sense than do contemporary psychologists. Emotion is only one type of affect. Young (p. 750) defines emotion as a disturbed affective process or state *"which originates in the psychological situation and which is revealed by marked bodily changes in smooth muscles, glands, and gross behaviors."* This definition suggests that emotional behavior is a relatively temporary state—a departure from the normal state of composure. Emotions involve perception and memory and always include an environmental factor, present or past.

Meyer (1956, pp. 13–32) has theorized how music arouses emotion. Central to his theory is the view that arrest or inhibition of a tendency to respond arouses emotion. An individual's tendencies to respond to music result from previous experiences with music of the style to which he or she is listening. From previous experiences, an individual develops expectations (tendencies to respond) regarding the types of patterns which might come next in the music. To the degree that the anticipated patterns are not forthcoming, i.e., they are delayed or do not come at all, *tension,* or *emotion,* is aroused. Some simple examples of delay of musical expectations include the deceptive cadence (V_7-vi, as in a G chord to an A chord in C major) instead of an authentic cadence (V_7-I, as in G to C) and the rapid repetitive alteration of I–V_7–I–V_7–I in a coda section, resulting in a "when will it end already" feeling.

Meyer's theory, which essentially is a conflict theory, is not without criticism. Miller (1992, p. 422) cites two deficiencies: (1) the theory lacks a satisfactory means for "sorting out affect or emotion after the arousal takes place," and (2) the theory does not provide "a good explanation of why pleasant emotions are aroused." Miller notes that most interruptions would seem to cause surprise, frustrations, or annoyances.

Nevertheless, listeners to Western music appear to learn that certain chords or sound terms imply certain other musical entities. When an appropriate expected musical consequent is delayed, suspense is aroused. However, Meyer recognizes that mere arousal of tension via the inhibition of musical expectations is of little import in itself. He maintains that for the tension or emotion to result in *aesthetic meaning,* it must be followed by a fulfillment of the expectation (e.g., the expected chord is reached; the composition finally comes to a clear end) and hence resolution of the tension.

Most recent applications of theories of emotion such as Meyer's to musical experience essentially elaborate and/or refine a basic theory of emotion, but reflect language and refinements consistent with the authors' theoretical perspectives (e.g., Dowling & Harwood, 1986, pp. 214–219). More will be said of these theories later.

The important point here is that theories of how music creates emotion are consistent with the contemporary psychological viewpoint that emotion is a relatively temporary disruption of a normal state. Further, emotion is seen as an essential component of aesthetic meaning, although emotion alone is, in Meyer's words, "aesthetically valueless" (p. 28).

Aesthetic

Aesthetic feeling is a particular type of affective behavior and is the outcome of aesthetic experience. The term *aesthetic* usually is used in relation to art and its value or meaning, although aesthetic feeling may result from interactions with phenomena of nature or from interactions with nonart objects or events. What makes some interactions *aesthetic* and others not has been subject to much discussion by philosophers, even to the point that aesthetics traditionally is viewed as a branch of philosophy. While it is recognized that philosophical theory and discussion have provided many valuable insights regarding the nature and value of aesthetic feeling and experience, the present discussion also recognizes aesthetic feeling and experience as psychological behaviors which are subject to study via the same methods that are used to examine other aspects of human behavior. Psychologists only recently have begun to study aesthetic behavior, while philosophical examination of the aesthetic has a long history. To the extent that psychologists will be able to substantiate philosophical theory regarding aesthetic behaviors, theory will be strengthened.

Common to most discussions of aesthetics is a concern for beauty, and definitions of beauty have their own difficulties. When one says something is beautiful, he or she is reflecting a value. What causes the individual to value this something as beautiful is subject to much debate. Some would hold that the beauty is inherent in the object or event because of its structure or form. In other words, beauty is a property of the object or event and remains so regardless of what an individual respondent might "feel." An opposing view is that "beauty is in the eyes of the beholder." Perhaps Saint Thomas Aquinas, as cited by Rader and Jessup (1976, p. 20), stated it best: "Let that be called *beauty*, the very perception of which pleases." The statement has two implications: First, beauty gives pleasure, and second, not everything that gives pleasure is beautiful, but only that which gives pleasure in immediate perception. Which position reflects the greater truth regarding the determination of beauty has been and will continue to be subject to debate and conjecture. The point here is that, for most people, beauty is the subject matter and stimulus for aesthetic experience and feeling. While the notion that response to beauty is the basis for the aesthetic response seems plausible, it should be noted that not all aestheticians and writers on aesthetics agree that the aspects of music which contribute to its aesthetic value fit neatly in the rubric of *beauty*.

Aesthetic experience is the term most often used to describe subjective, personal response to beauty or the other aesthetic qualities of an object, event, or phenomenon. Hargreaves (1986, p. 108) argues that the term is applicable to "more or less any reaction that any person might have to any work of art, defined in the broadest possible terms." For Hargreaves, a school girl's like-dislike reaction to a current pop record and a music critic's critique of a performance of a Beethoven symphony are both reflections of aesthetic experience. Other writers, however, are more delimiting in what they consider aesthetic experience.

The following discussion is based primarily on the descriptions of aesthetic experience offered by two advocates of aesthetic education, Bennett Reimer (1989, pp. 99–117) and Gerard L. Knieter (1971, pp. 3–20). Both recognize aesthetic experience as human experience, and while they also recognize beauty in nature and other objects and events that are not primarily intended to be art, they generally discuss aesthetic experience in relation to artworks.

Knieter cites five characteristics of an aesthetic experience: (a) focus, (b) perception, (c) affect, (d) cognition, and (e) its cultural matrix. *Focus* suggests that an individual must devote his attention to the artwork and respond thereto. *Perception* is viewed as the process through which sensory data are received and through which the individual becomes aware of the artwork. Knieter sees two basic types of *affect* occurring during the aesthetic experience, physiological change and feelingful reaction. Concomitant with aesthetic experience are changes in blood pressure, respiration, and electrodermal response. The feelingful reaction may vary from simple feeling to complex emotional sets. *Cognition* is a particularly important attribute of aesthetic experience, reflecting the intellectual processes involved: analysis, synthesis, abstraction, generalization, and evaluation. Knowledge and learning regarding the stylistic attributes of a musical work contribute greatly to the quality of an aesthetic experience. Finally, the *cultural matrix* is reflected in the aesthetic experience. Aesthetic values are learned within a cultural context.

Reimer emphasizes that an individual's interest and reactions must be absorbed by or immersed in the aesthetic qualities of the music to which the individual attends; the feelingful reaction must be to the expressive aesthetic qualities rather than to any symbolic designation. For Reimer, the aesthetic qualities of music conveyed by melody, harmony, rhythm, tone color, texture, and form are "expressive of or analogous to or isomorphic with the patterns of felt life or subjectivity or the conditions of livingness" (p. 102). The individual must be involved with the *embodied* meaning of music rather than with any symbolic designations it might have.[1] Reimer also maintains that aesthetic experience is valuable in and of itself, is not a means toward non-aesthetic experience, and serves no utilitarian purpose. Taken at face value this might suggest a contradiction with the authors' view that aesthetic experience serves a human

---

[1] *Embodied* musical meaning results from expectations *within* the music, whereas *designative* meaning refers to meaning *symbolized* by the music. The differences are discussed in more detail later in the chapter.

function and that music also serves other functions. This is not the case. While aesthetic experience may appear to have no purpose or *use,* it still serves a valuable *function,* providing an individual an opportunity for feelingful experience above and beyond the meeting of basic human needs. Maslow (1970, p. 5) contends that aesthetic experience is a basic human need, albeit one with which people become involved only when their physiological, safety, and certain psychological needs are met. Therefore, an aesthetic experience is valuable in and of itself to the experiencing individual; the very fact that the experience holds value for the individual suggests that it is functional to his or her well-being.

Reimer's final characteristic of an aesthetic experience is that it must involve the qualities of a perceptible "thing." The "thing" is the sensuous element, the "formed substance," containing the aesthetic qualities which an individual perceives and responds to.

Implicit in both Knieter's and Reimer's descriptions is that aesthetic experience requires psychological *involvement* with the aesthetic stimulus, *perception* of interacting events within the artwork, *cognition* of the inter play among the events within the aesthetic stimulus, and *feelingful* reaction thereto. Aesthetic experience differs from most affective experience in that it must involve perception and *cognition* of an aesthetic stimulus. There is something more than just an "oh how pretty" reaction. Yet, without the immediacy of the aesthetic stimulus, the affective behavior can not be an aesthetic behavior.

For an experience to be an aesthetic experience, it must result in feelingful reactions to perceived interactions of those aesthetic qualities contributing to the beauty of an artwork or other stimulus in which an observer (listener to music) is involved perceptually. Such a definition of aesthetic experience does not deny, however, that music and other aesthetic stimuli elicit many other significant affective responses. Certainly hearing a composition with which one has had previous associations may elicit feelings regarding those associations. For example, hearing the theme song of a previously seen movie generally elicits thoughts and feelings regarding the movie. To say, however, that this feeling is aesthetic is questionable; for Knieter and Reimer it probably lacks sufficient involvement with the auditory stimulus itself. On the other hand, the feelings elicited may be very meaningful to the individual. In the authors' view, such feelings reflect another type of affective response to music.

Other Definitions

Several additional terms will be mentioned briefly because each suggests a psychological construct with a substantial affective component. Essentially these constructs are covert and therefore inferred from an individual's behaviors (including verbal) relative to the objects, events, or phenomena that are the stimulus for the affective response. While the definitions are neither discrete nor exhaustive, they are believed to reflect the general meanings of the terms as used in the literature. The definitions are essentially the same as the authors have offered elsewhere (Boyle & Radocy, 1987, pp. 195–199).

Attitude, the most general term, connotes a predisposition toward mental or psychomotor activity with respect to a social or psychological object, event, or phenomenon. The predisposition may be either positive or negative, that is, reflecting either approach or avoidance activity. Kuhn (1979) notes that an attitude is relatively long term and stable and that any real changes in attitude necessarily take place over a considerable period of time.

Interest suggests feelings of concern, involvement, and curiosity. A clear demarcation between "attitude toward something" and "interest in something" is difficult to make, but it appears that in common usage interest is more often manifested through active participation or involvement with the object, event, or phenomenon, while attitude is considered more covert and suggests more of a value judgment.

Taste, as applied to music, usually suggests an element of connoisseurship, reflecting some agreement with the "experts" regarding quality and excellence. Kuhn equates taste with attitude, because both essentially imply covert predispositions, both are developed as a result of experience, and both appear to be long term in nature. However, all affective responses appear to be influenced by experience.

Preference is considered more overt, or behavioral, than taste or attitude in that preferences usually involve the act of making choices and indicating them in some overt manner. Abeles (1980) suggests that preference and taste actually represent a continuum from a short-term (preference) to a long-term (taste) commitment.

Price (1986) recognizes *behavior preferences* and *behavioral intentions* as two important modes for expressing preference. A behavioral preference involves demonstrating choices through nonverbal actions such as concert attendance or record purchase, while a behavioral intention requires the verbal expression of a choice one would make in a specific decision-making context.

Appreciation with respect to music appears to be used in both a narrow and broad sense. Lehman (1968, p. 25) notes that in the broad sense appreciation includes a major knowledge component—knowledge of musicians, notation, literature, instruments, history, and so forth. The narrower sense appears to place more emphasis on an individual's sensitivity to the aesthetic qualities.

Sensitivity usually implies perception of and responsiveness to sensory stimuli and reflects both cognitive and affective dimensions. In common usage it implies making both subtle discriminations and subtle feeling responses. Considering these connotations, it is not surprising that the term *aesthetic sensitivity* is much used in the literature.

Types of Affective Responses to Music

To suggest that aesthetic experience is the only important feeling response elicited by music is to deny the value of a broad spectrum of affective behaviors related to music. The present discussion does not purport to consider relative value of the respective types of affective behaviors in relation to aesthetic experience per se, but it does recognize that various affective experiences are important to greater or lesser degrees for many individuals. The relative values of the various affective modes differ for *individuals,* and it is unlikely that any given affective mode, even the aesthetic mode, is of greater or lesser value for all individuals.

The variety of affective responses to music is great. Concomitant with all types are *physiological reactions* of the autonomic nervous system. Hector Berlioz's descriptions of his reactions while listening to a piece of music, as reported by Schoen (1940, p. 103), included increased blood circulation, violent pulse rate, muscle contractions, trembling, numbness of the feet and hands, and partial paralysis of the nerves controlling hearing and vision. While it is doubtful that many individuals' physiological mechanisms are affected to the extent that Berlioz claimed, there is objective evidence that changes in certain physiological rates do accompany affective behaviors. Whether these changes themselves are affective behaviors is subject to interpretation. The behaviorist might insist that they are because they can be observed (via certain measuring instruments); another view, however, is that they are merely physiological correlates of affective behavior, because feelings by definition are psychological rather than physiological.

A common affective behavior is the *mood* or *character* response. In Western cultures certain musical sound patterns have come to be reflective of different psychological mood states. Certain music may be soothing or relaxing, other music may make an individual feel happy or sad, while still other music may elicit feelings of frustration or agitation. The range of moods that music may characterize is as great as the range of moods people can feel. There is no question that music can elicit mood response; further, within a given cultural context, many individuals tend to agree regarding the moods elicited by certain types and examples of music. While the variables underlying mood response are many, it should be noted that whatever mood response music elicits is much more than a response to any inherent mood or character of the music. Mood responses to music, just as virtually all other responses to music, are essentially determined by an individual's previous experience with music. *Learning underlies all musical behavior, affective or otherwise.*

Affective responses to music also may be influenced by an individual's *associations* with the music. The most common example of this is when an individual responds to the music's programmatic content. Feelings of this type usually relate to an event or story which the individual has previously associated with the music. The popularity of movie soundtrack recordings suggests that many people want to reexperience the narrative through listening to the music. The same type of associations are made with opera and musical comedy. The feeling response is to much more than the music itself. Listening to music of one's childhood or adolescence may evoke feelings from those years associated with that music. Lovers recall special occasions through "their song." Music's power to elicit strong feelings of experiences associated with it provides individuals with a mechanism for reexperiencing many significant events of their lives.

While philosophers and aestheticians have been greatly concerned with the wordless meaning of music, there has been relatively little study of the feelings evoked by the words of songs. One only has to listen to the words of folk, popular, and art music, however, to realize that the verbal messages of music are primarily affective. Feelings of love, frustration, and virtually every deep-seated and persisting type of human feeling that individuals hold toward one another have been verbalized through song. Feelings expressed or elicited through blues, country-western, rock, and rap music are primary examples of the affective impact of combining word meanings and music.

Words and music also have been combined to express and elicit affective reactions to all types of social, political, and religious issues. Music has been used as a persuasive tool throughout history. As noted in Chapters Two and Three, many of music's basic functions and applications are to sway feelings. There is little doubt that patriotic, social protest, and religious songs can arouse strong affective response. Such songs are symbols, are perceived and reacted to accordingly, and serve a legitimate and important function (Reimer, 1989, p. 121).

Many additional human behaviors related to music have an affective component in greater or lesser degree. Musical *preferences* (discussed in Chapter Nine), musical *interests,* musical *values, attitudes* toward music in general and toward various styles of music, and *appreciation* of music all reflect affective components. While these behaviors also depend in many respects on knowledge, their importance to music educators is great. Appreciation, values, and preferences are of essence to music education. Interests and attitudes are central to both the process and outcomes of music education.

Approaches to Studying Affective Responses to Music

Traditional approaches to the study of affective responses to music have involved (a) physiological measures, (b) adjective descriptors, (c) and philosophical inquiry. A fourth approach, which follows the work of Berlyne (1971, 1974), focuses on examination of empirical human response to musical stimuli. Termed *empirical aesthetics* in its broader sense, or *experimental aesthetics* in its narrower sense, this approach reflects a major development in music psychology.

Although the four approaches to the study of affective response to music overlap in several respects, they are discussed under separate headings: (a) physiological measures, (b) adjective descriptors, (c) philosophical aesthetics, and (d) psychological aesthetics.

Physiological Measures

Few musicians or psychologists deny that music can evoke changes in the rates of bodily processes, but there is little or no agreement regarding the degree to which these changes reflect affective responses to music. Affective behaviors are *psychological* behaviors, whereas measures of the rates of various bodily processes are *physiological* behaviors. The study of the relationships between physiological and psychological aspects of behavior is called *psychophysiology* (Sternbach, 1966, p. 3). If one is seeking to understand affective responses to music through the study of changes in the rates of certain bodily processes, then one should be engaged in psychophysiological research.

With few exceptions, research examining physiological responses to music stops short of examining any relationships between the two types of behaviors, thereby providing little insight regarding affective responses to music. Generally, such studies involve presenting a musical stimulus as the independent variable and using polygraph data regarding various physiological rates as the dependent variables. The underlying hypothesis of most studies is that the frequency and/or amplitude of the various bodily processes controlled by the autonomic nervous system reflect affective response to music. The most frequently studied dependent measures include heart rate, respiration rate, respiration amplitude, and electrodermal activity (skins responses, formerly called psychogalvanic reflex, galvanic skin response, or GSR). Other measures which have been used include *electroencephalography* (EEG)—a technique for recording various brain wave rhythms, *electromyography* (EMG)—a measure of muscle tension, *electrooculography* —a measure of eye movement, *pupillography* —a measure of pupil size, *electrogastrography* —a measure of gastrointestinal response, *pattelar reflex* —knee-jerk response, and the *pilomotor response* —movement of hairs on the skin.

Schoen (1927, 1940), Diserens and Fine (1939), Lundin (1967), and Farnsworth (1969) have summarized most of the early research on physiological responses to music, and readers interested in the particulars of such research should consult these sources. A brief general chronology of some of the major findings follows:

1880	Dogiel discovered that music influences blood circulation, heart rate, and respiration.
1888	Fere used music as a stimulus in studying galvanic skin response.
1895	Binet and Courtier compared pulse and respiration rate changes with changes in music.
1900	Fere discovered that isolated tones, scales, and tonal sequences energized muscles.
1906	Foster and Gamble concluded that music generally causes faster and shallower breathing regardless of loudness or mode.
1912	Weld recorded changes in pneumographic (breathing) and plethysmographic (blood supply) responses as a function of listening to music.
1918	Veselius reported that music without abrupt key changes can relieve high fever, high pulse rate, and hysteria.
1924	Wechsler observed that subjects' GSR curves changed when music was played.
1927	Hyde studied the effects of different kinds of musical selections on the cardiovascular responses of individuals fond of music, those indifferent or insensitive to music, and those of different nationality and training. She reported that people are psychologically and physiologically affected unfavorably by "tragic mournful tones" and favorably by "gay rhythmical melodies."
1932	Misbach studied the effects of isolated tonal stimuli on GSR, blood pressure, and pulse changes. He reported no significant pulse rate or blood pressure changes, although GSR changes were observed for tones of 512 HZ or higher, increasing in magnitude as frequency became higher.

1933	Wascho observed changes in pulse rate and blood pressure when different types of music were played. More definite rhythms and melodies yielded more definite physiological changes.
1934	Phares reported a positive relationship between amount of GSR change and the strength of the verbally reported pleasantness of music. She also reported, however, that the GSR results were of little value in her analysis of music appreciation.
1947	Dreher compared subjects' verbal reports and GSR responses to various types of music. Musically trained subjects showed a relationship between GSR and mood as measured by adjectives checked on the Hevner Adjective Circle; data for untrained subjects revealed no relationship.

The reader should recognize that, for the most part, the studies noted above merely describe physiological responses to various musical stimuli rather than true affective responses. They indicate particular physiological concomitants of affective response, but, with the exception of a few studies, no attempts were made to examine relationships between these physiological responses and affective responses.

Dainow's (1977) and Hodges's (1980b) excellent reviews and syntheses of the literature provide the basis for much of the following discussion. They review most of the studies noted above as well as some more recent research. Readers are encouraged to examine their excellent reviews and bibliographies.

Philosophers and musicologists long have maintained and sought to substantiate the existence of a relationship between heart rate and music. Most "substantiation," however, has just been rhetoric. Dainow's review of studies of heart rate in response to music provides virtually no support of the hypothesis that heart rate varies with musical tempo. Of eight studies examining the effects of music on heart rate, all but one failed to elicit any statistically significant change in heart rate. Some other studies suggested that any music will increase heart rate, although it was not clear whether these changes in heart rate were statistically significant for any of the studies. Another group of studies cited by Dainow did not produce any effects on heart rate. Dainow concludes that, "despite considerable research the relationship between HR and music is still unclear" (p. 212). Even if clear-cut relationships could be established between heart rate and tempo, it would provide little insight into the affective response.

Dainow notes that summarizing research on respiration rate or amplitude is particularly difficult because of the variety of experimental conditions. Some studies examine rate while others examine amplitude; further, some research sought to examine respiration rate in relation to tempo, while other research attempted to relate respiration to listeners' attention or enjoyment. Ries (1969), in one of the few studies which actually compared a physiological response to subjects' indicated enjoyment of musical examples, reported a .48 ($p < .01$) correlation coefficient between the two variables. Most other studies examined by Dainow, however, reported no clear-cut data regarding the relationship between respiration rate or amplitude and either a musical stimulus or verbal response. They merely described the responses to the musical stimuli. As was apparent for heart rate research, respiration research to date presents a confusing picture and provides little or no information regarding the affective response to music.

Dainow maintains that GSR experiments are even more incomplete and inconclusive than those for heart rate and respiration. He suggests that there is a general methodological "hodgepodge" in GSR research, noting that some studies measure magnitude and direction of response, some the number of deflections, and others the rising period or latency of response. Some have attempted to relate GSR to some ill-defined emotional response to music, while others have examined it in relation to stimulative versus sedative music or dissonant versus consonant sounds. Despite occasionally well-conceived studies such as Dreher's (1947) comparisons of verbal reports and GSR to different types of music, little can be concluded regarding GSR and affective response because of the many methodological problems in the various studies.

Hodges's (1980b) review corroborates Dainow's findings regarding contradictions in the research results on heart rate, respiration, and electrodermal skin response. Focusing on studies of the effects of *stimulative* music, which reflects high rhythmic activity, and *sedative* music, which is characterized by sustained legato melodies and minimal rhythmic activity, Hodges notes that, with respect to heart rate and pulse rate, (a) some studies resulted in increased rates for stimulative music and decreased rates for sedative music; (b) some studies resulted in increased heart and pulse rate for any music, whether stimulative or sedative; (c) some studies yielded changes in heart and pulse rates that were unpredictable; and (d) some yielded no change in heart or pulse rates for any music. Hodges notes similar contradictory results for studies of music's effects on respiration and electrodermal skin response.

Research on brain wave response to music has not focused primarily on brain waves as a measure of affect, but Hodges' conclusions regarding electroencephalographic (EEG) response should be noted. His review of EEG research revealed that (a) musicians produce more alpha brain waves than nonmusicians when listening to music, (b) children spend more time in alpha brain wave production during silence than during any of several conditions of aural stimuli, (c) musicians' and nonmusicians' brain waves are slightly more desynchronized during complex pitch discrimination tasks, and (d) there are significant variations in brain wave tracings both within and between musician and nonmusician groups.

The recent interest in hemispheric specialization and music has given rise to considerable research and much speculation regarding brain activity and musical processing. The research focus primarily has involved perceptual or conceptual responses to dichotic listening situations. Critical reviews of the research do not always interpret the research in the same way (Gates & Bradshaw, 1977a, 1977b; Hodges, 1978, 1980a; Radocy, 1978, 1979; Regelski, 1978; Webster, 1979), but two general conclusions appear to be receiving general acceptance:

> (1) hemispheric differences are to a considerable degree a function of the nature and complexity of the musical task, and (2) there are differences in the hemispheric activation on given musical tasks for musically trained and untrained subjects. (Boyle, Cole, Cutietta, & Ray, 1982), p. 10)

While much of the research on hemispheric specialization and music purportedly was undertaken to gain a better understanding of the affective response to music, partially in response to Regelski's (1978, p. 13) strong assertion that aesthetic thinking is a right hemisphere activity, little research actually has examined hemispheric specialization systematically as either an independent or dependent variable in musical affect. Tucker's (1981) comprehensive review of hemispheric specialization and emotion, however, suggests that both hemispheres are involved.

An exploratory investigation of right/left alpha brain wave ratios for liked and disliked music revealed no statistically differences in the ratios for liked and disliked music (Boyle, Cole, Cutietta, & Ray, 1982). In short, brain wave research, including that on hemispheric specialization and music, provides little or no insight regarding the affective response to music.

While the above discussion suggests that measurement of physiological rates as a basis for assessing affective response to music is fraught with problems, there remains a certain fascination with the notion that physiological responses reflect musical affect. In an effort to gain another perspective on the matter, Sloboda (1991) asked 83 music listeners to indicate (a) three "peak" emotional experiences they had when listening to music during the previous five years, (b) the music that elicited the peak experience, and (c) the nature of the physical response that had accompanied the experience. The most common responses, which were shared by a large majority of respondents, were shivers down the spine, laughter, lump in the throat, and tears. Sloboda's analysis of the responses suggests that respondents were able to pinpoint precise musical events that gave rise to the physiological response and that their responses were different for different types of musical structure. Later, Sloboda (1992) reported that when 67 regular listeners were asked to describe their most valued emotional experiences with music, 41 cited music as a change agent (as in relaxing feelings of tension), and 34 cited it as a way to intensify or release existing emotions.

Another recent study (DeVries, 1991) used Clynes's "sentograph" as a tool for assessing affective response to music.[2] DeVries examined responses of 30 people, some musicology students and some members of an amateur choir, to eleven short musical excerpts and observed that the subjects' responses were "fairly similar." Based on both visual and statistical analysis of the data, DeVries maintains that the sentograph "indeed measures the affective response to music" (p. 46). The theory is that "music directly activates the action programs that drive the expression of emotions," (p. 63) but notes that the movements are in response to only the *affective* content of the music. Obviously, this theory and approach will need further testing before receiving general acceptance as a measure of affective response to music.

Electromyography, or muscle tension, perhaps holds more promise as a reflection of affective response to music than any of the other physiological measures. Western music appears to organize sounds in which tension-resolution patterns are developed, and Dainow suggests that "it might be expected that inherently tense music could induce a corresponding physical or muscular tension in the listener" (p. 214). He cites research by Sears (1957, 1960), which provides evidence that music may alter muscle tension. The potential of electromyography for evaluating affective response to music, however, has yet to be explored adequately.

Clearly, physiological research to date provides little insight into the affective response to music. Reasons for this are difficult to pinpoint, although Dainow and Hodges suggest that many methodological issues are involved. Particular concerns include instructions to subjects, loudness of the musical stimuli, subject attention, and possible suppression of response due to fear of disturbing electrodes. Another major difficulty involves measurement of the psychological variable affect. In addition,

---

[2]The sentograph essentially measures finger pressure on a finger rest. The respondent is asked to express an emotion by applying pressure to the button. "The pressure applied to the button is measured over time, and in two directions: vertically (straight down) and horizontally (away from/towards the subject). The manner in which subjects push the button is thought to mirror their entire manner of movement" (p. 46). Analyses of the graphs of the responses, called "sentograms," allegedly represent "sentic states."

the sheer diversity of physiological variables themselves and the many aspects of each creates an overwhelming array of measurement and interpretation problems.

In a recent review of research on physiological response to music, Miller (1992) suggests that even if one can demonstrate that somatic changes are "in sync" with musical activities, it may be merely an instance of "phenomenology without psychology" (p. 419). He notes that the aspects of emotional behavior that are observable and measurable differ from emotional experiences, which he maintains are not measurable.

Finally, even if all of the measurement and research design problems can be resolved, it may be that responses of the autonomic nervous system are sufficiently unique to each individual, who also brings a unique experiential background to the measurement situation, that making predictions or generalizations about the affective response on the basis of physiological measurements is inappropriate. As Hahn (1954, p. 11) states, "an investigation of the physiological response may offer a clue but not a solution to the individual's psychological reactions."

Adjective Descriptors

Laymen, musicians, psychologists, and philosophers agree that music can reflect moods and evoke mood responses in listeners. Mood response to music, as other psychological responses to music, involves learning. Individuals within given cultural groups *learn* that music with certain characteristics reflects certain moods while music with other characteristics reflects different moods. Psychologists and philosophers have described moods in various ways, but as used in research related to music, *mood* generally refers to "relatively transient states . . . which can be cognized by individuals and designated with *words* [Italics not in original] (Eagle, 1971, p. 19).

The traditional approach to assessment of mood response has been through use of adjective descriptors, and most discussions of adjective descriptors as tools for assessment of response to music are labeled as discussions of mood response to music (e.g., Eagle, 1971, pp. 27–80; Farnsworth, 1969, pp. 79–86; Lundin, 1967, pp. 160–172). Eagle's discussion provides an exhaustive review of traditional literature using verbal descriptors as a basis for studying affective response to music. He notes that three basic methods have been used for gathering verbal descriptions: (a) adjective checklists, (b) the semantic differential, and (c) various types of rating scales. The most commonly used of the three methods has been the adjective checklist, and following is a brief chronology and summary of the major research using adjective checklists.

1927   Schoen and Gatewood presented ten musical selections to 32 female subjects on two separate occasions under similar testing conditions. Based on a frequency count of the adjectives checked for each selection, the researchers concluded that "a given musical selection will arouse a certain definite reaction and will arouse the same reaction on different occasions" (Schoen & Gatewood, 1927, p. 151).

1927   Gatewood (1927) presented a list of twelve adjective descriptors to 35 female subjects who were asked to check the moods elicited by each of ten selections. The study sought to examine the influence of rhythm, melody, harmony, and timbre on stated mood effects. Gatewood concluded that mood effects are dependent on definite musical elements.

1928   Heinlein studied adjectives checked in response to major and minor chords by 30 musically trained and untrained subjects. Two additional variables studied were intensity and pitch register. He found that mood effects were more a function of intensity than the chord per se. Further, pitch register also made a difference in which adjectives were checked. He concluded that "any fixity of feeling-tone in relation to a given mode is dependent upon training to react in a specific manner to a purely intellectual discrimination" (Heinlein, 1928, p. 140).

1935   Hevner (1935, 1936) developed an adjective checklist which has served as the basis for much subsequent research on mood response to music. She developed an adjective circle grouping 67 adjectives into eight clusters, each cluster containing adjectives of approximately the same meaning (See Figure 8-1). Listeners were asked to check the adjectives describing the mood of the musical excerpts heard. The intent was that as one progressed around the circle from cluster one to cluster eight there would be eight more-or-less discrete moods, representing a general trend of mood change through the respective clusters. Her results revealed a general consistency among subjects in the adjectives checked. She conducted a series of follow-up studies in the late 1930s to ascertain the effects of various elements of music (modality, rhythm, tempo, harmony, melody, and pitch) on mood response. From her series of studies she concluded that the major mode is "happy, graceful, and playful"; the minor mode is "sad, dreamy, and sentimental"; firm rhythms are "vigorous and dignified"; flowing rhythms are "happy, graceful, dreamy, and tender"; complex dissonant harmonies are "exciting, agitated, vigorous, and inclined toward sadness"; simple consonant harmonies are "happy, graceful, serene, and lyrical"; and differences in expressiveness caused by rising and falling of melodic line are not clear-cut, distinct, or constant (Hevner, 1936, p. 268). Hevner (1937) reported that slow tempos express "dignity, calmness, and sadness"; fast tempos, "restlessness and happiness." High pitches are "sprightly and humorous," while low pitches reflect "sadness, dignity, and majesty." She observed that responses were generally the same for listeners of all kinds, intelligent and less intelligent, trained and untrained (Hevner, 1939).

1952   Capurso (1952) developed a list of 105 musical selections to match six mood categories. He then asked 1,075 "nonmusical" subjects to listen to the selections and categorize them according to mood. He found that sixty-one selections had listener agreement at least 50 percent of the time.

1954   Farnsworth (1954) tested the internal consistency of the clusters of the Hevner Adjective Circle. He observed that several of the clusters did not describe internally consistent mood patterns and therefore did not justify the circle arrangement. He rearranged 50 of Hevner's adjectives into ten more consistent categories. (See Figure 8-2.)

1955   Sopchak (1955) developed a twelve-category adjective checklist which 553 college sophomores used in responding to fifteen compositions, five classical, seven popular, and three folk. Subjects also were asked to classify their own moods on a three-point scale: "cheerful" to "neutral" to "gloomy." A higher percentage of gloomy subjects responded to sorrow, joy, calm, love, eroticism, jealousy, wonder, and cruelty. Sopchak speculated that gloomy subjects have many tensions and thus more readily project into the music, while cheerful subjects may have less need to project into the music.

1960   Van Stone (1960) sought to ascertain mood differences associated with tone quality of music. Eight musical excerpts representing the eight clusters of the Hevner Adjective Circle were orchestrated and recorded by three ensembles—string, woodwind, and brass. Results indicated no significant differences among adjectival responses to the three types of ensembles. Apparently timbre change had little or no effect on mood response.

While mood response in terms of adjective checklists has been subject to considerable study, the more recently developed semantic differential

6
bright
cheerful
gay
happy
joyous
merry

7
agitated
dramatic
exciting
exhilirated
imipetuous
passionate
restless
sensational
soaring
triumphant

5
delicate
fanciful
graceful
humorous
light
playful
quaint
sprightly
whimsical

8
emphatic
exalting
majestic
martial
ponderous
robust
vigorous

4
calm
leisurely
lyrical
quiet
satisfying
serene
soothing
tranquil

1
awe-inspiring
dignified
lofty
sacred
serious
sober
solemn
spiritual

3
dreamy
longing
plaintive
pleading
sentimental
tender
yearning
yielding

2
dark
depressing
doleful
frustrated
gloomy
heavy
melancholy
mournful
pathetic
sad
tragic

Figure 8-1.

A	B	C	D	E
cheerful	fanciful	delicate	dreamy	longing
gay	light	graceful	leisurely	pathetic
happy	quaint	lyrical	sentimental	plaintive
bright			soothing	yearning
merry			tender	
playful			tranquil	
sprightly			quiet	

F	G	H	I	J
dark	sacred	dramatic	agitated	frustrated
depressing	spiritual	emphatic	exalting	
doleful		majestic	exciting	
gloomy		triumphant	exhilarated	
melancholic			impetuous	
mournful			vigorous	
pathetic				
sad				
serious				
sober				
solemn				
tragic				

Figure 8-2. Farnsworth's modification of the Hevner Adjective Circle.

technique offers another framework for eliciting subjects' responses to adjective descriptors. Essentially the technique attempts to measure subjects' views, perceptions, or concepts of various phenomena by use of a series of bipolar adjectives between which they make a response on a five- or seven-point continuum.[3] For example:

Concept: Mood

Happy	____ ____ ____ ____ ____	Sad
Light	____ ____ ____ ____ ____	Heavy
Humorous	____ ____ ____ ____ ____	Solemn

Eagle (1971) used the semantic differential technique in a study which sought to answer three questions: (a) Does existing stated mood affect rated mood response? (b) Does presentation order of music affect rated mood response to music? (c) Do similarly rated mood responses hold true for both vocal and instrumental music? Subjects were 274 undergraduate and graduate music majors who were asked to rate their own present mood on a ten-point scale and then respond to twenty musical selections in terms of five pairs of bipolar adjectives (good-bad, pleasant-unpleasant, bright-dark, depressed-elated, and happy-sad). The ten vocal

---

[3]Readers interested in more information on the semantic differential technique should consult Osgood, C.E., Suci, G.J., and Tannenbaum, P.H., *The Measurement of Meaning,* Urbana: University of Illinois Press, 1957.

excerpts included rock, folk, country-western, popular ballad, and hymns; instrumental excerpts included jazz, march semiclassical, and classical. Eagle found that the listener's existing mood does influence mood response to music, but order of presentation does not. In response to his third question, Eagle states that

> similar rated mood responses do not hold true for both vocal and instrumental music. A person responds differently to vocal music than to instrumental music, although both may seem to reflect the same mood qualities. (p. 171)

Eagle's (pp. 70–80) analysis of the literature using adjective descriptors as a measure of mood response revealed a number of research concerns. Only three studies mentioned the reliability of their testing instruments. Statistical analyses were not reported in more than half of the 43 studies he reviewed, and of the 20 reporting statistical data, nearly half used only frequency counts. Eagle did note, however, that eight of nine studies conducted since 1960 employed statistical analyses more sophisticated than frequency counts. Findings were not consistent regarding the importance of the elements in eliciting mood, although the review warranted the following broad generalization:

> Rhythm seems to be the primary element in evaluating mood responses to music. "Happiness" was the term used most often to describe fast tempi, major mode, consonant harmonies, and tunes pitched in high registers. "Excitement" or "agitation" described dissonant harmonies. (p. 79)

The semantic differential technique also is useful for assessing responses to music other than mood or character per se. Crozier (1974) and McMullen (1976, 1980, 1982a) are the major proponents of the technique. Building on the work of Osgood, Suci, and Tannenbaum (1957), whose research demonstrated that the bipolar technique is a viable tool for assessing affective response and identified three principal factors or dimensions (*evaluative, potency,* and *activity*) that account for most of the semantic loadings in factor analyses of responses on semantic differential scales, Crozier and McMullen each have identified two dimensions of affective meaning based on their subjects' semantic differential responses to musical stimuli.

Crozier's (1974, p. 85) data suggest that these dimensions are reflected in *pleasingness* and *interestingness* ratings, which are "evidently close to Osgood's Evaluative and Activity dimensions, respectively." Both vary with *uncertainty* or information content (in information theoretic terms) of the musical sequences heard, but in different ways. The former is related curvilinearly, and the latter is related linearly.

The *dimensional approach* for relating verbal responses to musical stimuli, according to McMullen (1976), appears to be closely related to the adjective checklist approach in that both seek

> to define verbally the affective domain or stimulus variables that influences these response dimensions. The dimensional approach seeks a statistical grouping of adjectives that contain similar meaning for the response dimension, while the Hevner Checklist uses individual adjectives which collectively form a mood pattern. Additionally, both approaches seek to define the variables in the stimulus that influence such responses, the dimensional approach by defining general dimensions such as activity/uncertainty that conceivably could apply to many art forms, while the researchers employing the checklist primarily have used variables associated with the analysis of musical structure. (p. 2)

McMullen examined the relationship between response to the Hevner Adjective Circle and some previously defined dimensions of *evaluation* (pleasing, beautiful, good), *potency* (interest, powerful, rugged), and *activity* (complex, clear, order). His data indicated that there is some merit in Hevner's concept of arranging her adjective checklist in a circle; two dimensions of semantic space, which he interprets as subfactors of the evaluative dimension, emerged. McMullen goes on to suggest that a third factor, associated with the activity dimension, might have emerged if additional activity-related adjectives had been used in the study.

Analysis of adjective descriptors into underlying dimensions holds much potential for assessing affective response to music and musical experience, and the approach is receiving increased usage. One of the most elaborate applications of the technique is Asmus's (1985) multidimensional instrument for the measurement of affective response to music. Called the *9-Affective Dimensions* (9-AD), Asmus's technique yielded nine dimensions of affect, which he named *Evil, Sensual, Potency, Humor, Pastoral, Longing, Depression, Sedative,* and *Activity*. Others who have used the dimensional approach to assessment of affective response to music include Gabrielsson (1973, 1979), Hargreaves and Coleman (1981), and Hylton (1981). While the dimensional approach, whether involving basic factor analytic techniques or even more sophisticated multidimensional scaling techniques, holds much promise for analyzing adjective descriptor data, Hargreaves (1986, p. 125) cautions that "any dimensional model is ultimately restricted by the range of musical stimuli on which it is based, as well as on the subjects and response measures adopted." Further, the interpretation of the dimensions that emerge involves subjective judgments by the researcher. Hargreaves suggests that dimensional approaches to the study of musical responses are still in their infancy and do not yet provide an adequate basis for drawing any firm conclusions about the broad dimensions of responses to music (p. 128).

Philosophical Inquiry

Philosophical explanations regarding the value or meaning of artistic phenomena and experience have been a part of Western culture since the time of Plato, who is considered the founder of philosophical aesthetics (Hofstadter & Kuhns, 1964, p. 3). The range and diversity of views that have been offered regarding the value and meaning of art (and music in particular) have resulted in a philosophical quagmire, often engulfing those who are not well schooled in aesthetics. While philosophical inquiry by nature arouses divergent viewpoints, it is believed that a cursory examination of some of the classical viewpoints may contribute to the understanding of the affective response to music, particularly since philosophical aesthetics represents the traditional and longest standing approach to the study of people's responses to arts phenomena.

Berlyne (1974, p. 2) suggests that *speculative aesthetics* is the most apt term for disciplines traditionally called philosophical.

> They depend heavily on deduction — from definitions of concepts, from self-evident principles, from generally accepted propositions, from an author's own beliefs, intuitions, and experience. To a large extent, their method is "hermeneutic," i.e., they rely heavily on interpretive examination of particular texts, particular specimens of literary, musical, or visual art. Their ultimate criterion of validity is whether they leave the reader with a feeling of conviction.

Berlyne sees two divisions of speculative aesthetics: traditional *philosophical* aesthetics, usually taught in a university department of philosophy, and *art theory,* which usually is taught in the respective art, music, or literature departments. Philosophical aesthetics includes general statements regarding arts phenomena and their intent, value, or meaning, while art theory involves more examination of individual art works, art styles, and artists. Music courses that concern art theory as defined by Berlyne are music history, music appreciation, music literature, and to a degree, form and analysis courses. As should be apparent, there is much overlap among the various types of courses, and aesthetics comprises only one concern of a course. Speculative aesthetics generally is viewed as subjective in approach; other approaches to the study of affective response are considered to be objective, although it is recognized that verbal descriptions of music may be subjective. The present discussion examines only philosophical aesthetics.

Readers interested in examining some of the classic aesthetic theories should consult a traditional text, such as Weitz's (1970) *Problems in Aesthetics* or Hofstadter and Kuhn's (1964) *Philosophies of Art and Beauty,* or any of several more recent sources that summarize, review, and/or synthesize various philosophical positions (e.g., Davies, 1994; Higgins, 1991, Reimer & Wright, 1992). However, a sampling of some of the various theories' basic tenets suffices to illustrate the dilemma philosophical aesthetics holds for the uninitiated. Plato viewed art as *imitation* of an ideal—the beautiful and the good. Aristotle also viewed art as imitation, but in a different sense; for him imitation was the realization of form in a sensory medium and therefore art was a revelation of reality.

Rousseau considered art as *expression*. French classicism turned art into arithmetical problems, while German romanticism sought explanations in metaphysical terms. Shiller viewed art as the most sublime form of play. Maritain suggested that all art begins for functional reasons and is a value of the practical intellect. Croce maintained that art is *intuition*. Schopenhauer saw music as the art *par excellence* because it "objectifies the world directly" and is "independent of the phenomenal world." Dewey viewed art as experience, reflecting the tension-release patterns of everyday life. Some other theories, as capsulized by Schwadron (1967, p. 33),[4] include:

> Freud, desire and unconsciousness; Santayana, reason; Langer, symbolic transformation; Garvin, feeling response; Stravinsky, speculative volition; Schoenberg, logical clarity; Leichtentritt, logical imagination; and Hindemith, symbolic craftsmanship.

To facilitate a modicum of order in dealing with aesthetic theories related to music, several writers have grouped aesthetic theories according to basic philosophical position (Meyer, 1956, pp. 1–3; Schwadron, 1967, pp. 34–47; Reimer, 1989, pp. 14–37). The basic viewpoints are summarized below.

The two most basic positions usually are classified as the *absolutist* and *referentialist* viewpoints, or in Schwadron's terminology, the *isolationist* and *contextualist*. Essentially, absolutist (isolationist) theories consider music's value or meaning to be the result of the musical sounds themselves and nothing more. For an absolutist, there is no musical meaning beyond that inherent in the sounds themselves. Meyer (1956, pp. 2–3) sees an additional distinction within the absolutist framework. An absolutist may be a *formalist*, who contends that musical meaning is primarily intellectual and based on perception and understanding of the formal structural relationships within a composition, or an *expressionist*, who views these structural relationships as capable of exciting feelings and emotions in the listener. The essential point regarding absolutist theories, however, is that any meaning or value derived from the music must be in

---

[4]For the novice to the study of aesthetics, Schwadron's highly readable and relatively short text remains an excellent introduction to the basic "isms" and more arcane aspects of aesthetics.

terms of the musical sounds and nothing else. Eduard Hanslick (1891) is generally recognized as one of the earliest proponents of the absolutist position. For Hanslick and other absolute formalists, the value and meaning of music are derived entirely from the musical structure. In Hanslick's extreme view, the "true" music lies in the musical score; any performance is an imperfect representation of the structure contained within the score.

Absolute expressionism has gained a certain acceptance in recent years. This view holds that the meaning of music must come not only from the music itself, but from its *expressive* or *aesthetic qualities* rather than its structure or form. Cook (1990), who questions the extent to which listeners give attention to formal details, contrasts "musical listening," where people listen for aesthetic gratification, with "musicological listening," where they listen to establish musical facts or formulate theories. Absolute expressionism's major proponent, Bennett Reimer (1989), argues very eloquently that this philosophical position should be the basis for contemporary music education philosophy.

The other basic position, i.e., the view that the meaning of music involves more than the sounds themselves, including extramusical ideals, emotions, stories, and even spiritual states (Sullivan 1927, pp. 27–37) is labeled the *referentialist* or *contextualist* position. Nearly all advocates of this position are expressionists; i.e., they view music as expressive of human experiences, although they also recognize that it can have other extramusical connotations.

Expressionism appears to be receiving considerable attention in some of the recent literature. Kivy (1980) has offered a theory of expression which has been well received, although it is not without criticism (Davies, 1994). Davies offers another theory of expression. Examination of these theories is beyond the scope of the present discussion, but readers interested in gaining an understanding of expressionism are encouraged to examine the work of Kivy and Davies.

A third position noted by Schwadron (1967, p. 42) is *relativism.* The relativist position allows for the development of personally derived value criteria and recognizes that values are relative to and conditioned by cultural groups and historical periods. "For the relativist, musical meaning is a psychological product of expectation, an outgrowth of stylistic experience and cultural orientation" (Schwadron, p. 47).

Schwadron's (1984) review of research in music philosophy and aesthetics recognizes another direction of contemporary philosophical aesthetics: *phenomenology.* He cites thirteen doctoral dissertations completed between 1974 and 1983 that were concerned with "the phenomenology of music." Following, and borrowing metaphors from, philosophical trends in the aesthetics of visual arts, phenomenological examination of music focuses on sound as *perceived* rather than physical sound.

Smith (1979, p. 54) views phenomenology as "an overcoming of metaphysics" and argues the need to develop appropriate language for sound instead of continuing to depend on visual metaphors. The phenomenology of music is still an emerging and evolving aesthetic philosophy, but its underlying focus on music as a perceptual phenomenon is more in keeping with contemporary psychological persuasions than the positions of traditional philosophical aesthetics.

Clifton's (1983) *Music as Heard: A Study in Applied Phenomenology* has been recognized as the most systematic application of phenomenological analysis to musical experience (Rao, 1992). Rao maintains that Clifton's view of music as " 'the outcome of a collaboration between a person and real or imagined sounds' provides a humanistic, perceiver-oriented approach to musical aesthetics" (p. 52). Individuals concerned with understanding the affective response to music will gain an important perspective by examining Clifton's and others' writings in the phenomenology of music.

Another contemporary philosophical position that recognizes the importance of auditory perception is Harrell's (1986, pp. 23–28) *theory of partial recall.* Concerned with the explanation of *depth metaphor* in music criticism, Harrell argues that ascribing qualities of profundity to a musical work in essence describes one's experiencing of it and reflects the value it holds for the individual. Harrell theorizes that music characterized as "deep" or "profound" may trigger memory for, or *partial recall* of, prenatal auditory experiences which most likely emanated positive emotional qualities and states. Because the human fetus has a fully developed auditory mechanism from about the age of five months, but is devoid of visual and tactual sensory mechanisms and language as "ways of knowing" during these positive emotional experiences, the associated auditory experiences (sounds) hold increased importance. Harrell suggests that music to which the quality of *depth* is ascribed (and depth may be ascribed to music of any culture or style, *not just Western art music*) may enable a listener to "momentarily 'be in touch' with a [positive emotional] state that was pre-linguistic as well as pre-visual and pre-tactual" (p. 28). She goes on to argue that music requiring visual explication for artistic import, particularly film music, may lack the qualities of depth that music recognized as profound through auditory perception may hold.

From this cursory examination of philosophical aesthetics, no clear-cut answers emerge regarding the affective response to music. No position has been substantiated by empirical methods. Most information offered remains purely speculative and as a result leads many individuals concerned with understanding affective response to accept some other philosophical positions noted by Schwadron (1967, pp. 34–35): complacency, eclecticism, skepticism, and agnosticism. Such philosophical positions, however, are not conducive even to attempting to understand affective response to music. The authors encourage those readers who find themselves reflecting one of the latter philosophical positions to examine not only the section immediately below, but particularly the subsequent section on meaning in music.

Psychological Aesthetics

Advocates of *psychological aesthetics* examine affective behavior in terms of human interaction with and response to musical sounds. Berlyne (1974, p. 4), whom many consider the founder of contemporary psychological aesthetics, equates psychological aesthetics with *empirical aesthetics*, which he defines as the study of aesthetic behavior through observation, using methods and objectives similar to empirical science. The bases for psychological aesthetics lie in several disciplines, especially psychology, physiology, and speculative aesthetics.

In contrast to philosophical aesthetics, psychological aesthetics has a relatively short history. Although Berlyne (1974, p. 5) traces its roots back to the work of Fechner in the 1860s and 1870s, he notes that its early products were relatively sparse and not very enlightening prior to 1960. Since about 1960, however, there has been a marked increase of interest in the discipline, which has been characterized by some new approaches, techniques, aims, and ideas.

Psychological aesthetics may involve any of three basic methodologies: (a) *correlational studies,* which examine how two or more factors vary in relation to one another, (b) *content analysis and description,* which involve measurement of artistic and other artifacts of specific social groups or historical periods, and (c) *experimental aesthetics,* which examines aesthetic response through experimental methods, i.e., seeking through systematically varying some factors to determine their causal effect on affective behavior. Berlyne maintains that experimental methodology offers the greatest potential for understanding aesthetic response to music and outlines basic criteria and premises that underlie what he terms the *new experimental aesthetics.*

For research to qualify as the "new" experimental aesthetics, it must possess one or more of four features: (a) a focus on the collative (structural or formal) properties of the musical stimulus, (b) a concentration on motivational questions, (c) study of nonverbal as well as verbally expressed judgments, and (d) efforts to establish links between aesthetic phenomena and other psychological phenomena. In addition, there are three basic premises of the new experimental aesthetics.

First, a work of art is analyzed in information-theoretic terms; i.e., it is comprised of elements, each of which can transmit *information* of four types: (a) semantic, (b) expressive, (c) cultural, and (d) syntactic. Berlyne recognizes some overlap among the four types of information, but notes that the four information sources also emit independent information, thus setting up a competition among them. More information from one generally allows less from the other sources.

The second theoretical premise is that artworks are collections of symbols in accordance with the conception of signs and symbols in the semiotic movement.[5] Artworks have properties in common with objects or events that they signify, and they serve as symbols for communication of artists' values regarding which objects or events deserve attention.

The third theoretical premise is that an artwork serves as a stimulus pattern whose collative properties give it a positive intrinsic hedonic value. Variables for measuring "hedonic value" include degree of pleasure, preference, or utility, which usually are measured via verbal expressions, and such nonverbal variables as reward value and incentive value. An artwork that has "positive intrinsic hedonic value" is pleasurable or rewarding in itself and not because it serves as a means to an end. Berlyne hypothesizes that positive hedonic values are a function of *arousal*—through a moderate increase in arousal or through a decrease in arousal when arousal has reached an uncomfortable high. The "arousal potential" of an artwork's stimulus pattern for an individual depends on many factors, including intensity, association with, or resemblance to experientially significant events, and collative properties.

McMullen (1982a), another strong proponent of psychological aesthetics, expanded on Berlyne's concept of arousal, or *activation* as some call it. He notes that the key concept of arousal—the degree of action or activity by an individual—is the same whether viewed from a cognitive or behavior perspective. He argues that the basic reason for including the concept of arousal at the core of psychological aesthetics is that it provides a bridge between what is perceived—the music—and the related feeling response.

When a person listens to and processes acoustic properties of music, he or she is, according to McMullen, responding perceptually in terms of the music's "energy" and "structure," which in combination serve to arouse or activate the listener. Both McMullen and Berlyne suggest that

---

[5]Readers interested in information on the semiotic movement should consult Chapter 6 of D.E. Berlyne's *Aesthetics and Psychobiology* (New York: Appleton-Century-Crofts, 1971).

this activation or arousal provides the framework for the aesthetic response to music.

Dependent variables for experimental aesthetics may include verbal ratings, psychophysiological measures, and behavioral measures. As noted in the earlier discussion of adjective descriptors, the semantic differential has become the predominant framework for verbal ratings, and much of the research using adjective descriptors is considered part of the contemporary psychological aesthetics movement. Three classes of scales are used: (a) *descriptive scales,* in reference to collative properties of stimulus patterns, (b) *evaluative scales,* reflecting hedonic value, and (c) *internal state scales,* for assessing subjects' reactions or mood while exposed to a stimulus. Psychophysiological measures generally are used as indicators of "arousal" rather than as attempts to measure "affect" as in much of the previously cited psychophysiological research. Behavioral measures generally are *exploratory time* (in music, *listening time*) or *exploratory choice* (in music, *listening choice*). Exploratory time variously has been interpreted as a measure of intensity of orientation time, the intensity of attention, or perceptual curiosity, while exploratory choice is viewed as an index of "incentive value" or "utility" (Berlyne, 1974, pp. 13–14).

Independent variables in experimental aesthetics generally reflect the *approach* to experimentation. The *synthetic* approach involves a more-or-less laboratory approach in which particular variables are isolated for manipulation and study, while the *analytical* approach examines reactions to art and other aesthetic stimuli taken from real life. While there are obvious advantages to the synthetic approach, McMullen (1978) argues that there is a great need for music psychologists to examine musical behaviors from the latter perspective. He maintains that the psychology of music reflects too much the one-sided position of psycho*acoustics* rather than psycho*music.* Berlyne (1974, p. 18) notes that both synthetic and analytic approaches are necessary, but he too recognizes that the synthetic approach has been the dominant approach for much research. Independent variables generally are structural or formal characteristics, i.e., the collative characteristics of the artwork, and their effects frequently are evaluated within an information theory framework.

Research in psychological aesthetics continues to develop in several directions. The psychophysiological approaches, using measures of various physiological rates as dependent measures, and the adjective descriptor approach, particularly studies of dimensionality reflected in the descriptors, have received renewed emphasis and direction from the theory, methodology, and research of contemporary psychological aesthetics. The major developments in psychological aesthetics, however, seem to be emerging through research using experimental methodology that focuses on the collative variables of musical stimuli such as "complexity, novelty/familiarity, redundancy/uncertainty, and orderliness, and various measures of 'aesthetic' response including liking, interestingness, and subjective familiarity and complexity" (Hargreaves, 1986, p. 110). The collative variables generally serve as independent variables, and the various measures of aesthetic response the dependent. Relationships within and between the two classes of variables obviously are highly complex, and examination of them is fraught with many semantic, measurement, methodological, and theoretical problems and issues. The present discussion is intended to serve as an introduction to the theory and issues and to provide an overview of some of the research directions using experimental methodology. Readers interested in more information on contemporary experimental aesthetics should examine Hargreaves's (1986, pp. 110–122) and his colleagues' (Sluckin, Hargreaves, & Coleman, 1982) thorough and lucid reviews of the literature and issues.

Research in music using the theory and methodology of experimental aesthetics appears to be spearheaded by one of Berlyne's associates, J.B. Crozier (Crozier, 1974, pp. 27–90); Bragg & Crozier, 1974, pp. 91–108). In the United States, Patrick McMullen seems to be the chief proponent (McMullen, 1976, 1977, 1982a, 1982b; McMullen & Arnold, 1976). Perhaps the strongest research thrust in recent years comes through the work of David Hargreaves and his colleagues in the Leicester Aesthetics Research Group in England (e.g., Hargreaves, 1982, 1984, 1986, pp. 110–122; Hargreaves & Coleman, 1981; Sluckin, Hargreaves, & Coleman, 1982).

Much of these scholars' research has been related to what Smith and Cuddy (1986) term the "classical model of aesthetic preference," the *optimal-complexity model.* At least some aspect of the theory pervades most research in experimental aesthetics. The theory's origin is generally attributed to Berlyne (1971), but it has been tested and modified over the years by a number of researchers, including Heyduk (1975), Davies (1978), and Walker (1981). Because many of the issues and problems central to research in experimental aesthetics are grounded in the assumptions of the optimal-complexity model, the balance of the present discussion will examine research in experimental aesthetics as it relates to the theory's assumptions, which Smith and Cuddy (pp. 17–18) conveniently have summarized:

1. The critical aspect of a stimulus that determines its hedonic, or positive affective value, is its complexity. Complexity is measured by the amount of variability or uncertainty associated with an event. In terms of information theory, it is directly related to the amount of information conveyed by an event and indirectly related to redundancy.

2. The relation between complexity and affective value may be described by an inverted U-shaped curve. In other words, an intermediate level of complexity elicits maximum positive affect; lower and higher levels of complexity elicit less positive affect.

3. The effect of stimulus exposure (repetition, training, practice) is to lower stimulus complexity and, by consequence, to alter the affective values of stimulus patterns. For example, a pattern whose preexposure complexity was on the high side of the optimal point of complexity would move toward the optimal point with repetition, and its attractiveness would increase. The pattern formerly at the optimal point would become lower than optimal complexity, and its attractiveness would decrease. The result is that a higher level of complexity, as measured by the preexposure scale, is now required to elicit maximum positive affect.

Most of the general assumptions of the optimal-complexity model relate to the effects of the stimulus's collative attributes. However, the collative attributes of a musical stimulus are not simple, isolated variables.

Complexity, which seems to be the central variable, may be either *objective,* a function of the stimulus attributes varied according to some systematic and objective procedure, or *subjective,* the apparent perceived complexity that is assumed to be a function of the interaction between the stimulus's objective complexity and the listener's musical knowledge, experience with the musical style and/or idiom, and familiarity with the particular musical stimulus.[6] In reality, most collative variables are *relativistic;* i.e., their qualities depend on the interaction between the structural attributes of the musical stimulus and the listener's prior experience with music in general, with the style and/or idiom, and with the particular piece. Subjective complexity is similar to the notion of *conceptual meaning,* discussed in Chapter Six.

If complexity is relativistic and is measured in terms of the musical stimulus, as the optimal-complexity model assumes, then the uncertainty/certainty continuum, another generally accepted collative variable, also must be considered relativistic, i.e., a function of both stimulus structure (*structural redundancy*) and the listener's experience with such music (*cultural redundancy*), with the net effect being *perceptual redundancy.*

Research tends to support the first general assumption. Crozier (1974) used a synthetic approach to examine the effects of uncertainty in melodic structure. He found that variations in information, i.e., varying levels of uncertainty, affected subjects' ratings of "pleasingness" and "interestingness." Further, he reported a "remarkably high degree" of interpredict-

_____

[6]The constructs *objective* and *subjective complexity* are borrowed and adapted from Hargreaves (1986, pp. 116–117).

ability between mean verbal ratings and nonverbal measures of exploratory behavior.

McMullen and Arnold's (1976) study of the effects of distributional redundancy on preference and interest response for rhythmic sequences also suggests that redundancy influences both preference and interest. Preference tended to increase as redundancy decreased to a point, after which preference began to decrease; interest generally increased as redundancy decreased.

Smith and Cuddy (1986) examined the effects of (objective) harmonic complexity on 36 university psychology students' "pleasingness" ratings of 20 melodic sequences. The melodic stimuli previously had been classified into five levels of complexity "according to rules defining tone sets and tone progressions in classical Western European music" (p. 21). Essentially, the level of uncertainty or redundancy, as reflected by degree of tonality or tonal strength, was the variable of concern to the present discussion. Results indicated that pleasingness ratings varied with level of objective harmonic complexity. Analysis of data according to subjects' level of musical training revealed that pleasingness ratings also varied according to level of musical training. They concluded that the data supported the first assumption of the optimal-complexity model; i.e., the critical importance of stimulus complexity.

The second general assumption of the optimal-complexity model, that the relationship between complexity and affective value may be described by an inverted U-shaped curve, suggests that a person will like more, prefer more, or be more pleased by music at an optimal-complexity level (i.e., moderately complex) for him or her than by music that is either very simple or very complex. Research testing this assumption includes both studies that attempt to vary the objective complexity (information or redundancy) and studies that use subjective complexity (perceived or judged complexity).

Research examining the effects of both types of complexity generally is supportive of the inverted U-shaped curve hypothesis. Smith and Cuddy (1986) cite five studies using tone sequences with varied information content (i.e., complexity) as the independent variable that support the inverted U-shaped curve hypothesis (Berlyne, 1971; Crozier, 1974; Vitz, 1966a, 1966b; and Walker, 1981). However, they also cite studies showing positive linear (monotonic) relationships between amount of information and judged preference (Vitz, 1962, 1964).

Hargreaves's review of studies of subjective complexity and liking for musical excerpts is similarly supportive of the hypothesis. He notes the Crozier (1974) and McMullen and Arnold (1976) studies cited above, as well as some of the studies cited by Smith and Cuddy. Other studies cited as supportive of the inverted U-shaped curve hypothesis include Heyduk (1975), Radocy (1982), and Hargreaves and Castell (1986).

Heyduk (1975) varied the harmonic and rhythmic content of four brief piano compositions so that they reflected different levels of objective complexity. Subjects' "liking" ratings of the resultant versions of varying objective complexity provided strong support for the inverted U-shaped curve hypothesis and the general assumptions of the optimal-complexity model.

Radocy (1981) tested Walker's (1981) version of the optimal-complexity model, the "hedgehog" theory, so-named because Walker views the one central idea of the theory as being applicable to many situations, just as the European hedgehog has one response to fatigue, stimulation, or fright, namely rolling into a ball. Using 15 instrumental excerpts from Western art music as stimuli, Radocy asked college music and nonmusic majors to rate each excerpt in terms of complexity, familiarity, and preference. Results revealed that excerpts rated as moderately complex were the most preferred, despite a strong positive linear relationship between familiarity and preference. It also was concluded that perceived complexity or lack thereof is more than just a matter of familiarity.

Hargreaves and Castell (1986) compared the preferences of subjects of different age levels, which were assumed to reflect different levels of enculturation with music, for four types of melodic sequences, ranging from very familiar melodies to "near" and "far" statistical approximations of music. Ratings of the familiar melodies and the unfamiliar folk song melodies yielded inverted U-shaped relationships with increasing age, but with a later peak for the unfamiliar melodies. The statistical approximations to music were preferred less as the subjects' age increased. Data were interpreted as supporting the inverted U-shaped curve hypothesis, as well as Hargreaves' contention that *stimulus familiarity* serves as a key explanatory variable in tests of the optimal-complexity model.

Although research generally supports the theory's assumption that complexity and affective value may be described by an inverted U-shaped curve, the role of familiarity is not quite as clear as Hargreaves suggests. Research related to the theory's third assumption, that repeated exposure to a stimulus (i.e., increasing familiarity) serves to lower stimulus complexity, has yielded contradictory results.

Hargreaves's (1984) study of the effects of repetition on "liking" of music examined the hypothesis that the liking curve would, with repeated hearings of the music, reflect a U-shaped curve. Using musical pieces in four styles, he conducted two experiments, one with adults and one with university students, asking them to rate the pieces on seven-point scales for liking and familiarity. Excerpts for the adult group were played three times, those for the other group four times. For the adult group, which heard easy listening and avant-garde jazz excerpts, familiarity ratings increased with repetitions, but results were different for the different styles. For the easy listening music, which appeared to be at about the listeners' optimal level of subjective complexity, liking ratings declined with repetitions, but for the avant-garde music, which probably was above the listeners' optimal level of subjective complexity, the liking ratings increased with repetition. For the university students, who heard avant-garde jazz, pop, and classical excerpts, liking curves also varied with style. Ratings for the avant-garde excerpts did not change, but those for the pop and classical excerpts generally supported the inverted U-shaped curve. Apparently the inverted U-shaped curve predicts preference well within in styles but not between styles.

Smith and Cuddy (1986), whose study was discussed above in relation to the first assumption of the optimal-complexity model, also examined repetition effects. Their data revealed that for four of the five levels of complexity, subjects' "pleasingness" ratings increased with repetition. However, on a postrepetition test, which contained some repeated sequences and some nonrepeated sequences, the repetition effects did not carry over, leading the authors to conclude that "the degree to which we appreciate repetition depends in part on the initially perceived complexity of the repeated excerpt" (p. 31). They go on to suggest that "mere repetition does not necessarily lead to cognitive reorganisation; if it does not, the evaluation of rule complexity will be unaffected by repetition" (p. 31).

Hargreaves's (1986, pp. 118–122) excellent review of the literature on repetition and liking led him to conclude that "the results of approximately half of the studies seem to support the inverted U-shaped hypothesis, whilst the other half show a positive monotonic 'mere exposure' relationship between familiarity and liking" (p. 119). He acknowledges that the contradictory results could be the result of differences in experimental designs and procedures, but he argues quite convincingly that they may be due to the variations in the ranges of the familiarity variable sampled in the experimental stimuli. He maintains that studies showing linear relationships between repetition and preference could just be sampling the beginning or ending part of the U-shaped curve, depending on the initial complexity level of the stimuli for the subjects. He goes on to note that this view is in accord with Lundin's (1967) earlier review of the repetition literature, in which he noted that popular music tended to attain a maximal pleasantness level at an early repetition, while classical excerpts, which presumably were more complex, reached their affective maximum during later repetitions. Smith and Cuddy's (1986) discussion of the research on repetition effects essentially concurs with Hargreaves's explanation for the seemingly contradictory results from repetition studies.

As may be apparent, the experimental aesthetics approach to understanding the affective response to music has developed a workable research paradigm, which has generated considerable data. However, it also is apparent that the research paradigm needs refinements so that more consistent data might be forthcoming. While a number of factors may contribute to the inconsistent data, future research should scrutinize some of the variables very carefully. The research appears to be overly dependent on verbal ratings as measures of liking, pleasingness, preference, etc., with little consideration given to the reliability of such ratings. Certainly, the assumptions of the optimal-complexity model and the complex interrelationships among the collative variables warrant further careful examination. The examination of familiarity has been almost solely in terms of particular pieces, whereas Meyer's (1956, 1967) applications of information theory as a model for meaning in music, which is discussed in the next section, suggests that familiarity with style, idiom, or rules of musical grammar seems to be of even greater importance. The apparent relativistic nature of collative variables suggests that *individuals,* as well as groups, will differ greatly in their perception of and response to musical stimuli; consequently, there is great need to study individual differences in addition to group differences, which have been the primary concern of researchers to date.

While discussions of cognitive and affective responses to music generally are separated for convenience, there is need for more studies, such as Smith and Cuddy's (1986), which seek to examine both perceptual and cognitive underpinnings of affective behavior. Finally, researchers need to give greater consideration to the role of enculturation and the sociocultural context within which data are gathered. In short, major developments in experimental aesthetics have occurred during the past few decades, but refinement of research variables and methodology is still necessary if psychological aesthetics is to provide satisfactory answers for those seeking to understand the affective response to music.

Meaning in Music

As may be apparent from the preceding discussion, there is a broad gap between philosophical and psychological aesthetics. Philosophers tend to talk to philosophers, and psychologists tend to talk to psychologists. Philosophers tend to be concerned with whether music's value and import come from within the music or from its referents, while psychologists have examined the affective response to music in terms of psycho-physiological, verbal, or behavioral response to music. However, information theory, with its constructs related to redundancy, appears to offer a viable means for bridging the gap between aesthetic theory and musical response,[7] and Leonard B. Meyer's work toward this end provides some direction not only for philosophical aestheticians and psychological aestheticians, but for anyone concerned with understanding the affective response to music.

Meyer (1956, pp. 1–42) espouses a theory of musical meaning based on a theory of emotion and expectation. The relationships between his theory of musical meaning and information theory are explored in another publication, *Music, the Arts, and Ideas* (Meyer, 1967). This section examines Meyer's theories of emotion and meaning in music as well as some of the parallels between his theories and information theory.

Meyer's theory of musical meaning is based on his *theory of emotion,* which has the same basic tenets as Dewey's *conflict theory of emotion.* "Emotion or affect is aroused when a tendency to respond is arrested or inhibited" (Meyer, 1956, p. 14). Emotional responses are dependent on the relationship between a stimulus (music) and a responding individual. Originally, the theory suggested that a musical stimulus must produce a tendency for an individual to respond in a particular way. A stimulus that arouses no tendency to respond or that is satisfied without delay can not arouse emotion.

Reimer and Wright (1992) note that Meyer subsequently revised his theory of musical meaning to recognize that a tendency to respond is most likely not limited to a single particular response, but results in a tendency to respond in terms of a weighted set of musically probable events. They describe the revision as it relates to information theory:

> The most probable event produces the least information; the most unlikely event produces the most information. Thus, Meyer's theory of musical meaning can be modified to this: musical meaning arises when a listener, uncertain of the music's progress, objectively or tacitly estimates the probabilities of the music's continuation. When less probable events occur, the music is experienced as meaningful or informative. To Meyer, music is as meaningful as it is informative. (Reimer & Wright, p. 214)

The most meaningful events are those that are neither so direct (highly probable) as to appear trite nor those that are so elusive (highly

[7]Besides the work of Berlyne, Crozier et al., significant work has been conducted by Abraham Moles (1966, *Information Theory and Esthetic Perception,* Urbana: University of Illinois Press). In addition, much of Roederer's (1995) work in the psychophysics of music, previously noted in Chapter Four, utilizes information theory as a framework for examining responses to aural stimuli.

improbable) as to appear ridiculous to a listener knowledgeable of the style of music heard. This is somewhat analogous to the inverted U-shaped curve with respect to liking or pleasingness ratings and complexity.

Meyer differentiates between emotion per se and the emotional experience: the latter includes an awareness and cognition of a stimulus situation that always involves specific stimuli. Thus, affective experiences with music require *musical* stimuli.

Musical affective experience is distinguished from affective experience in everyday life. Tensions created by tendencies to respond in everyday life may go unresolved, whereas those aroused by music usually are resolved within a musical framework. Music can serve as both stimulus and as meaningful resolution to such tendencies; in life, that which creates the tension usually can not serve to resolve it.

Tensions, which may be either conscious or subconscious, are rooted in expectations. Music arouses expectations in various ways. Listeners to Western music *learn* (consciously or subconsciously) that certain "sound terms" (melodic, rhythmic, or harmonic patterns, phrases, etc.) imply certain other musical entities. When the expected musical consequent is delayed, suspense is aroused. In Meyer's (1956, p. 28) words,

> The greater the buildup of suspense, of tension, the greater the emotional release upon resolution. This observation points up the fact that in aesthetic experience emotional pattern must be considered not only in terms of tension itself but also in terms of the progression from tension to release. And the experience of suspense is aesthetically valueless unless it is followed by a release which is understandable in the given context.

A musical consequent that will fulfill such expectations is dictated by the possibilities and probabilities of the style of the musical composition in question. When seen in this light, stylistic knowledge becomes essential; without knowledge of a musical style or idiom, a listener's expectations lack a basis for focus, other than the unexpected.

In summary, Meyer's theory of emotion is a theory of expectation, which necessarily has certain cultural and stylistic presuppositions. His central hypothesis is that "affect or emotion felt is aroused when an expectation—a tendency to respond—activated by the musical stimulus situation, is temporarily inhibited or permanently blocked" (Meyer, 1956, p. 31). Without the essential expectations, affective possibilities are extremely limited.

While the question of musical meaning is centered on the opposing views of the absolutists and the referentialists, much of the confusion concerning it may be attributed to the different views regarding the definition of meaning. The following definition suffices for Meyer:

"Anything acquires meaning if it is connected with, or indicates, or refers to something beyond itself, so that its full nature points to and is revealed in that connection" (1956, p. 34). Meaning is defined in terms of the relationship between a stimulus and the thing it points to or indicates, but such a relationship must be perceived by the listener. Meaning thus arises out of a triadic relationship among (a) a stimulus, (b) that to which it points, and (c) the conscious observer.

Meyer maintains that music's meaning has been further muddled by aestheticians' failure to state explicitly that to which musical stimuli point. He recognizes two types of musical meaning: *designative* and *embodied.* The designative meaning of a musical stimulus may indicate events or consequents that differ from itself in kind, i.e., nonmusical events. Embodied meaning refers to those in which the stimulus and consequent are of the same kind, i.e., both musical. Designative meaning regards that which music represents, while embodied meaning regards structural interrelationships within the music. Meyer is far more concerned with embodied meaning: For him, one musical event has meaning because it points to and makes the listener expect another musical event. Embodied musical meaning, therefore, is a product of musical expectations, developed as a result of past experiences with music of a given style. Music that does not arouse expectations of a subsequent musical consequent is meaningless for the listener. Because expectation is so much a product of stylistic experience, music in a style with which a listener is totally unfamiliar holds little meaning for the listener.

A knowledge of style implies that learning has taken place; thus, the perception of meaning can not take place without involving cognition. The affective and intellectual responses to music can not be separated. They both depend on the same perceptual processes, stylistic habits, and mode of mental organization. The same musical processes give rise and shape to both types of experience. Meyer maintains that the formalists' and expressionists' conceptions of aesthetic experience are complementary rather than contradictory. They are considered not different processes, but different ways of experiencing the same process. "Whether a piece of music gives rise to affective experience or to intellectual experience depends upon the disposition and training of the listener" (1956, p. 40).

People who have been taught that musical experience is primarily emotional probably will experience delay of expectation as affect. The trained musician probably will listen in more technical terms and tend to make musical processes an object of conscious consideration. Regardless of the way in which one views the delay of expectations, Meyer's theory of expectation may explain it.

Meyer (1967, pp. 5–21) notes striking parallels between his theory of musical meaning and information theory, and he hypothesizes that "the psychostylistic conditions which give rise to musical meaning, whether affective or intellectual, are the same as those which communicate information" (1967, p. 5). Meyer specifically argues that it is music's embodied meaning that is most consistent with information theory.

As discussed in Chapter Six, information theory is a system for quantifying the amount of uncertainty in a stimulus. The greater the amount of *information,* the greater the *uncertainty* of meaning or response. The amount of information a listener receives from a musical stimulus is a function of two basic variables: (a) the extent to which the structural characteristics of the music conform to fundamental organizational laws of Gestalt psychology and (b) the listener's previous experience with the given musical style. The greater the perceptual redundancy of the music, the more predictable the musical response.[8]

Variables Contributing to Musical Meaning

Variables contributing to musical meaning may be classified under two broad categories: (a) those related to the structural (collative) characteristics of the musical stimulus and (b) those related to the listener, particularly the experiential variables. McMullen (1978) conveniently groups the variables related to musical structure under three headings: *order, complexity,* and *energy.*

He notes that order is closely related to a traditional aesthetic principle of "unity in variety." Order within musical structure appears to be a function of the amount of structural redundancy in a composition; e.g., tonality and rhythmic redundancy appear to contribute greatly to musical meaning, but systematic investigation of the effects of order in musical structure had received little attention from researchers until recent years.

Complexity of musical structure, a construct not unrelated to order, is currently receiving much attention from psychological aestheticians, although much of the research examines it as a perceived or subjective variable rather than as an objective structural attribute of music. As discussed previously, the authors believe that complexity, as all collative variables, is relativistic and that responses to complexity are result from interaction between the structural attributes of the musical stimulus and the listener's prior experience with music in general, with the given musical style and/or idiom, and with the particular music heard. How-

---

[8]The relationship of perceptual redundancy to *structural* and *cultural* redundancy is discussed in Chapter Six.

ever it is examined, structural complexity is a critical variable in musical response, as demonstrated by its centrality to the optimal-complexity model of musical preference.

Energy is the quality that reflects stimulation or drive. Variables such as tempo and dynamics generally are recognized as primary contributors to energy, but other variables such as melodic and harmonic movement also appear to contribute. Some of the earlier work regarding mood response, as reported by Lundin (1967, pp. 160–177) and Farnsworth (1969, pp. 83–90), examined some of these variables, although it appears that many of the tentative conclusions reached were artifacts of the particular musical examples and evaluative measures employed.

McMullen (1980, 1982a) suggests that people's connotative verbal descriptions of music, traditionally mood response as indicated by adjective descriptors, have taken on greater import as reflections of musical meaning. Rather than just connoting some mood or other meaning external to the musical stimulus, he maintains that studies of dimensionality in the connotative labels (adjective descriptors) provide evidence for an *interpretive paradigm*. The proposed paradigm is relativistic in that it considers

> connotative vocabulary to be the result of a relationship between acoustical properties external to the human senses and their resultant perception as music, the human experience of and/or resulting from that perception and then, and only then, translating that human experience into overt form, in this case connotative vocabulary. (McMullen, 1982a, p. 49)

McMullen also offers a theoretical model, derived primarily from dimensional research, suggesting that the perceived dimensions of *energy* and *structure* are experienced as forms of *activation* or arousal. He hypothesizes that if the experience of perceiving music is related to activation (arousal), "when connotative labels (either in prose form or individual words) are used as descriptors of responses to music, these labels represent some combination of the two covert dimensions—activation and evaluation" (McMullen, 1982a, p. 52). In short, he argues that activation (arousal) and evaluation are the covert bipolar dimensions, reflecting respective continua from high to low activation and positive to negative evaluative judgments, that are operative in determining the *meaning* of a given connotative word.

As may be apparent, McMullen's views are consistent with Meyer's theory of musical meaning. If a musical stimulus fails to arouse any tendencies to respond, it is meaningless.

Variables related to the listener are many and complex. Perhaps of greatest importance are the variables related to the listener's previous experiences with music. From infancy on, individuals have many varieties of experiences with music. They develop expectations regarding its structure (embodied meaning) as well as its referents (designative meaning). In addition to expectations, formal musical training and the resultant learning, associations with particular musical examples and styles, as well as all of an individual's informal musical learning are variables that appear to affect musical meaning.

In conclusion, the efforts of previous researchers in examining the effects of selected variables is acknowledged; they have contributed much to the understanding of musical meaning. However, it also is apparent that research efforts related to musical meaning, or the affective response to music, are still in their infancy, and much effort must be directed toward examining the effects of the variables noted here (as well as many others) before any "final truth" is reached regarding affective responses to music.

Summary

1. *Affect* is a broad term referring to a wide variety of human feeling responses.
2. *Emotion* is a particular type of affect reflecting a relatively temporary disturbance from a normal state of composure.
3. *Aesthetic* feeling results from certain types of experiences with artworks, natural phenomena, or other objects or events in which beauty, artistic value, or meaning may be perceived.
4. *Aesthetic experience* requires perceptual involvement with interacting attributes within artworks (or natural phenomena or other objects or events), perception of beauty or meaning therein, and a feeling reaction thereto; it is more than just "oh how pretty."
5. Other types of affective response to musical stimuli (besides the aesthetic) include *mood* or character responses, *association* responses, *intrasubjective* responses, reactions to word meanings of songs, preferences, interests, attitudes, values, and appreciations.
6. Four basic approaches to study of the affective response to music have been through (a) psychophysiological research, (b) adjective descriptor research, (c) philosophical inquiry, and (d) psychological aesthetics research.
7. Concomitant with affective responses are physiological reactions of the autonomic nervous system.
8. Although physiological reactions, particularly heart rate, respiration rate, and electrodermal responses, to music have been examined for nearly a century, such research provides little insight into the affective response to music.

9. Early research using adjective descriptors focused on assessment of mood response to music, but more recent research using dimensional analysis techniques on semantic differential data has sparked a renewed interest in adjective descriptors as tools for understanding affective behaviors.

10. Speculative aesthetics is of two basic types: *philosophical aesthetics*, which seeks to make general statements regarding arts phenomena and their intent, value, or meaning, and *art theory*, which in music is incorporated in such courses as music history, literature, analysis and which involves examination of individual compositions, styles, and composers.

11. Basic philosophical aesthetic positions include the *absolutist*, which views the value or meaning of music as resulting from the musical sounds themselves, and the *referentialist*, which views music as reflecting more than sounds themselves; the referentialist position may include extramusical ideas, emotions, stories, and even spiritual states.

12. Psychological aesthetics, particularly with the renewed emphasis on *experimental aesthetics*, utilizing methods of empirical science, focuses on the collative properties of aesthetic stimuli, examines motivational questions, studies nonverbal as well as verbal behavior, and seeks to establish links between aesthetic phenomena and other psychological phenomena.

13. Research in psychological aesthetics has focused on the optimal-complexity model of music preference, in which an individual's "liking," "pleasingness," or "preference" response to a musical stimulus is hypothesized to reflect an inverted U-shaped curve with respect to complexity.

14. The collative variables of a musical stimulus (complexity, novelty/familiarity, uncertainty/redundancy) are relativistic.

15. An apparent parallel exists between Leonard B. Meyer's theory of musical meaning, which views meaning in terms of expectations, and information theory, which offers a promising model for examining affect resulting from musical uncertainty.

16. Variables contributing to musical meaning are of two broad classes: (a) those related to the structural (collative) characteristics of a music stimulus and (b) those related to the listener, particularly the experiential variables.

References

Abeles, H. F. (1980). Responses to music. In D. A. Hodges (Ed.), *Handbook of music psychology* (pp. 105–140). Lawrence, KS: National Association for Music Therapy.

Asmus, E. P., Jr. (1985). The effect of time manipulation of affective responses to a musical stimulus. In G. C. Turk (Ed.), *Proceedings of the Research Symposium on the Psychology and Acoustics of Music* (pp. 97–110). Lawrence: The University of Kansas.

Berlyne, D. E. (1971). *Aesthetics and psychobiology.* New York: Appleton-Century-Crofts.

Berlyne, D. E. (Ed.) (1974). *Studies in the new experimental aesthetics: Steps toward an objective psychology of aesthetic appreciation.* New York: Halsted Press.

Boyle, J. D., & Radocy, R. E. (1987). *Measurement and evaluation of musical experiences.* New York: Schirmer Books.

Boyle, J. D., Cole, H. W., Cutietta, R., & Ray, W. J. (1982). Electrocortical responses to music: An exploratory study concerning affect and familiarity. In P. R. Sink (Ed.), *Proceedings of the Research Symposium on the Psychology and Acoustics of Music* (pp. 10–18). Lawrence: The University of Kansas.

Bragg, B. W., & Crozier, J. B. (1974). The development with age of verbal and exploratory responses to sound sequences varying in uncertainty level. In D. E. Berlyne (Ed.), *Studies in the new experimental aesthetics: Steps toward an objective psychology of aesthetic appreciation* (pp. 91–108). New York: Halsted Press.

Capurso, A. (1952). The Capurso study. In *Music and your emotions* (56–86). New York: Liverright Publishing.

Clifton, T. (1983). *Music as Heard: A study in applied phenomenology.* New Haven: Yale University Press.

Cook, N. (1990). *Music, imagination, and culture.* Oxford: Clarendon Press.

Crozier, J. B. (1974). Verbal and exploratory responses to sound sequences varying in uncertainty level. In D.E. Berlyne (Ed.), *Studies in the new. experimental aesthetics: Steps toward an objective psychology of aesthetic appreciation* (pp. 27–90). New York: Halsted Press.

Dainow, E. (1977). Physical effects and motor responses to music. *Journal of Research in Music Education, 25,* 211–221.

Davies, J. B. (1978). *The psychology of music.* London: Hutchinson & Co.

Davies, S. (1994). *Musical meaning and expression.* Ithaca, NY: Cornell University Press.

DeVries, B. (1991). Assessment of the affective response to music with Clynes's sentograph. *Psychology of Music, 19,* 46–64.

Diserens, C.M., & Fine, H. (1939). *A psychology of music.* Cincinnati: College of Music.

Dowling, W. J., & Harwood, D. L. (1986). *Music cognition.* Orlando, FL: Academic Press.

Dreher, R. E. (1947). The relationship between verbal reports and galvanic skin response. Unpublished doctoral dissertation, Indiana University.

Eagle, C.T., Jr. (1971). Effects of existing mood and order of presentation of vocal and instrumental music on rated mood responses to that music. Unpublished doctoral dissertation, The University of Kansas.

Farnsworth, P. R. (1954). A study of the Hevner adjective list. *Journal of Aesthetics and Art Criticism, 12,* 97–103.

Farnsworth, P. R. (1969). *The social psychology of music* (2nd ed.). Ames: The Iowa State University Press.

Gabrielsson, A. (1973). Adjective ratings and dimension analyses of auditory rhythm patterns. *Scandinavian Journal of Psychology, 14,* 244–260.

Gabrielsson, A. (1979). Dimension analyses of perceived sound quality of sound-reproducing systems. *Scandinavian Journal of Psychology, 20,* 159–169.

Gates, A., & Bradshaw, J. L. (1977a). Music perception and cerebral asymmetries. *Cortex, 13,* 390–401.

Gates, A., & Bradshaw, J. L. (1977b). The role of the cerebral hemispheres in music. *Brain and Language, 4,* 403–431.

Gatewood, E. L. (1927). An experimental study of the nature of musical enjoyment. In M. Schoen (Ed.), *The effects of music* (pp. 78–120). Freeport, NY: Books for Libraries Press.

Hahn, M. E. (1954). A proposed technique for investigating the relationship between musical preferences and personality structure. Unpublished doctoral dissertation, The University of Kansas.

Hanslick, E. (1957). *The beautiful in music* (G. Cohen, trans.). New York: Liberal Arts Press. (Originally published 1854, translation, 1891)

Hargreaves, D. J. (1982). The development of aesthetic reactions to music. *Psychology of Music, Special Edition,* 51–54.

Hargreaves, D. J. (1984). The effects of repetition on liking for music. *Journal of Research in Music Education, 32,* 35–47.

Hargreaves, D. J. (1986). *The developmental psychology of music.* Cambridge: Cambridge University Press.

Hargreaves, D. J., & Castell, K. C. (1986). Development of liking for familiar and unfamiliar melodies. Paper presented at the Eleventh International Research Seminar of the International Society for Music Education, Frankfurt, West Germany.

Hargreaves, D. J., & Coleman, A. M. (1981). The dimensions of aesthetic reactions to music. *Psychology of Music, 9,* 15–20.

Harrell, J. G. (1986). *Soundtracks, A study of auditory perception, memory, and valuation.* Buffalo, NY: Prometheus Books.

Heinlein, C. P. (1928). The affective characters of the major and minor modes in music. *The Journal of Comparative Psychology, 8,* 101–142.

Hevner, K. (1935). Expression in music: A discussion of experimental studies and theories. *Psychological Review, 42,* 186–204.

Hevner, K. (1936). Experimental studies of the elements of expression in music. *American Journal of Psychology, 48,* 246–268.

Hevner, K. (1937). The affective value of pitch and tempo in music. *American Journal of Psychology, 49,* 621–630.

Hevner, K. (1939). Studies of expressiveness in music. *Proceedings of the Music Teachers National Association* (pp. 199–217).

Heyduk, R. G. (1975). Rated preference for musical composition as it relates to complexity and exposure frequency. *Perception and Psychophysics, 17,* 84–91.

Higgins, K.M. (1991). *The music of our lives.* Philadelphia: Temple University Press.

Hodges, D. A. (1978). Spit-brain research: A new frontier. In E. P. Asmus, Jr. (Ed.), *Proceedings of the Research Symposium of the Psychology and Acoustics of Music* (pp. 71–93). Lawrence: The University of Kansas.

Hodges, D. A. (1980a). Neurophysiology and musical behavior. In D. A. Hodges (Ed.), *Handbook of music psychology* (pp. 195–224). Lawrence, KS: National Association for Music Therapy.

Hodges, D. A. (1980b). Physiological responses to music. In D. A. Hodges (Ed.), *Handbook of music psychology* (pp. 393–400). Lawrence, KS: National Association for Music Therapy.

Hofstadter, A., & Kuhns, R. (Eds.) (1964). *Philosophies of art and beauty.* New York: The Modern Library.

Hylton, J. (1981). Dimensionality in high school student participants' perceptions of the meaning of choral singing experience. *Journal of Research in Music Education, 29,* 287–304.

Kivy, P. (1980). *The corded shell: Reflections on musical expression.* Princeton: Princeton University Press.

Knieter, G. L. (1971). The nature of aesthetic experience. In *Toward an aesthetic education* (pp. 3–20). Washington, D. C.: Music Educators National Conference.

Kuhn, T. L. (1979). Instrumentation for the measurement of attitudes. Paper presented at the meeting of the College Music Society, San Antonio, Texas.

Lehman, P. R. (1968). *Tests and measurements in music.* Englewood Cliffs, NJ: Prentice-Hall.

Lundin, R. W. (1967). *An objective psychology of music* (2nd ed.). New York: Ronald Press.

McMullen, P. T. (1976). Influences of distributional redundancy in rhythmic sequences on judged complexity ratings. *Council for Research in Music Education, 46,* 23–30.

McMullen, P. T. (1977). Organizational and technical dimensions in musical stimuli. Paper presented at the MENC Eastern Division Conference, Washington, D.C.

McMullen, P. T. (1978). Music and empirical aesthetics: Present and future directions. Paper presented as the Symposium on the Psychology and Acoustics of Music, Lawrence, The University of Kansas.

McMullen, P. T. (1980). Music as a perceived stimulus object and affective responses: An alternative theoretical framework. In D. A. Hodges (Ed.), *Handbook of music psychology* (pp. 183–193). Lawrence, KS: National Association for Music Therapy.

McMullen, P. T. (1982a). Connotative responses to musical stimuli: A theoretical explanation. *Council for Research in Music Education, 71,* 45–57.

McMullen, P. T. (1982b). Empirical aesthetics: An overview. In P. E. Sink (Ed.), *Proceedings of the Research Symposium on the Psychology and Acoustics of Music 1982* (pp. 48–55). Lawrence: The University of Kansas.

McMullen, P. T., & Arnold, M. J. (1976). Preference and interest as functions of distributional redundancy in rhythmic sequences. *Journal of Research in Music Education, 24,* 22–31.

Maslow, A. H. (1970). *Motivation and personality* (2nd ed.). New York: Harper & Row.

Meyer, L. B. (1956). *Emotion and meaning in music.* Chicago: The University of Chicago Press.

Meyer, L. B. (1967). *Music, the arts, and ideas.* Chicago: The University of Chicago Press.

Miller, R. F. (1992). Affective response. In R. Colwell (Ed.), *Handbook of research on music teaching and learning* (pp. 414–424). New York: Schirmer Books.

Moles, A. (1966). *Information theory and esthetic perception* (J. E. Cohen, Trans.). Urbana: University of Illinois Press.

Osgood, C. E., Suci, G. C., & Tannenbaum, P. H. (1957). *The measurement of meaning.* Urbana: University of Illinois Press.

Price, H. E. (1986). A proposed glossary for use in affective response literature in music. *Journal of Research in Music Education, 34,* 151–159.

Rader, M., & Jessup, B. (1976). *Art and human values.* Englewood Cliffs, NJ: Prentice-Hall.

Radocy, R. E. (1978). Cerebral dominance and music perception: Stop the fad. In E. P. Asmus, Jr. (Ed.), *Proceedings of the Research Symposium of the Psychology and Acoustics of Music* (pp. 120–130). Lawrence: The University of Kansas.

Radocy, R. E. (1979). Hemispheric specialization in music perception: It all depends. Paper presented at the national meeting of the National Association for Music Therapy, Dallas.

Radocy, R. E. (1982). Preference for classical music: A test for the hedgehog. *Psychology of Music, Special Issue,* 91–95.

Rao, D. B. (1992). Thomas Clifton. In B. Reimer & J. E. Wright (Eds.), *On the nature of musical experience* (51–60). Niwot, CO: The University Press of Colorado.

Regelski, T. A. (1978). *Arts education & brain research.* Reston, VA: Music Educators National Conference.

Reimer, B. (1989). *A philosophy of music education* (2nd ed.). Englewood Cliffs, NJ: Prentice-Hall.

Reimer, B., & Wright, J.E. (Eds.) (1992). *On the nature of musical experience.* Niwot, CO: The University Press of Colorado.

Ries, H.A. (1969). GSR and breathing amplitude related to emotional reactions to music. *Psychonomic Science, 14,* 62–64.

Roederer, J.G. (1995). *Introduction to the physics and psychophysics of music* (3rd ed.). New York: Springer-Verlag.

Schoen, M. (Ed.) (1927). *The effects of music.* New York: Harcourt, Brace.

Schoen, M. (1940). *The psychology of music.* New York: Ronald Press.

Schoen, M., & Gatewood, E. L. (1927). An experimental study of the nature of musical enjoyment. In M. Schoen (Ed.), *The effects of music* (pp. 131–183). New York: Harcourt, Brace.

Schwadron, A. A. (1967). *Aesthetics: Dimensions for music education.* Washington, D.C.: Music Educators National Conference.

Schwadron, A. A. (1984). Philosophy and aesthetics in music education: A critique of the research. *Council for Research in Music Education, 79,* 11–32.

Sears, W. W. (1957). The effects of music on muscle tone. In E. T. Gaston (Ed.), *Music therapy 1957.* Lawrence, KS: Allen Press.

Sears, W. W. (1960). A study of some effects of music upon muscle tension as evidenced by electromyographical recordings. Doctoral dissertation, The University of Kansas.

Sloboda, J.A. (1991). Music structure and emotional response: Some empirical findings. *Psychology of Music, 19,* 110–120.

Sloboda, J.A. (1992). Empirical studies of emotional response to music. In M.R. Jones & S. Holleran (Eds.), *Cognitive bases of musical communication* (pp. 33–46). Washington, D.C.: American Psychological Association.

Sluckin, W., Hargreaves, D. J., & Coleman, A. M. (1982). Some experimental studies of familiarity and liking. *Bulletin of the British Psychological Society, 35,* 189–194.

Smith, F. J. (1979). *The experiencing of musical sound: Prelude to a phenomenology of music.* New York: Gordon and Breach Science Publishers.

Smith, K. C., & Cuddy, L. L. (1986). The pleasingness of melodic sequences: Contrasting effects of repetition and rule-familiarity. *Psychology of Music, 14,* 17–32.

Sopchak, A. L. (1955). Individual differences in responses to different types of music in relation to sex, mood, and other variables. *Psychological Monographs, 69* (11), 1–20.

Sternbach, R. A. (1966). *Principles of psychophysiology.* New York: Academic Press.

Sullivan, J. W. N. (1927). Music as expression. In J. W. N. Sullivan, *Beethoven, his spiritual development* (27–37). New York: New American Library.

Tucker, D. M. (1981). Lateral brain function, emotion, and conceptualization. *Psychological Bulletin, 89,* 19–46.

Van Stone, J. K. (1960). The effects of instrumental tone quality upon mood response to music. In E. Schneider (Ed.), *Music therapy 1959.* Lawrence, KS: Allen Press.

Vitz, P. C. (1962). Preference for sequences of tones and the rate of information presentation. *Dissertation Abstracts International, 23,* 4440.

Vitz, P. C. (1964). Preference for rates of information presented by sequences of tones. *Journal of Experimental Psychology, 68,* 176–183.

Vitz, P. C. (1966a). Affect as a function of stimulus variability. *Journal of Experimental Psychology, 71,* 74–79.

Vitz, P. C. (1966b). Preference for differing amounts of visual complexity. *Behavioral Science, 11,* 105–114.

Walker, E. L. (1981). Hedgehog theory and music education. In R. G. Taylor (Ed.), *The documentary report of the Ann Arbor Symposium* (pp. 37–328). Reston, VA: Music Educators National Conference.

Webster, P. R. (1979). Music and brain asymmetry: Some basic concerns and thoughts toward a model. In *Proceedings report of the second annual Loyola symposium: Hemisphere laterality and music.* New Orleans: Loyola University.

Weitz, M. (Ed.) (1970). *Problems in aesthetics* (2nd ed.). New York: MacMillan.

Young, P. T. (1973). Feeling and emotion. In B. B. Wolman (Ed.), *Handbook of general psychology* (pp. 749–771). Englewood Cliffs, NJ: Prentice-Hall.

CHAPTER NINE

MUSICAL PREFERENCES

People vary in their preferences for any sensory experiences in which they have a choice. Personal preferences for certain foods, paintings, home decor, clothing, food, and music are rooted in individual biological needs, cultures, training, and experience. Preferences are not always consistent, and they can be modified. What is preferred in one instance is not necessarily preferred in another.

People often use the terms *preference* and *taste* interchangeably, but a distinction occasionally is made on the basis of commitment. Abeles (1980, p. 106) suggests that taste implies a relatively long-term value for or commitment to a broad class of objects or events, while preference implies a more immediate and specific choice within a set of possibilities. One might have a taste for white wines or Romantic orchestral music and preferences for a particular rhine or chablis, or particular works of Liszt or Strauss. The difference between preference and taste may be a matter of perspective, and, while semantically interesting, probably is of little consequence in studying factors which influence making musical choices.

Musical preference is an area of longstanding interest in the psychology of music. What factors influence a person's musical evaluations are of continuing concern, and a simple preference of one musical work over another may have meaning beyond the musical decision. Psychologists may use expressed musical preferences to assess personality via deviations from population trends regarding musical choices. Some believe that "illogical" aesthetic reactions differentiate psychotics and paranoids from "normals," and alcoholics from other psychotics (Cattell & Anderson, 1953). Hahn (1954) found that individual musical choices reflected clinical personality assessments. Choices also depended on aesthetic values and individual needs for sensual pleasure. Researchers often explore relationships between and among various aspects of personality and musical preferences. Payne (1980) found that among trained musicians, extraverts had a greater preference for "emotional" music while introverts had a greater preference for music with a more "formal" structure. Glasgow, Cartier, and Wilson (1985) found "conservative" listeners preferring familiar rather than unfamiliar classical music to a greater extent than "liberal" listeners. Dollinger (1993) found that extraversion related positively to preference for jazz and excitement seeking related positively to preference for hard rock. He also found that people's openness to diverse experiences related to their enjoyment of musical styles other than popular music. Rawlings et al. (1995) found that a personality factor called "toughmindedness" or "psychoticism" (Eysenck & Eysenck, 1976) relates to a preference for hard rock music and dissonant sounds. The relationship of personality and musical preferences is tenuous due to idiosyncratic behavior.

This chapter examines determining what is "good" music, particular preferences, various musical, psychological, and social influences on preference, and alterations of preference.

What Is "Good" Music?

What music is "good" is, of course, a matter of judgment. Reasons for individuals judging particular music as superior to other music may include musical characteristics, such as forms, tempos, orchestral colors, and lyrics. Extramusical associations ("Darling, our song . . . ") and societal pressures may be influential. Preferences may be based on simple enjoyment, fervent intellectualization, or ideas of what one "ought" to prefer. Group preference tendencies exist; they are not solely a matter of individual choices. Group tendencies arouse concern for what good music really is—what *should* be preferred?

One traditional view of "good" music is that that which is good is good because of inherent aspects of the musical stimulus. In such a view, melodic, harmonic, and formal ideals characterize good, even great music. If the listener is educated properly in such ideals, his or her preferences will conform to some aesthetic ideal. The view that good music owes its goodness to its structure represents a formalistic (Meyer, 1956; Reimer, 1989) or *isolationist* (Schwadron, 1967) position regarding musical aesthetics: The music's value supposedly is inherent in the music itself.[1]

Music, indeed all art, has properties that arouse people. The so-called "collative" variables of novelty, surprise, complexity, and ambiguity, related to form and structure, influence the observer's response. Instability can lead to discomfort; incongruity may increase attention (Berlyne, 1971). The essence of Meyer's (1956) theory regarding musical enjoyment,

---

[1]Hanslick's 1854 view that the real music is contained in a musical score and can be only approximated in any audible performance represents an extreme formalist position, with philosophical roots in Plato. For a discussion, see Higgins (1991, pp. 20–35).

discussed earlier, is that the delay of musical expectancy promotes pleasure through the ultimate dissipation of resulting frustration. Complex music, as long as it is not *too* complex, is more likely than simple music to be preferred over a longer period. McMullen and Arnold (1976) showed a tentative relationship between rhythmic redundancy and preference; the less the dominance of one rhythmic figure, the less the redundancy and the greater the preference, to a certain point.[2]

If music's inherent or "objective" structure is of particular importance, then Adorno's (1976) oft-cited hierarchy of listeners has particular implications. His hierarchy suggests that structural awareness is of the greatest importance in serious listening; his highest classification is the *expert*, who can hear musical structures completely and properly order all formal nuances. The hierarchy then runs "down" through a *good listener*, who hears beyond musical details but lacks structural awareness, a *culture consumer*, mainly concerned with information about music, a nonintellectual *emotional listener*, a *protest listener*, an *entertainment listener*, and, finally, an *indifferent, unmusical*, or *antimusical listener*. Adorno believes that music primarily is an intellectual event, although he does state that one must understand music's social characteristics in order to understand music.

In contrast to the view that good music is "good" because of its structure is a view that preferred music is preferred because of its individual values and utilities rather than any inherent goodness. Whereas Adorno indicates that a criterion of individual taste would deprive "great" music of what makes it great, Chancellor (1974/1975) says that all art is ambiguous and acquires its values from subjective, pluralistic, and relativistic determinants. Hamm, Nettl, and Byrnside (1975) tie music to society and culture and allow for individual utility and personal gratification. In its extreme, such a view represents a *referential* (Meyer; Reimer) or a *contextual* (Schwadron) aesthetic position: Music is meaningless except to the extent that it communicates extramusical messages. A school of aesthetic *relativism* (Schwadron) allows for different value systems for different musical styles and recognizes the importance of musical structure while allowing for cultural and functional variability in musical preference.

Individual critics, musicians, and listeners may continue to explain musical preferences on the basis of inherent musical properties, but it

---

[2]Much contemporary (1995) popular music suggests that considerable amounts of rhythmic redundancy are desirable, at least in music popular for short periods of time. The music often has a dominant syncopated or anapestic accompanying figure (zoom POW zoom POW) that is louder than the melodic line and helps obscure the lyrics.

may be more fruitful psychologically to study preference in terms of people's expressions of preference. "Good" music is good because people *desire* it, due to their moods, backgrounds, training, experiences, prejudices, and beliefs. Some people want complexity. Some want simplicity. Some want strong narrative suggestions; some want an exercise in tracking and labelling musical form. Some preferences are predictable; others are not. It depends on the person making the choice.

Existing Musical Preferences

No formula exists for predicting individual musical preferences reliably, although particular groups tend to prefer particular musical styles. Most investigations have been directed toward preferences for Western art ("classical") music. Often, investigations rely on some sort of polling of representative groups and archival records (e.g., printed programs) of what is performed. A few studies have related listener characteristics to musical preferences.

Any measure of musical preference is imperfect. People may not respond honestly to questions regarding their preferences; reasons for attending live performances selectively include nonmusical ones, such as social visibility. Examining collections of recordings may be useful, but individuals vary in the extent to which they can afford an extensive collection, and possessing a recording tells little about how often the owner listens to it. Analyses of what is performed or broadcast are subject to biases of conductors, wealthy patrons, and advertisers. Scholarly discussions of music reflect musical preferences, but with editorial biases.

Regardless of what a listener bases a musical preference judgment upon, the judgment represents a subjective impression of musical desirability. As with sensory impressions, magnitude estimation, measurement by matching one sensory continuum with another (often numbers but not necessarily so) is a viable technique if one is willing to accept matching impressions as measurement (Radocy, 1986). Aesthetic judgments may be prothetic in nature; investigators have observed psychophysical phenomena, such as a tendency to hear the second member of a pair of ambiguous stimuli as having "more" of the property in question, in affective measurements (Koh, 1965; 1967). Perhaps magnitude estimation or some other technique which does not require counting units may enable quantification of preferences in a meaningful way.

Summaries of some representative investigations of preference follow.

Surveys and Classical Music Preferences

Keston and Pinto (1955) investigated the relationships between college students' musical preferences, as indicated by preferential choices of musical excerpts, and eight variables: introversion-extroversion, masculinity-femininity, age, educational level, gender, formal musical training, music recognition ability, and intelligence. The investigators considered a selection of "classical" music rather than "pop concert" music, "dinner" music, or currently popular music as a "correct" answer. The study showed that people with greater amounts of musical training and experience who were willing to spend the time required for concentrated listening tended to prefer classical music. Of course, this is *correlational* evidence, an indication that people who tend to score highly on one variable score highly on others. Training, recognition, introversion, and gender do not "cause" a preference for classical or any other style of music.

Farnsworth's (1966) eminence rankings are milestones in the study of preference for art music and changes across time. Based on polls of American Musicological Society members in 1938, 1944, 1951, and 1964, the rankings list composers in order of their perceived eminence. "Eminence" apparently means perceived contributions to music history and worthiness of study. In the final year, the "top five" composers in order were Bach, Beethoven, Mozart, Haydn, and Brahms. The rankings were relatively stable across the sampling years, and they always showed a notable absence of twentieth century composers. The American Musicological Society hardly is representative of typical listeners, and one could criticize Farnsworth's polls because of lack of currency, disproportionate attention to European composers, and possible inconsistency in exactly what the respondents evaluated, but the rankings do show that musical preferences within one style have some degree of consistency— they are not solely a matter of individual scholars' whimsy. Of course, eminence and preference are not identical. Farnsworth (1969) reports polls showing less than perfect relationship between perceived eminence and enjoyment of particular composers. On one occasion, expressed preference may be based on eminence; on another, it may be based on enjoyment.

Poland (1970) conducted a content analysis of three music history texts, two music theory texts, Farnsworth's rankings, and the then most recent issue of the Schwann catalog.[3] The thirty composers cited most

---

[3]The Schwann catalogs, published by W. Schwann, Inc. of Boston, list available recordings of classical music by composer and title. The relative amounts of space required to list the works of various composers provide some indication of those composers' popularities as indicated by the marketplace.

frequently in each text, Farnsworth's top thirty names, and the thirty composers receiving the most space in Schwann overlapped considerably: Although the seven sources theoretically could yield 210 names, only seventy-one names appeared, thereby indicating considerable agreement among the various authors, Farnsworth's respondents, and the recording industry regarding whose music merits attention.

Poland then counted the total number of citations for each of the seventy-one composers in the combined five texts and listed the sixty composers who had at least one full column of Schwann listings. While not identical, the two lists contained remarkable similarities regarding composer nationality and historical period. About 59 percent of the combined citations were of works by German composers. Ten percent were of French works, 9 percent were Russian, 7 percent were Italian, and slightly less than 3 percent were American. The remaining 12 percent accounted for the rest of the world, and all of those citations were to works of European composers, except for the Brazilian Villa-Lobos.

Analysis of historical periods represented by Poland's combined citations showed that 19 percent were baroque, 26 percent were classical, and 34 percent were romantic. The text list showed 0.3 percent of the citations for the years 500 BC to 1450. 3.8 percent for the renaissance, and 17 percent for a "modern" (1915–1955) period. The corresponding Schwann list percentages were zero, zero, and 20.

Perhaps most reassuring or discouraging, depending on one's viewpoint, 52 percent of the text citations were to just eleven composers, nine of whom were German. Just five composers had one-third of all the citations; in order, they were Beethoven, Bach, Mozart, Brahms, and Haydn. (Although in a different order, these five Germanic composers are Farnsworth's top five.) Poland's investigation suggested that the core of formal collegiate musical study was built around works of "the three B's" plus Mozart and Haydn. Perhaps preferences are perpetuated.

The apparent reverence for the past which emerges from descriptive research such as that of Farnsworth and Poland as well in analyses of orchestral programs may trouble advocates of contemporary music. People wonder whether a "gap" exists between contemporary composers and their prospective audiences and to what it might be attributable.

J. Mueller (1967) believed that an "aesthetic gap" indeed separated twentieth century composers and audiences to an extent unseen earlier in music history. Favorable initial criticism of works of Beethoven and others and the rate of new works' appearances in nineteenth century European concert programs suggest that the claim that "good" music is never appreciated initially just is not substantiated. Mueller noted that new music never is equally "new"; novelties vary in their public interest and adoption. The contemporary composer often is experimental and pays a price through nonconformity which strains an audience's ears and lacks perceptual redundancy. Mueller suggested that composers need to make more effort to understand their audiences.

Although inherent musical properties do not guarantee "good," "great," or "truthful" music, many people may prefer the lyric melodies, relatively predictable tonal and harmonic patterns, symmetric rhythms, extensive repetitions, and orchestral colors available in the music of eighteenth and nineteenth century composers. The widespread availability of recordings of many styles and eras means that twentieth century composers must compete with the music of previous generations (Hamm, Nettl, & Byrnside, 1975).

Popular Music

In general, investigators have not assessed preferences for popular music to the degree they deserve. A view that popular music appeals to only some broad undifferentiated mass, victimized by an inferior culture, is just not true. All people have specific and individual tastes (Denisoff, 1976). With the onset of television (which radically altered network radio), development of FM broadcasting, changes in recording technology, and the rise of an affluent youth culture in the 1950s and succeeding cultures since, radio stations developed numerous formats centered on various musical styles, several of which could be called "popular" as a way of marketing audiences to advertisers.

In the United States, and by extension to much of the world, the development of separate popular music cultures has many implications for musical preferences. From roughly 1930 to the early 1950s, popular music was aimed predominantly at an adult white middle class culture. Music popular with one generation generally was popular with another. Country, African-American, and folk styles were alive and well, but they had largely a regional appeal. After about 1955, popular music became extensively fragmented, with each style having its own values and sociological bases. Country, soul, and folk styles acquired national audiences; rock music became the music of youth (Frith, 1981; Hamm, Nettl, & Byrnside, 1975). Today, audiences exist for numerous styles, often with confusing and conflicting labels. In a survey of the then existing radio formats, Barnes (1988) identified the following music-based styles, many of which (but not all) represent a type of popular music: adult contemporary (basically rock but not "hard" rock), album-oriented rock (a bit "wilder"), beautiful music, big band, contemporary hit radio (a melange of basically rock-like styles), classical, contemporary Christian radio, country, easy listening, gold (basically older rock music), Hispanic, jazz (rare), "music of your life" (essentially from the one-dominant-style pre-rock period), new age, nostalgia, quiet storm (a format aimed at primarily African-American audiences), and urban contemporary. "Alternative" rock is a force in some areas.[4]

Popular music does not lack aesthetic bases. Frith (1985) indicates that popular music fulfills four social functions: It helps individuals in self-identity, relates public and private emotional lives, shapes popular memory and sense of time, and becomes something possessed, as in members of a group proclaiming "this is *our* music." Four aesthetic factors enable fulfillment of the social functions. One factor is popular music's "intentional" complexity, due to manipulation of individual sounds within simple forms, rather than the "extensional" complexity of art music, due to extension of basic themes through various compositional devices such as augmentation, variation, and counterpoint. Another is use of the voice as an expressive instrument, beyond any particular words. A third factor is the possibility of analyzing and classifying popular music into ideological categories; a fourth, which, of course, exists for art music as well, is the association of particular sounds with particular times and places.

Within popular styles, preferences may change quite rapidly. A somewhat different phenomenon is the convergence toward one popular style. In visiting American music classrooms, the writers have noticed that overt group musical preferences narrow with advancing grade level. First, second, and third graders generally will listen to brief excerpts of a variety of musical styles without undue protest. The children accept the sound of a trained soprano, ethnic musics, and ambiguous electronic sounds. In fourth grade and beyond, students will cover their ears, cringe, and look around to ascertain that sufficient numbers of peers are doing the same thing. The preferred music becomes rock or, occasionally, country.

About twenty years ago, studies by Greer, Dorow, and Hanser (1973), Greer et al. (1973), and Greer, Dorow, and Randall (1974) showed decreasing interest in nonrock music with advancing grade level. Assessments of attitudes toward music conducted as part of the National Assessment of Educational Progress showed increasing rock preferences with increasing age. More extensive studies, with consideration of location as well as grade and age, are needed to ascertain the extent to which rock's dominance continues today, especially given the diversity of available styles.

---

[4]Labels attached to musical styles may be quite confusing. One can gain thorough familiarity with a style only by listening to it, and styles constantly evolve. Consequently, any documentation of stylistic categories is open to interpretation.

Summary of Existing Preferences

Existing preferences for Western art ("classical") music show a strong tendency to prefer music of the eighteen and nineteenth centuries. Such preferences may result from contemporary composers' excessive deviations from compositional norms as well as from listeners' personal qualities. Popular music requires investigation, although American popular music clearly is "popular" over much of the world. In the elementary school years, American students' preferences appear to converge toward rock or country music, which may make comprehensive education in a variety of musical styles difficult, especially beyond the first years of elementary school.

Influences on Musical Preferences

Musical preferences are more than an interaction of inherent musical characteristics and individual psychological and social variables. Societal pressures influence preferences. A person making a musical choice considers opinions of other persons who are significant in his or her life, as well as cultural messages in and about the music.

Experiments by Greer, Dorow, and Hanser (1973) and Dorow (1977) suggested that teacher approval could influence elementary school students' preferences. Shortly after the Second World War, Rigg (1948) showed that the rate of increased enjoyment for repeated compositions could be altered by providing propaganda-based information regarding Nazi Germany. Johnstone and Katz (1957) found that peers influenced teenage girls' musical preferences, with highly popular girls conforming more closely to neighborhood norms regarding songs and disk jockeys than did less popular girls. Inglefield (1974) showed that ninth graders tended to alter their expressed musical preferences, especially for jazz, to conform to those of acknowledged peer leaders. Such studies require a cautious interpretation because public expression of a view in accordance with that of an authority figure, peer leader, or perceived acceptable sentiment does not necessarily mean private belief.

Abeles (1980) extensively reviewed literature regarding musical preference and taste. He concluded that personality factors and emotional states are related to preference, but further exploration of the specific nature of those relationships is necessary. Little evidence exists that gender has any consistent influence on preferences. Socioeconomic status and musical preference show diverse relationships; Abeles believes that a lack of standardized measures of socioeconomic status complicates such studies. Correlational evidence suggests uncertain and modest relationships between musical aptitude or achievement and preference.

In examining studies in which researchers manipulated variables to investigate their effects on preferences, Abeles noted that long-term musical training may result in increased preference for "classical" or "concert" music, but effects of short-term training are unclear. One variable which clearly does influence preference is *repetition:* Familiarity enhances preference—to a point.

Abeles's review of literature regarding longer-term commitments (i.e., musical taste) suggests that women generally attach more importance to "classical" music than do men, that racial differences in taste exist, and that social class and political views may interact to influence taste. Although no "standardized" taste exists, mass media, peer groups, and musical experience all may influence taste.

LeBlanc (1982) created a detailed comprehensive model of the sources of variation in musical preference and taste. His hierarchical classification sorts variables which influence the listener as well as variables which result from the listener's actions in making preferential judgments. While the model does not predict what judgment any particular listener will make regarding a piece of music, it is quite useful in detailing many of the processes that comprise a preference judgment.

The "bottom" level of LeBlanc's model includes nine classes of input variables that characterize the situation in which the listener experiences the music. Four classes are primarily properties of the musical stimulus: physical (acoustical) properties, complexity, referential meaning, and performance quality. Media, peer group, family, authority figures, and incidental conditioning complete the input variables. The relative importance of the input variables will vary with individuals; the model makes no suggestion that any one variable class is more or less important than any other.

The input variables and interactions among them lead into LeBlanc's seventh level, physiological enabling conditions. The listener's auditory pathway must be able to receive the musical input, his or her brain must recognize pertinent extramusical variables as relevant to the music, and he or she must be sufficiently free from pain or other physiological emergency.

When a listener encounters the input variables, he or she will receive them to the extent that physiological enabling conditions permit. However, without basic attention, LeBlanc's sixth level, no further meaningful musical awareness or judgment can occur. Thus, this level is a "gate": If the "gate" is closed, the music is largely meaningless. Whether or not to give "basic" attention to a stimulus is a conscious choice. The most elegant lesson in music appreciation goes for naught if the listener, for whatever reason, elects to not give the music attention.[5]

At the fifth level, the listener's current affective state "filters" the musical input to which the listener has elected to give basic attention. The individual's mood will influence his or her further musical processing and judgments. For example, "happy" music usually will interact differently with a "sad" mood than will "sad" music.[6]

Auditory sensitivity (which here means sensitivity to particular aspects of musical sounds, not basic perception or reception), musical ability and training, personality, gender, ethnic group, socioeconomic status, and maturity are relatively stable personal characteristics which comprise LeBlanc's fourth level. A person may be especially sensitive to phrasing, particular timbres, or rhythms, perhaps overly so in relation to other aspects. Performance skill on a particular instrument may sensitize the listener to literature featuring that instrument; an experienced French horn player certainly has a different sensitivity to Strauss's *Till Eulenspiegel* or the Mozart horn concerti than a listener who is unfamiliar with the horn. Remembering what was heard formerly as a guide to what one is hearing now can be crucial for organization.

So, input variables characterizing the listening experience comprise a musical stimulus. The listener attends to that stimulus to the extent that he or she is physiologically able and personally willing. After interaction with the current affective state, the musical input is influenced by personal characteristics and interactions among them. Now comes a change from variables that influence the listener to variables that result from the listener's actions.

The change occurs at the model's level three, where the listener actively *processes* the input. Processing may include labelling stimulus aspects, such as the formal sections, instruments, style, and likely composer. The listener may consider extramusical aspects, including images of what the music may "say" or "mean." He or she may establish musical expectancies, which then are confirmed or disconfirmed.

After actively processing the input at the third level, the listener makes a decision at the second level: He or she either decides that a judgment is possible or decides that more information is necessary. When desired, the listener seeks further information, of a musical or

---

[5]By definition, if the listener gives conscious attention to what is intended to be background music, the ersatz background music is failing in its function. Since background music is intended to be heard *"but not actively or purposely listened to"* (Mussulman, 1974, p. 93; italics added), LeBlanc's model can not apply to true background music.

[6]This by no means reduces music's potential to alter a mood. The current affective state may change as the listener experiences the music.

nonmusical nature, through repeated listening with heightened attention: New input passes "up" the hierarchy.

At the very "top" of LeBlanc's hierarchy is the preference judgment, a decision based on the combination of all the variables at the lower levels. The listener *accepts* or *rejects* the musical input. In the event of acceptance, the model assumes repetition until satiation. As stimulus conditions change, or as listener conditions change, the judgment may change.

People will vary in their relative importance of the model's variables and variable categories, but almost all individuals who are able to hear music will share many of the model's aspects. Even people who generally are considered "deviant" or "different" in some way—be it due to mental retardation, a physical, sensory, or motor impairment, or social deviation—are influenced by many of the variables, and do process the input in some way. While the *amount* of perceived stimulus complexity, authority figure influence, basic attention, or other influence variables may differ drastically (in either direction) from what most other people experience, there will be *some* amount.

Complexity, one of LeBlanc's input variables, may be an especially important influence on musical preference. As used here, complexity refers to how intricate, ornate, or confusing a stimulus appears; it is a matter of subjective judgment. In appearance, function, and operation, an automobile is more complex than a toy wagon. To Western listeners, a Bach fugue usually appears more musically complex than a European or American folk song. In information theory terms, a lack of redundancy results in excessive information, which increases complexity. Complexity may be a function of uncertainty, unfamiliarity, and a resulting lack of expectancy. As is the case with other psychological constructs, complexity never can be measured directly, but it can be estimated and quantified by evaluating stimulus properties or people's behaviors.

Investigators may analyze complexity multidimensionally through factor analysis and/or multidimensional scaling of semantic differential, Likert scale, or paired or triadic comparison data. Possible underlying dimensions may relate to melodic direction and ornamentation, harmonic changes and textures, rhythmic regularity, and the degree to which the music meets expectancies.[7] A simpler approach to measuring complexity may be based on observers' immediate impressions of apparent complexity. In such a *global* approach, *why* something seems relatively complex or simple is not immediately important; it is enough to say that a stimulus has a certain amount of complexity because of the

---

[7]For a discussion of factor analysis, multidimensional scaling, and other multivariate techniques in the context of experimental research, see Asmus and Radocy (1992).

way people react to it. A global approach recognizes that people may vary considerably in why they make particular complexity judgments. For some listeners, an overall impression of a piece of music may include a degree of apparent complexity which defies analysis. For others, rhythm, harmony, melody, or another musical property may override other properties as a basis for complexity. The authors lean toward a global approach to measuring apparent complexity.

Conceiving musical preference as a function of complexity is not new. Berlyne (1971) and McMullen (1980) alluded to musical affect having a particular relationship to music's structural complexity, a relationship describable as an inverted U-shaped curve, in mathematical terms, a *quadratic* function.[8]

One important development regarding preference as a quadratic function of complexity is Walker's (1980) "hedgehog" theory, so named because the theory has one explanation for many situations, just as the spiny little European animal rolls into a ball in response to many stimuli. Walker (p. 1) states the theory in his own words as "Psychological events nearest optimum complexity are preferred. Occurrence produces simplification." The theory presumes an optimal complexity level for any stimulus class, including music. Preference is highest when the stimulus is at the optimal complexity level. Excessive complexity results in less preference, as does excessive simplicity. Too much complexity causes the listener to cease attempting to process the stimulus; too much simplicity causes boredom. As a stimulus recurs, as in repeated listening to a musical composition, it theoretically simplifies. If the stimulus moves closer to the optimum complexity level, preference increases; if it moves further away, preference decreases. If optimal complexity changes, the curve shifts in one direction or the other, and a particular stimulus's relative position on the newly shifted curve may change.

Although optimal complexity levels vary among and within individuals, each individual has an optimal complexity level for a stimulus class at any particular time. A group of people can provide an average estimate of the complexity of each object in a stimulus set, such as a collection of musical examples. Heyduk (1975), employing four compositions specifically composed to vary in complexity and a 13-point rating scale, demonstrated the expected complexity-preference relationship as well as reduced complexity with repetition.

Using "real" examples of Western art music rather than contrived examples, Radocy (1982) investigated preference as a function of com-

---

[8]In a quadratic function, as variable X increases, variable Y increases—for a while. Then as variable X continues to increase, variable Y decreases: Hence, the descriptive use of "inverted U."

plexity and familiarity, and complexity as a function of familiarity. As would be expected if a quadratic relationship exists, subjects indeed preferred the examples that they judged as moderately complex. In general, the more familiar the example, the more it was preferred. Although familiarity is supposed to produce simplification, there was no simple relationship between familiarity and judged complexity. A systematic procedure featuring repetition within the confines of a designated time period may be necessary for occurrence to produce simplification. Hargreaves (1984) later found that repetitions over weekly intervals caused changes in preference, presumably due to changes in optimal complexity levels.

Desired or optimal complexity may interact with the social situation in which the music is heard, as Konecni (1982) demonstrated in a series of studies. In one study, subjects working on a relatively complex task preferred to listen to simpler melodies than subjects working on simple tasks. In other studies, an experimental confederate selectively aroused some subjects by insulting them as they worked on nonmusical tasks. In a study where subjects could choose to hear simple or complex melodies following their work times, insulted subjects preferred simpler melodies while uninsulted subjects had no particular preference for simple or complex melodies. In a study where subjects had a chance for vengeance by administering what they thought were painful electric shocks to the confederate, Konecni formed four listening groups from combinations of simplicity, complexity, and comfortable or excessively loud loudness levels. A control group deliberated in silence; the listening groups heard their assigned condition as "background" music while deciding whether or not to shock the accomplice. Uninsulted subjects generally were not aggressive toward the accomplice, except for uninsulted subjects who were exposed to loud complex melodies: These subjects were statistically as aggressive as the insulted control group members! (Konecni suggests that people aroused by loud complex music may overreact to relatively mild annoyances that they ordinarily would ignore.) Insulted subjects who heard loud complex melodies during deliberation periods were the most aggressive. Moderate aggression characterized insulted subjects who heard relatively soft complex melodies or loud simple melodies. Insulted subjects who heard softer *simple* melodies showed aggression that was significantly lower than insulted control group subjects, and, in a few cases, lower than that of some uninsulted subjects who heard loud complex melodies. Melodies varying in complexity apparently have different effects on antisocial behavior, both as functions of themselves and in combination with anger.

Performer identification regarding gender and race may play a role in expressed preferences. Killian (1990) found that junior high students, particularly males, generally preferred performers of the same race and gender as their own. McCrary (1993) found that African-American middle school students gave stronger preferences to the music for which they identified the performer as African-American. White students were nearly equal in their preferences for African-American and white performers.

Altering Preferences

Musical preferences may be altered. One's less preferred style may become a more preferred style, and a listener may broaden his or her range of choices. Much music requires learning through formal instruction before a listener may experience more than some sort of sound bath. K. Mueller (1970) stressed that listeners cannot hear accurately because they are not taught to hear musical details.[9] After studying college and high school students' thematic recognition ability and finding that typical students showed positive responses toward diverse styles, including classical and jazz, Duerksen (1968) noted the potential for developing and expanding preferences through education. Zenatti (1993) believes that musical taste is partly cognitive, so enhanced cognitive processing ability should facilitate taste for more complex contemporary musical styles.

Seventh graders who were encouraged to be creative in activities related to contemporary music outscored a control group, who followed an existing curriculum guide, on a test of musical understanding (Archibeque, 1966). Interestingly, all seventh graders in the study developed an interest in contemporary music regardless of prior training, grades, or initial attitudes.

Repetition, a process for making the unfamiliar familiar, may be useful in altering and expanding musical preference. Mull (1940) had undergraduate musicians listen to obscure works of Bach, Chopin, and Brahms, and raise their hands to indicate "high spots." With repeated listening, as the music became more familiar, the lengths of the "high spots" increased. Listeners evidently became aroused by anticipation of newly familiar sections and raised their hands in anticipation. Getz (1966) found that seventh graders' preferences for string ensemble excerpts increased over ten weeks as a result of familiarity through repetition.

---

[9]To "hear musical details" means to hear various nuances, recall necessary information for recognizing musical form, and relate a myriad of factual information about the music and its performance. A listener's ability to verbalize about the music is evidence of detailed hearing. Hierarchical perceptual structuring, discussed earlier, where "details" of a musical surface structure are subsumed into a deeper structure, may exist without formal musical instruction as a result of experience in a musical culture.

Faster tempos usually elicited greater preference. Schuckert and McDonald (1968) found that four- to six-year-old children altered their musical preferences between jazz and classical music after being required to listen individually to the lesser preferred style during quiet play periods. While previous research (LeBlanc, 1981; LeBlanc & Cote, 1983; LeBlanc et al., 1988) amply demonstrates that children usually prefer fast to slow music, Moskovitz (1992), assessing fourth graders' selections of fast vs. slow music, found that repetition of slow baroque, classical, romantic, and atonal art music increased preferences for slow excerpts.

Familiarity through repetition will not guarantee an increase in preference, of course. As a prelude to attending concerts featuring contemporary woodwind quintets, elementary, junior high school, and high school students in a midwestern city heard tapes in advance to familiarize them with the music (Hornyak, 1966). Familiarity indeed increased the elementary students' positive response to the contemporary compositions, but it made no difference for junior high pupils. The high school students showed a *less* positive response as a result of preliminary hearing. Cook (1990, p. 174) cautions that instructing people about particular music will not automatically increase enjoyment, and that enjoying music does not require understanding its structural details (pp. 164–165).

In a broad sense, style rather than specific examples may be the basis for familiarity. In a study of the effects of attending an in-school opera performance, Sims (1992) found that attendance had a positive effect on attitudes toward attending opera, opera singing, and the performers, as indicated by significant differences in favor of fifth and sixth graders who attended the opera. Fourth graders were consistently more positive, with little difference between those who saw the opera and those who did not. Opera is a form for which young people generally do not care (LeBlanc, 1981; LeBlanc & Sherrill, 1986; Thompson, 1991).

In a study relating undergraduate nonmusic majors' multicultural attitudes and their preferences for and knowledge of music of Africa, China, India, Indonesia, Japan, Korea, the Middle East, and Thailand, Fung (1994) found a significant relationship between overall scores on a multicultural attitude inventory and overall preference scores. There was no significant relationship between preference and recognition. Significant relationships existed between the students' years of study of foreign language and overall preference, as well as between year in school and overall preference. Apparently, certain social familiarity and attitudes may influence preference when all of the music is relatively unfamiliar.

Musical preferences can be altered, but the direction of alteration is not always predictable. The philosophical question of whether or not preferences *should* be altered is not answered satisfactorily. Music educators and critics should remember that musical preferences result from a complex interaction of personal and social factors, all of which are not under the control of any one institution. An expansion of preferences may be attempted in educational settings with reasonable chances of success, but a reordering of musical preferences in some arbitrary direction is questionable. Given the many variables that interact to influence preference, the relative flexibility of younger students, and the importance of musical expectations, one thing that music education can and should do is to provide preschool and elementary school children with a wide variety of experiences in listening to, performing, and creating many musical styles.

Summary

The major points in this chapter include the following:
1. Musical preferences result from a complex mixture of musical and human characteristics.
2. "Good" music may be "good" because of inherent structural aspects; it may be "good" because of what people say about it in context.
3. Preferences may be related to various personality aspects.
4. Group tendencies exist in musical preference, especially for certain predominantly German composers of Western art music.
5. The apparent reverence for the past observed in classical music is a new occurrence in music history; it probably is attributable to perpetuation of tradition through formal education and the widespread availability of music from different eras as well as radical creations of nonconforming contemporary composers.
6. Popular music exists in many continually evolving forms; each has its own cultural orientation, sociological base, and market.
7. The preferences of many American school children focus increasingly on rock or country music with advancing grade levels.
8. Musical preference and taste are a function of many variables, including variables in the music, short-term and long-term variables in the listener, and variables in the conditions under which the music is experienced.
9. Musical preferences may be altered and expanded through education, but the results are not always predictable.

References

Abeles, H. F. (1980). Responses to music. In D. A. Hodges (Ed.), *Handbook of music psychology* (pp. 105–140). Lawrence, KS: National Association for Music Therapy.

Adorno, T. W. (1976). *Introduction to the sociology of music* (E. B. Ashton, trans.). New York: Seabury Press.

Archibeque, C. P. (1966). Developing a taste for contemporary music. *Journal of Research in Music Education, 14,* 142–148.

Asmus, E. P., & Radocy, R. E. (1992). Quantitative analysis. In R. Colwell (Ed.), *Handbook of research on music teaching and learning* (pp. 141–183). New York: Schirmer Books.

Barnes, K. (1988). Top 40 radio: A fragment of the imagination. In S. Frith (Ed.), *Facing the music* (pp. 8–50). New York: Pantheon Books.

Berlyne, D. E. (1971). *Aesthetics and psychobiology.* New York: Appleton-Century-Crofts.

Cattell, R. B., & Anderson, J. C. (1953). The measurement of personality and behavior disorders by the IPAT music preference test. *Journal of Applied Psychology, 37,* 446–454.

Chancellor, G. R. (1975). Aesthetic value in music: Implications for music education from the classic literature of the field (Doctoral dissertation, Northwestern University, 1974). *Dissertation Abstracts International, 35,* 6493A. (University Microfilms No. 75-7886)

Cook, N. (1990). *Music, imagination, and culture.* Oxford: Clarendon Press.

Denisoff, R. S. (1976). Massification and popular music: A review. *Journal of Popular Culture, 9,* 886–894.

Dollinger, S. (1993). Research note: Personality and music preference: Extraversion and excitement seeking or openness to experience? *Psychology of Music, 21,* 73–77.

Dorow, L. G. (1977). The effect of teacher approval/disapproval ratios on student music selection and concert attentiveness. *Journal of Research in Music Education, 25,* 32–40.

Duerksen, G. L. (1968). A study of the relationship between the perception of musical processes and the enjoyment of music. *Council for Research in Music Education, 12,* 1–8.

Eysenck, H. J., & Eysenck, H. B. G. (1976). *Psychoticism as a dimension of personality.* London: Hodder and Stoughton.

Farnsworth, P. R. (1966). Musicological attitudes on eminence. *Journal of Research in Music Education, 14,* 41–44.

Farnsworth, P. R. (1969). *The social psychology of music* (2nd ed.). Ames: Iowa State University Press.

Frith, S. (1981). *Sound effects.* New York: Pantheon Books.

Frith, S. (1985). Towards an aesthetic of popular music. In R. Leppert & S. McClary (Eds.), *Music and society: The politics of composition, performance and reception* (pp. 133–149). Cambridge: Cambridge University Press.

Fung, C. V. (1994). Undergraduate nonmusic majors' world music preference and multicultural attitudes. *Journal of Research in Music Education, 42,* 45–57.

Getz, R. P. (1966). The effects of repetition on listening response. *Journal of Research in Music Education, 14,* 178–192.

Glasgow, M. R., Cartier, A. M., & Wilson, G. D. (1985). Conservatism, sensation seeking, and music preference. *Personality and Individual Differences, 6,* 395–396.

Greer, R. D., Dorow, L., & Hanser, S. (1973). Music discrimination training and the music selection behavior of nursery and primary level children. *Council for Research in Music Education, 35,* 30–43.

Greer, R. D., Dorow, L., & Randall, A. (1974). Music listening preferences of elementary school children. *Journal of Research in Music Education, 22,* 284–291.

Greer, R. D., Dorow, L. G., Wachhaus, G., & White, E. R. (1973). Adult approval and students' music selection behavior. *Journal of Research in Music Education, 21,* 345–354.

Hahn, M. E. (1954). A proposed technique for investigating the relationship between musical preferences and personality structure. Unpublished doctoral dissertation, University of Kansas.

Hamm, C. E., Nettl, B., & Byrnside, R. (1975). *Contemporary music and music cultures.* Englewood Cliffs, NJ: Prentice-Hall.

Hargreaves, D. J. (1984). The effects of repetition on liking for music *Journal of Research in Music Education, 32,* 3547.

Heyduk, R. G. (1975). Rated preference of musical compositions as it related to complexity and exposure frequency. *Perception and Psychophysics, 17,* 84–91.

Higgins, K. M. (1991). *The music of our lives.* Philadelphia: Temple University Press.

Hornyak, R. R. (1966). An analysis of student attitudes toward contemporary American music. *Council for Research in Music Education, 8,* 1–14.

Inglefield, H. G. (1974, March). Conformity behavior reflected in the musical preferences of adolescents. Paper presented at the meeting of the Music Educators National Conference, Anaheim, CA.

Johnstone, J., & Katz, E. (1957). Youth and popular music: A study of the sociology of taste. *American Journal of Sociology, 62,* 563–568.

Keston, M. J., & Pinto, I. M. (1955). Possible factors influencing musical preference. *Journal of Genetic Psychology, 86,* 101–113.

Killian, J. N. (1990). Effect of model characteristics on musical preferences of junior high students. *Journal of Research in Music Education, 38,* 115–123.

Koh, S. D. (1965). Scaling musical preferences. *Journal of Experimental Psychology, 70,* 79–82.

Koh, S. D. (1967). Time-error in comparison of preferences for musical excerpts. *American Journal of Psychology, 80,* 171–185.

Konecni, V. J. (1982). Social interaction and musical preference. In D. Deutsch (Ed.), *The psychology of music* (pp. 497–516). New York: Academic Press.

LeBlanc, A. (1981). Effects of style, tempo, and performing medium on children's music preference. *Journal of Research in Music Education, 29,* 143–156.

LeBlanc, A. (1982). An interactive theory of musical preference. *Journal of Music Therapy, 19,* 28–45.

LeBlanc, A., Colman, J., McCrary, J., Sherrill, C., & Malin, S. (1988). Tempo preferences of different age music listeners. *Journal of Research in Music Education, 36,* 156–168.

LeBlanc, A., & Cote, R. (1983). Effects of tempo and performing medium on children's music preference. *Journal of Research in Music Education, 31,* 57–66.

LeBlanc, A., & Sherrill, R. (1986). Effect of vocal vibrato and performer's sex on children's music preference. *Journal of Research in Music Education, 34,* 222–237.

McCrary, J. (1993). Effects of listeners' and performers' race on music preferences. *Journal of Research in Music Education, 41,* 200–211.

McMullen, P. T. (1980). Music as a perceived stimulus object and affective responses: An alternative theoretical framework. In D. A. Hodges (Ed.), *Handbook of music psychology* (pp. 183–193). Lawrence, KS: National Association for Music Therapy.

McMullen, P. T., & Arnold, M. J. (1976). Preference and interest as functions of distributional redundancy in rhythmic sequences. *Journal of Research in Music Education, 24,* 22–31.

Meyer, L. (1956). *Emotion and meaning in music.* Chicago: University of Chicago Press.

Moskovitz, E. M. (1992). The effect of repetition on tempo preference of elementary children. *Journal of Research in Music Education, 40,* 193–203.

Mueller, J. H. (1967). The aesthetic gap between consumer and composer. *Council for Research in Music Education, 15,* 151–158.

Mueller, K. (1970). The other side of the record. *Council for Research in Music Education, 21,* 22–31.

Mull, H. K. (1940). Preferred regions in music compositions and the effect of repetition upon them. *American Journal of Psychology, 53,* 583–586.

Mussulman, J. A. (1974). *The uses of music: An introduction to music in contemporary life.* Englewood Cliffs, NJ: Prentice-Hall.

Payne, E. (1980). Towards an understanding of music appreciation. *Psychology of Music, 8,* 31–41.

Poland, B. W. (1970). The content of graduate studies in music education: Music history and music theory. In H. L. Cady (Ed.), *Graduate studies in music education* (pp. 9–28). Columbus, OH: Ohio State University School of Music.

Radocy, R. E. (1982). Preference for classical music: A test for the hedgehog. *Psychology of Music, Special,* 91–95.

Radocy, R. E. (1986). On quantifying the uncountable in musical behavior. *Council for Research in Music Education, 88,* 22–31.

Rawlings, D., Hodge, M., Sherr, D., & Dempsey, A. (1995). Toughmindedness and preference for musical excerpts, categories and triads. *Psychology of Music, 23,* 63–80.

Reimer, B. (1989). *A philosophy of music education* (2nd ed.). Englewood Cliffs, NJ: Prentice-Hall.

Rigg, M. C. (1948). Favorable versus unfavorable propaganda in the enjoyment of music. *Journal of Experimental Psychology, 38,* 78–81.

Schuckert, R. F., & McDonald, R. L. (1968). An attempt to modify the musical preferences of preschool children. *Journal of Research in Music Education, 16,* 39–45.

Schwadron, A. A. (1967). *Aesthetics: Dimensions for music education.* Washington: Music Educators National Conference.

Sims, W. (1992). Effects of attending an in-school opera performance on attitudes of fourth-, fifth-, and sixth-grade students. *Council for Research in Music Education, 114,* 47–58.

Thompson, K. P. (1991). An examination of the consistency of junior high students' preferences for general music activities. *Update, 9* (2), 11–16.

Walker, E. L. (1980). *Psychological complexity and preference: A hedgehog theory of behavior.* Monterey, CA: Brooks/Cole.

Zenatti, A. (1993). Children's musical cognition and taste. In T. J. Tighe & W. J. Dowling (Eds.), *Psychology and music: The understanding of melody and rhythm* (pp. 177–196). Hillsdale, NJ: Lawrence Erlbaum Associates.

CHAPTER TEN

MUSICAL ABILITY AND ITS DEVELOPMENT

The measurement and prediction of musical ability and music learning are two traditional areas of the psychology of music. The first and second editions of this text reflected the tradition by devoting a single chapter to each area. Among the beneficial developments arising from contemporary research in the cognitive psychology of music is an expanding awareness of musical ability's nature and development. While an exact definition remains and probably will remain elusive, music psychologists now generally see musical ability as far more than test scores or a specific ability to "succeed" musically. Also, the study of human learning and the nature of intelligence suggests a need for a more fluid application of learning theories to the teaching and learning OF music. Recent years have seen extensive reviews of knowledge, increased understanding of a developmental sequence in musical ability, and continuing interest in multiple intelligence theory. Accordingly, this chapter interweaves a presentation of musical ability and music learning, and considers aspects of musical development and musical abnormalities. Capsules of traditional learning theories and time-honored ways of assessing musical ability also appear.

Extended Definitions

Ability suggests being "able" to do something. A person with musical ability is able to perform, create, or, perhaps, analyze music if given an opportunity. Unfortunately, people interchange the terms talent, musicality, capacity, and aptitude with ability, and opinions differ regarding the permissible degree of interchange. The definition of learning may be more clear, but one must distinguish learning from other developmental phenomena, and recognize that learning is not an automatic consequence of teaching. The following definitions represent the authors' views.

Ability is a broad term referring to being "able" to do something, regardless of how a person acquired the necessary knowledge, skills, and experience. It defies precise definition. Performing, composing, analyzing, and recalling music may be parts of musical ability. The authors hold that aptitude and capacity are within ability, and that achievement, while "off to the side, may be evidence of ability."

Aptitude, narrower than ability but broader than capacity, refers to the part of ability resulting from a combination of genetic endowments and environmental experiences with music other than formal music education. Since much of music educators' concerns for musical ability relate to predicting a potential student's musical success prior to providing opportunity for musical training, musical ability's measurement problems often are problems of measuring musical aptitude.

Capacity, a narrower term yet, refers to a part of a person's ability that he or she possesses as a result of genetic endowment and maturation. To the extent that musical capacity increases, it increases regardless of environmental influences. Superior auditory detection or discrimination ability may be a matter of capacity, although one would need to learn labels for expressing those discriminations.

Achievement refers to specific musical accomplishment, often the result of specific instruction. Reading notation, playing a specific piece of music, knowing the names of the conductors of ten major symphony orchestras, and recognizing all of the themes of Beethoven's symphonies and relating them within their formal structures exemplify specific achievement. To assess musical aptitude or capacity via tasks that require specific achievement is inappropriate, but past achievements nevertheless may indicate musical ability, which in turn may suggest possibilities for further achievements.

Other terms related to musical skill or accomplishment include *talent,* an imprecise term designating some obvious indication of ability, usually related to performance, and *musicality,* another imprecise term, referring to a state of being "musical," i.e., of being sensitive to changes in a musical stimulus. An inexperienced performer may show musicality when he or she tapers a phrase or varies dynamic levels without teacher direction; musicality also simply may mean interest in music.

Development refers to the growth and maturation process through which people go as they move from an embryonic stage, through birth, childhood, and adolescence, to an adult stage. It could include the "disdevelopment" through which many elderly people must pass. Development includes the results of physical, emotional, and cognitive maturity; it inevitably interacts with learning. Musically, people pass through stages from the earliest awareness of sounds to, at least in some cases, thorough musical literacy. Many people never "develop" beyond a stage of simple musical recognition and singing.

Learning is an observable change in behavior, due to experience, which is not attributable to anything else. (The authors pattern this definition after that which Bower and Hilgard (1981, p. 11) offer in their authoritative text.) According to this definition, without some behavioral change between two points in time, no learning has occurred in that time span. Someone who already can recite major and minor key signatures cannot "learn" to do it, although he or she obviously learned the signatures in the past. Furthermore, someone who needs to ascertain that an individual indeed has learned something requires observable evidence in behavioral form. Showing a student how to produce a trumpet tone or telling him or her how to recognize ternary form is insufficient; learning has not occurred until the previously unable student can play a tone or identify an ABA form. While some authorities may recognize so-called "latent" or "hidden" learning, i.e., the student "knows" but somehow can not show what he or she knows, latent learning is nonfunctional or even nonexistent from the standpoint of anyone, such as a music teacher, who requires tangible evidence of learning: If someone "knows," he or she can demonstrate that knowledge.

The qualification in the learning definition of "not attributable to anything else" excludes behavioral changes resulting from maturation or genetic programming. An infant does not "learn" to breathe or to shake violently in the presence of a sudden loud sound; an adolescent boy does not "learn" to grow facial hair. Breathing occurs naturally; the startle response is a reflex action, and the newly hirsute young man is displaying a secondary sexual characteristic.

With the possible exception of "automatic" perceptual subprocesses, such as eardrum and basilar membrane movement and reflexive startle responses to loud music, the development of any musical behavior requires learning, even when "musical behavior" is conceived very broadly. Genetic and maturational processes or the lack thereof will influence the forms of particular behaviors; consider the qualities of children's, men's, and women's voices, and the seventeenth century castrati. But people do not organize, analyze, or perform specific musical sounds as a result of instinct or secreted hormones. They *learn* to react to and with music.

Selected Influences on Musical Ability

The development of musical ability depends on what is *in* as well as what is *around* a person. The exact importance of heredity and environment is uncertain, although both conditions obviously are influential. This section discusses various influences.

Auditory Acuity

Music is an aural art form, so, logically, sufficient hearing sensitivity is an essential part of musical ability. Hearing impaired individuals will have difficulty experiencing music in a normal manner.[1] Musicians view various hearing ailments with alarm; contemporary performing musicians in rock bands and symphony orchestras may wear hearing protection to preserve their hearing. However, acuity, while a minimal necessity for hearing music, bears little relationship to musical ability beyond the most basic level.

In a study of continuing importance, Sherbon (1975) administered tests of melody, harmony, visual music recognition, musical memory, pitch, loudness, and timbre to undergraduate musicians and nonmusicians. Sherbon tested each subject for hearing threshold and diplacusis.[2] The musicians outperformed the nonmusicians on all but the loudness and timbre tests. However, the two groups did not differ in acuity or diplacusis, and neither acuity nor diplacusis showed a significant relationship to any of the seven sets of test scores. From the standpoint of being "able" to accomplish the required tasks, superior hearing acuity made no difference.

Genetics

Genetic endowment for specific musical accomplishment is unlikely, except for the extent to which such endowment might contribute to other abilities that might facilitate musical accomplishment: Perhaps some singers have naturally resonant vocal tracts that facilitate singing with a desirable quality; some pianists may benefit from long finger spans; fast reflexes may facilitate mastering wind instrument fingerings. These are rather specific aspects. In terms of overall musical ability, what Farnsworth (1969) called "DAR[3]-like studies," showing how Bach and Mozart were in "musical families," are as much evidence for a stimulating musical environment as they are for a strain of musically superior beings. As of yet, research has found no true musical gene or chromosome.

Belief that musical ability is largely innate does persist. Bentley (1966), basing his view in part on observing highly diverse levels of musical

---

[1] The reader should not assume that music is irrelevant for hearing impaired individuals. There are many degrees of hearing impairment, and many deaf individuals do involve themselves with music. For a discussion of music's importance in deaf culture, see Darrow (1993).

[2] Sherbon tested for *binaural diplacusis,* a condition in which an identical frequency sounds with a different pitch in each ear.

[3] The Daughters of the American Revolution (DAR) is an organization of American women who believe that their ancestors were involved in some way in the War of American Independence (1775–1783). Tracing ancestry may be especially important for such an organization, hence Farnsworth's potentially pejorative use of the term. The authors mean no offense.

ability in relatively homogeneous groups of children, maintained that musical abilities are mostly a matter of innate capacity. Scheid and Eccles (1975) suggested that the physical size of the right cerebral hemisphere's planum temporale, located just behind the primary auditory cortex, indicates genetically-coded musical ability. They called for postmortem examinations of the brains of high-ability and low-ability musicians. Twenty years later, Schlaug et al. (1995), employing positron emission topography, examined the living brains of 30 musicians and compared them with the brains of matched nonmusicians. They found a larger *left* planum temporale in musicians who had absolute pitch; such a difference did not exist between other musicians and nonmusicians. If the planum temporale can grow with environmental stimulation, neither postmortem evidence nor morphometric evidence from living brains is valid as evidence of genetically acquired differences.[4] Aggleton, Kentridge, and Good (1994) found a greater incidence of lefthandedness and mixed dominance for handedness among orchestral performers, composers, and singers of both sexes as compared with the general population, but handedness by itself is hardly a genetic predictor of musical ability.

People do differ in nonenvironmental ways, of course; it is silly to pretend that anyone can accomplish anything, given the right opportunities and education. Someone whose adult height is 150 cm (about 4 ft 11 in) is not likely to play on a professional basketball team; a child born with Down syndrome (once called Down's syndrome or mongolism) is unlikely to become a professional musician, although such a child still may have satisfying experiences with music. Nevertheless, while differences in musical ability due to innate differences in people theoretically are possible, the evidence for influence of the planum temporale, handedness, or any "natural" physiological or neurological structure is tenuous.

Musical Home

A musical home nurtures the development of musical ability. Encouragement from parents and siblings and a supportive environment may be critical. The development of absolute pitch through imprinting, discussed in Chapter Four, is but one example: The critically-timed, label-sensation connections require teaching and reinforcement. Performance is more likely later in life when young children are encouraged to perform and rewarded for doing so. The all important musical expectancies, discussed extensively in the context of information theory,

---

[4]Indeed, Schlaug et al. caution that they have no evidence regarding just how the observed planum temporale asymmetries came to exist.

hierarchical perceptual structuring, and Meyer's theory of musical enjoyment, arise from experience in a musical culture, and a supportive home enhances that culture. In a study of very young children's vocalizations, Ries (1982) found that children from a closely-knit, family-centered subculture sang spontaneous songs with definite tonality at the age of thirty months, despite evidence that tonality usually is unstable until approximately the age of five years (Dowling, 1982). A home that encourages active music making may accelerate development in comparison with a home where musical experiences are generally passive, as in listening to recordings.

Physical Features

Physical features such as teeth alignment and lip, hand, and finger sizes (which of course reflect genetic influences) may influence performing ability regarding particular instruments. The upper lip protrusion known as a Cupid's bow makes it difficult to form the characteristic flute embouchure. Children with tiny fingers have difficulty covering clarinet fingerholes, and a pronounced overbite makes forming a trumpet embouchure difficult. Dental trauma, vocal nodules, and physical debilitation resulting from muscular overuse or misuse may cause serious difficulties for experienced performers. Ability in a specific performance medium is only a part of musical ability, however. If physical influences on overall musical ability are important, they should relate to many aspects of musical ability.

Creativity

Composition and improvisation obviously require creativity; the composer or performer creates a new arrangement of sounds. Performance of notated music may be creative (although some may say it is more recreative), and a person can listen in creative ways. Since music is at least partly a creative art form, attempts to relate musical ability to some general creative ability are logical, but explaining musical ability as a function of creativity is largely unsuccessful, partly because neither musical ability nor creativity are defined adequately.

Creativity may require production, or it simply may be a process. Guilford (1957) stressed that creative ability consists of numerous factors: Fluency, flexibility, originality, and evaluative factors are particularly important for a creative artist. Moore (1966) concluded that creativity requires above average intelligence, but it is not synonymous with intelligence. Radocy (1971) suggested that creativity may be in the eyes and ears of the beholder: If an observer judges some product or act as creative, rather than ordinary, unmusical, "wrong," or bizarre, it *is* creative, at least for the observer.

Although dated and subject to criticism, the Getzels and Jackson (1962) study of creativity and intelligence remains relevant because of the view of creativity implied by the researchers' measuring techniques. They identified creativity through tests requiring multiple associative responses to stimulus words, suggestions of novel and nonstereotyped uses for common objects, detection of simple geometric figures hidden within complex patterns, composition of endings for four fables, and composition of mathematical problems from four paragraphs containing numerical statements. Getzels and Jackson compared two student groups, one deemed highly intelligent and one highly creative, for fantasy via stories the students wrote about pictures and via pictures they drew to portray given situations. Running throughout is a presumption that the creative student is inventive, nonconforming, and prone to unconventional and even bizarre ideas. For example, a creative student, when asked to depict children playing tag in a schoolyard, submitted a blank white paper and said that the children were playing during a blizzard. The student describing a picture of a man in an airplane seat as a scientist, travelling to the moon, who is about to be consumed by a mass of protoplasm that he mistakenly believes is a pillow, also was creative. Or were the students sarcastic? Or "creative" in avoiding effort?[5] Any student with a sense of humor and ability to spot absurdities in daily life probably could be highly creative if creativity is synonymous with inventiveness.

Musical ability may relate to creativity in many facets of music, especially in composition, improvisation, and arranging, but divergent thinking, inventiveness, and bizarre behavior are hindrances in the context of ordinary musical development and instruction. Creativity may characterize the musically able, but without discipline and direction, creativity is insufficient to make a person musically successful.

Intelligence

Intelligence logically is an important influence on musical ability. A relatively intelligent person ought to be able to cope with musical prob-

---

[5]Turning in a blank paper with a "creative" label may remind the reader of other clever student responses to assignments. Mehrens and Lehmann (1973) describe the student who, in response to a physics test question regarding measuring the height of a tall building by using a barometer, proposed several creative answers, including offering to give the building superintendent the barometer if the superintendent would tell him how tall the building was. More brazen, perhaps, was the student who, when asked to write a 500-word English theme about an object in his room, wrote, "In my room is a clock. The clock goes tick-tock, tick-tock,...." Are these students creative?

lems with more success than a relatively unintelligent person, if one defines intelligence as coping with intellectual demands of the environment. As with creativity, definition problems have clouded the relationship of intelligence and musical ability. Different measurement tools and different conceptions of intelligence imply different definitions. We will consider some traditional relationships, the phenomenon of the idiot savant, and current conceptions of a "musical" intelligence.

Intelligence in the traditional sense of academic abilities may not be essential for musical ability. Gordon (1968) reported that musical aptitude scores often related only slightly to intelligence, although, in European studies, performance ratings related more highly to intelligence. He found (not surprisingly) that his own musical aptitude measures were better predictors of musical success, as measured by etude performance, teacher ratings, and a notation test after three years of instruction, than were intelligence tests. Yet, the logic that intelligence *ought* to be related to musical success persists.

Sergeant and Thatcher (1974) demonstrated that apparent weak relationships between tests of musical ability and intelligence likely are a statistical artifact caused by the tests' less-than-perfect reliability and validity. Correlation techniques, often used to relate musical ability and intelligence, are such that a relatively small change in absolute rank on one variable as compared with absolute rank on another variable can produce a spuriously low relation. On the basis of three experiments employing various measures of intellectual and musical abilities, where data were analyzed via analysis of variance and trend analysis, Sergeant and Thatcher concluded that all highly musical people appear to be highly intelligent, but not all highly intelligent people are highly musical: The relationship goes far more in one direction than in the other. Musical ability requires an interaction between intelligence and appropriate environmental stimulation. Phillips (1976) also suggested a close relationship between musical ability and intelligence, believed to result from a common environmental cause: A home promoting musical ability also is likely to promote intelligence.

Idiots savant constitute a continuing dilemma for a close relationship of intelligence, conceived as intellectual ability, and musical ability. An idiot savant[6] is a person of subnormal intelligence who displays remarkable ability in one or more narrow areas. Anastasi and Levee (1960)

---

[6]A "savant" is a scholar, so an idiot savant is an "idiotic scholar." While today "idiot" is a pejorative term connoting personal stupidity or irresponsibility, at one time it had a relatively precise technical meaning. A "moron" was a person in the highest functioning group of individuals having subnormal intelligence, an "imbecile" was in the middle group, and an "idiot" was in the lowest group.

reported a case of a thirty-eight-year-old man with exceptional keyboard ability. He appeared to concentrate only when he played the piano, often for six to nine hours daily. He was an excellent sight reader and could play by ear; his preference was for music of the classic period. He also had a phenomenal verbatim memory for printed passages and events which occurred one month or more in the past. Brain damaged due to encephalitis, the man did not walk until eighteen months and did not talk until age five. He hummed tunes before he talked, and a speech therapist taught him to speak by using song lyrics.

Sloboda, Hermelin, and O'Connor (1985) described the case of NP, an idiot savant residing in a residential home for autistic persons. Although NP displayed bizarre behaviors, rarely produced spontaneous speech, avoided looking at people, and had minimal verbal intelligence, he was delighted to play the piano, and he had a phenomenal ability to memorize music. In a comparison with the memorization skills of a professional pianist, NP easily "outmemorized" the professional in the task of memorizing a piece by Grieg, but he did not do well at all in memorizing an atonal work by Bartok. The investigators reported error rates of 8 percent for NP and 63 percent for the professional on the Grieg; for the Bartok, the corresponding rates were 80 and 14 percent. Of considerable interest to students of cognitive musical processing, NP's ability apparently is based in structures and relations of tonal music. Readers may find further documentation of profound musical abilities accompanying profound intellectual deficits in Miller (1989).

Idiots savant are considerably less of a problem in multiple intelligence theory, where intelligence is conceived as a collection of loosely related skills. Historically, psychologists have conceived of intelligence as a set of loosely related specific skills (Thurstone, 1947) or as a set of closely related skills, dominated by one general factor (Spearman, 1927). Parallel beliefs regarding musical ability are found in Seashore's (1938) "theory of specifics" and Mursell's (1937) "omnibus theory." Occasionally, people group the two respective schools of thought as "foxes" (a fox has many ways to avoid predators) and "hedgehogs" (a hedgehog has basically one response—rolling into a ball—to many situations) (Gardner, 1993; Walker, 1980).

Gardner (1993) developed a theory of multiple intelligences which includes a *musical* intelligence, as well as linguistic, logical-mathematical, spatial, bodily-kinesthetic, and personal intelligences. His criteria for an intelligence (pp. 62–67) include (a) potential isolation by brain damage; (b) the existence of idiots savant and prodigies (e.g., NP and Mozart); (c) identifiable core operations, such as sensitivity to pitch or rhythm relations; (d) a developmental history which leads to expert performance; (e) evolutionary history; (f) support from experimental psychological tasks; (g) support from psychometric findings; and (h) the ability to encode the information with which an intelligence deals in a symbol system. For Gardner, an investigator may not measure any person's intelligence adequately in one testing session, as is usually the case with studies comparing musical ability or aptitude scores with scores on a verbal intelligence measure. It might be better to measure the discrepancy between what a person can do initially and what the person can do a month after instruction, in accordance with Vygotsky's (1978) *zone of proximal development.* In any case, the intelligences do not exist in anything approaching equal amounts. A concept of a separate musical intelligence, which has its own developmental sequence, offers opportunities for assessing a person's current musical ability as a present stage in the development of musical intelligence.

Gender and Race

Gender presents an apparent paradox regarding musical ability. Girls dominate in many school musical organizations, which can be verified by examining membership lists and attending concerts and music festivals. In a nationwide examination of performers' gender as indicated by schools' and colleges' concert programs from over a thirty-year period, Zervoudakes and Tanur (1994) found that the proportion of female players among those playing historically "male" instruments (bassoon, saxophone, French horn, trumpet, trombone, euphonium, tuba, contrabass, percussion) increased, but so did the proportion of females among those playing historically "female" instruments (flute, oboe, clarinet, violin, viola).[7] Zervoudakes and Tanur conclude that gender-based segregation for instrument types has increased at the high school and college levels, although not at the elementary school level. Yet, except for certain types of vocalists, many, if not most, professional performers are males. Much of this results from sexual stereotyping and discrimination, not any inherent gender-based differences in musical ability.

Stereotypes do persist. In the nineteenth century, many middle class American females were encouraged to become musically proficient but not *too* proficient if they wanted to retain their social stature; males who studied music risked being labelled as effeminate (Koza, 1990). During the late nineteenth and early twentieth centuries, when vast numbers of

---

[7]Zervoudakes and Tanur based their instrumental gender classifications on previous research regarding gender stereotyping of instruments (Abeles & Porter, 1978; Delzell & Leppla, 1992). One could argue about any particular classification, especially if one has experienced proficient performers of the opposite gender.

people from eastern and southern Europe came to the United States and established numerous ethnic subcultures, many immigrant parents expected their children to study an instrument—often stereotyped as violin for the boys, piano for the girls (Rubin, 1973; Tawa, 1982). Over half a century ago, Gilbert (1942) administered musical aptitude measures to 500 male and 500 female college students. In general, the females outscored the males, but not when musically untrained females were compared with untrained males. Only 231 males had any musical training; their average amount was two years. Four hundred females had an average of three-and-one-half years of private lessons. The social stereotype of women being more "artistic" was a self-perpetuating one, in Gilbert's opinion, as a result of musical training being given more readily to females. (Most of Gilbert's subjects, male and female, attended expensive private schools and were from high socioeconomic levels.) Much more recently, Koza (1994), in a study of illustrations in music-related textbooks used in middle schools, found that females were underrepresented in illustrations, despite their high degree of involvement in school music, and illustrations tended to reflect gender-based stereotypes, such as depicting females as amateurs, rather than professionals.

On the basis of data gathered in the creation, design, and improvement of musical aptitude tests for elementary school children, Bentley (1966) concluded that there are no inherent gender differences in musical ability. At certain ages, many boys begin to associate musical activity, particularly singing, with feminine roles as a result of classroom gender-based stereotypes.

Figgs (1976), reviewing literature on gender discrimination and stereotypes, concluded that women have been encouraged to excel only to a certain degree (nineteenth century style?), be dependent, and avoid specialization. Stigmas regarding who should play certain instruments and who should occupy certain roles in music education have not dissipated completely. Human differences in musical ability exist, but gender differences are a cultural artifact.

Just as social conditions and beliefs may perpetuate gender-based stereotypes and encourage or discourage musical involvement, so may racial and ethnic-based expectancies encourage or discourage musical development. Such differences are cultural, not the result of any inherent differences due to being born into any particular ethnic group. African-Americans do not necessarily "have rhythm," nor are they necessarily rap artists. Not all Italians are singers. Not all Hungarians are violinists. While one may argue legitimately that "understanding" a particular musical culture requires longstanding experiences in that culture, such "understanding" results from cultural immersion, not inherent ethnicity.

Summary of Influences on Musical Ability

Musical ability is relatively uninfluenced by hearing, genetics, and physical features, provided minimal perceptual and physical capacities are present. Gender and race are irrelevant psychologically, although certainly not sociologically. Creativity is too ill-defined to be very helpful in predicting musical ability and its likely growth. Idiots savant to the contrary, it is difficult to be highly musically able without being reasonably intelligent, although one must recognize the possibility, even the probability, of different forms of intelligence, with varying relationships and interactions among them. The constituents of musical ability vary with how they are conceptualized, defined, and measured. Although the major determinants of musical ability are not understood, it probably results from interaction of *audition, physical coordination, intelligence,* and *experience.* Attempts to measure and predict musical ability have yielded interesting descriptive information, and, in recent years, a sequence of musical development has emerged.

Normal Musical Development and Learning

Development, defined above as "the growth and maturation process through which people go as they move from an embryonic stage, through birth, childhood, and adolescence, to an adult stage," and learning, defined as "an observable change in behavior, due to experience, which is not attributable to anything else," are intertwined. Development may connote more of a natural "unfolding" of abilities with advancing age while learning may connote the result of deliberate effort, but they are related intimately. We shall review some basic learning theories and then present a developmental sequence. The reader should remember that learning occurs during development, and learning fosters development.

Theoretical Bases

One traditional classification of learning theories is the two-fold categorization into *behavioral-associationist* (or stimulus-response, or trial-and-error) theories and the *cognitive-organizational* (or cognitive-field, or insightful) theories. Distinctions are not always clearcut, but, essentially, behavioral-associationists tend to take an empirical approach to studying learning and view it in terms of behavioral sequences, habit acquisition, and trial-and-error. Cognitive-organizational theorists, often employing a more rational approach, are more concerned with central brain processes, structuring and restructuring of cognitive fields, and insightful problem solving (Bower & Hilgard, 1981, pp. 2–8). Notterman and Drewry (1993) identify seven schools of thought or "paradigms" of learning: functionalism, associationism, "dialectical-materialist" psychology, behaviorism, Gestalt psychology, Freudian psychoanalysis, and cognitive psychology. (One may group the first four schools into the behavioral-associationist camp and the remaining three into the cognitive-organizational.) Regardless of labels and classifications, no one theory accounts for all learning phenomena. No theory which survives in the literature completely lacks utility. As Lathrop (1970) noted during an earlier time when music educators were "discovering" learning theory, learning theory does not offer instant explanations of or solutions to music learning problems. Nevertheless, theoretical frameworks may be useful in planning instruction, developing curricula, and questioning reasons for particular professional practices. The theories discussed below represent the two major schools. In addition to the theorists' own works, authoritative bases include Bower and Hilgard, Hilgard and Bower (1975) (an older edition), Bugelski (1971), LeFrancois (1982), the Music Educators National Conference publication *Documentary Report of the Ann Arbor Symposium* (Taylor, 1981), and Notterman and Drewry.

Behavioral-associationist theories. E. L. Thorndike (1932) viewed learning as resulting from the connection of stimuli with responses through loosely conceived "bonds." Proper use of reward and reinforcement would help establish the bonds. A "satisfying state of affairs" would strengthen connections; established connections could be strengthened through reward for practice. While the bonds themselves lack physical reality, Thorndike's positions regarding the importance of reinforcement and the need to specify just what is to be learned are important.

I. P. Pavlov (1927), a Nobel-prize winning physiologist in 1904, established the classical conditioning paradigm (ding-slurp), refined to a high degree in his well-known experiments with dogs. The paradigm, also known as Pavlovian conditioning, operates, schematically, as

$$
\begin{array}{lll}
(1) & & \text{US—UR} \\
(2) & (\text{CS}) & \text{US—UR} \\
(3) & & \text{CS—CR,}
\end{array}
$$

where (1) an unconditioned stimulus naturally elicits an unconditioned response, as in a hungry dog salivating in response to meat powder, a person leaping because of a sudden loud noise, or a person blinking an eye because a puff of air is directed at it; (2) the conditioned stimulus—a ringing bell, a verbal command, or some other signal—precedes the unconditioned stimulus; (3) eventually the conditioned stimulus elicits the same response, now a conditioned response. With judicious reinforcement by occasional presentation of the unconditioned stimulus, the precision of the conditioned response may be increased.[8] Failure to present the unconditioned stimulus eventually will cause the linkage to break; the response is "extinguished." Conditioning is not limited to "lower" animals; among humans, student fear of particular teachers, reactions to particular functional household objects at certain times of day, and special behaviors of trained troops or marching bands exemplify conditioning. It is very difficult to apply Pavlov's system except in narrow areas because the requisite unconditioned stimulus-unconditioned response links are seldom apparent, and extinction of undesirable generalization to similar stimuli by withholding the unconditioned stimulus is not always practical.

E. R. Guthrie (1952) stressed contiguity, as did Pavlov, but found the classical conditioning paradigm too restrictive. Rather than viewing learning as the substitution of one stimulus for another, Guthrie conceptualized the stimulus as being conditioned to the response. Guthrie believed that a person would connect a movement (covert or overt) that *changed* a stimulus ("shut it off") *to* that stimulus. Future occurrences of an identical stimulus would be met with the movement; if the stimulus changed, a different movement would be necessary. Learning supposedly occurs in one trial, at full strength. Guthrie's theory handles the obvious criticism that complex tasks, such as playing a piece on the piano, are not learned in one trial by conceiving a complex task as a myriad of simpler tasks, each of which is learned in one trial. In Guthrie's system, reinforcement is important because it "protects" behavior from new associations; strengthening responses is nonexistent. Learning is habit formation, and once a person learns a habit, he or she never can "unlearn" or "break" the habit—he or she can only replace it. A student who finally stops habitually playing a notated F♯ as F in a particular piece has replaced the incorrect habit with the correct one. Guthrie's theory is flexible, albeit somewhat lacking in precision; its utility probably lies in its constructs of habit replacement and the all-or-none occurrence of parts of a complex task at definite points in time. The wisdom of practicing for a performance in situations simulating the expected performance conditions as closely as possible also flows from Guthrie's theory.

A strict behavioral conception of learning may have reached its zenith

---

[8]Among other stimuli, Pavlov employed tones. By selective presentation of an unconditioned stimulus, he was able to make some dogs salivate to A = 440 Hz but not generalize to 441 Hz!

in B. F. Skinner's views, where *operant conditioning*, in which an emitted response is strengthened and made more likely through selective reinforcement, is the basis for learning.[9] If an encaged pigeon pecks at a particular spot and receives food as a consequence, the pigeon is more likely to peck at that spot again and can learn to do it when requiring food. If a cat escapes from a cage by a certain combination of movements, that combination is more likely to occur when the cat is recaged; the cat can learn to escape. If a baby "discovers" that dropping a toy from the crib brings Mother's solicitous attention, the baby is more likely to drop the toy again; the baby learns to fetch Mother. A series of selective reinforcements can build rather intricate chains of behavior. Reinforcement may occur continuously, in which case the experimenter, "behavior manager," or teacher rewards each and every desired response, or intermittently, where only selected desired responses are rewarded. Many arrangements are possible; Bower and Hilgard (1981, p. 180) indicate that responses developed under variable time interval reinforcement schedules are unusually resistant to extinction.

In theory, the proper reinforcement schedule added to opportunities arranged in the proper sequence virtually guarantees the stimulus discrimination and response differentiation necessary for performing clearly structured tasks. Skinner's work is a basis for linear programmed instruction, in which learning proceeds, relatively error-free, in small sequential steps according to a structured presentation of the material. While Skinner was rather unsuccessful in accounting for development of verbal behavior, study of reinforcement schedules may be quite beneficial in encouraging development of precisely defined skills. Constant praise, as most experienced music teachers recognize, becomes ineffective; a variable praise schedule will, in the long run, motivate more students to higher goals. Secondary reinforcers, such as praise, do work with many human learners, and a careful structuring of reinforcement is a powerful learning aid. Greer (1981) presents a useful review of manipulations of reinforcement contingencies in studies pertaining to music education. Skinner's 1938 and 1953 texts present his system in detail; his *Beyond Freedom and Dignity* (1971) presents his case that people are not "free" because they always are subject to environmental controls. Skinner believed that systematic planned positive controls would be superior to existing quasi-random controls.

Cognitive-organizational theories. Many developments in cognitive views

---

[9]In operant, "Skinnerian," "R–S," or "instrumental" conditioning, the organism *emits* a response as part of naturally occurring behavior. In classical, "Pavlovian," or "S–R" conditioning, the stimulus *elicits* or "pulls out" the response.

of learning flow from the work of the Gestalt psychologists, of whom Kohler, Wertheimer, and Koffka were leaders. Those German psychologists primarily were interested in perception, but perception extends to learning; in the Gestalt view, learning is a matter of perceptual organization. Gestalt theories have a contemporary importance in theories about aspects of music perception; some melodies are inherently easier to organize (and learn) than others. Phenomena mentioned earlier in this text, such as auditory stream segregation and the tonal hierarchy, are related to Gestalt considerations. Because of what the authors feel is the continuing relevance of Gestalt views, they have elected to give extra attention to classical Gestalt theory.

One should not simply equate "Gestalt" with "nonbehaviorism" or assume that all cognitive theories are Gestalt. Gestalt theory is a specific set of organizational principles in the service of "good figures." The term Gestalt may mean shape or form as a stimulus attribute, or it may mean an entity in itself. For the advocate of a Gestalt view of learning, problem solving is structuring and restructuring perceptual relations to make "good figures" or "good Gestalts." Gestalt theorists make much of insightful behavior, which stimulus-response theorists generally do not consider; insight requires grasping the proper relations.

In Gestalt theory, learning requires coherence rather than association. The theory's essence is the *Law of Pragnanz* (compactness), which states that psychological organization is toward "good" or "harmonious" figures. Four sublaws of the Law of *Pragnanz* help clarify just what a "good" or "harmonious" figure is.

The *Law of Proximity* states that one groups elements to make a figure in accordance with the elements' nearness or proximity to each other. A person is more likely to group the pattern 11 11 11 11 as four twos rather than two fours or one two and two threes. With tones, people are more likely to group sounds that are closer in pitch as a melodic idiom or figure; Lundin's (1967) melodic principle of propinquity (see Chapter Six) is grounded in the Law of Proximity.

If not overridden by proximity, objects or events with similar attributes, such as shape, color, or timbre, will group together in accordance with the *Law of Similarity.* A listener often will hear a musical idiom containing groups of four sixteenth notes, as in

as a duet when played by one instrument such as a clarinet: The last three notes of each group are in a different register than the first and are within a semitone; they are "similar." (From a frequency standpoint they also are "proximate.")

The *Law of Common Direction* refers to grouping on the basis of extrapolated completion. The incomplete lower case cursive letter *d* easily can look like *cl,* but a reader can see it as a *d* from the context of the word. Incomplete notes and clefs abound in music manuscript, but experienced performers generally have no difficulty interpreting them.

The *Law of Simplicity* refers to a perceptual preference for smoothness, regularity, and symmetry as compared with roughness, irregularity, and asymmetry; it relates to making perceptual order out of chaos.

Careful perceptual organization can facilitate music learning. For example, music manuscript that violates the principle of rhythmic spacing[10] is asking for trouble, especially with inexperienced performers, because of the Law of Proximity. The Law of Simplicity suggests that a teacher should begin "music appreciation" with novice listeners by using music with predictable and readily perceivable forms. Kohler's (1929) text is a good source for exploring classical Gestalt viewpoints.

Piaget, the Swiss biologist, founded a theory of *genetic epistemology,* a melange of formal logic and psychology. Developed from observations of children in natural settings, the theory hypothesizes four major developmental stages through which all children must pass in order to become mentally mature adults.

In the initial *sensorimotor* stage, lasting from birth until about two years of age, the child essentially moves from a type of motor intelligence to a more symbolic intelligence as voluntary movements replace reflexive behavior. During the sensorimotor stage, the child acquires object permanence, i.e., moves from a literal state of "out-of-sight, out-of-mind" to recognition that a toy or other object exists even when it is not in the child's immediate environment.

In the *preoperational* stage, lasting roughly from ages two through seven, the child moves through various illogical and incomplete concepts. Perception dominates reason, as in a child saying that a higher or wider container holds more beads than a lower or narrower container, despite seeing equal amounts of beads placed in each container. LeFrancois (1982, pp. 228–229) indicates that a peculiar transductive reasoning, in

---

[10]The principle of rhythmic spacing is a convention that requires the empty spaces following notes to be proportional to the note values; e.g., more space should follow a quarter note (crotchet) than an eighth note (quaver). Similarly, the amount of space occupied by two successive eighth notes should be about what a single quarter note would occupy.

which the child goes from specific instance to specific instance, as in assuming that any two animals that give milk belong to the same species, characterizes the preoperational stage.

From roughly ages seven through eleven or a little older, the child is in the stage of *concrete operations,* a time during which thought processes depend on a concrete framework. One aspect of the stage is the child's effort to learn conservation, i.e., the recognition that changes can occur in an object's form or spatial arrangement without changing the object's other attributes. In volume relations, a conserving child recognizes that two initially identical amounts of water remain identical when they are poured into containers of different shapes, but a nonconserving child may insist that suddenly there is more water in a wide shallow pan than in a tall test tube, or vice versa. When the water is poured back into the original identical containers, the same child will quite easily say that the amounts of water are identical.

Pflederer (1967) identified five types of music conservation: (1) *identity,* where thematic material maintains its essential characteristics across various permutations; (2) *metrical groupings,* in which the listener recognizes and discriminates among meters despite changes in note value distributions within measures; (3) *augmentation and diminution,* recognition that respective lengthening and shortening of a melodic passage's note values does not change the basic tonal relations; (4) *transposition,* where a change in frequency level does not alter perception of tonal configurations; and (5) *inversion,* where the listener recognizes an inverted simultaneous or successive interval. While conservation is of interest to some music researchers and teachers, partly because children in the concrete operations stage often are beginning formal musical training and conservation is necessary for form perception and musical analysis, conservation's arrival time will vary greatly with individuals. All aspects of a developmental stage must occur; attempts to accelerate conservation are highly questionable.

Piaget's final major stage is *formal operations,* where the child is capable of formal propositional thinking and can combine various grouping operations. The adolescent now can consider diverse possibilities, make "what if" judgments, and organize principles into networks. While the child/adolescent may not be "wise," he or she now is a mental adult.

Equilibration is the self-regulated process which is the basis for psychological development and learning in Piaget's system. It includes *assimilation,* in which a new environmental experience is accepted into the existing cognitive structure, and *accommodation,* in which the cognitive structure is altered to take cognizance of a new reality. Learning problems may result when the learner ignores details in a "new" stimulus and assimilates rather than accommodates.

Recent years have seen increasing criticism of Piaget's system, partly because of the difficulty of applying the theory in detail. Serafine (1980), in a rather negative review, notes that Piaget sought to study how the "mind" becomes capable of thought, language, and knowledge, and was rather unconcerned with learning and individual differences. She also believes that music conservation tasks may lack validity because of possible confusion of aural perception difficulties with lack of conservation. Gardner (1993, pp. 20–22), while crediting Piaget with developing important broad guidelines for child development, believes that research shows that Piaget's stages are far more continuous and gradual in their transitions than Piaget indicated. Furthermore, Piaget's operations are more content specific than they might theoretically appear; for example, a child might exhibit conservation with some materials but not with others. Piaget's theory probably is most applicable to the development of "scientific" thinking in Western literate societies; it may be less applicable to the arts and to other cultures.

Despite the real danger of overcategorizing children in stages on the basis of ungeneralizable evidence and unwarranted concern with conservation, Piaget's work remains valuable because it clearly shows that children are not miniature adults. Music teachers must present material to children in ways in which the children are ready to assimilate or accommodate it. Excessively hypothetical questions (what if . . .) without concrete referents are unsuited to a child in the stage of concrete operations. The relevant Hilgard and Bower (1975) chapter provides a comprehensive overview of Piaget's theories. Piaget's *The Psychology of Intelligence* (1950) and *The Psychology of the Child* (1969), coauthored by Piaget and Inhelder, discuss his work and views in detail.

We will conclude this section with brief mention of a lesser known but increasingly more frequently cited theorist: Vygotsky. Especially interested in children's development of "inner speech" and thought as well as how formal instruction might expand mental operations, Vygotsky believed that higher cognitive processes differ qualitatively from fundamental sensory processes. Social interaction is critical for intellectual development. A *zone of proximal development* (ZPD) represents the difference between a person's current ability level or achievement and what that person might be able to do if given instruction and opportunity. In the sense of intelligence testing, musical or otherwise, a greater ZPD might indicate higher intelligence; conversely, more efficient or appropriate instruction might widen the ZPD. Day (1983) and translations of Vygotsky's

(1962; 1978) works provide insights into Vygotsky's theory and philosophy and the functional importance of the ZPD.

Musical Development Across Age-Based Stages

Musical ability proceeds through a developmental sequence, running from basic sensory perceptions through complex abstract musical reasoning. The sequence is flexible, fluid, and subject to modification. To some extent, having such a sequence is quite natural: Musical behavior is one form of human behavior, and most behaviors become more sophisticated and skilled in a developmental manner. A supportive and nurturing environment must interact with any natural aspects of musical behavior in order for someone to develop to the fullest extent musically. Normative information regarding what occurs when may be quite valuable in planning for music instruction. Much remains to be learned about the sequence, its individual steps, and the discrete nature of steps and developmental stages, but the literature suggests an overall pattern. In addition to the cited references, the following discussion generally is based on the research and descriptions of Dowling and Harwood (1986), Gardner (1993), and Hargreaves and Zimmerman (1992). A capsulization of the information appears in Radocy (1994).

As Kuhl (1989, p. 379) indicates, part of being a "normal" human is production of a species-specific sound. The human's signal identifies its producer as human. Infants engage in a "canonical babbling," i.e., a highly repetitive emission of consonant-vowel combinations, as in "ma-ma-ma-ma" or "da-da-dada." Such babbling occurs initially regardless of the language in the home, parental attributes, or, within wide limits, the infant's general motor and intellectual abilities. As part of their prespeech sounds, babies may make individual tone-like sounds and produce short babbling patterns that suggest definite, albeit considerably variable, itch.[11] The patterns may vary in loudness and musical contour, thereby suggesting a certain amount of rudimentary musical expression.

Musical stimuli, which often have relatively steady pitches and repetitive rhythms, stand out from other sounds. Infants may give attention to sources of musical sounds in their immediate environments and may respond with interest to a change in their aural surroundings, such as a different voice or instrument performing a previously heard melody. Babies as young as four months may notice changes in beat and tempo.

---

[11]Nettl's (1956) theory of language differentiation, noted in Chapter Two, proposes that humans originally communicated with a mixture of sounds which were neither speech nor music. The initial sound production of humans may microcosmically represent Nettl's evolutionary process.

Slightly older babies may respond to changes in contour, but transpositions to new keys are unlikely to arouse any interest.

Trehub (1993), summarizing various studies, notes that infants are sensitive to contour but not individual pitch and interval changes. Interestingly, they occasionally can discriminate ascending from descending two-tone patterns, even though older children and even some adults may have difficulty. Infants show a tendency to group rhythms, as in hearing XXXOOO (where X and O represent contrasting timbres or loudnesses) as two groups of three. Pauses between contrasting groups lack salience, but pauses within groups catch infants' attention.

Around two years of age, children begin to produce sound sequences that contain successive intervals which are found in their surrounding musical culture. *Spontaneous song,* an active creation of (to the children) musically logical sequences commonly occur during play and other periods of auditory expression. Most children gradually mix more and more imitations of songs they hear around them (*learned song*) into their creations; by approximately four years of age, learned song largely has replaced spontaneous song. Curiously, musicians may deem composition as a skill which few possess or a skill which requires intensive and lengthy study. Yet, while many of their creations defy accurate notation, many children as a matter of natural development pass through a highly creative musical stage in which they do considerable "composing" within the scope of spontaneous song.

In addition to reflecting the surrounding musical culture through their songs, children learn cultural conventions and stereotypes by singing. In a study where children aged three through six years learned to discriminate between tonal and atonal songs, children as young as age three could discriminate *if* they were among the more competent singers, as demonstrated by singing "Happy Birthday" (Dowling, 1988). Simple songs evidently facilitate learning cultural scale patterns, even without formal training. Once the child learns the patterns, he or she continues to use them, even when the specific behaviors that led to acquisition of the patterns are forgotten.

As with any developmental sequence, the musical development of babies and young children may vary considerably, and some babies may show remarkable skills. Ries's (1982) study of the spontaneous and learned song of 48 Canadian children remains illustrative. Employing naturalistic inquiry methods, Ries observed the children, ranging in age from seven to thirty-two months, in their homes, where they were able to perform before their parents and others with whom they were familiar. While extensive variation existed, Ries generally found that babies do sing in an expressive manner, with style, articulation, and vocal quality.

Prelanguage babies are expressive vocally even without specific words. Her data suggested a developmental sequence of pitch or melody at seven months, articulation (separation of sounds rather than wailing) at eleven months, and very simple rhythms until nineteen months, when words were added. Children employed pulse and meter at thirty months. Learned songs developed more slowly than spontaneous song. As mentioned earlier, Ries found that thirty-month old children could sing spontaneous songs with definite tonality, although other research (Dowling & Harwood, 1986) suggests that tonality remains unstable until around age five or six. These children were from a closely knit family-centered subculture, and Ries's results are atypical, but they do suggest that young children, ready in some cases for preschool, may be capable of rather advanced musical behaviors.

As children continue to mature and approach kindergarten (still the beginning of formal schooling for many children in the United States), their songs become longer. Tonal centers are more stable, even for those who previously fluctuated widely in their relationships to any home tone; rhythm patterns become steadier. Eventually, children, at widely varying rates, discover that certain musical properties may remain the same while others change. Intervalic structure and melodic contour remain the same even though the song changes in its tonal center. Tones and silences retain the same relative durations even though tempo may vary. Words seem to be especially relevant for children in learning a song; learning words or fragments of words (such as the "E–I–E–I–O" section of "Old MacDonald Had a Farm") may precede learning pitches.

Commenting on children's aural perception of musical events, Pick and Palmer (1993) note the sensitivity of five-year-old children to musical contour. Children can recognize transposed melodies and indicate that the same melody in different tonalities indeed is the same melody. They point out that young infants also are sensitive to contour, but with immersion in one's musical culture, sensitivity to contour and intervals within melodies increases.

The study of children's visual representations of musical sounds may be illuminating. In a study of five- through seven-year-old children, Davidson and Scripp (1988) found increasing sophistication in notation schemes with advancing age, with pitch emerging as a primary basis for organization. The researchers found that the children employed five types of systems. In a *pictorial system,* the child simply portrayed a song title or events within the song through pictures or icons, as in drawing a boat for "Row, Row, Row Your Boat." In an *abstract patterning system,* the child usually used lines or dots to represent relationships among melodic tones and phrases. Icons and words alternated flexibly in a *rebus system.*

Children employing a *text system* wrote words with suggestions of ordered grouping, something like poetry. In a *combination/elaboration system,* the child used abstract symbols and words to represent simultaneously the song's words and musical dimensions—this system did not focus primarily on the words or use pictures or icons. Changing percentages in the relative use of each system across the three ages suggest the increasing sophistication in notating songs:

Age	%Pictorial	%Abs.Patt.	%Rebus	%Text	%Comb/elab
5	26	43	8	18	5
6	8	41	13	23	15
7	3	28	5	36	28

Bamberger (1991) presents elaborate descriptions of children's pictorial representations of music. Children reflect their grouping of sonic events into various simple metric and phrase groupings, which become building blocks for more complex patterns.

In a study comparing four- to eight-year-old children's invented notations, Gromko (1994) found a relationship between measures of musical understanding and portrayed awareness of pitch and rhythmic relationships. Understanding, a variable based on factor analysis of the children's scores on Gordon's (1979) *Primary Measures of Music Audiation,* was more related to notational sophistication than to the children's age.

As children continue to mature until about age nine, musical ability tends to increase, largely as a matter of further cultural immersion. The sounds of the surrounding musical culture, including sounds from media as well as sounds produced in the home by children, parents, and siblings, build musical expectancies and a sense of what is appropriate musically and what is not. Children become increasingly familiar with predominant scales, intervals, harmonic conventions, metric organization and subdivisions, as well as a specific repertoire of music. Even without formal instruction or any idea of correct labels for what they hear, the children build their musical expectancies and develop preferences. The authors strongly believe that this is a crucial time for developing intelligent and musically sophisticated future audiences and performers. Music educators and caregivers should exploit children's flexibility and openness to diverse musical styles during the preschool and early elementary school years before they become locked into any one style. Overly narrow musical experiences lead to restrictive expectancies, which lead to restrictive preferences.

Further progress beyond the level of learning songs from the surrounding culture, creating similar songs, and a sensitivity to differing musical styles requires formal music instruction, especially in music performance, but also in developing more sophisticated analytical and listening skills and the ability to read and employ conventional music notation. Cultures and individuals within cultures differ greatly in the importance they place on formal instruction; many Western cultures create a musically elite group of performers and composers and a large group of consumers. In the United States, relatively few people develop their musical abilities beyond those present around age nine.

People who do pursue formal musical study into adulthood may become skillful performers, some even reaching the level of expertise discussed in Chapter Seven. Some individuals may become composers and arrangers. Others may become highly sophisticated listeners. A few may become widely adept in all fields of music. Of course, many music students will settle for less than "superstardom" or its equivalent, whether due to a lack of "talent," a lack of motivation, or stronger interests in fields of endeavor other than music.

Musical Abnormalities

"Normal" musical development is wide ranging, although much of it occurs in most humans who have anything approaching "normal" sensory and intellectual abilities (and even in some who do not). Yet, conditions exist that are well beyond even the wide range of "normal" human musical behaviors. Labelling phenomena as abnormal is a matter of judgment, and musicians, teachers, and others working with music should not be too quick to consider someone's musical behavior as abnormal simply because it is different. However, some individuals just cannot or do not respond to music, and some respond in remarkably unusual ways. The authors have elected to discuss briefly amusia, monotonism, and synesthesia.

Amusia is a broad term, literally meaning "without music." Including diverse abnormalities and difficulties, which may or may not result from some traumatic event, amusia usually refers to some problem in music perception or cognition. Other perceptual difficulties such as aphasia may or may not accompany amusia. Marin (1982) reviews numerous case studies and other reviews and identifies six major hierarchical classifications of amusia.

Difficulties in the basic psychoacoustical perception of properties within a tone are at Marin's lowest level. These include inability to detect changes in basic tonal properties and having difficulty with sound localization. The second level includes what Marin calls (p. 472) "disorders of precategorical auditory perception." Inability to notice that different pitches, chords, timbres, and loudness levels are indeed different characterizes this level, as does perception problems with musical intervals. Difficulties in actual categorization and labelling of elementary structures such as chords, intervals, melodies, and scales, and sensing octave equivalence and perceiving rhythm patterns are deficiencies at the third level. Marin's fourth level includes more complex difficulties in melodic and rhythmic discrimination, and the fifth level includes difficulties in reading music. The sixth and highest hierarchical level regards learning complex perceptions, such as stylistic characteristics of individual composers, melodic conventions, and thematic treatments.

Monotonism, where a person seems to sing only one tone, regardless of the musical situation, is an especially frustrating form of amusia. Among music teachers, it is an article of faith that there are no (or at least very few) true monotones, but one does find people with pitch matching problems and people who sing with a restricted range. Choral music teachers occasionally encounter a "droning" phenomenon among adolescent males, where the boys sing consistently below the designated pitch and usually produce only a few separate tones. Vocal remediation techniques are beyond the scope of this text, and some pitch problems are not simply from inadequate singing, but guided practice may do wonders for many monotones and near-monotones.

The phenomenon of *synesthesia* perhaps should not be considered as an abnormality, although the phenomenon is hardly "normal." While the various amusias clearly are a deficit, the person with true synesthesia has additional ways of experiencing the environment. Synesthesia is a multisensory response to a stimulus. In addition to hearing a tone, the respondent experiences the tone simultaneously in a non-auditory way, such as by seeing a color or smelling an aroma. The experience is one of conscious sensation, not merely verbal association.

In *chromesthesia* (the sound-color type of synesthesia), a consistent relation exists between color brightness and tonal pitch: Bright colors accompany low pitches; dark colors accompany high pitches. Unlike dual *spoken* vowel-color sensations, where red and yellow often accompany "ah;" white accompanies "ay" (as in "late"), "eh" (as in "let"), "ih" (as in "bit"), and "ei" as in "beet"; red and black accompany "o" (as in "home"); and blue, brown, or black go with "oo" (as in "boot"), *tone-color* sensations are rather idiosyncratic (Marks, 1975). Haack and Radocy (1981) described a case study of an art teacher who experienced dramatic tone-color sensory linkages.

As with other unusual phenomena, the musician, music teacher, music therapist, or other person working with music should recognize that the person reporting the multisensory synesthetic experience quite likely is describing a real experience. The person is not necessarily ill in any way!

Measurement and Prediction of Musical Ability and Learning

There are many ways to measure musical ability. A high level of musical achievement clearly indicates musical ability, at least of the sort necessary for achievement in the designated medium. Measurement of ability prior to successful pursuit of a career is more challenging.

Musical ability is defined operationally, rather than constitutively, by the particular means of measurement.[12] Some measures stress basic discrimination skills; others require more "musical" tasks. Some measures require prior musical achievement. Instrument manufacturers have published "tests" on which almost anyone who is marginally literate may score well.

This book is not a measurement text; only three published measures are discussed below. Readers who wish to investigate other tests and necessary considerations in test development should consult Boyle and Radocy (1987) and scan *Dissertation Abstracts International*, as well as examine older texts by Colwell (1970), Lehman (1968), and Whybrew (1971). Test development remains a common doctoral research project, and modern technology enables fairly sophisticated test design and administration. Boyle (1992) presents a detailed discussion of typical tasks which testmakers employ to test musical ability.

Some Approaches

An experienced observer may assess musical ability by means of educated guessing. Children vary in the extent to which they actively seek to make and listen to sounds, "natural" though such activity may be. Children with older musically successful siblings may themselves be successful. Any child who asks for musical experiences certainly should be welcomed and encouraged. But educated guesses may be misleading, particularly if they stress overt indicators. Discovering "latent" musical ability requires a more formal assessment. In order to illustrate diverse approaches, three representative tests are discussed below.

The *Seashore Measures of Musical Talents* (Seashore, Lewis, & Saetveit, 1960) appeared initially in 1919 and were revised extensively in 1939. By 1994, the battery was out-of-print; despite its pioneering status and long history of use, the construct of musical ability the battery embodies

---

[12]An operational definition specifies how a trait will be recognized in a specific instructional or research setting, while a constitutive definition is a dictionary-style definition.)

evidently made it obsolete in light of contemporary constructs and attitudes. The measures are discussed here because they so closely exemplified a particular school of thought, a belief that musical ability, especially regarding aptitude, is rooted in psychoacoustical discriminations.

The term "measures" rather than the singular reflected Seashore's view that musical ability consisted of loosely related specific sensory capacities. Each of the six particular measures was a measure of one narrow skill; together, the measures yielded a musical profile that showed a pattern of auditory acuity. No total score was possible, in accordance with Seashore's theory of specifics.

The Seashore pitch, loudness, time, and timbre tests required judgments of paired tones. The subject respectively indicated whether the second tone was higher or lower, stronger or weaker, longer, and same or different in comparison with the first tone. Many of the differences were rather subtle, subtle enough that the fidelity of sound reproduction equipment and acoustical aspects of the testing environment could affect scores. Plomp and Steeneken (1973) demonstrated the variability of sound pressure level in reverberant sound fields and the place dependence of sound sensations for steady-state tones. The rhythm test required indicating whether the second short monotonic rhythm pattern in a pair differed from the first; in the tonal memory test, the subject indicated which tone differed in the second version of a pair of short tonal patterns.

Seashore believed that auditory abilities had a physiological limit, so scores on his tests would not change appreciably over time, except as a function of misunderstood directions and experience in taking tests. Research (Wyatt, 1945) showed convincingly that training procedures indeed could raise subjects' Seashore scores.

The person who equates musical ability with the Seashore tests' perceptual tasks or believes that such tasks are an important part of musical ability still may find the tests useful. They were fairly reliable and valid for what their creators claimed to measure. Someone who believes that music is more than analysis of psychoacoustical differences and short-term retentions may prefer a more "musical" test; today's *zeitgeist* certainly favors more musical and less atomistic approaches than that of Seashore.

Wing (1961) developed the *Standardised Tests of Musical Intelligence,* a battery of seven tests which do provide a total score. All stimuli are piano tones. In the chord analysis and pitch sections, the subject respectively must evaluate individual chords for the number of tones contained therein and indicate whether the second of paired chords contains a tone within it higher or lower than the first chord. The memory, rhythmic accent, harmony, intensity, and phrasing sections require comparisons of paired melodies, some of which are rather lengthy. In the memory section, the subject must indicate which one of three to ten tones is altered in the second version. The other tests require the subject to indicate if the second melody is the same or which one he or she prefers regarding the property in question.

Wing (1954) believed that musical ability is largely innate, not necessarily related to intelligence, and not influenced by environment, views which are difficult to sustain today in light of other evidence. The tests may be useful for someone who believes in the importance of melodic, harmonic, and rhythmic discrimination.

Gordon's (1965a) *Musical Aptitude Profile* is one of the most comprehensive prediction measures. Each of the seven subsections, each of the three major sections, and the total battery all yield a score. The subject's basic task is to evaluate paired phrases; the stress is on what Gordon called *imagery* or *sensitivity*. [13]

The tonal imagery section contains a melody subsection, in which the subject must indicate whether the second phrase is an embellished melodic variation of the first ("same") or a different melody, and a harmony subsection, in which the subject labels the second phrase as having a lower voice the same as, or different from, the lower voice of the first.

One subsection of rhythm imagery requires the subject to indicate whether the second phrase's tempo accelerates, retards, or stays the same. The second rhythm imagery subsection asks for a same-different comparison regarding metrical accents.

Gordon's musical sensitivity section contains three subsections. In each, the subject must indicate which of two performances sounds better. In the phrasing subsection, musical expression is varied. Endings differ, rhythmically and melodically, in the balance subsection. In a "style" subsection, tempo differences predominate.

The Gordon test is lengthy and expensive, but it is thorough, includes an excellent manual, and was based on eight years of research. Gordon (1965b) believes that the battery minimizes musical achievement. The person who believes that sensitivity to tonal and rhythmic variation and nuance in a musical context is a vital aspect of musical ability may find the *Musical Aptitude Profile* useful.

The Seashore, Wing, and Gordon measures, selected by the authors because of historical importance, illustrate diverse approaches to measur-

---

[13]In later work, Gordon developed a series of tests of *audiation,* i.e., recalling or creating musical sound without its physical presence. Presumably, audiation requires evaluating an immediate series of auditory impressions. The difference between "imagery" and "audiation" may be somewhat pedantic; for a discussion of some of Gordon's audiation measures, see Boyle and Radocy (1987, pp. 151–153).

ing musical ability. More precisely, they are measures of musical *aptitude*, intended to assess ability without requiring specific musical knowledge. In order for a person to use these or any other measures with belief in their utility, that person must be convinced of the measures' *validity*. In addition, he or she must believe that a one-time testing is valid.

Validity

Any test's validity refers to how well the test measures what it is supposed to measure. Validity must not be confused with *reliability*, the consistency with which a test measures whatever it is measuring.[14] While a test must be reliable in order to be valid, a test may be quite reliable and yet be invalid, as in using a highly reliable final examination for a music history class as a measure of musical aptitude with kindergarten children.

Test constructors estimate reliability by correlating two forms of the same test, correlating two administrations of the same form, or correlating scores on two halves of the test. In addition, internal consistency techniques may estimate the average interitem correlation. An authoritative discussion of classical reliability techniques appears in Stanley (1971). Reliability estimates theoretically may range from -1.00 to $+1.00$; negative estimations are rare. The closer to $+1.00$, the more reliable the test.

Given sufficient reliability, a number which usually should be .80 or higher (in the authors' opinion), a test needs a sufficient rationale for *why* it is a test of whatever it is supposed to test in order to be valid. Since musical ability is not defined clearly, no ability measure is completely valid.

If a purported measure of musical ability is valid as a predictor of musical success, a logical way to validate such a test is to administer it to a large representative sample, measure the sample's musical success later, and look for a strong positive relationship between scores and success. This often is called criterion-related or predictive validity, and a problem may exist with the criterion's validity. Musical success often means achievement in a formal instructional setting. Children particularly may be "unsuccessful" because of organizational and personality problems rather than musical problems. Teacher ratings easily are influenced by nonmusical variables. Correlating a new with an old test presumes that the old test is sufficiently valid.

Validity may be a matter of how well the test represents a designated body of material. This is called content validity and is more readily

---

[14]A more technical definition is that reliability is the proportion of overall variability in the test scores that is due to genuine differences in the property being measured.

appropriate for achievement than for aptitude measures. It requires a fairly complete specification of just what a musically able person should be able to do.

Construct validity, the extent to which a test measures ability in accordance with underlying theoretical constructs of ability, is difficult to establish. Invalidity may be a failure of the test or a failure of the theory.

Whatever the test's claims for validity, the prospective test user personally must decide whether the test appears valid. Someone who believes that musical ability truly is largely a matter of fine sensory discriminations of isolated tonal stimuli might be comfortable with the Seashore battery or another test with similar characteristics. Someone who believes that "sensitivity" to underlying structures is important might endorse the Gordon *Musical Aptitude Profile*. Someone who believes that no one-time testing can possibly assess the likelihood of future accomplishment adequately may believe that no conventional test is appropriate.

Importance of Nonmusical Variables

Given the facts that musically able people may be able in other areas and that evaluators of musical success may employ nonmusical criteria, it is reasonable to examine the idea that additional nonmusical variables might increase the accuracy with which one might predict musical success. Two studies employing multiple regression analysis, a technique for relating a series of predictor variables to a criterion variable, illustrate utility for nonmusical or extramusical predictors of musical success.

Using students from a university laboratory school, Rainbow (1965) found that interest in music and socioeconomic background, along with pitch discrimination and tonal memory, were significant predictors of teacher ratings of elementary students' musical abilities. For junior high school students, the significant predictors were academic intelligence, gender, and relatives' participation in music, along with prior musical achievement. Teacher ratings for high school students were significantly predicted by home enrichment and interest in music, as well as pitch discrimination and tonal memory. For all school levels taken together, academic intelligence, home enrichment, interest in music, and socioeconomic background, as well as tonal memory and musical achievement were the significant predictors.

Hedden (1982) studied the effectiveness of attitude toward music, self-concept in music, musical background, academic achievement, and gender as predictors of the musical achievement of fifth and sixth-grade students in two schools. His most significant predictor, accounting for 25 percent of the variance in musical achievement in one school and 40 percent in the other, was academic achievement. Addition of the self-concept measure in one school and the attitude measure in the other increased the respective amounts of "accounted for" variance to 34 and 61 percent respectively. The other variables, including musical background, were not effective predictors. (While Rainbow used teacher ratings as a criterion variable, Hedden used a formal test, the *Music Achievement Tests* (Colwell, 1969).)

What Should We Measure?

While formal measures of musical and nonmusical variables may aid in measuring and predicting musical ability, no one test is likely to be adequate by itself. A reliable and valid battery that tests musical skills which the investigator deems important in combination with tests of intellectual ability, academic achievement, prior opportunities for musical stimulation, and, where necessary, physical attributes probably offers the best approach to making judgments of musical ability on which to make decisions regarding student recruitment, selection, and counseling. As understanding of sequential musical development increases, Sloboda's (1985) belief that "musical expertise" consists of awareness of musical structures, such as melodies, harmonies, rhythms, and underlying "deep" structures may have increasing utility: Assessing where a person is in some sequential development of musical awareness and sensitivity may be beneficial for assessing musical ability.

There is no substitute for providing an *opportunity* for success, of course; the chance to do something usually is the best predictor of whether a person is able to do something. The zone of proximal development, mentioned earlier, conceivably could be assessed by requiring a series of ordered tasks: Perhaps more musically able persons have wider zones of proximal development; i.e., they are more able to profit from musical instruction.

Philosophically, one can question the selection and development of a musical elite. While such an elite may be "natural" in a competitive society, particularly when resources are limited, some of the world's peoples do not recognize a musical elite. Blacking (1973) discusses at length the Venda people of South Africa, for whom musicmaking is more of a social than a technical experience. The Venda recognize that some individuals may be better performers than others, but the possibility of *anyone* being unmusical is alien to their culture.

The risk of allowing an "unmusical" person to try to learn to play an instrument or develop sophisticated listening skills hardly is in the same class as allowing a person who wishes to be a pilot but seems potentially to have little ability to fly an airplane to enroll in flight school. Pursuit of a musical career by a person lacking successful musical achievements is dubious, but a child who has had no musical training should not be denied musical opportunity. We know enough about musical ability and normal musical learning to know that these are complex areas, with many facets. We do not know enough about musical ability and learning to use them as barriers. And music educators should not be desirous of establishing musical barriers.

Practical Suggestions Regarding Music Education

A student brings his or her experiences, strengths, and weaknesses to the music learning situation. As the reader easily may surmise, instruction and learning involve numerous aspects, and no one theoretical explanation is completely adequate. While the authors respect important aspects of many theories (e.g., children's brains are organized differently from those of adults, behaviors may be altered through reinforcement contingencies, stimulus organization facilitates learning, they are not "true believers" in any one theory. Nevertheless, a large amount of literature as well as personal experience suggests particular principles for guiding instructional planning and evaluation. While no recipe for successful teaching exists, useful suggestions for applying some of what we know about musical learning and development flow from theoretical work and research. The following ideas, based on and expanded from Radocy (1982) and Boyle and Radocy (1987), are presented from the teacher's standpoint.

Clear specification of what students are to learn and how the teacher will evaluate their learning provides content, context, and structure. For musical performance, specification of what to learn includes descriptions of intermediate steps, which involve structured practice. General instructions to "practice" are less useful than specification of what and how to practice. In particular, students need to practice in meaningful musical segments—phrases rather than measures, musical sections rather than printed lines. While it is necessary to practice troublesome spots, including even individual tones, at varied tempi, the student should incorporate those isolated spots, at appropriate tempi, into the musical flow as soon as practical.

Evaluation should be in accordance with finding information to enhance students' musical experiences. The information should improve performance, expand knowledge, and facilitate revising curricula and instruction. Evaluation should not be a scare tactic.

In instruction and evaluation, a teacher must avoid excessive abstraction with younger students. One does not have to be a Piagetian "true believer" to recognize that young children often require specific concrete examples of musical situations. Duple and triple meter, ascending and descending phrases, simple binary and ternary forms, and other basic musical organizations are abstract, largely meaningless labels unless they are attached to meaningful aural examples. For students of any age, the provision of models and examples is beneficial. It is especially important for young children to have opportunities to *experience,* through movement, singing, or instrument playing, musical activities that exemplify the musical concepts we desire them to develop.

While music educators may argue about the relative importance of music reading, much musical learning is and will continue to be based on what is represented in musical notation. Accordingly, musical notation should be as clear and neat as possible. Excessively small notation, carelessly written manuscript, and notation that violates the principle of rhythmic spacing invite needless difficulty in reading; spaces following notes should be proportional to note values, e.g., more space should follow a quarter note (crotchet) than an eighth note (quaver). While there may be traditions to uphold, and, in vocal music, alignment of words with notes may be a consideration, the vocal style of separate flags for each note is more difficult to organize in relation to beats than the instrumental style of grouping notes via beams and ligatures.

While people may disagree about the theoretical role of reward and reinforcement, and people will vary greatly in what is rewarding and how often reward must occur, everyone needs some form of reward at some time. Accordingly, a learner's demonstrations of desired behaviors merit praise; tangible rewards should accompany music learning. Saying such things as "good job," awarding stripes and medals for band uniforms, and other tokens of appreciation may be of considerable value in maintaining interest and motivation.

Motivation is critical. Modern students usually are able to hear high quality recorded performances in a variety of musical styles, but they may lack the patience to spend the time and effort to make their performance sound like their auditory images. This requires motivation, not only toward long-term goals, but also toward shorter-term goals necessary for musical progress along the way. Maintaining motivation requires the teacher to provide opportunity for rewards, intrinsic as well as extrinsic, and to make the experience of learning music basically positive.

Teachers should treat failure to learn as failure to *learn,* not failure as a person. Errors require correction, not guilt. While teachers must address undesirable, counterproductive, or "off task" behavior, when possible, chastisement should occur in private. One interesting aspect of human interaction is the way in which many people find it easier to provide negative than positive criticism. An ensemble director may chastise one student who is late for rehearsal without praising any of the other students who arrived on time. A critique of a performance may stress wrong notes and other flaws with little mention of positive aspects. While error-free learning may be impossible, and error recognition and correction is essential, recognition of a performance's positive aspects may help sustain a student's desire to correct errors and improve.

Especially for younger learners, frequent spaced instruction is superior to less frequent concentrated instruction. Meeting twice a week for thirty minutes each allows more opportunity for reward and error correction and less time for practicing mistakes than meeting once a week for sixty minutes.

Musical activity should not be used as a threat or punishment. Parents should not discipline children for sundry offenses by forcing extra practice, and teachers should not call extra rehearsals out of anger rather than for attaining musical goals. Also, the possible use of negative reinforcement in releasing students early from practice or study time is questionable: Should teachers "reward" students for musical accomplishment by reducing the students' experience with music?

One need not believe that the theoretical importance of practice is to protect prior learning in order to realize benefits of practicing for specific performances under a variety of conditions. Seemingly trivial things such as the location of music stands or seating position on stage can distract relatively novice performers unless they have learned to make adaptations and adjustments. Acoustical conditions vary among performance sites; touring ensembles may find it advantageous to simulate varied amounts of reflection.

Lastly, making music is more than *re*creation; it is a creative process. One needs to tolerate experimentation and new ideas, and yet insist on disciplined expression of the results.

Summary

This chapter's key summative points include the following:
1. *Ability* is a broad term, denoting having the necessary skills and experience to do something; it is broader than *aptitude*, which denotes ability minus the results of formal instruction, and *capacity*, which denotes genetic endowment.
2. *Development* is a process of growth and maturation, which is partly dependent on learning.
3. *Learning* is a change in observable behavior that is not attributable to anything else.

4. Musical ability is not dependent on superior auditory acuity.
5. The influence of genetic endowment on musical ability is uncertain; much evidence of musical accomplishment is intertwined with environmental factors.
6. While not everyone can learn anything, a nurturing environment is crucial for developing musical ability.
7. Physical features are unimportant in musical ability, except to the extent that particular performance media may be involved.
8. While some musical behavior is creative, creativity is too ill-defined as a construct to be valuable as a predictor of musical ability.
9. Intelligence may be related to musical ability; that relationship may be a function of how the properties are conceptualized and measured.
10. The *idiot savant,* a person of generally highly limited intelligence who possesses remarkable skills in one area, which could be music, presents complications for relating musical ability and intelligence, unless the conception of intelligence is multifaceted.
11. Neither gender nor ethnicity are valid predictors of musical ability.
12. Musical ability probably results from an interaction of audition, physical coordination, intelligence, and experience.
13. Theories of learning include *behavioral-associationist* and *cognitive-organizational* theories.
14. The theories of *Thorndike* (stimulus-response connections resulting from consequences), *Pavlov* (becoming conditioned to some signal that then elicits a response), *Guthrie* (a movement becoming associated at full strength with a stimulus), and *Skinner* (emitted responses shaped to desired behavior through judicious use of reinforcement) exemplify behavioral-associationist theories.
15. The theories of the *Gestalt* psychologists (learning is a matter of perceptual organization) and of *Piaget* (learning is a developmental unfolding through several stages of maturation) exemplify cognitive-organizational theories.
16. Piaget's stages are useful in showing that children fundamentally differ from adults mentally, but the stages are not as rigid as once thought and may be more appropriate in areas other than music.
17. *Vygotsky's zone of proximal development,* the difference between what a person can do and what he or she might do if given instruction, may be useful in assessing musical ability and learning.
18. Musical development proceeds through a sequence from birth into adulthood, partly due to innate developments but also due to musical experience.
19. Infants naturally make sounds and notice their auditory environments.

20. Young children proceed through a stage of *spontaneous song,* which usually is replaced by *learned song.*
21. Young children generally are more sensitive to melodic contour than to intervalic detail within a melody.
22. Words seem to be especially important for children in learning songs.
23. Children's created notations show increasing sophistication, not only with advancing age but also with advancing musical understanding.
24. *A child's preschool and early elementary school years are crucial for developing musical expectancies and preferences.*
25. While much musical learning and development seem to occur as a result of immersion in a musical environment, progress beyond that of the early elementary school years usually requires formal instruction.
26. *Amusia* refers to the absence of some musical skill, which may be productive or perceptual.
27. *Synesthesia* is a multisensory response to a single stimulus; a common form is experiencing a color as a visual sensation along with hearing a tone (*chromesthesia*).
28. The tests of *Seashore, Wing,* and *Gordon* represent diverse traditional measures of musical aptitude.
29. *Validity,* the extent to which a test measures what it is supposed to measure, is a major concern; using any test to assess any form of musical ability implies agreement with the testmaker's concept of validity.
30. Especially in formal instructional settings, nonmusical or extramusical variables may be useful predictors of musical ability and achievement.
31. A variety of indicators should constitute measures of musical ability.
32. There is no substitute for providing *opportunity* for learning music.
33. One need not be a "true believer" in any theory of learning or evaluation in order to make practical applications of theories to instruction and evaluation.

References

Abeles, H. F., & Porter, S. Y. (1978). Sex stereotyping of musical instruments. *Journal of Research in Music Education, 26,* 65–75.

Aggleton, J., Kentridge, R., & Good, J. (1994). Handedness and musical ability: A study of professional orchestral players, composers, and choir members. *Psychology of Music, 22,* 148–156.

Anastasi, A., & Levee, R. F. (1960). Intellectual defect and musical talent: A case report. *American Journal of Mental Deficiency, 64,* 695–703.

Bamberger, J. L. (1991). The mind behind the musical ear: How children develop musical intelligence. Cambridge, MA: Harvard University Press.

Bentley, A. (1966). *Musical ability in children and its measurement.* New York: Random House.

Blacking, J. (1973). *How musical is man?* Seattle: University of Washington Press.

Bower, G. H., & Hilgard, E. R. (1981). *Theories of learning* (5th ed.). Englewood Cliffs, NJ: Prentice-Hall.

Boyle, J. D. (1992). Evaluation of music ability. In R. Colwell (Ed.), *Handbook of research on music teaching and learning* (pp. 247–265). New York: Schirmer Books.

Boyle, J. D., & Radocy, R. E. (1987). *Measurement and evaluation of musical experiences.* New York: Schirmer Books.

Bugelski, B. R. (1971). *The psychology of learning applied to teaching* (2nd ed.). Indianapolis: Bobbs-Merrill.

Colwell, R. (1969). *Music achievement tests 1 and 2.* Chicago: Follett Educational Corporation.

Colwell, R. (1970). *The evaluation of music teaching and learning.* Englewood Cliffs, NJ: Prentice-Hall.

Darrow, A.-A. (1993). The role of music in deaf culture: Implications for music educators. *Journal of Research in Music Education, 41,* 93–100.

Davidson, L., & Scripp, L. (1988). Young children's musical representations: Windows on musical cognition. In J. A. Sloboda (Ed.), *Generative processes in music: The psychology of performance, improvisation, and cognition* (pp. 195–230). Oxford: Clarendon Press.

Day, J. D. (1983). The zone of proximal development. In M. Pressley & J. R. Levin (Eds.), *Cognitive strategy research: Psychological foundations* (pp. 155–175). New York: Springer-Verlag.

Delzell, J. K., & Leppla, D. A. (1992). Gender associations of musical instruments and preferences of fourth-grade students for selected instruments. *Journal of Research in Music Education, 40,* 93–103.

Dowling, W. J. (1982). Melodic information processing and its development. In D. Deutsch (Ed.), *The psychology of music* (pp. 413–429). New York: Academic Press.

Dowling, W. J. (1988). Tonal structures and children's early learning of music. In J. A. Sloboda (Ed.), *Generative processes in music: The psychology of performance, improvisation, and composition* (pp. 113–128). Oxford: Clarendon Press.

Dowling, W. J., & Harwood, D. L. (1986). *Music cognition.* Orlando, FL: Academic Press.

Farnsworth, P. R. (1969). *The social psychology of music* (2nd ed.) Ames: Iowa State University Press.

Figgs, L. (1976). The ms. mess. *Kansas Music Review, 38* (3), 24–25.

Gardner, H. (1993). *Frames of mind* (10th anniversary ed.). New York: Basic Books.

Getzels, J. W., & Jackson, P. W. (1962). *Creativity and intelligence: Explorations with gifted students.* New York: Wiley.

Gilbert, G. M. (1942). Sex differences in musical aptitude and training. *Journal of General Psychology, 25,* 19–33.

Gordon, E. E. (1965a) *Musical aptitude profile.* Boston: Houghton-Mifflin.

Gordon, E. E. (1965b). The musical aptitude profile: A new and unique musical aptitude test battery. *Council for Research in Music Education, 6,* 12–16.

Gordon, E. E. (1968). A study of the efficiency of general intelligence and musical aptitude tests in predicting achievement in music. *Council for Research in Music Education, 13,* 40–45.

Gordon, E. E. (1979). *Primary measures of music audiation.* Chicago: G. I. A. Publications.

Greer, R. D. (1981). An operant approach to motivation and affect: Ten years of research in music learning. In R. G. Taylor (Ed.), *Documentary report of the Ann Arbor symposium* (pp. 102121). Reston, VA: Music Educators National Conference.

Gromko, J. E. (1994). Children's invented notations as measures of musical understanding. *Psychology of Music, 22,* 136–147.

Guilford, J. P. (1957). Creative abilities in the arts. *Psychological Review, 64,* 110–118.

Guthrie, E. R. (1952). *The psychology of learning* (rev. ed.). New York: Harper & Row.

Haack, P. A., & Radocy, R. E. (1981). A case study of a chromesthetic. *Journal of Research in Music Education, 29,* 85–90.

Hargreaves, D. J., & Zimmerman, M. P. (1992). Developmental theories of music learning. In R. Colwell (Ed.), *Handbook of research in music teaching and learning* (pp. 377–391). New York: Schirmer Books.

Hedden, S. K. (1982). Prediction of musical achievement in the elementary school. *Journal of Research in Music Education, 30,* 61–68.

Hilgard, E. R., & Bower, G. H. (1975). *Theories of learning* (4th ed.). Englewood Cliffs, NJ: Prentice-Hall.

Kohler, W. (1929). *Gestalt psychology.* New York: Liveright.

Koza, J. E. (1990). Music instruction in the nineteenth century: Views from *Godey's lady's book,* 1830–77. *Journal of Research in Music Education, 38,* 245–257.

Koza, J. E. (1994). Females in 1988 middle school textbooks: An analysis of illustrations. *Journal of Research in Music Education, 42,* 145–171.

Kuhl, P. K. (1989). On babies, birds, modules, and mechanisms: A comparative approach to the acquisition of vocal communication. In R. J. Dooling & S. H. Hulse (Eds.), *The comparative psychology of audition: Processing complex sounds* (pp. 379–419). Hillsdale, NJ: Lawrence Erlbaum Associates.

Lathrop, R. L. (1970). Music and music education: A psychologist's view. *Music Educators Journal, 56* (6), 47–48.

LeFrancois, G. R. (1982). *Psychology for teaching* (4th ed.). Belmont, CA: Wadsworth.

Lehman, P. R. (1968). *Tests and measurements in music.* Englewood Cliffs, NJ: Prentice-Hall.

Lundin, R. W. (1967). *An objective psychology of music* (2nd ed.). New York: Ronald Press.

Marin, O. S. M. (1982). Neurological aspects of musical perception and performance. In D. Deutsch (Ed.), *The psychology of music* (pp. 453–477). New York: Academic Press.

Marks, L. E. (1975). Synesthesia: The lucky people with mixed-up senses. *Psychology Today, 9* (1), 48–52.

Mehrens, W. A., & Lehmann, I. J. (1973). *Measurement and evaluation in education and psychology.* New York: Holt, Rinehart, and Winston.

Miller, L. K. (1989). *Musical savants: Exceptional skill in the mentally retarded.* Hillsdale, NJ: Lawrence Erlbaum Associates.

Moore, R. (1966). The relationship of intelligence to creativity. *Journal of Research in Music Education, 14,* 243–253.

Mursell, J. L. (1937). *The psychology of music.* New York: Norton.

Nettl, B. (1956). *Music in primitive cultures.* Cambridge: Harvard University Press.

Notterman, J. M., & Drewry, H. N. (1993). *Psychology and education: Parallel and interactive approaches.* New York: Plenum Press.

Pavlov, I. P. (1927). *Conditioned reflexes.* London: Clarendon Press.

Pflederer, M. (1967). Conservation laws applied to the development of musical intelligence. *Journal of Research in Music Education, 15,* 215–223.

Phillips, D. (1976). An investigation of the relationship between musicality and intelligence. *Psychology of Music, 4* (2), 16–31.

Piaget, J. (1950). *The psychology of intelligence.* New York: Harcourt, Brace, Jovanovich.

Piaget, J., & Inhelder, B. (1969). *The psychology of the child.* New York: Basic Books.

Pick, A. D., & Palmer, C. F. (1993). Development of the perception of musical events. In T. J. Tighe & W. J. Dowling (Eds.), *Psychology and music: The understanding of melody and rhythm* (pp. 197–213). Hillsdale, NJ: Lawrence Erlbaum Associates.

Plomp, R., & Steeneken, H. J. M. (1973). Place dependence of timbre in reverberant sound fields. *Acustica, 28,* 50–59.

Radocy, R. E. (1971). Thoughts on creativity. *Kansas Music Review, 33* (5), 16–17.

Radocy, R. E. (1982). Applying selected learning principles to music instruction: Some practical suggestions. *Update, 1* (1), 11–13.

Radocy, R. E. (1994). Musical ability. In V. S. Ramachandran (Ed.), *Encyclopedia of human behavior* (Vol. 3, pp. 257–263). San Diego, CA: Academic Press.

Rainbow, E. L. (1965). A pilot study to investigate the constructs of musical aptitude. *Journal of Research in Music Education, 13,* 3–14.

Ries, N. L. L. (1982). An analysis of the characteristics of infant-child singing expressions. (Doctoral dissertation, Arizona State University, 1982). *Dissertation Abstracts International, 43,* 1871A. (University Microfilms No. 82–23, 568)

Rubin, R. (1973). *Voices of a people: The story of Yiddish folksong* (2nd ed.). New York: McGraw-Hill.

Scheid, P., & Eccles, J. C. (1975). Music and speech: Artistic functions of the human brain. *Psychology of Music, 3* (1), 21–35.

Schlaug, G., Jancke, L., Huang, Y., & Steinmetz, H. (1995). In vivo evidence of structural brain asymmetry in musicians. *Science, 267,* 699–701.

Seashore, C. E. (1938). *Psychology of music.* New York: McGraw-Hill.

Seashore, C. E., Lewis, L., & Saetveit, J. G. (1960). *Seashore measures of musical talents.* New York: The Psychological Corporation.

Serafine, M. L. (1983). Piagetian research in music. *Council for Research in Music Education, 62,* 1–21.

Sergeant, D., & Thatcher, G. (1974). Intelligence, social status, and musical abilities. *Psychology of Music, 2* (2), 32–57.

Sherbon, J. W. (1975). The association of hearing acuity, diplacusis, and discrimination with musical performance. *Journal of Research in Music Education, 23,* 249–257.

Skinner, B. F. (1938). *The behavior of organisms: An experimental analysis.* New York: Appleton-Century-Crofts.

Skinner, B. F. (1953). *Science and human behavior.* New York: Macmillan.

Skinner, B. F. (1971). *Beyond freedom and dignity.* New York: Alfred A. Knopf.

Sloboda, J. A. (1985). *The musical mind: The cognitive psychology of music.* Oxford: Clarendon Press.

Sloboda, J. A., Hermelin, B., & O'Connor, N. (1985). An exceptional musical memory. *Music Perception, 3,* 155–170.

Spearman, C. (1927). *The abilities of man: Their nature and measurement.* New York: Macmillan.

Stanley, J. C. (1971). Reliability. In R. L. Thorndike (Ed.), *Educational measurement* (pp. 356–442). Washington: American Council on Education.

Tawa, N. (1982). *A sound of strangers: Musical culture, acculturation, and the post-Civil War ethnic American.* Metuchen, NJ: Scarecrow Press.

Taylor, R. G. (Ed.), *Documentary report of the Ann Arbor symposium.* Reston, VA: Music Educators National Conference.

Thorndike, E. L. (1932). *The fundamentals of learning.* New York: Teachers College Press.

Thurstone, L. L. (1947). *Multiple-factor analysis: A development and expansion of "the vectors of the mind."* Chicago: University of Chicago Press.

Trehub, S. E. (1993). The music listening skills of infants and young children. In T. J. Tighe & W. J. Dowling (Eds.), *Psychology and music: The understanding of melody and rhythm* (pp. 161–176). Hillsdale, NJ: Lawrence Erlbaum Associates.

Vygotsky, L. S. (1962). *Thought and language* (E. Hanfmann & G. Vakar, eds.). Cambridge, MA: M.I.T. Press.

Vygotsky, L. S. (1978). *Mind in society* (M. Cole, ed.). Cambridge, MA: Harvard University Press.

Walker, E. L. (1980). *Psychological complexity and preference: A hedgehog theory of behavior.* Monterey, CA: Brooks/Cole.

Whybrew, W. H. (1971). *Measurement and evaluation in music* (2nd ed.). Dubuque, IA: W. C. Brown.

Wing, H. D. (1954). Some application of test results to education in music. *British Journal of Educational Psychology, 24,* 161–170.

Wing, H. D. (1961). *Standardised tests of musical intelligence.* The Mere, England: National Foundation for Educational Research.

Wyatt, R. F. (1945). Improvability of pitch discrimination. *Psychological Monographs, 58* (2). (Whole No. 267)

Zervoudakes, J., & Tanur, J. M. (1994). Gender and musical instruments: Winds of change? *Journal of Research in Music Education, 42,* 58–67.

CHAPTER ELEVEN

FUTURE RESEARCH DIRECTIONS

The previous two editions of this text concluded with a prediction of future directions in research. When the authors were completing the first edition, considerable interest in hemispheric specialization abounded, some of which was of a serious research nature and some of which was due to ill-guided attempts at educational reform. The authors anticipated that the future would bring considerable research to bear on the topic; they also believed that synesthesia would be of growing interest. Events showed that research in hemispheric specialization certainly did continue, but nothing happened to make the first edition's conclusion basically vary: The human brain is a complex organ, in contact with all of its sections. Music may be a product of either hemisphere, of both acting together, or of neither. Specialization for music depends on the nature of the musical task and the experience of the performer or listener. Synesthesia is an occasionally mentioned phenomenon: Experiencing a stimulus is more than one sensory mode simultaneously may relate to modern concern for multimedia presentations.

The second edition's concluding chapter predicted increased interest in multiple intelligence and expertise. The multiple intelligence idea, exemplified by Howard Gardner's (1993)[1] work, indeed found favor with students of musical ability. The study of expertise is exemplified by some of Sloboda's work, discussed in Chapter Seven. The ideas remain important; efforts to develop assessments of musical intelligence that recognize its numerous facets should continue. The development of expertise is a logical extension.

For the present edition, the authors elected to express caution regarding potential fads and overreactions to sundry information regarding musical phenomena. Strictly speaking, we are not predicting research—we are warning that a little knowledge of musical behavior can be misleading or even dangerous.

Music has value in and of itself, but, of course, music is highly useful as a catalyst for or an accompaniment to other activities. Much of this

---

[1] Curiously, Gardner's 1993 "edition" is identical to the 1983 edition, except for a brief introductory chapter.

text discusses various commercial, therapeutic, and social functions of music. One must be careful not to make extravagant claims for music. Research in musical behavior often lags behind practice, and much experimental research necessarily sacrifices some reality in the interest of control. Yet, a parsimonious attitude toward purported claims for music, an attitude that recognizes that research may show inadequacies of a particular belief, is wise.

Hemispheric specialization remains one area for caution. There is no question that such specialization exists in humans, but the cerebral hemispheres are not at war with themselves! Musical behavior involves both hemispheres, so educational reformers, marketers, and persons anxious to nurture creativity should not claim that music somehow rescues the noble free associative right hemisphere from the fetters of the tyrannically linear left hemisphere. Particular musical tasks indeed may require right hemisphere (or left hemisphere) involvement, but most people have intact brains and use diverse parts of it, as the occasion requires.

Occasionally, people may view the study of music as a means for furthering another goal. Music certainly may be motivating and function as a reward for other activity, as was addressed in earlier chapters. Music may keep otherwise uninterested students in school. Music may facilitate a recovery process, help people cope with stress or grief, and provide, through active music making or passive listening, a catharsis for many of life's trials and tribulations. But do students become better readers or solvers of mathematical problems or painters or computer programmers because they study music? Do "toxins" in the body disappear, or do cancer cells disappear, or do personality disorders disappear if the patient hears the right music? Does intoning a "correct" pitch connect the person with some cosmic destiny? As absurd as these questions may seem, the authors have heard educators who regard music as the solution to all curricular problems and therapists or "healers" who regard music as a cure or opening to a new life.

The purported "Mozart effect" illustrates taking minimal information and making it into something well beyond what it represents. In a letter to the editor of *Nature*, Rauscher, Shaw, and Ky (1993) reported a comparison of three groups of college students, one of which listened to Mozart's D major sonata (K488), another of which listened to an unspecified relaxation tape, and the other of which sat in silence for ten minutes prior to taking tests of spatial reasoning. The test scores were converted to the equivalence of intelligence scores, in accordance with instructions for the *Stanford-Binet Scale of Intelligence* (Thorndike, Hagen, & Sattler, 1986). The group that had listened to Mozart showed statistically significantly higher scores than the others. The investigators carefully cautioned that their results were temporary and did not extend beyond the particular spatial reasoning tasks. They called for further research regarding additional styles, and noted that musicians might react differently than nonmusicians. Popular media ignored the researchers' cautions and promulgated a story that music could make a person "smarter." A periodical of the Music Educators National Conference headlined an unsigned article in the February 1995 *Teaching Music*[2] with "Music Makes You Smarter"! It is a long way from a temporary gain in a restricted test setting to being "smarter."

The "Mozart effect" does seem to be a real phenomenon in carefully limited situations. Rauscher, Shaw, Levine, and Ky (1994) reported the results of two experiments at a meeting of the American Psychological Association. In one experiment, where college students were tested on their ability to imagine the result of a series of paper folding and cutting operations, the students who listened to ten minutes of the Mozart sonata outscored students who either listened to other aural stimuli or sat in silence for the ten minute preparation times over a period of five days. In the other experiment, three- and four-year-old children who underwent eight months of piano and voice experiments in preschool were superior to children who had not had the musical experiences in assembling puzzle pieces. The researchers believe that they have shown how music may enhance cognitive spatial-temporal development. Evidently, similar cortical areas are involved in the types of musical processing and spatial processing addressed in their experiments.[3] Again, the investigators call for more research. A causal effect between different kinds of tasks, as opposed to merely a correlational one, *is* exciting. But this hardly justifies claiming that music makes a person "smarter"!

Music therapy is a well-established profession, and many therapeutic applications of music and associated sounds exist. Yet purported claims may stretch credulity, especially when sounds are packaged as a cure. For example, a presentation at a recent meeting of the National Association for Music Therapy (Clendenon-Wallen, 1994) extolled "healing with sound." Essentially, a "healer" analyzes a person's vocal spectrum for missing frequencies in the chromatic octave. Each missing sound has alleged physical and emotional correlates. Missing C's supposedly indi-

---

[2] *Teaching Music* is a nonscholarly adaptation of the older refereed *Music Educators Journal.* It functions mostly as a newsletter to express current interests of the headquarters staff of the Music Educators National Conference and rarely employs the expertise of the research community.

[3] An elaborate description of a neural model from which the investigators drew underlying theoretical support appears in Leng, Shaw, and Wright (1990).

cate hormonal problems, or constipation, or listlessness. Missing D's indicate low self-esteem, liver or gall bladder problems, or problems with blood sugar or cramping. Exposure to the "missing" tones allegedly vibrates the body, removes "blockages," opens "chakras," and allows "body energy" to flow through the body and heal it. The tonal exposure purportedly removes "heavy metals and toxins." Placebo effects are powerful, and belief in a technique may make a difference in the technique's efficacy. But should we replace medicines and dietary principles with tones?

Clearly, systematic inquiry is necessary to describe the actual conditions under which music *is* beneficial in educational and therapeutic situations. While the music is no substitute for the surgery itself, patients undergoing surgery often may benefit from hearing chosen sedative music before anesthesia and during recovery. While music does not make a person a better mathematician or author, using music as a means of relaxation prior to or immediately following intensive intellectual activity may be cathartic. The operative verb is *may*—and research can help locate the when and where.

So, we anticipate an ever-continuing flow of various claims for music as an educational and therapeutic medium. Music has powerful influences on a person's mind and body. Researchers will have to examine the validity of claims in relation to documented influences.

References

Clendenon-Wallen, J. (1994). *Healing with sound.* Paper presented at the meeting of the National Association for Music Therapy, Orlando, FL.

Gardner, H. (1993). *Frames of mind* (10th anniversary ed.). New York: Basic Books.

Leng, X., Shaw, G. L., & Wright, E. L. (1990). Coding of musical structures and the trion model of cortex. *Music Perception, 8,* 49–62.

Rauscher, F. H., Shaw, G. L., & Ky, K. N. (1993). Music and spatial task performance. *Nature, 365,* 611.

Rauscher, F. H., Shaw, G. L., Levine, L. J., & Ky, K. N. (1994, August). *Music and spatial task performance: A causal relationship.* Paper presented at the meeting of the American Psychological Association, Los Angeles.

Thorndike, R. L., Hagen, E. P., & Sattler, J. M. (1986). *The Stanford-Binet scale of intelligence.* Chicago: Riverside.

AUTHOR INDEX

Citations to jointly authored works are listed by the first author only. For example, the Getzels and Jackson study is listed here only as Getzels.

SUBJECT INDEX

387